Yusei Matsui

I think what an author has to be the most careful about when creating historical fiction is getting too absorbed in history.

The more you learn about history, the more you realize how much deeper you can go, and if you get too obsessed, you'll leave the reader behind.

While this series may be based on historical fact, it's primarily a work of entertainment, so I want to approach the history with a certain degree of lightness and looseness.

Yusei Matsui was born on the last day of January in Saitama Prefecture, Japan. He has been drawing manga since elementary school. Some of his favorite manga series are *Bobobo-bo Bo-bobo*, *JoJo's Bizarre Adventure*, and *Ultimate Muscle*. Matsui learned his trade working as an assistant to manga artist Yoshio Sawai, creator of *Bobobo-bo Bo-bobo*. In 2005, Matsui debuted his original manga *Neuro: Supernatural Detective* in *Weekly Shonen Jump*. In 2007, *Neuro* was adapted into an anime. His next series, *Assassination Classroom*, captured imaginations worldwide and was adapted to anime, video games, and film. In 2021, *The Elusive Samurai* began serialization in *Weekly Shonen Jump*.

THE ELUSIVE SAMURAI
VOLUME 2
SHONEN JUMP Edition

**Story and Art by
Yusei Matsui**

Translation & English Adaptation John Werry
Touch-Up Art & Lettering Chi Wang
Designer Jimmy Presler
Editor Mike Montesa

NIGEJOZU NO WAKAGIMI © 2021 by Yusei Matsui
All rights reserved.
First published in Japan in 2021 by SHUEISHA Inc., Tokyo.
English translation rights arranged by SHUEISHA Inc.

The stories, characters, and incidents mentioned
in this publication are entirely fictional.

Printed in Canada

Published by VIZ Media, LLC
P.O. Box 77010
San Francisco, CA 94107

10 9 8 7 6 5 4 3 2 1
First printing, September 2022

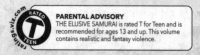

PARENTAL ADVISORY
THE ELUSIVE SAMURAI is rated T for Teen and is
recommended for ages 13 and up. This volume
contains realistic and fantasy violence.

viz.com

THE STO[redacted]

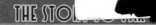

Hojo Tokiyuki was heir to the Kamakura shogunate, but when Ashikaga Takauji suddenly rebelled, Tokiyuki lost everything, including his home and family. Suwa Yorishige is sheltering him in Shinano, but Ogasawara Sadamune from western Shinano is searching for Hojo survivors and is closing in. As Tokiyuki disguises himself to conceal his identity, a game of hide-and-seek begins in which he hopes to learn from Sadamune's impeccable archery skills!

ASHIKAGA TAKAUJI

In secret communication with Emperor Go-Daigo, he overthrew the Kamakura shogunate. Handsome, dauntless, and charismatic, his popularity is immense. Tokiyuki views him as the Hojo clan's enemy.

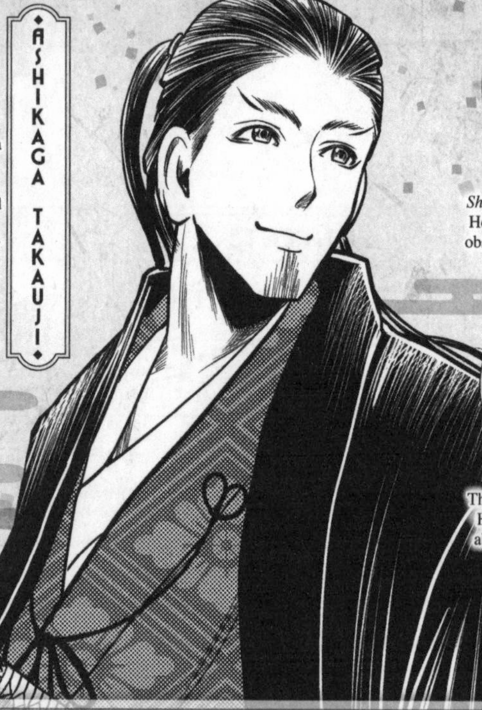

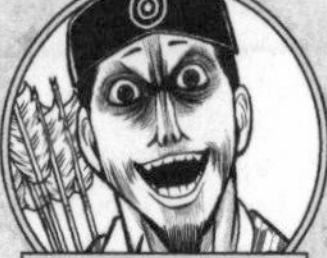

OGASAWARA SADAMUNE

Shugo (governor) of Shinano. He possesses keen powers of observation that are positively threatening, and he's an excellent archer.

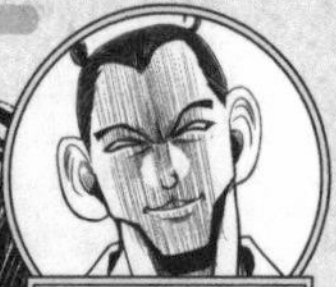

ICHIKAWA SUKEFUSA

The Shinano shugo's assistant. He uses his infernal hearing ability to support Sadamune.

GUIDE TO STATS

1333
ABILITIES
NANBOKU-CHO COMPATIBILITY
MARTIAL ARTS
SAVAGERY
INTELLIGENCE
LOYALTY
POLITICS
CHAOS
LEADERSHIP
INGENUITY
CHARM
RUNNING AND HIDING
CREST
SKILL
NOTE
COMMENTS

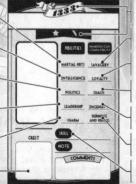

- Individual combat strength, including swordsmanship, archery, and horsemanship
- Overall ability, including knowledge, quick thinking, and strategy
- Mastery of internal affairs, scheming, and power struggles
- Ability to coordinate political entities and allied military forces
- Ability to attract others
- Family crest, clothing pattern, etc.
- Character's importance in that year
- Ability to fight and survive in violent times
- Attribute providing strength when needed
- Ability to adapt to changing circumstances
- Inventiveness and will to create a new world
- Adaptability to a time when much happens in secret
- Characteristic skill

THE ELUSIVE SAMURAI

2

CONTENTS

CHAPTER 8: DOG SHOOTING 1333

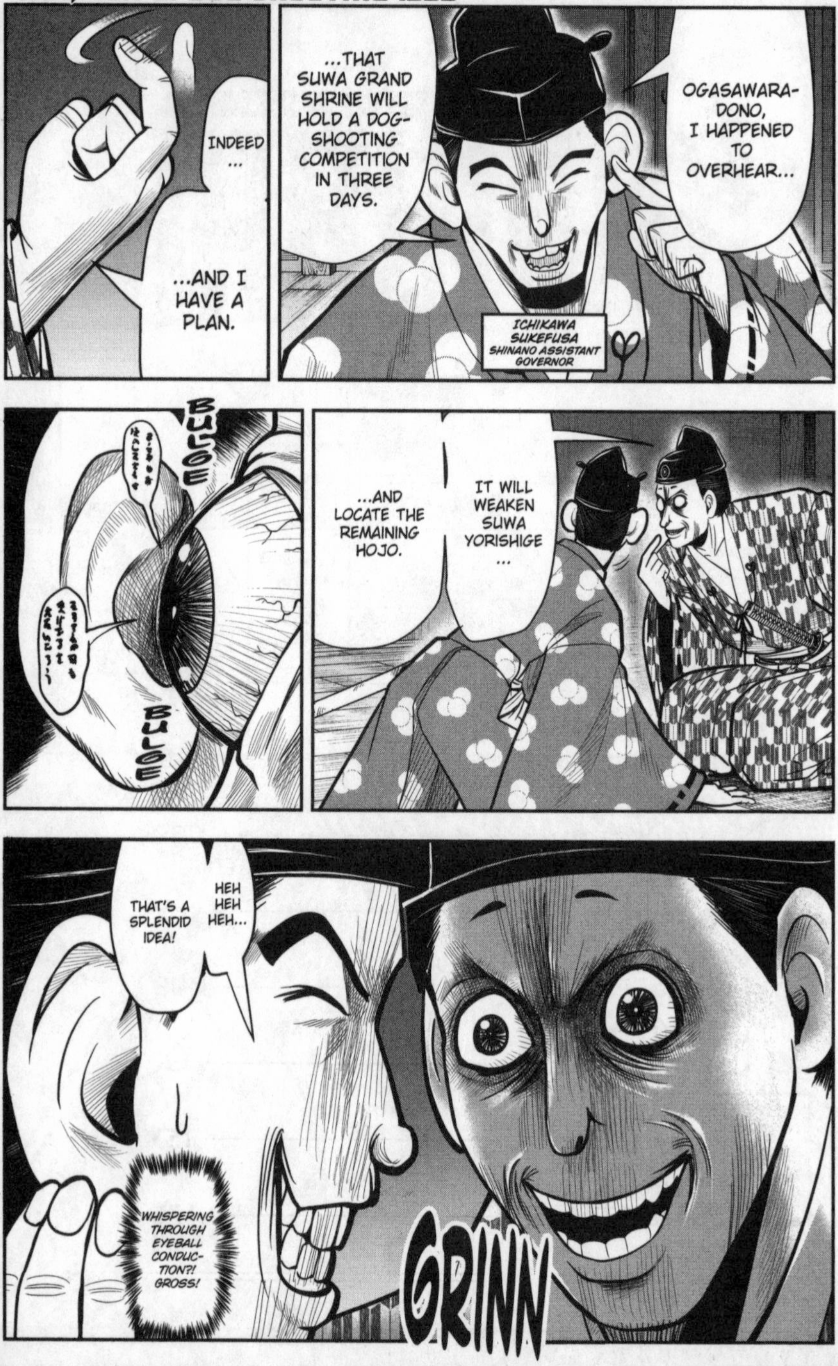
OGASAWARA-DONO, I HAPPENED TO OVERHEAR...
...THAT SUWA GRAND SHRINE WILL HOLD A DOG-SHOOTING COMPETITION IN THREE DAYS.
ICHIKAWA SUKEFUSA SHINANO ASSISTANT GOVERNOR
INDEED...
...AND I HAVE A PLAN.
IT WILL WEAKEN SUWA YORISHIGE...
...AND LOCATE THE REMAINING HOJO.
BULGE
BULGE
HEH HEH HEH...
THAT'S A SPLENDID IDEA!
GRINN
WHISPERING THROUGH EYEBALL CONDUCTION?! GROSS!

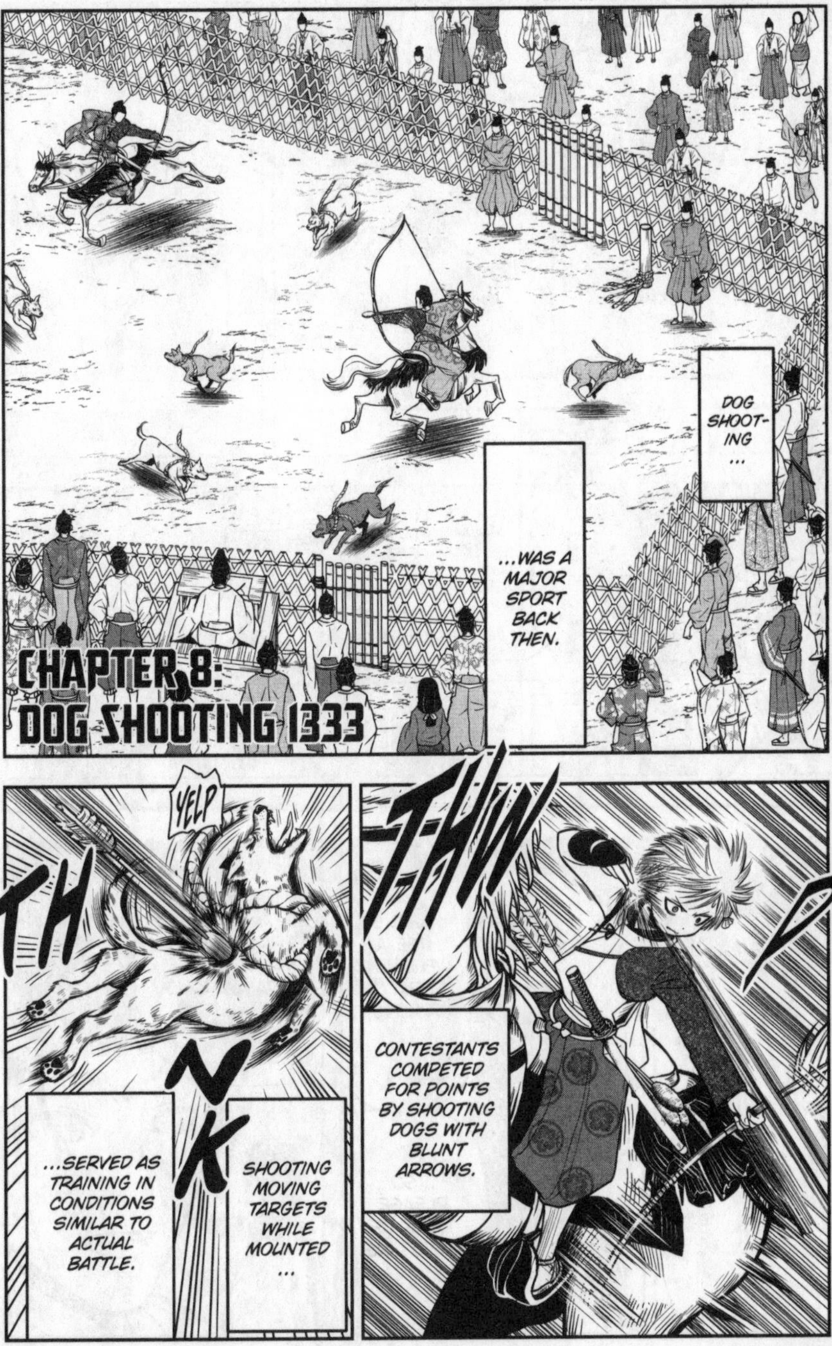
DOG SHOOTING...
...WAS A MAJOR SPORT BACK THEN.
CHAPTER 8: DOG SHOOTING 1333
T-THWI
P
CONTESTANTS COMPETED FOR POINTS BY SHOOTING DOGS WITH BLUNT ARROWS.
YELP
TH
N
K
SHOOTING MOVING TARGETS WHILE MOUNTED...
...SERVED AS TRAINING IN CONDITIONS SIMILAR TO ACTUAL BATTLE.

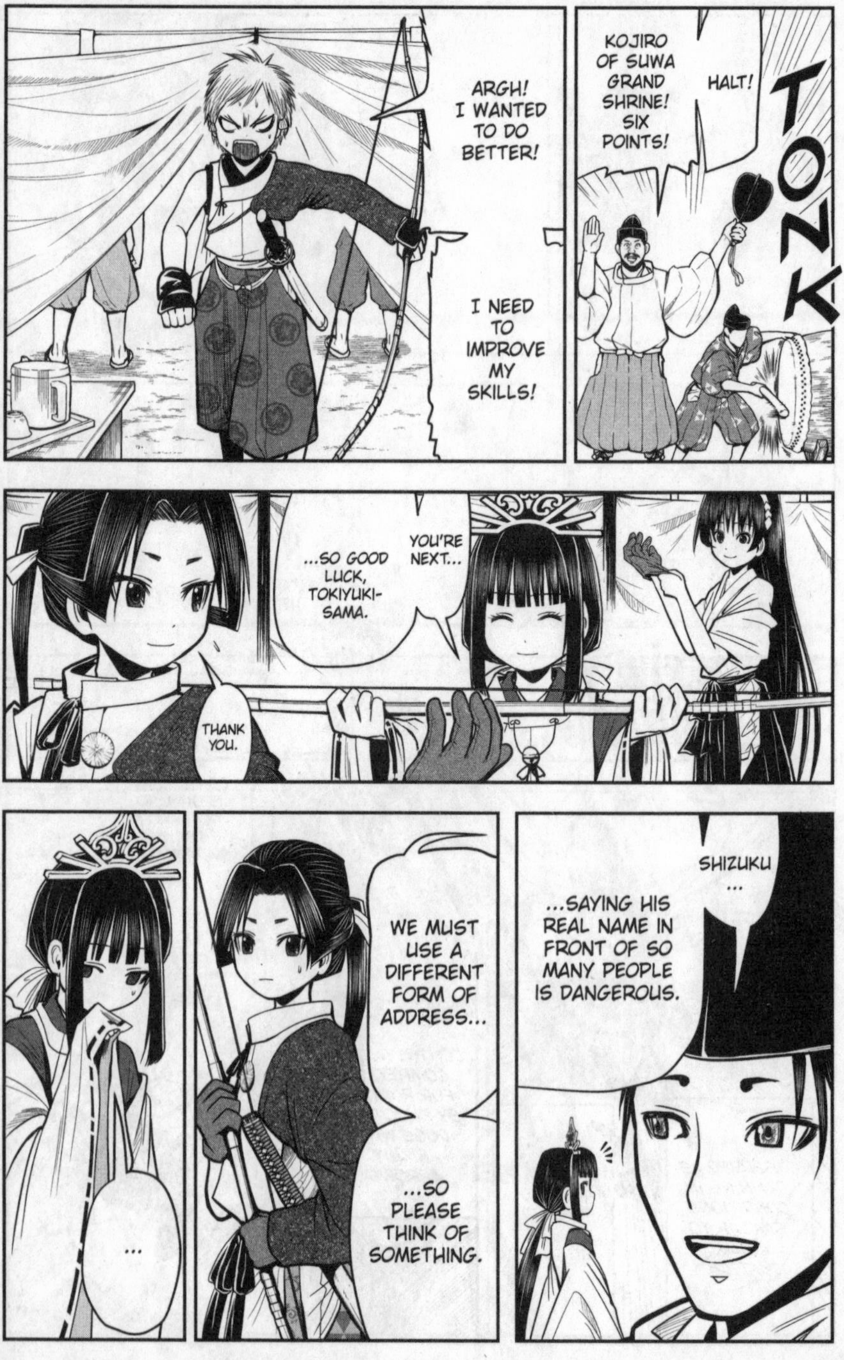
TONK
HALT!
KOJIRO OF SUWA GRAND SHRINE! SIX POINTS!
ARGH! I WANTED TO DO BETTER!
I NEED TO IMPROVE MY SKILLS!
YOU'RE NEXT...
...SO GOOD LUCK, TOKIYUKI-SAMA.
THANK YOU.
SHIZUKU ...
...SAYING HIS REAL NAME IN FRONT OF SO MANY PEOPLE IS DANGEROUS.
WE MUST USE A DIFFERENT FORM OF ADDRESS...
...SO PLEASE THINK OF SOMETHING.
...

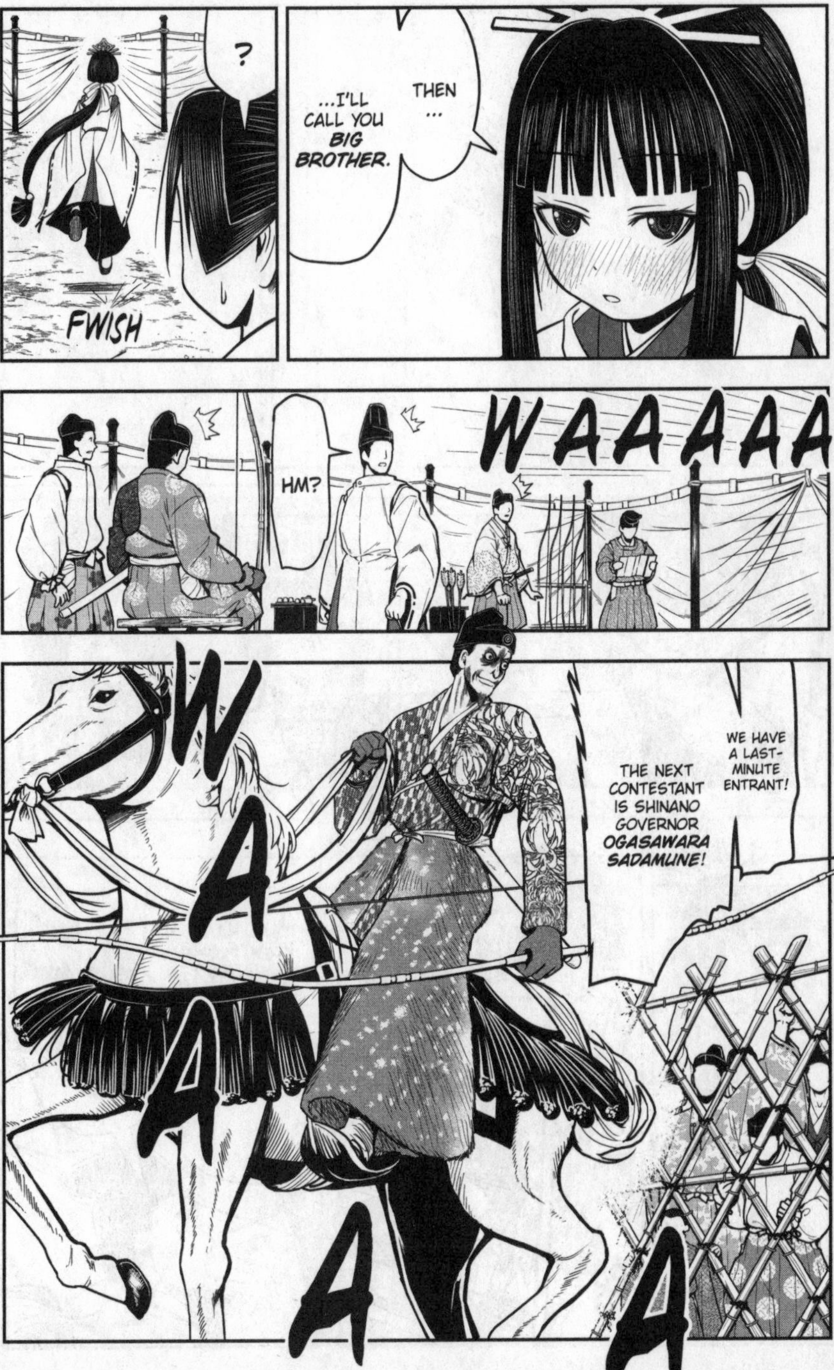

THEN ...
...I'LL CALL YOU BIG BROTHER.
?
FWISH
WAAAAAA
HM?
WE HAVE A LAST-MINUTE ENTRANT!
THE NEXT CONTESTANT IS SHINANO GOVERNOR OGASAWARA SADAMUNE!
WAAAA

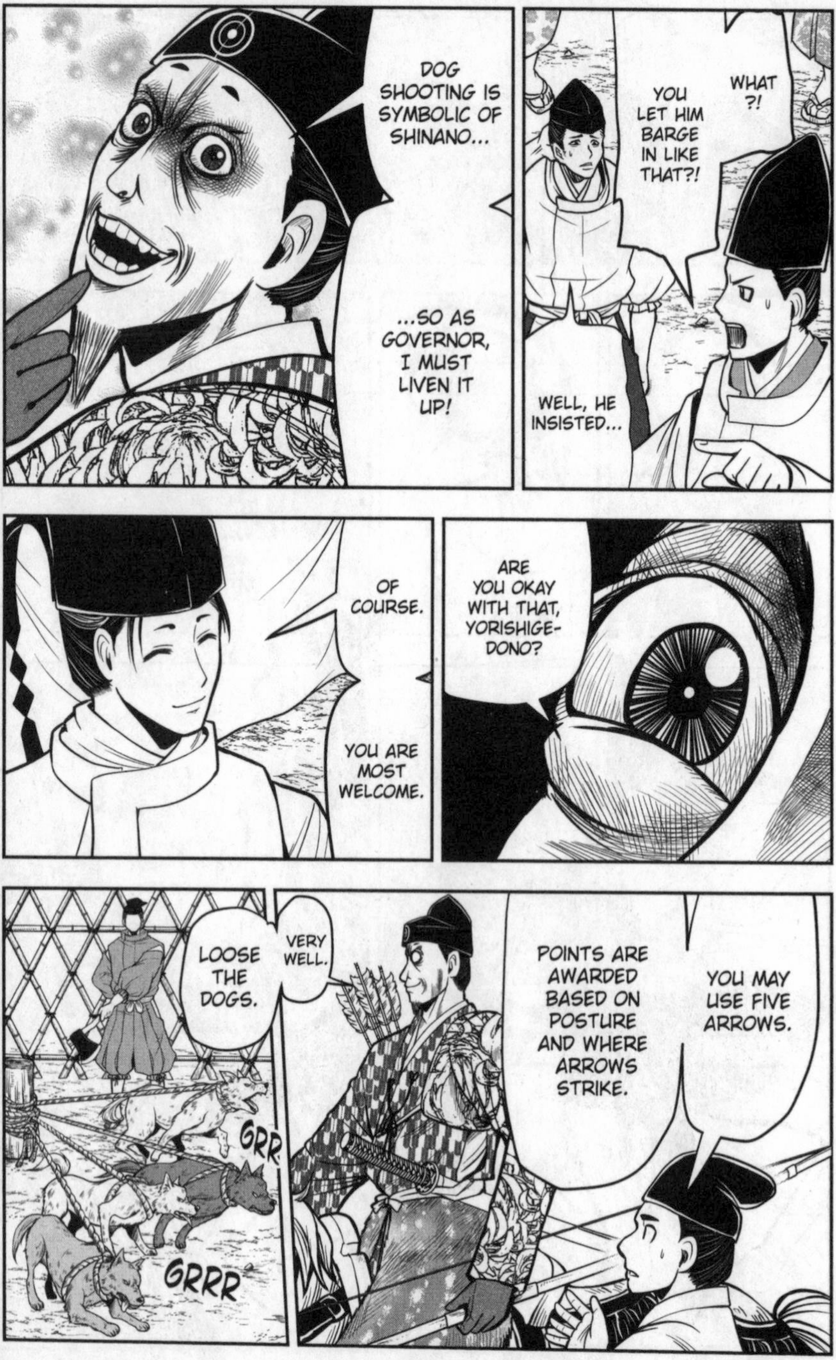
WHAT?!
YOU LET HIM BARGE IN LIKE THAT?!
WELL, HE INSISTED...
DOG SHOOTING IS SYMBOLIC OF SHINANO...
...SO AS GOVERNOR, I MUST LIVEN IT UP!
ARE YOU OKAY WITH THAT, YORISHIGE-DONO?
OF COURSE.
YOU ARE MOST WELCOME.
YOU MAY USE FIVE ARROWS.
POINTS ARE AWARDED BASED ON POSTURE AND WHERE ARROWS STRIKE.
VERY WELL.
LOOSE THE DOGS.
GRR
GRRR

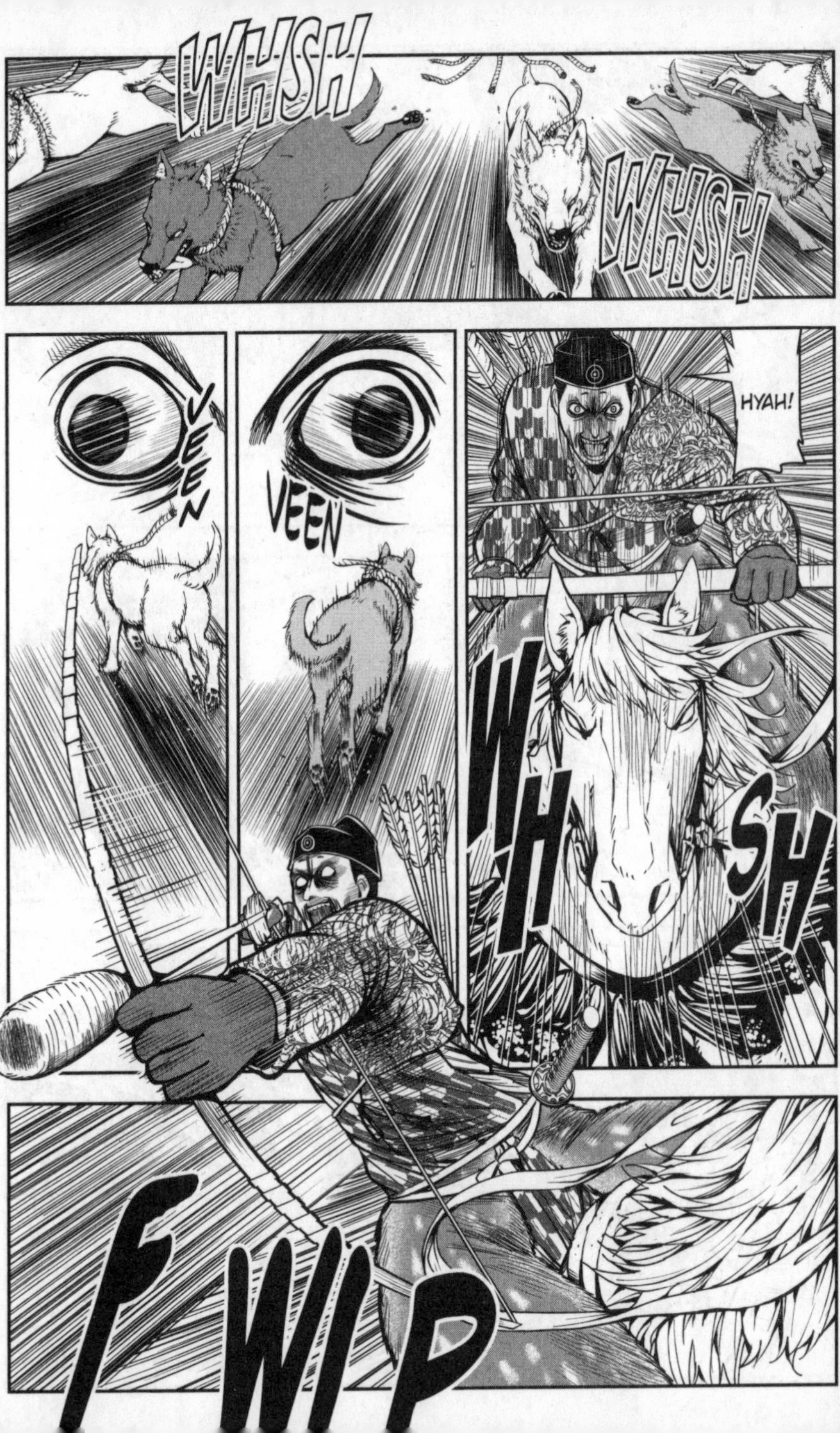
WHSH
WHSH
HYAH!
WHSH
VEEN
VEEN
FWIP

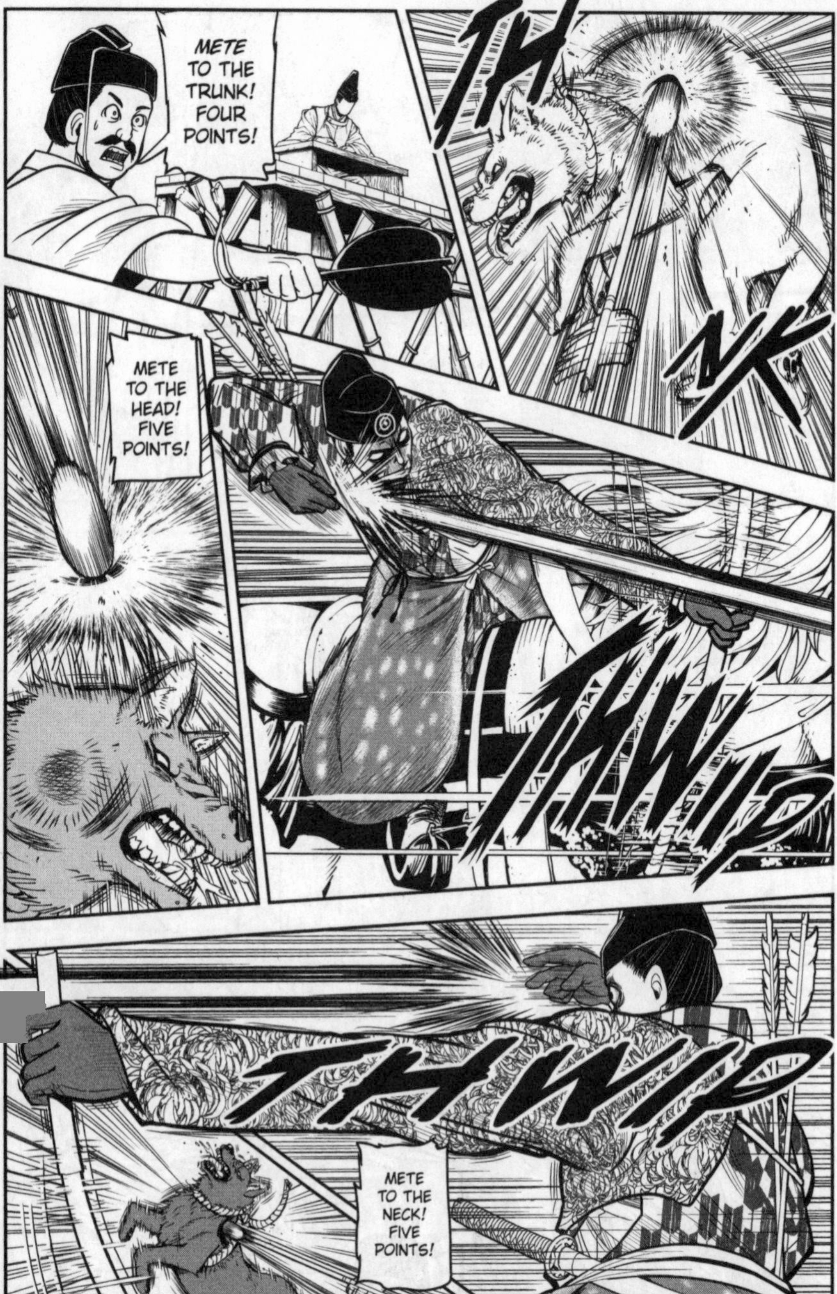
TH
NK
METE TO THE TRUNK! FOUR POINTS!
THWIP
METE TO THE HEAD! FIVE POINTS!
THWIP
METE TO THE NECK! FIVE POINTS!

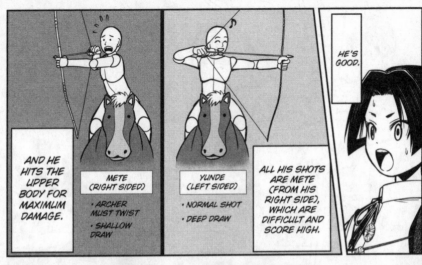

HE'S GOOD.
ALL HIS SHOTS ARE METE (FROM HIS RIGHT SIDE), WHICH ARE DIFFICULT AND SCORE HIGH.
YUNDE (LEFT SIDED)
• NORMAL SHOT
• DEEP DRAW
METE (RIGHT SIDED)
• ARCHER MUST TWIST
• SHALLOW DRAW
AND HE HITS THE UPPER BODY FOR MAXIMUM DAMAGE.
IS YORI-SHIGE-DONO...
...TREMBLING IN FEAR?
TRMBL
TRMBL
IS HE AFRAID OF SADAMUNE'S SKILL?
TRMBL
NO, YOU DON'T UNDERSTAND!
IN THE FUTURE, THIS IS CALLED ANIMAL CRUELTY...
...BUT IT'S NORMAL NOW...
...SO PLEASE DON'T COMPLAIN!!
WHO ARE YOU TALKING TO?!
TRMBL
TRMBL
TRMBL

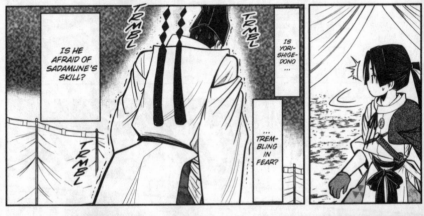

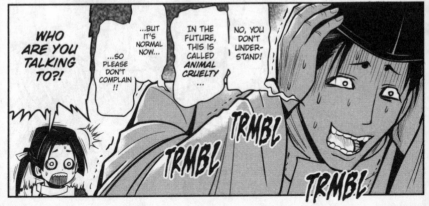

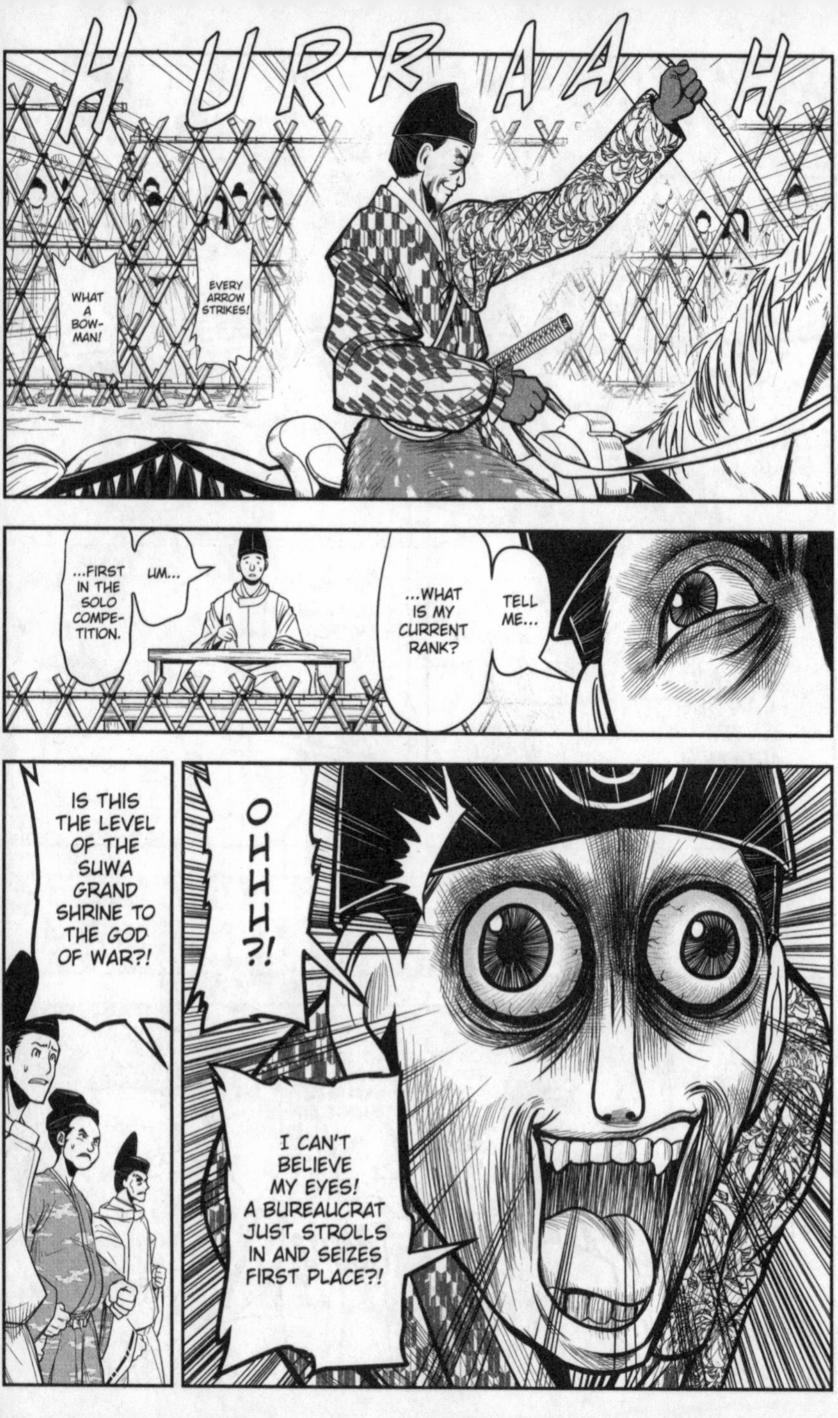
HURRAAH
EVERY ARROW STRIKES!
WHAT A BOW-MAN!
TELL ME...
...WHAT IS MY CURRENT RANK?
UM...
...FIRST IN THE SOLO COMPETITION.
OHHH?!
I CAN'T BELIEVE MY EYES! A BUREAUCRAT JUST STROLLS IN AND SEIZES FIRST PLACE?!
IS THIS THE LEVEL OF THE SUWA GRAND SHRINE TO THE GOD OF WAR?!

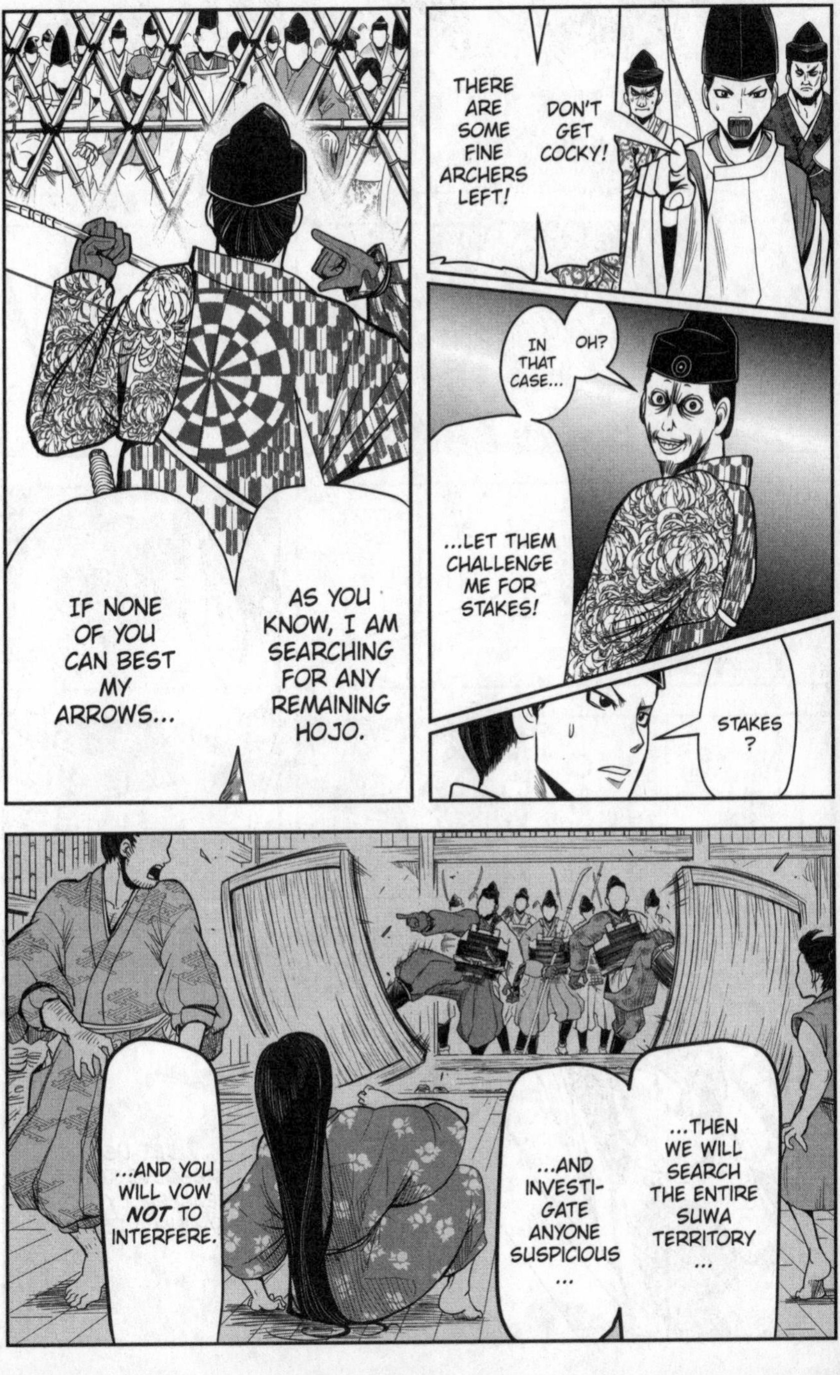
DON'T GET COCKY!
THERE ARE SOME FINE ARCHERS LEFT!
OH?
IN THAT CASE...
...LET THEM CHALLENGE ME FOR STAKES!
STAKES?
AS YOU KNOW, I AM SEARCHING FOR ANY REMAINING HOJO.
IF NONE OF YOU CAN BEST MY ARROWS...
...THEN WE WILL SEARCH THE ENTIRE SUWA TERRITORY...
...AND INVESTI-GATE ANYONE SUSPICIOUS...
...AND YOU WILL VOW *NOT* TO INTERFERE.

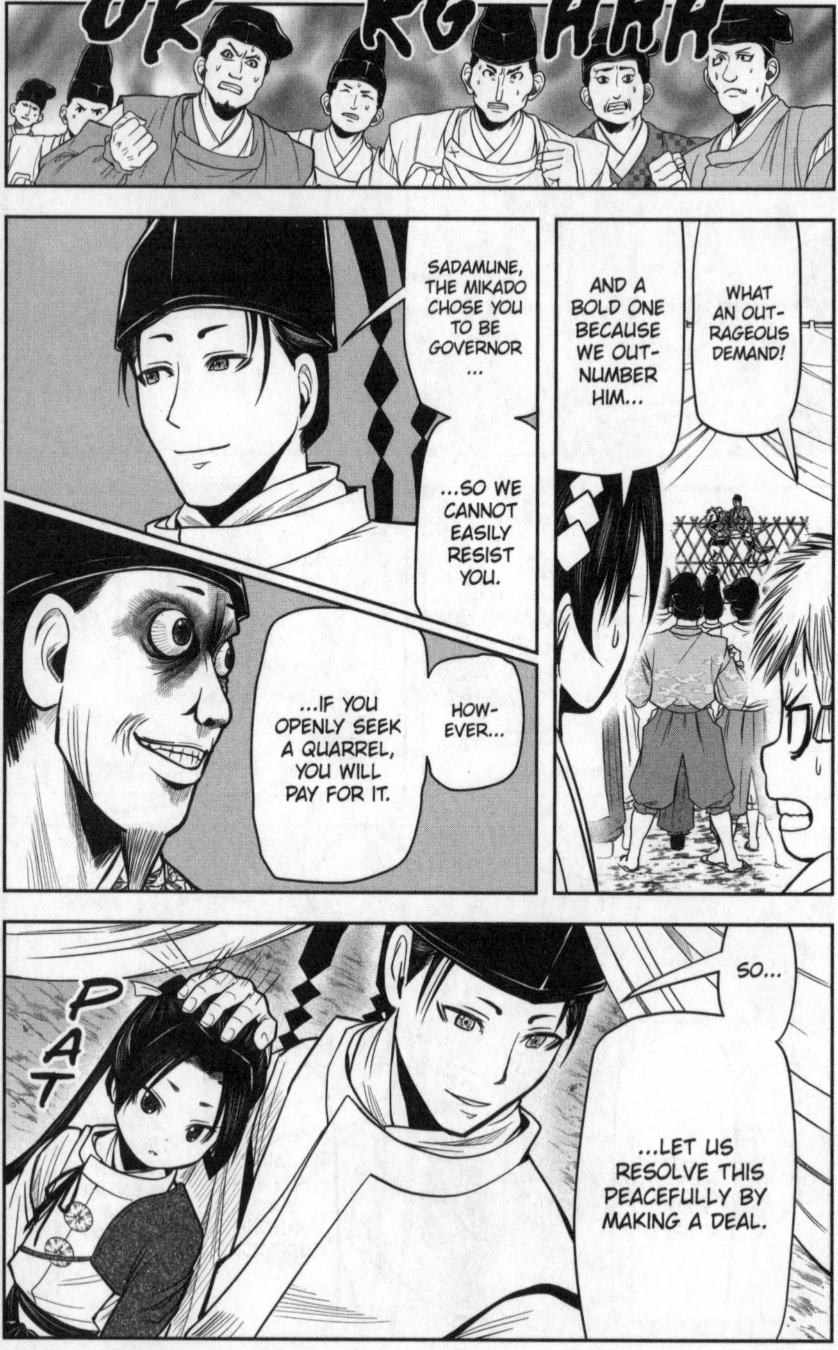
URRGHHH
WHAT AN OUT-RAGEOUS DEMAND!
AND A BOLD ONE BECAUSE WE OUT-NUMBER HIM...
SADAMUNE, THE MIKADO CHOSE YOU TO BE GOVERNOR ...
...SO WE CANNOT EASILY RESIST YOU.
HOW-EVER...
...IF YOU OPENLY SEEK A QUARREL, YOU WILL PAY FOR IT.
SO...
PAT
...LET US RESOLVE THIS PEACEFULLY BY MAKING A DEAL.

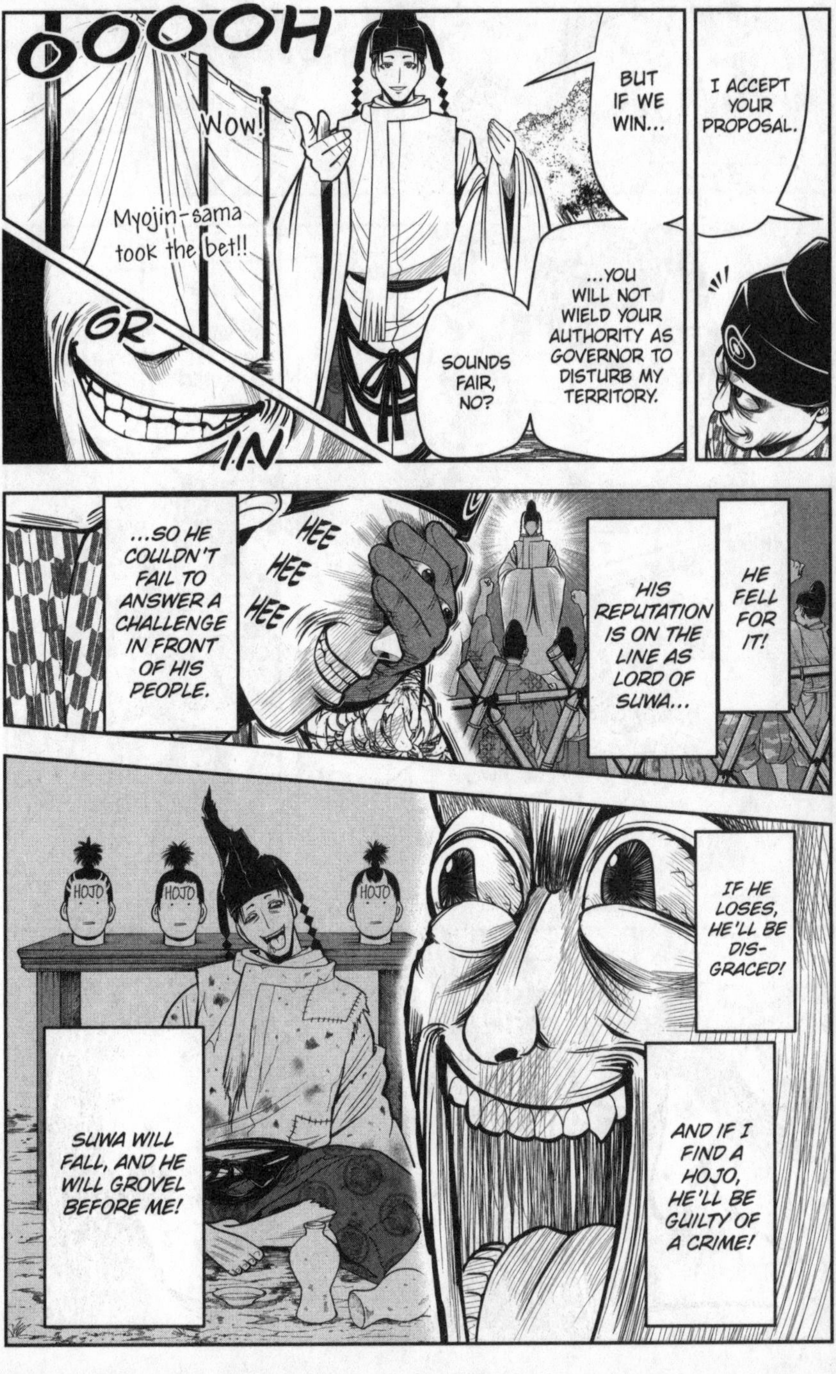
I ACCEPT YOUR PROPOSAL.
BUT IF WE WIN...
...YOU WILL NOT WIELD YOUR AUTHORITY AS GOVERNOR TO DISTURB MY TERRITORY.
SOUNDS FAIR, NO?
OOOOH
Wow!
Myojin-sama took the bet!!
GRIN
HE FELL FOR IT!
HIS REPUTATION IS ON THE LINE AS LORD OF SUWA...
HEE HEE HEE
...SO HE COULDN'T FAIL TO ANSWER A CHALLENGE IN FRONT OF HIS PEOPLE.
IF HE LOSES, HE'LL BE DIS-GRACED!
AND IF I FIND A HOJO, HE'LL BE GUILTY OF A CRIME!
HOJO
HOJO
HOJO
SUWA WILL FALL, AND HE WILL GROVEL BEFORE ME!

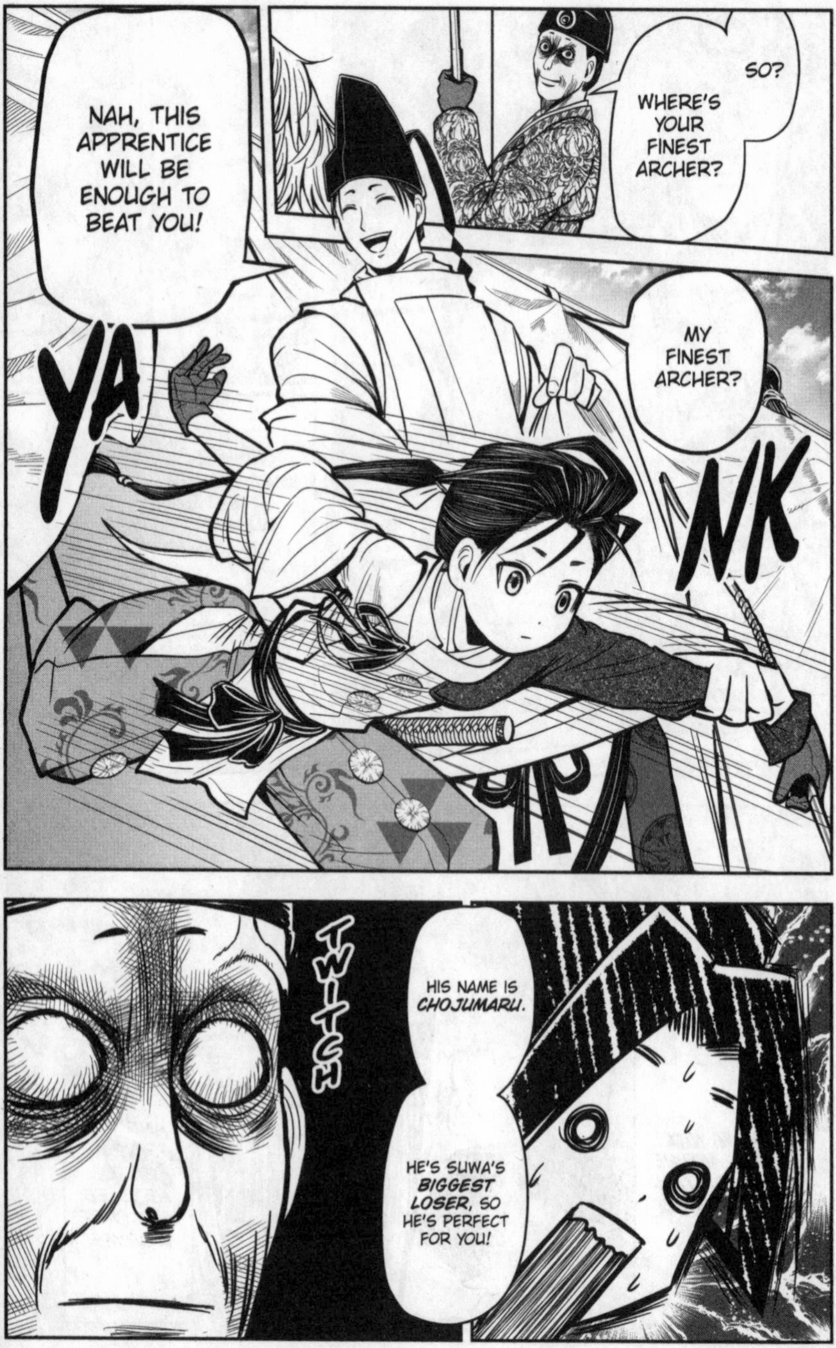
SO?
WHERE'S YOUR FINEST ARCHER?
MY FINEST ARCHER?
NAH, THIS APPRENTICE WILL BE ENOUGH TO BEAT YOU!
YANK
HIS NAME IS *CHOJUMARU*.
HE'S SUWA'S ***BIGGEST LOSER***, SO HE'S PERFECT FOR YOU!
TWITCH

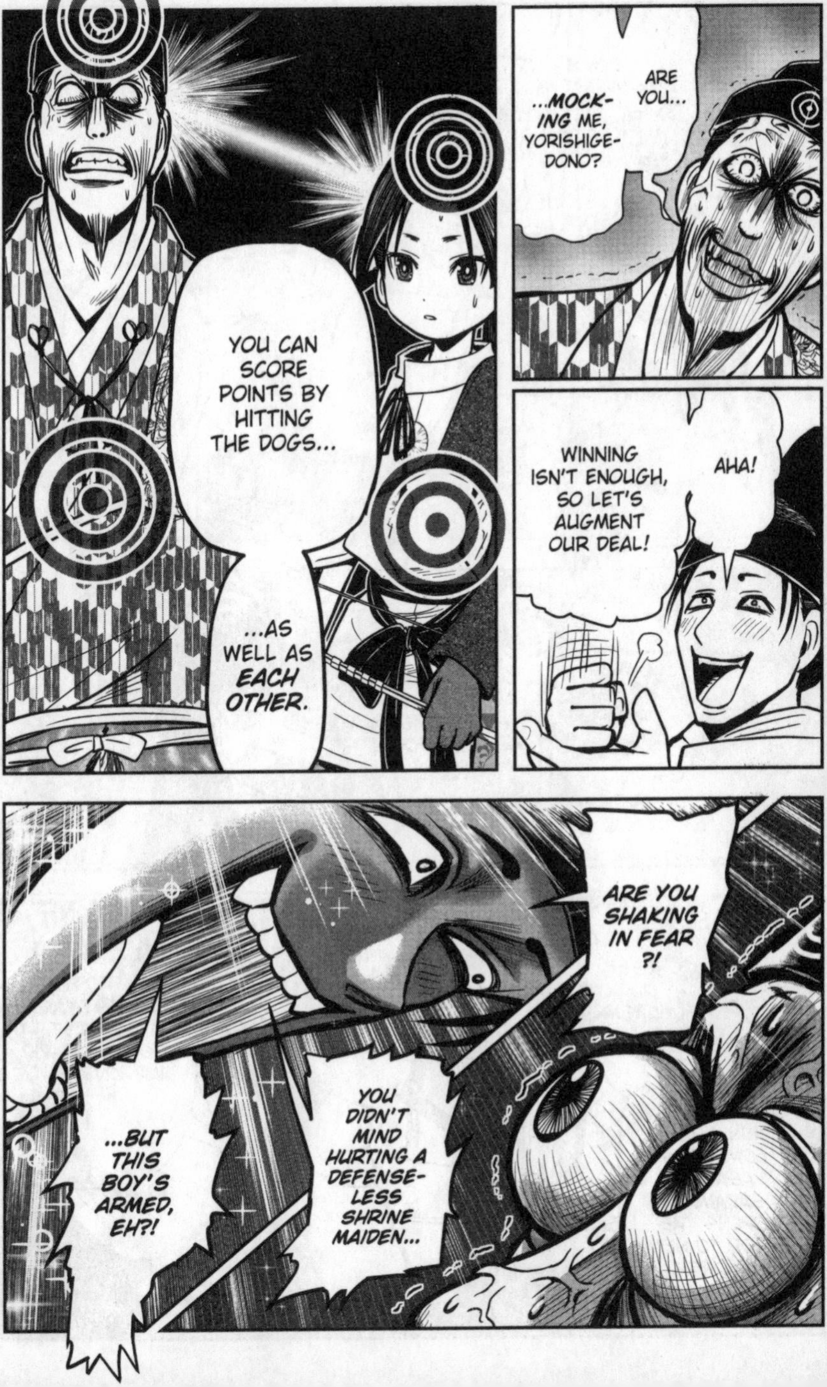
ARE YOU...
...MOCKING ME, YORISHIGE-DONO?
AHA!
WINNING ISN'T ENOUGH, SO LET'S AUGMENT OUR DEAL!
YOU CAN SCORE POINTS BY HITTING THE DOGS...
...AS WELL AS EACH OTHER.
ARE YOU SHAKING IN FEAR?!
YOU DIDN'T MIND HURTING A DEFENSELESS SHRINE MAIDEN...
...BUT THIS BOY'S ARMED, EH?!

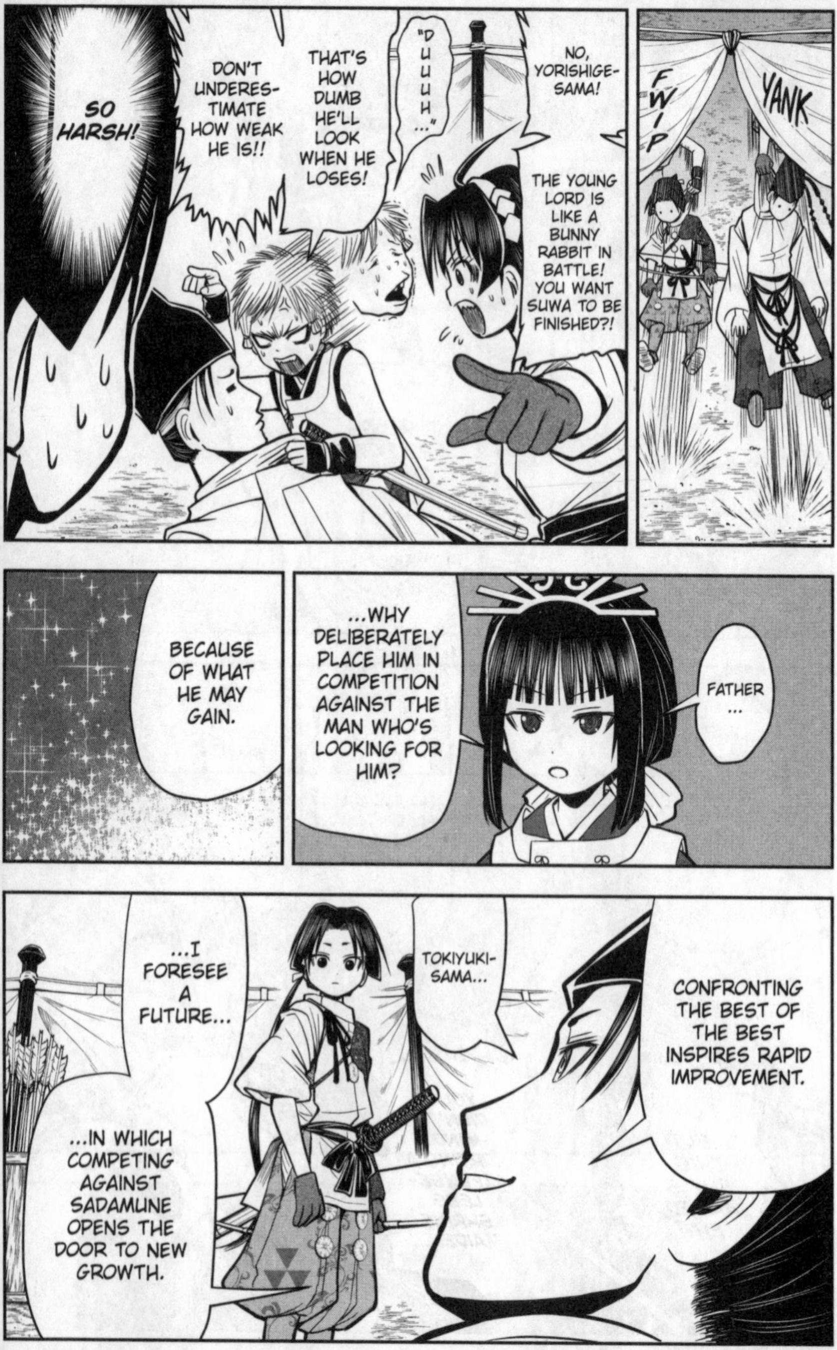
YANK
FWIP
NO, YORISHIGE-SAMA!
THE YOUNG LORD IS LIKE A BUNNY RABBIT IN BATTLE! YOU WANT SUWA TO BE FINISHED?!
"DUUUH..."
THAT'S HOW DUMB HE'LL LOOK WHEN HE LOSES!
DON'T UNDERESTIMATE HOW WEAK HE IS!!
SO HARSH!
FATHER...
...WHY DELIBERATELY PLACE HIM IN COMPETITION AGAINST THE MAN WHO'S LOOKING FOR HIM?
BECAUSE OF WHAT HE MAY GAIN.
CONFRONTING THE BEST OF THE BEST INSPIRES RAPID IMPROVEMENT.
TOKIYUKI-SAMA...
...I FORESEE A FUTURE...
...IN WHICH COMPETING AGAINST SADAMUNE OPENS THE DOOR TO NEW GROWTH.

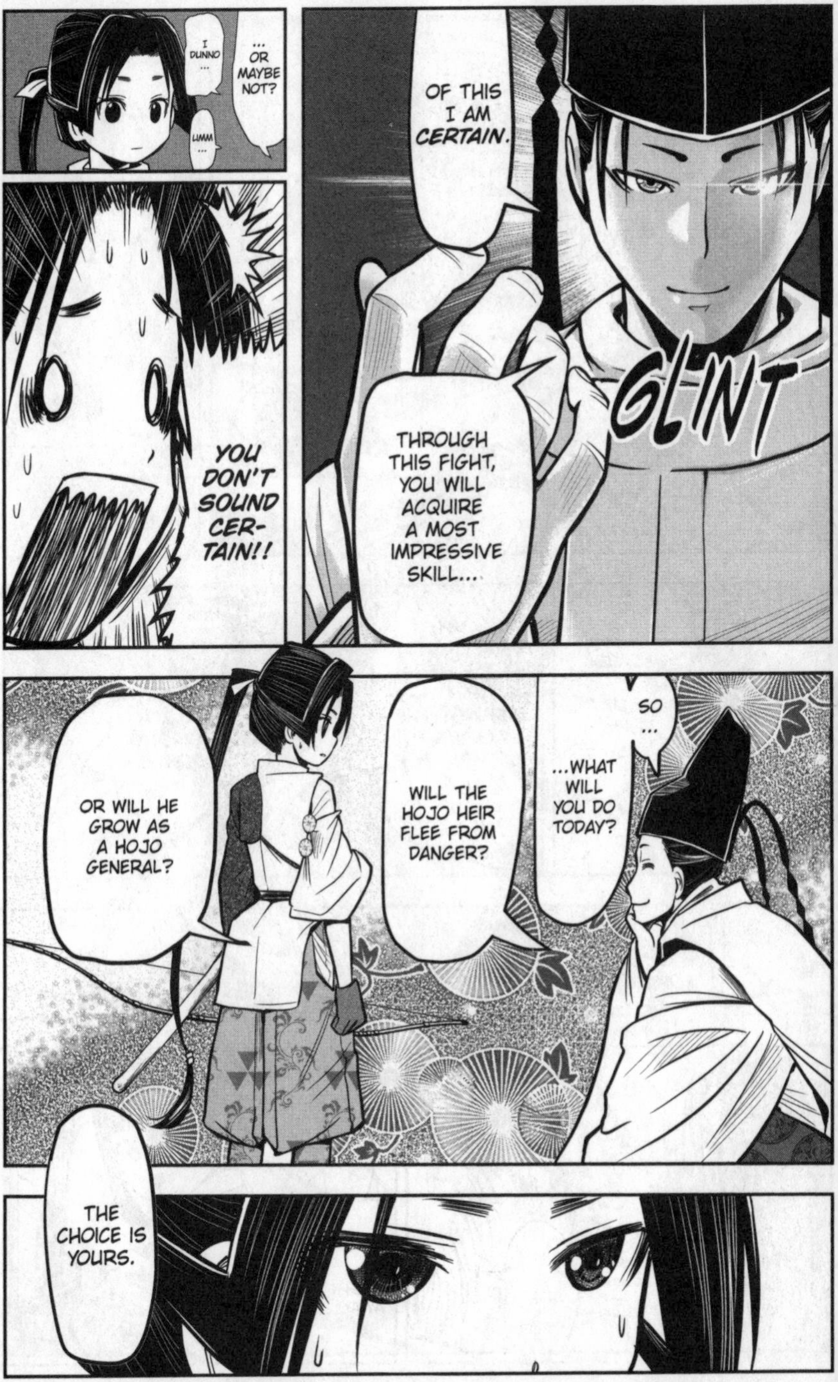
OF THIS I AM CERTAIN.
THROUGH THIS FIGHT, YOU WILL ACQUIRE A MOST IMPRESSIVE SKILL....
GLINT
...OR MAYBE NOT?
I DUNNO...
UMM...
YOU DON'T SOUND CERTAIN!!
SO...
...WHAT WILL YOU DO TODAY?
WILL THE HOJO HEIR FLEE FROM DANGER?
OR WILL HE GROW AS A HOJO GENERAL?
THE CHOICE IS YOURS.

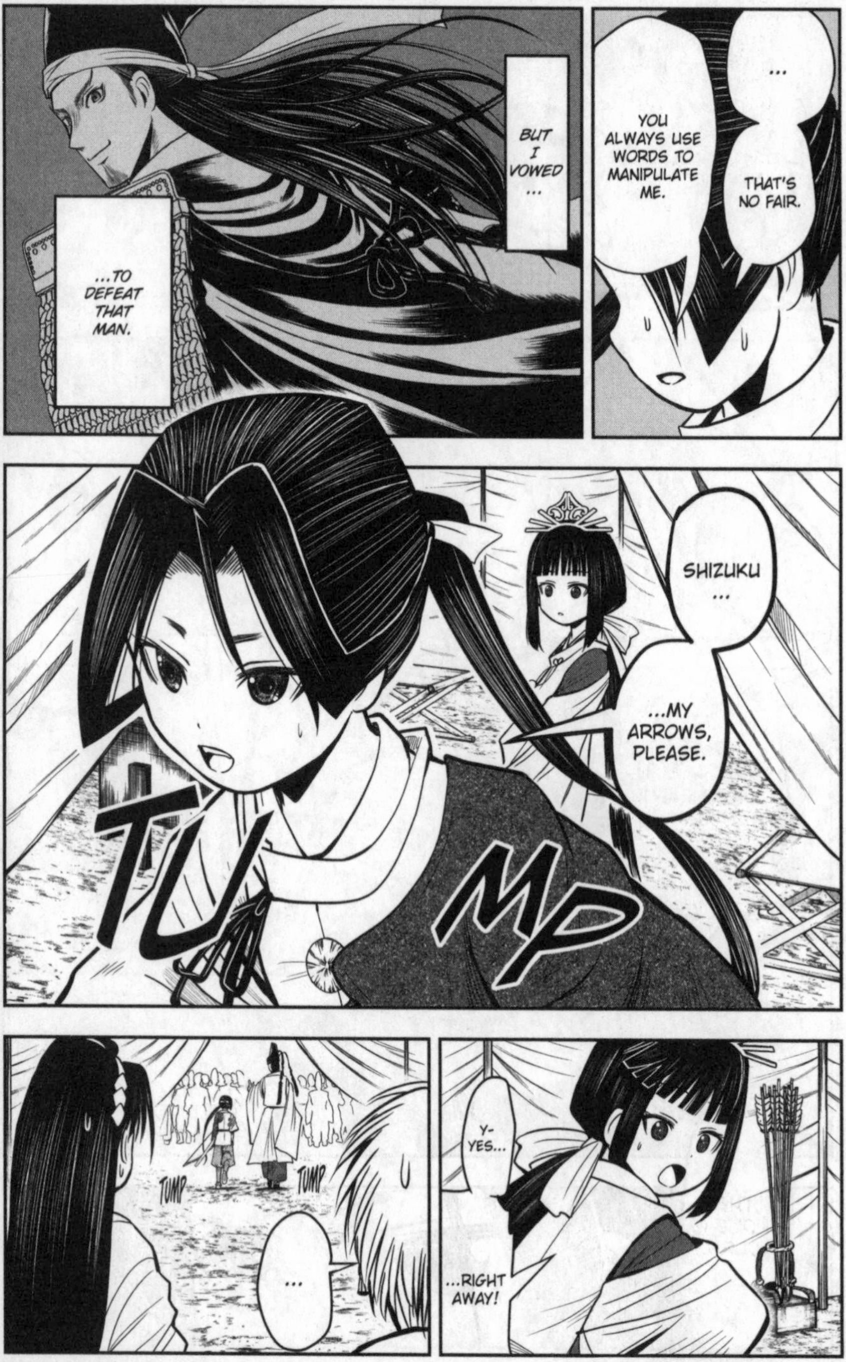
...
THAT'S NO FAIR.
YOU ALWAYS USE WORDS TO MANIPULATE ME.
BUT I VOWED ...
...TO DEFEAT THAT MAN.
SHIZUKU ...
...MY ARROWS, PLEASE.
TUMP
Y-YES...
...RIGHT AWAY!
TUMP
TUMP
...

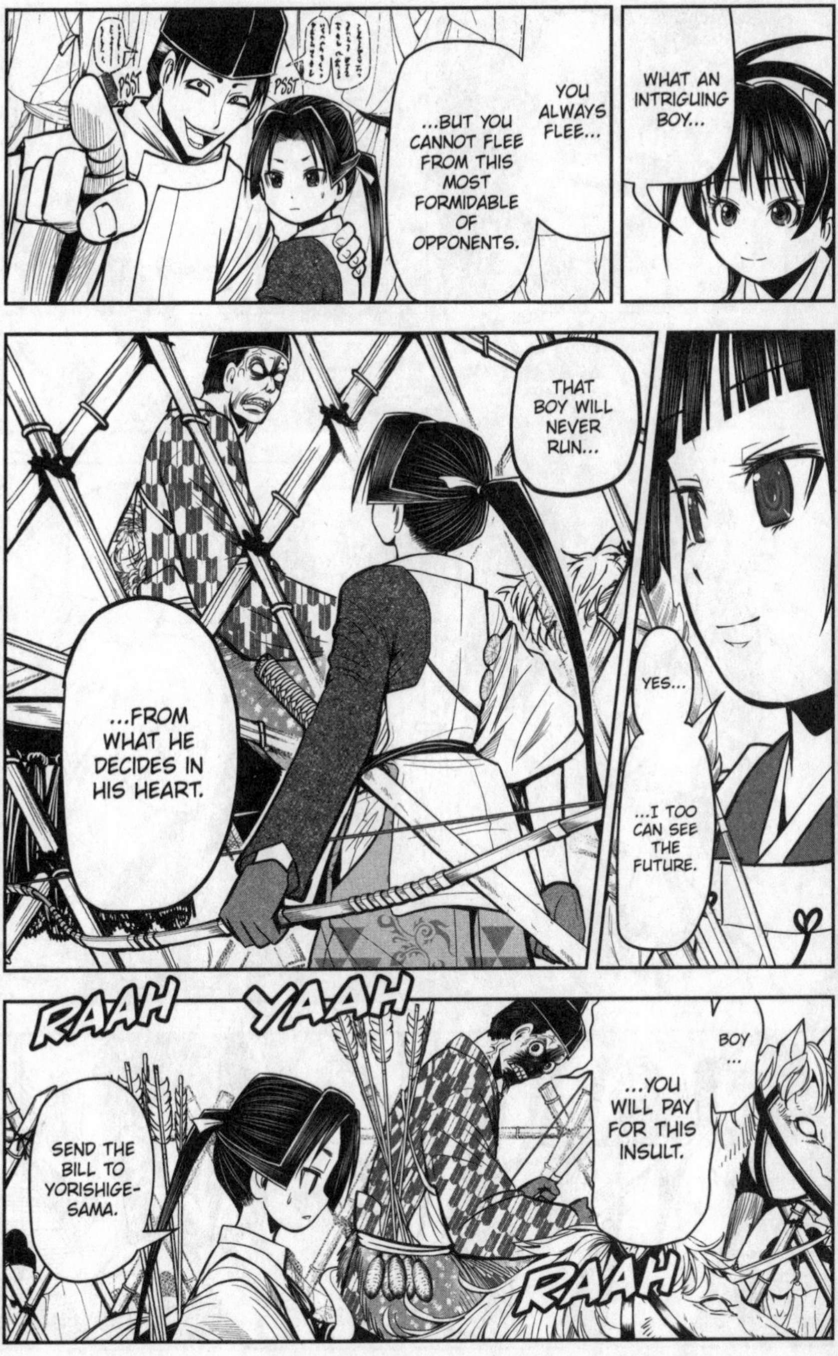
WHAT AN INTRIGUING BOY...
YOU ALWAYS FLEE...
...BUT YOU CANNOT FLEE FROM THIS MOST FORMIDABLE OF OPPONENTS.
PSST
PSST
THAT BOY WILL NEVER RUN...
YES...
...I TOO CAN SEE THE FUTURE.
...FROM WHAT HE DECIDES IN HIS HEART.
BOY...
...YOU WILL PAY FOR THIS INSULT.
YAAH
RAAH
RAAH
SEND THE BILL TO YORISHIGE-SAMA.

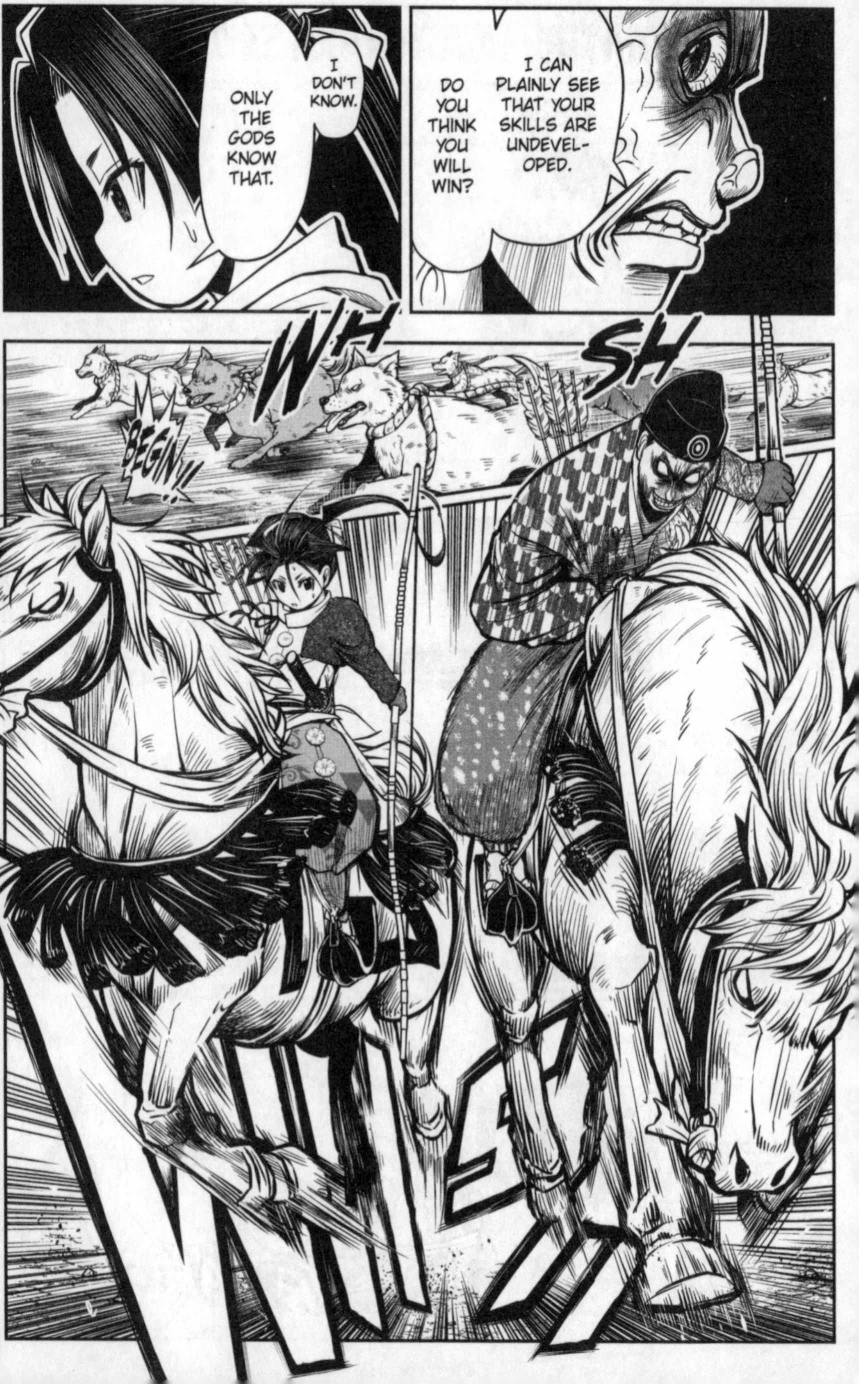
I CAN PLAINLY SEE THAT YOUR SKILLS ARE UNDEVELOPED.
DO YOU THINK YOU WILL WIN?
I DON'T KNOW.
ONLY THE GODS KNOW THAT.
SH
WH
BEGIN!!

ILLUSTRATING OGASAWARA SADAMUNE

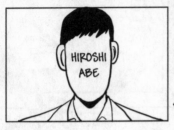

HIROSHI
ABE

1. HIROSHI ABE IS KNOWN FOR HAVING BIG EYES, SO I START WITH AN IMAGE OF HIM.

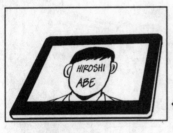

HIROSHI
ABE

2. I IMPORT THAT TO THE COMPUTER AND TRACE IT.

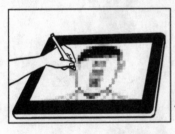

3. I DRAW OVER EVERYTHING SO NOTHING OF THE ORIGINAL IMAGE REMAINS.

4. ***ALL DONE!***

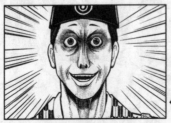

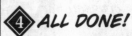

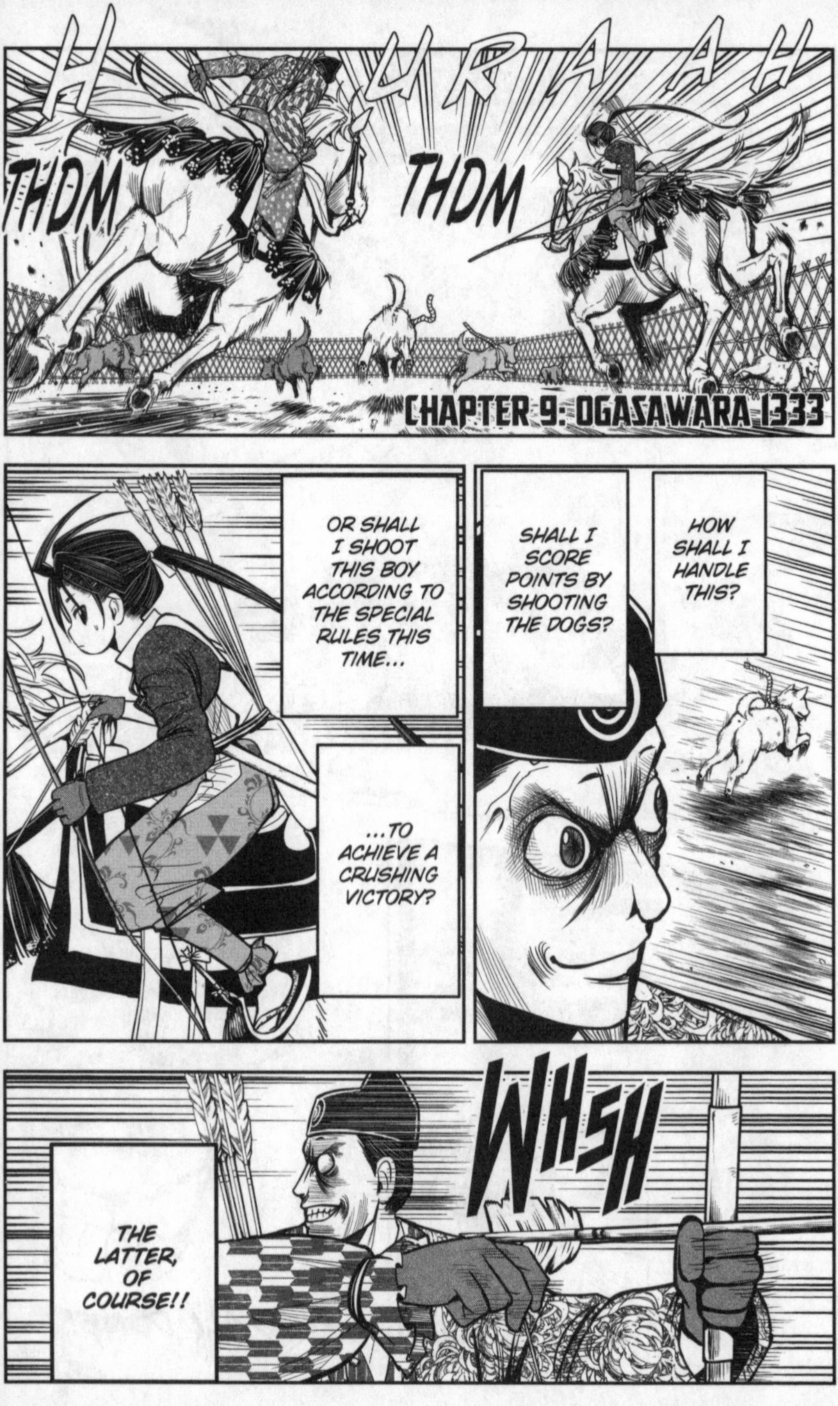
HURAAH
THDM
THDM
CHAPTER 9: OGASAWARA 1333
HOW SHALL I HANDLE THIS?
SHALL I SCORE POINTS BY SHOOTING THE DOGS?
OR SHALL I SHOOT THIS BOY ACCORDING TO THE SPECIAL RULES THIS TIME...
...TO ACHIEVE A CRUSHING VICTORY?
WHSH
THE LATTER, OF COURSE!!

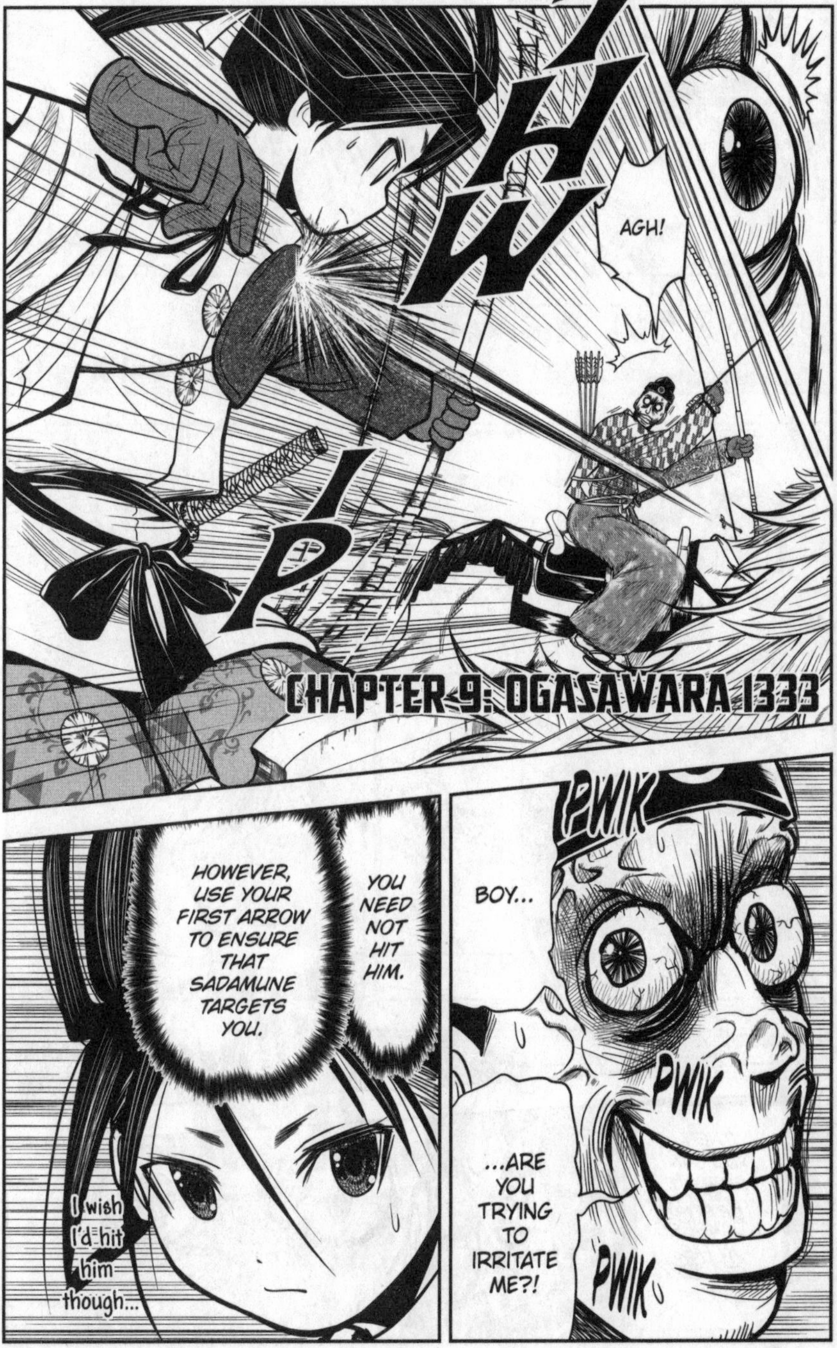
AGH!
CHAPTER 9: OGASAWARA 1333
PWIK
BOY...
PWIK
...ARE YOU TRYING TO IRRITATE ME?!
PWIK
YOU NEED NOT HIT HIM.
HOWEVER, USE YOUR FIRST ARROW TO ENSURE THAT SADAMUNE TARGETS YOU.
I wish I'd hit him though...

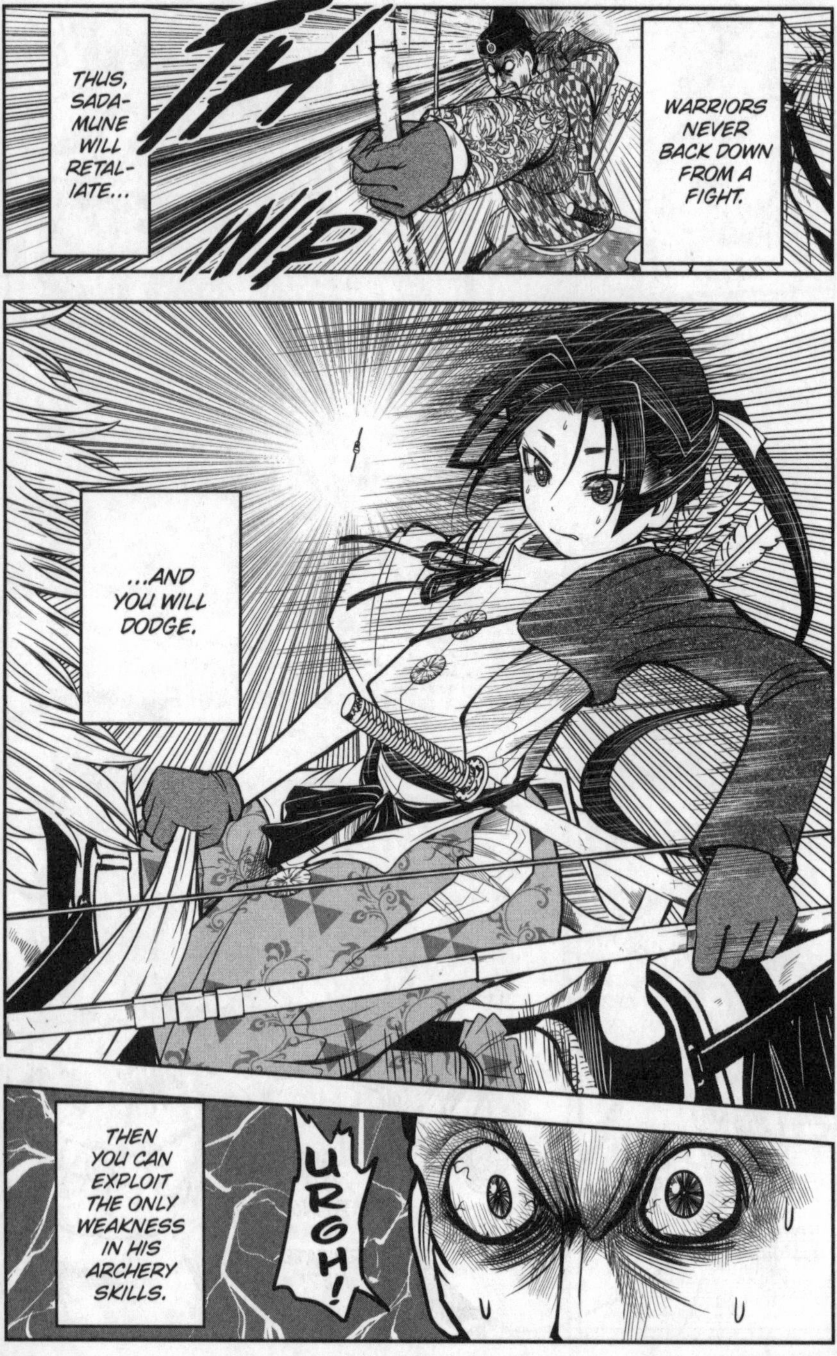
WARRIORS NEVER BACK DOWN FROM A FIGHT.
THWIP
THUS, SADA-MUNE WILL RETAL-IATE...
...AND YOU WILL DODGE.
URGH!
THEN YOU CAN EXPLOIT THE ONLY WEAKNESS IN HIS ARCHERY SKILLS.

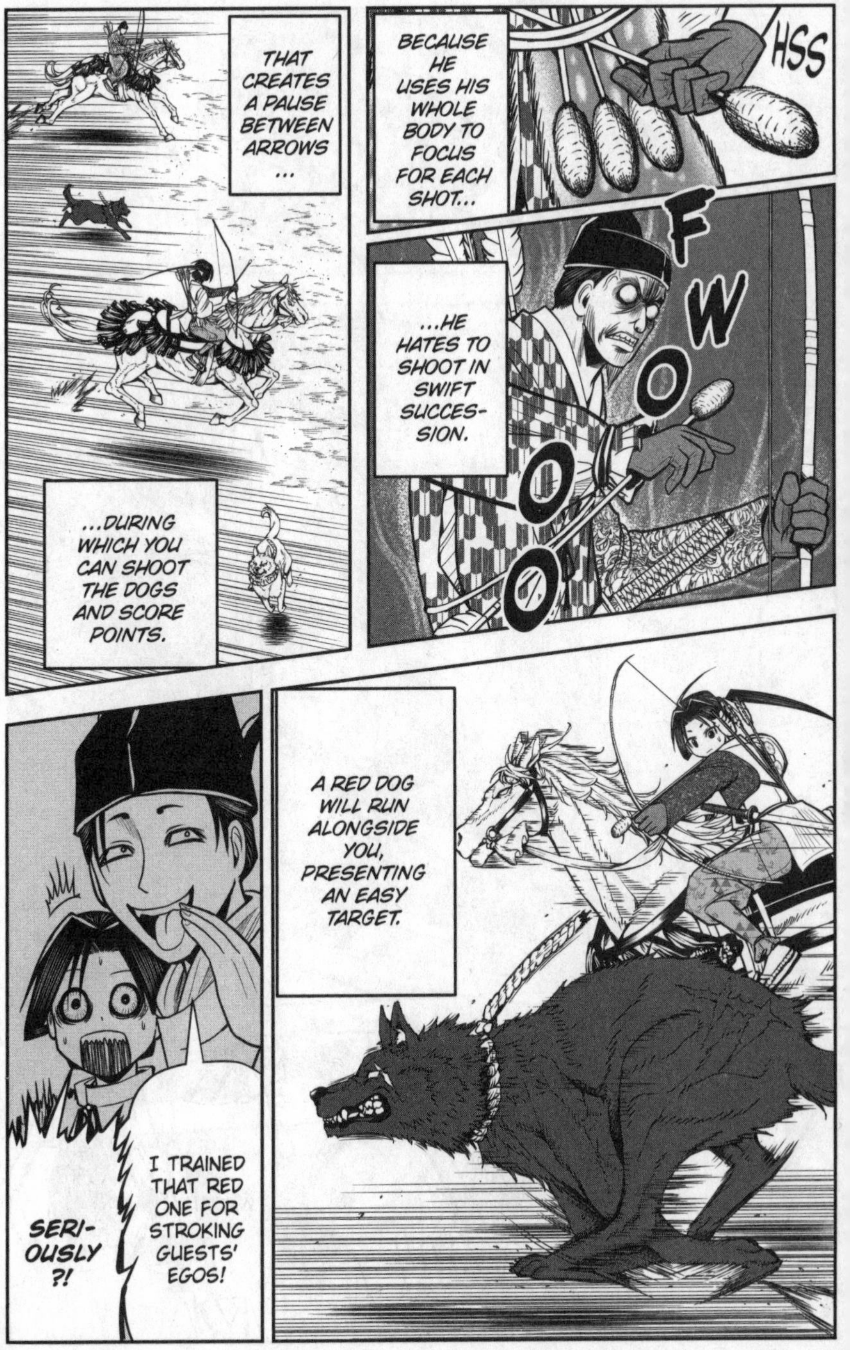

BECAUSE HE USES HIS WHOLE BODY TO FOCUS FOR EACH SHOT...
HSS
...HE HATES TO SHOOT IN SWIFT SUCCESSION.
FWOOOO
THAT CREATES A PAUSE BETWEEN ARROWS ...
...DURING WHICH YOU CAN SHOOT THE DOGS AND SCORE POINTS.
A RED DOG WILL RUN ALONGSIDE YOU, PRESENTING AN EASY TARGET.
I TRAINED THAT RED ONE FOR STROKING GUESTS' EGOS!
SERIOUSLY?!

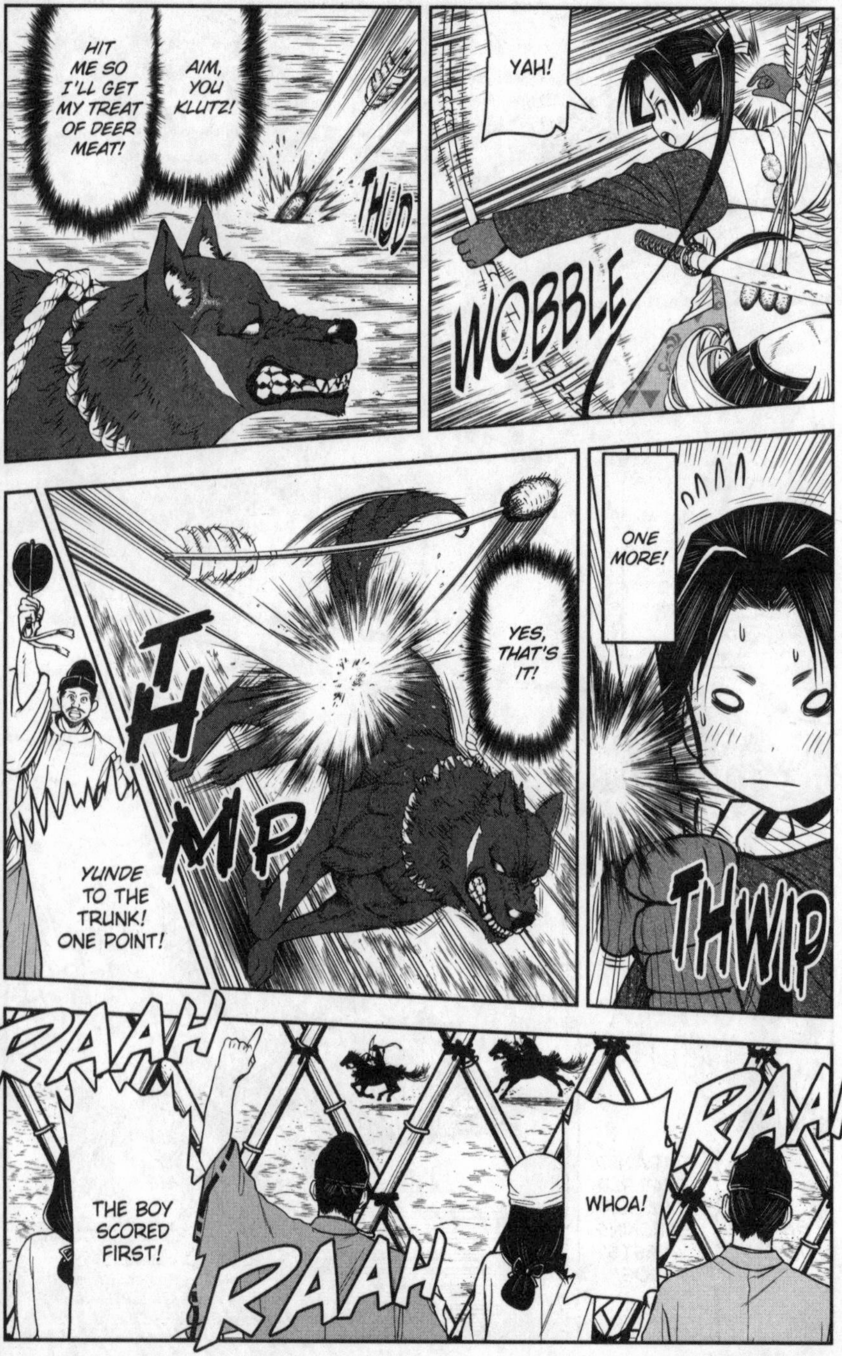
YAH!
WOBBLE
AIM, YOU KLUTZ!
HIT ME SO I'LL GET MY TREAT OF DEER MEAT!
THUD
ONE MORE!
THWIP
YES, THAT'S IT!
THMP
YUNDE TO THE TRUNK! ONE POINT!
RAAH
WHOA!
THE BOY SCORED FIRST!
RAAH
RAAH

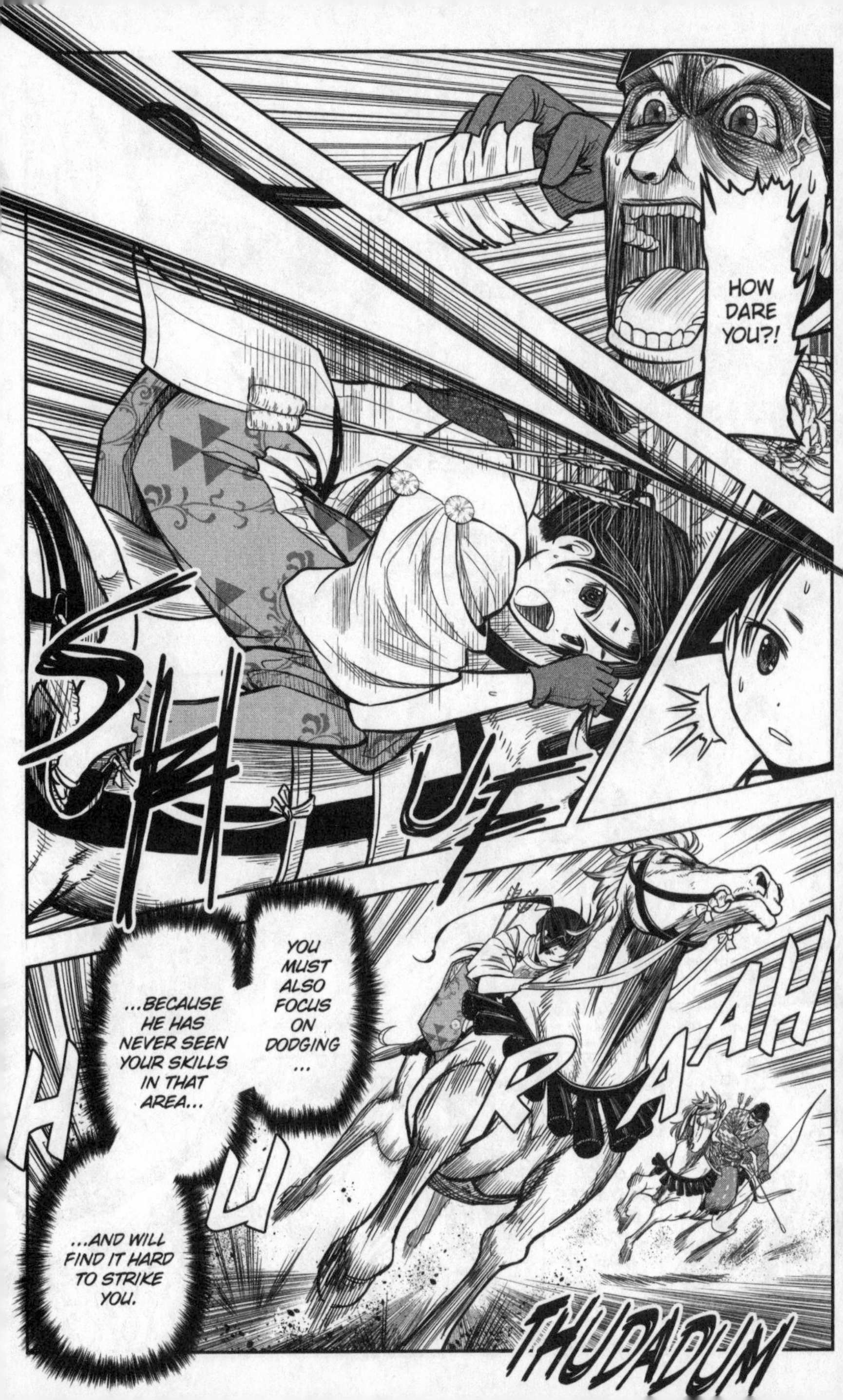
HOW DARE YOU?!
SHHUF
YOU MUST ALSO FOCUS ON DODGING...
...BECAUSE HE HAS NEVER SEEN YOUR SKILLS IN THAT AREA...
...AND WILL FIND IT HARD TO STRIKE YOU.
HURAAAH
THUDADUM

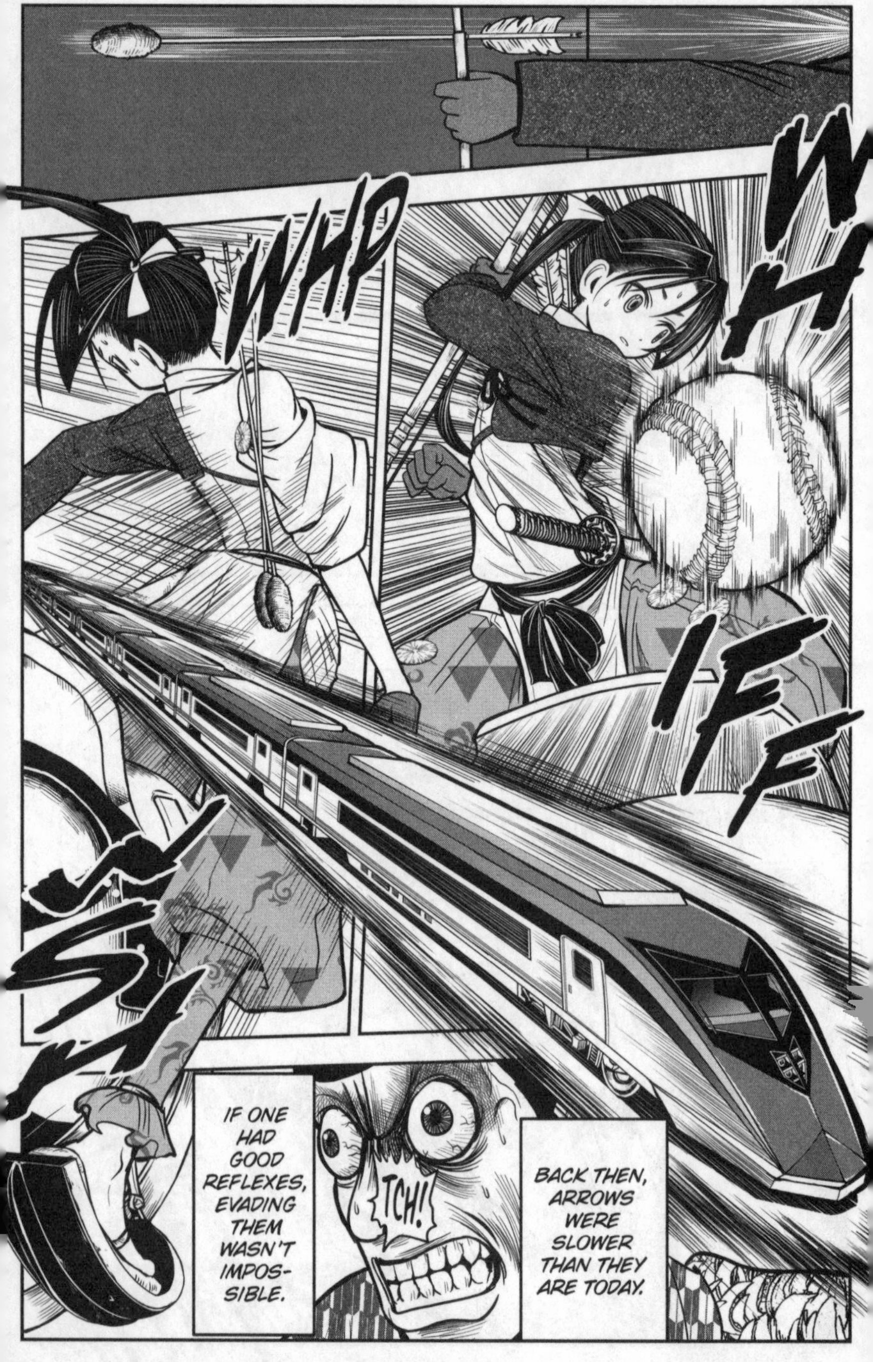
WHP
BACK THEN, ARROWS WERE SLOWER THAN THEY ARE TODAY.
TCH!
IF ONE HAD GOOD REFLEXES, EVADING THEM WASN'T IMPOSSIBLE.

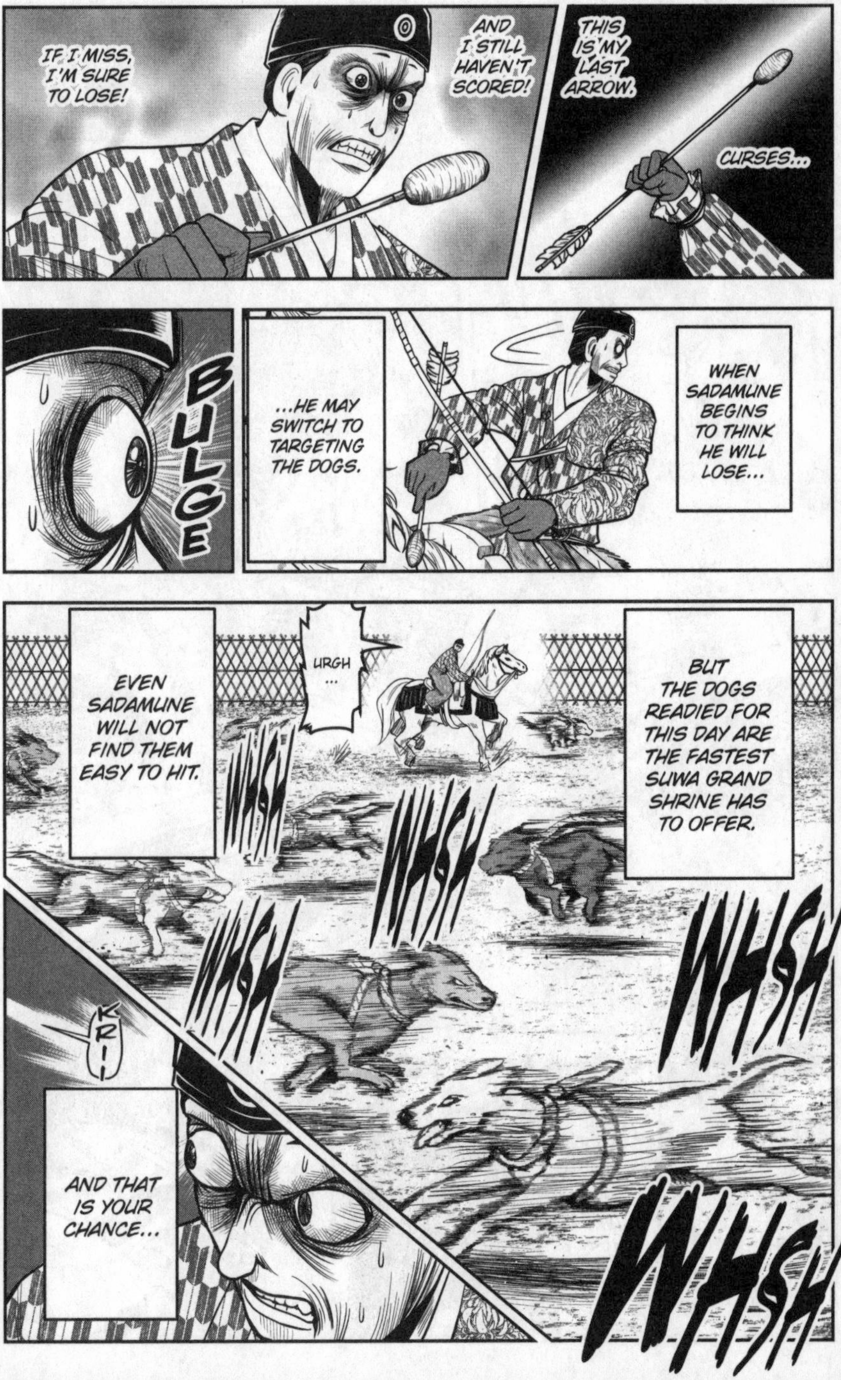
THIS IS MY LAST ARROW.
CURSES...
AND I STILL HAVEN'T SCORED!
IF I MISS, I'M SURE TO LOSE!
WHEN SADAMUNE BEGINS TO THINK HE WILL LOSE...
...HE MAY SWITCH TO TARGETING THE DOGS.
BULGE
BUT THE DOGS READIED FOR THIS DAY ARE THE FASTEST SUWA GRAND SHRINE HAS TO OFFER.
URGH ...
EVEN SADAMUNE WILL NOT FIND THEM EASY TO HIT.
WHSH
WHSH
WHSH
WHSH
WHSH
KRII
AND THAT IS YOUR CHANCE...

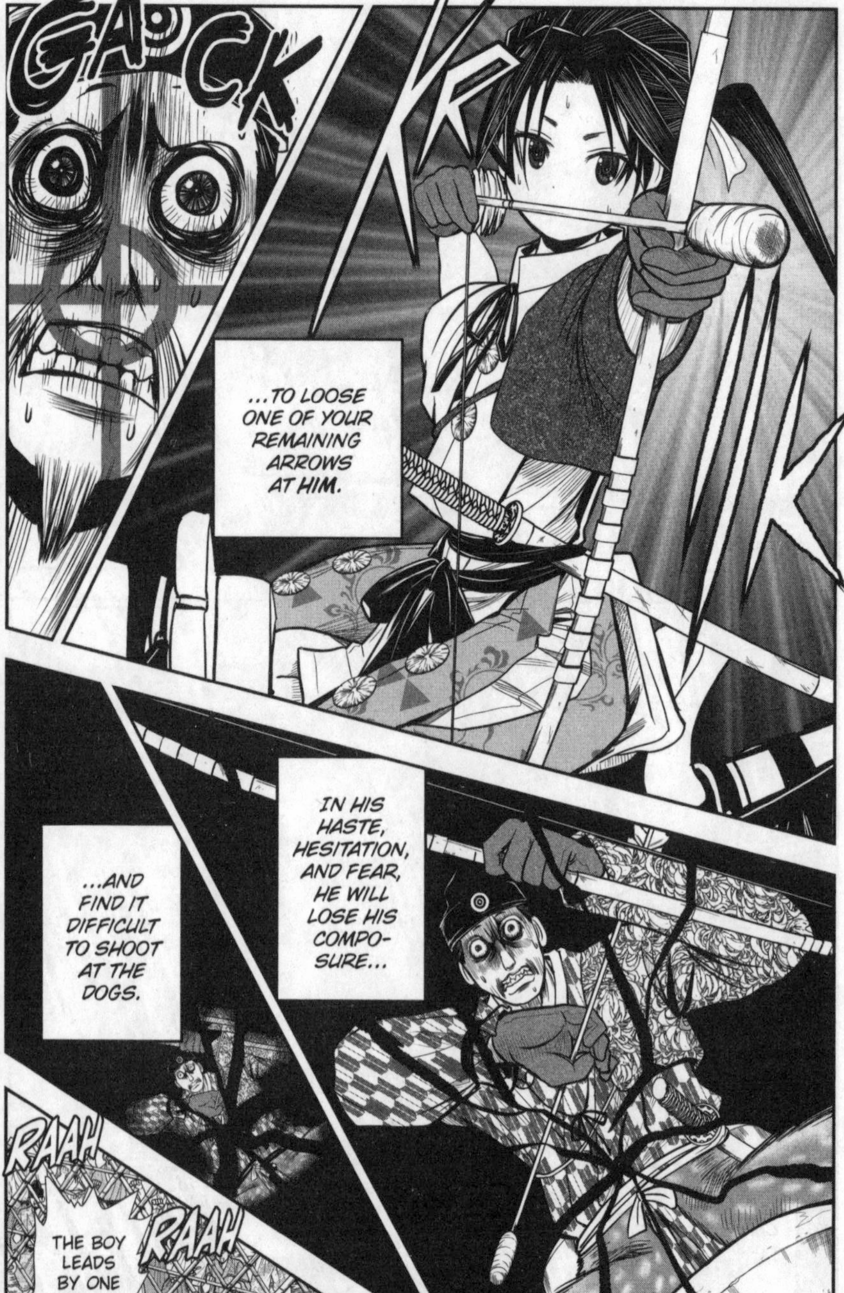
KRIK
...TO LOOSE ONE OF YOUR REMAINING ARROWS AT HIM.
GACK
IN HIS HASTE, HESITATION, AND FEAR, HE WILL LOSE HIS COMPOSURE...
...AND FIND IT DIFFICULT TO SHOOT AT THE DOGS.
RAAH
RAAH
THE BOY LEADS BY ONE POINT!
RAAH

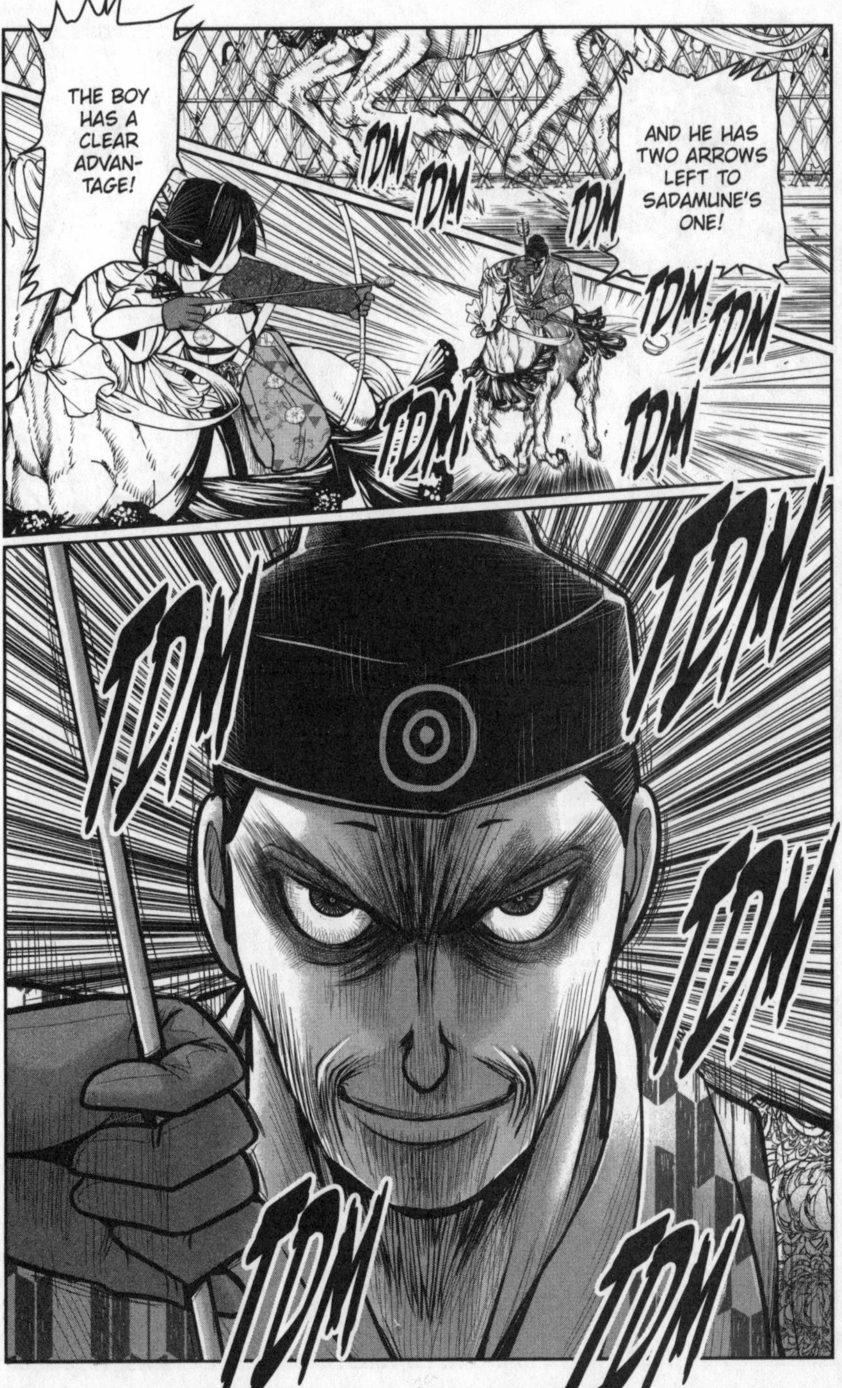
THE BOY HAS A CLEAR ADVAN-TAGE!
AND HE HAS TWO ARROWS LEFT TO SADAMUNE'S ONE!
TDM TDM TDM TDM TDM TDM TDM
TDM TDM TDM TDM TDM

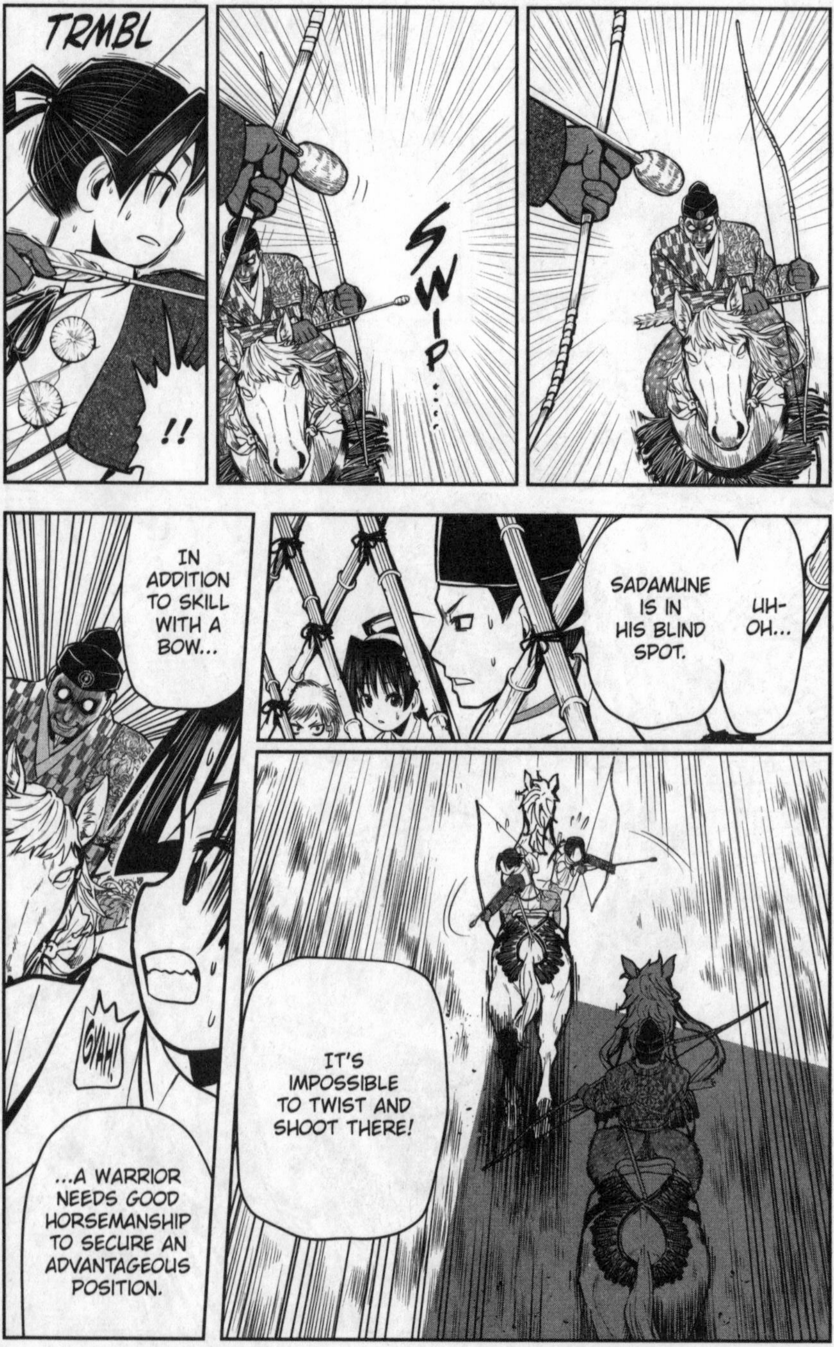
SWIP...
TRMBL
!!
UH-OH...
SADAMUNE IS IN HIS BLIND SPOT.
IT'S IMPOSSIBLE TO TWIST AND SHOOT THERE!
IN ADDITION TO SKILL WITH A BOW...
GYAH!
...A WARRIOR NEEDS GOOD HORSEMANSHIP TO SECURE AN ADVANTAGEOUS POSITION.

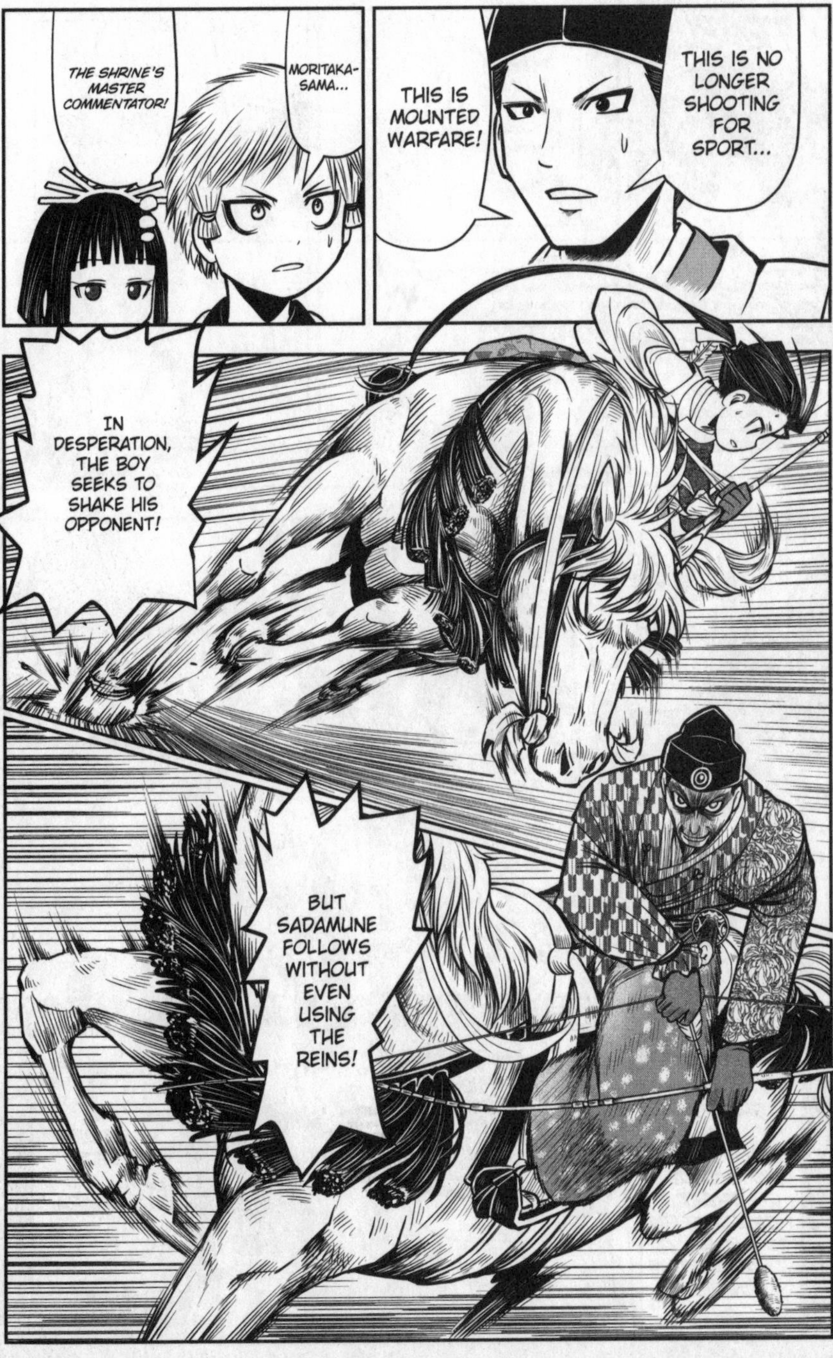
THIS IS NO LONGER SHOOTING FOR SPORT...
THIS IS MOUNTED WARFARE!
MORITAKA-SAMA...
THE SHRINE'S MASTER COMMENTATOR!
IN DESPERATION, THE BOY SEEKS TO SHAKE HIS OPPONENT!
BUT SADAMUNE FOLLOWS WITHOUT EVEN USING THE REINS!

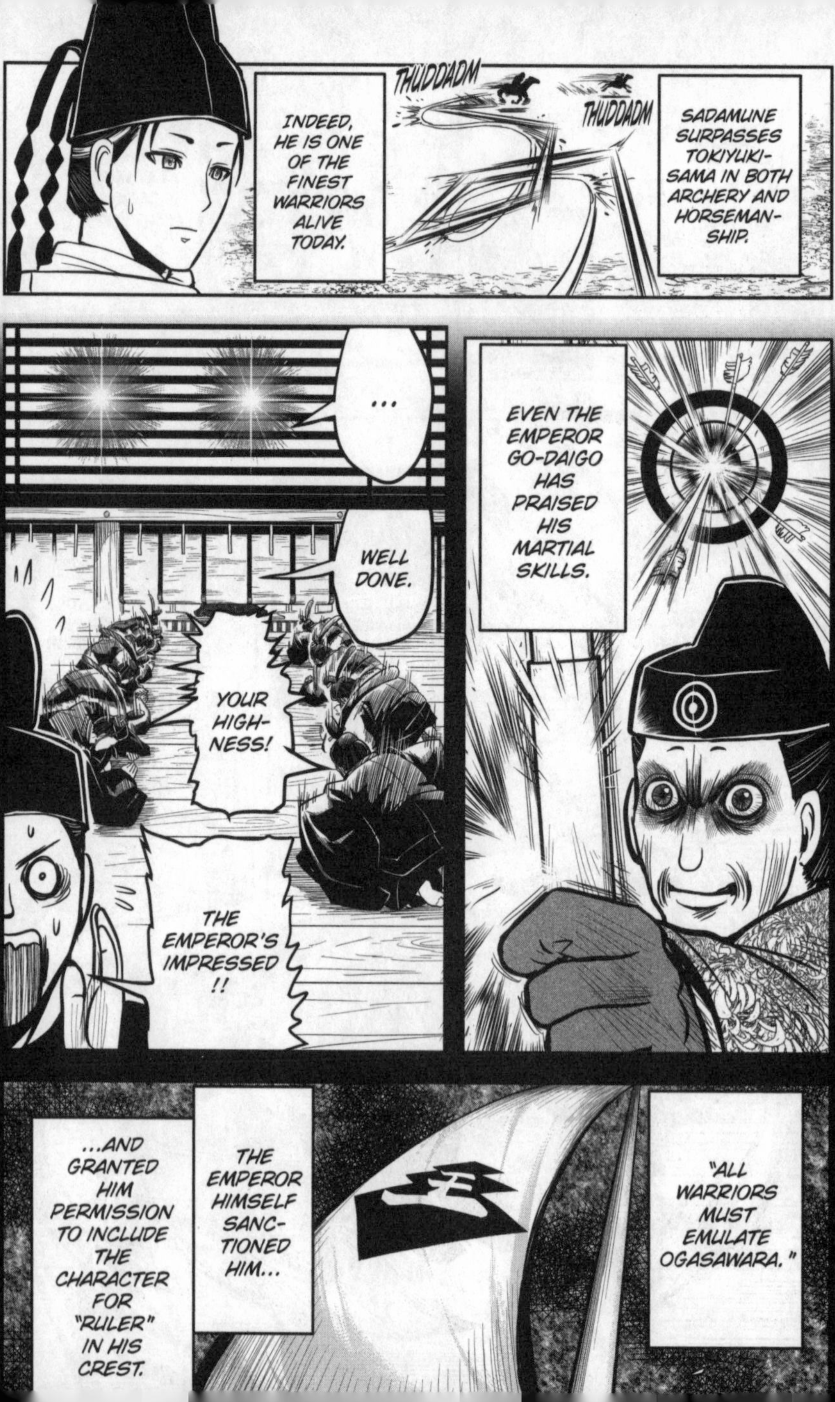
SADAMUNE SURPASSES TOKIYUKI-SAMA IN BOTH ARCHERY AND HORSEMAN-SHIP.
THUDDADM
THUDDADM
INDEED, HE IS ONE OF THE FINEST WARRIORS ALIVE TODAY.
EVEN THE EMPEROR GO-DAIGO HAS PRAISED HIS MARTIAL SKILLS.
...
WELL DONE.
YOUR HIGH-NESS!
THE EMPEROR'S IMPRESSED !!
"ALL WARRIORS MUST EMULATE OGASAWARA."
THE EMPEROR HIMSELF SANC-TIONED HIM...
...AND GRANTED HIM PERMISSION TO INCLUDE THE CHARACTER FOR "RULER" IN HIS CREST.

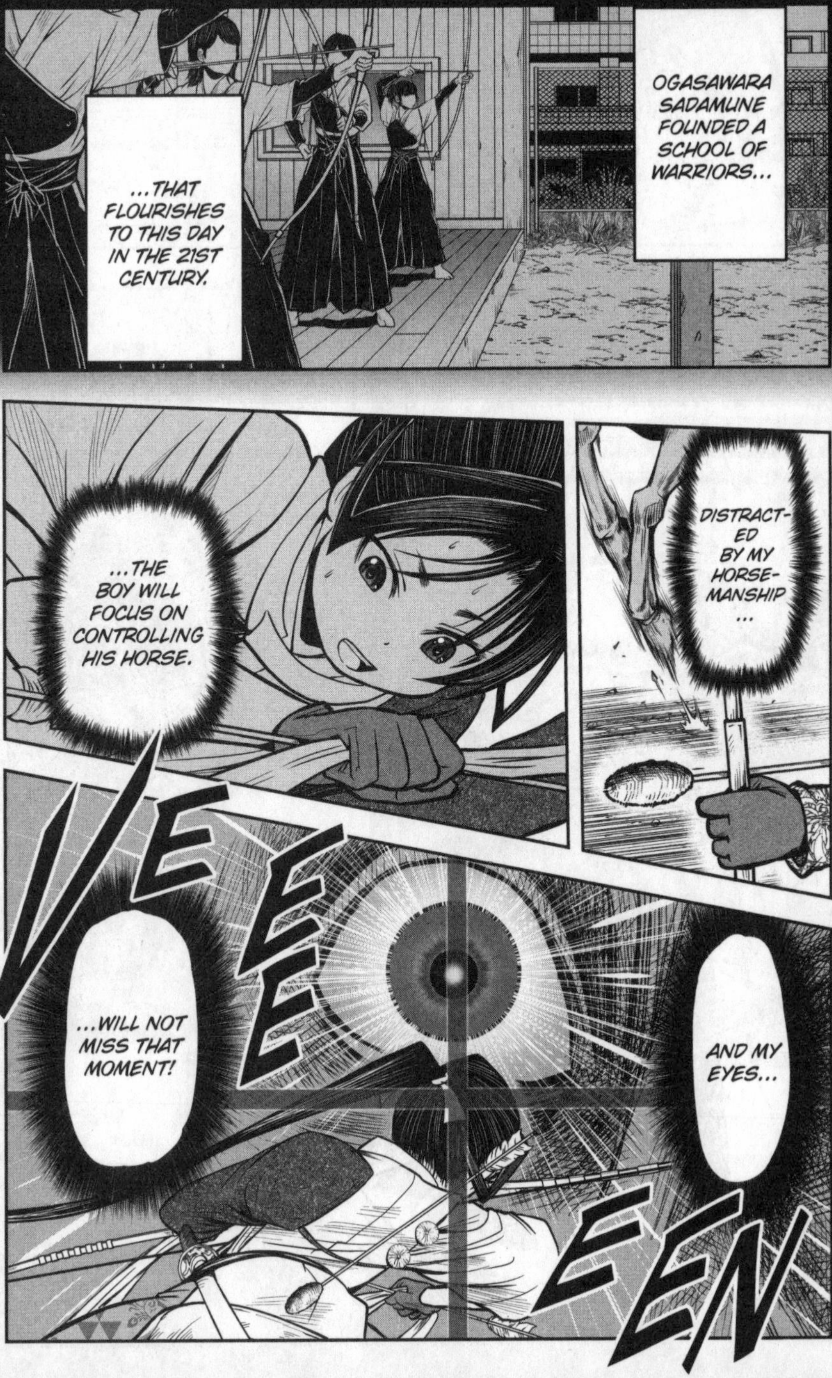
OGASAWARA SADAMUNE FOUNDED A SCHOOL OF WARRIORS...
...THAT FLOURISHES TO THIS DAY IN THE 21ST CENTURY.
DISTRACTED BY MY HORSEMANSHIP...
...THE BOY WILL FOCUS ON CONTROLLING HIS HORSE.
AND MY EYES...
...WILL NOT MISS THAT MOMENT!
VEEEEEN

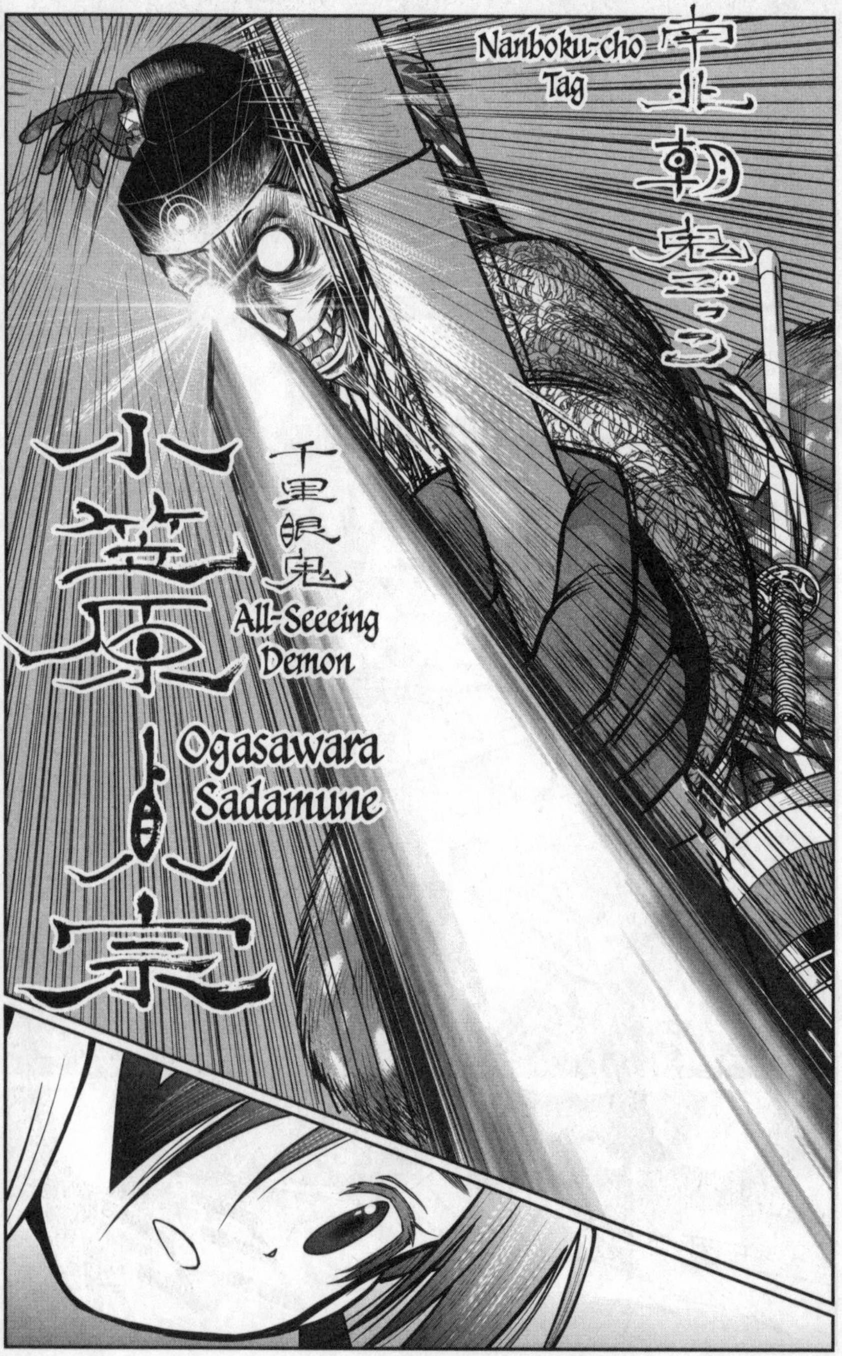
南北朝鬼ごっこ
Nanboku-cho Tag
千里眼鬼
All-Seeeing Demon
小笠原貞宗
Ogasawara Sadamune

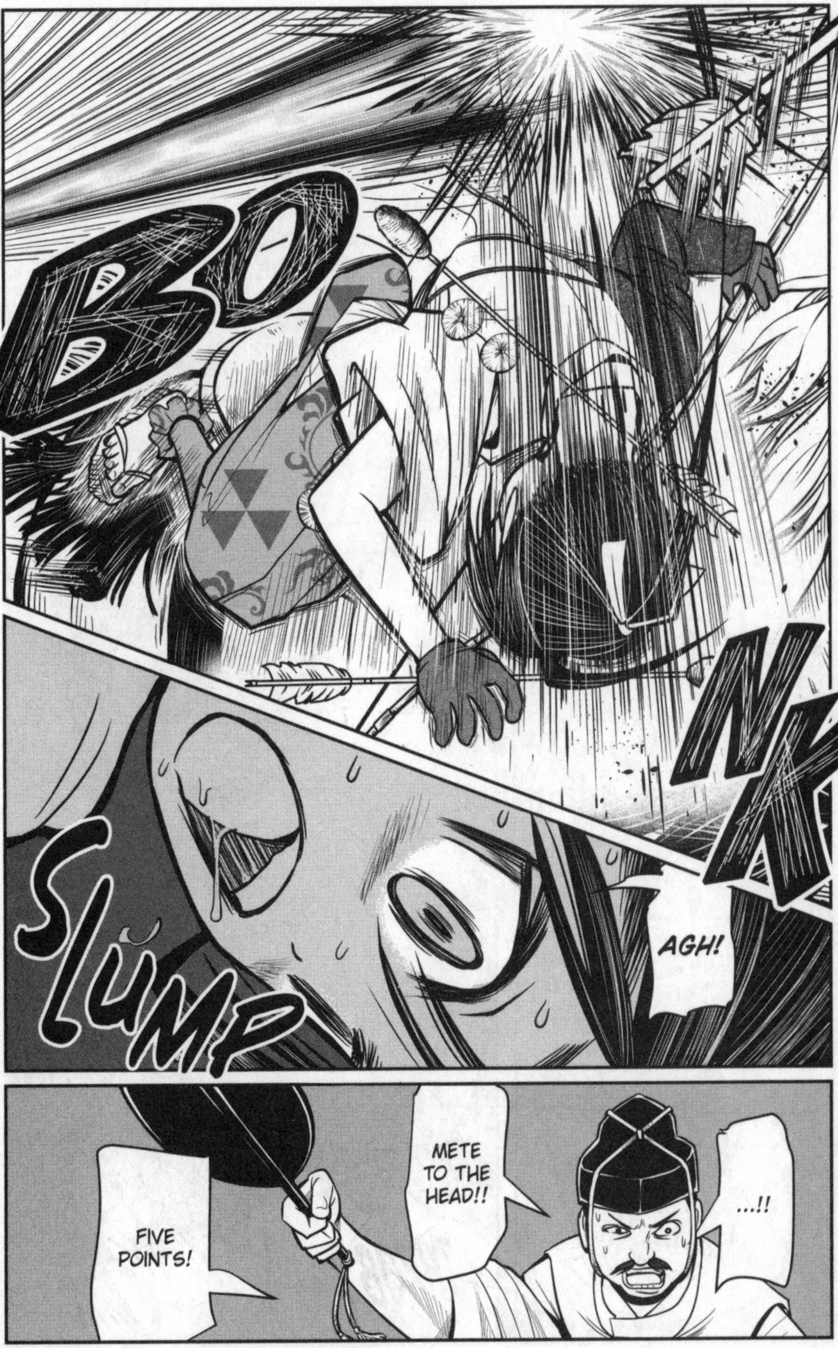
BO
NK
AGH!
SLUMP
...!!
METE TO THE HEAD!!
FIVE POINTS!

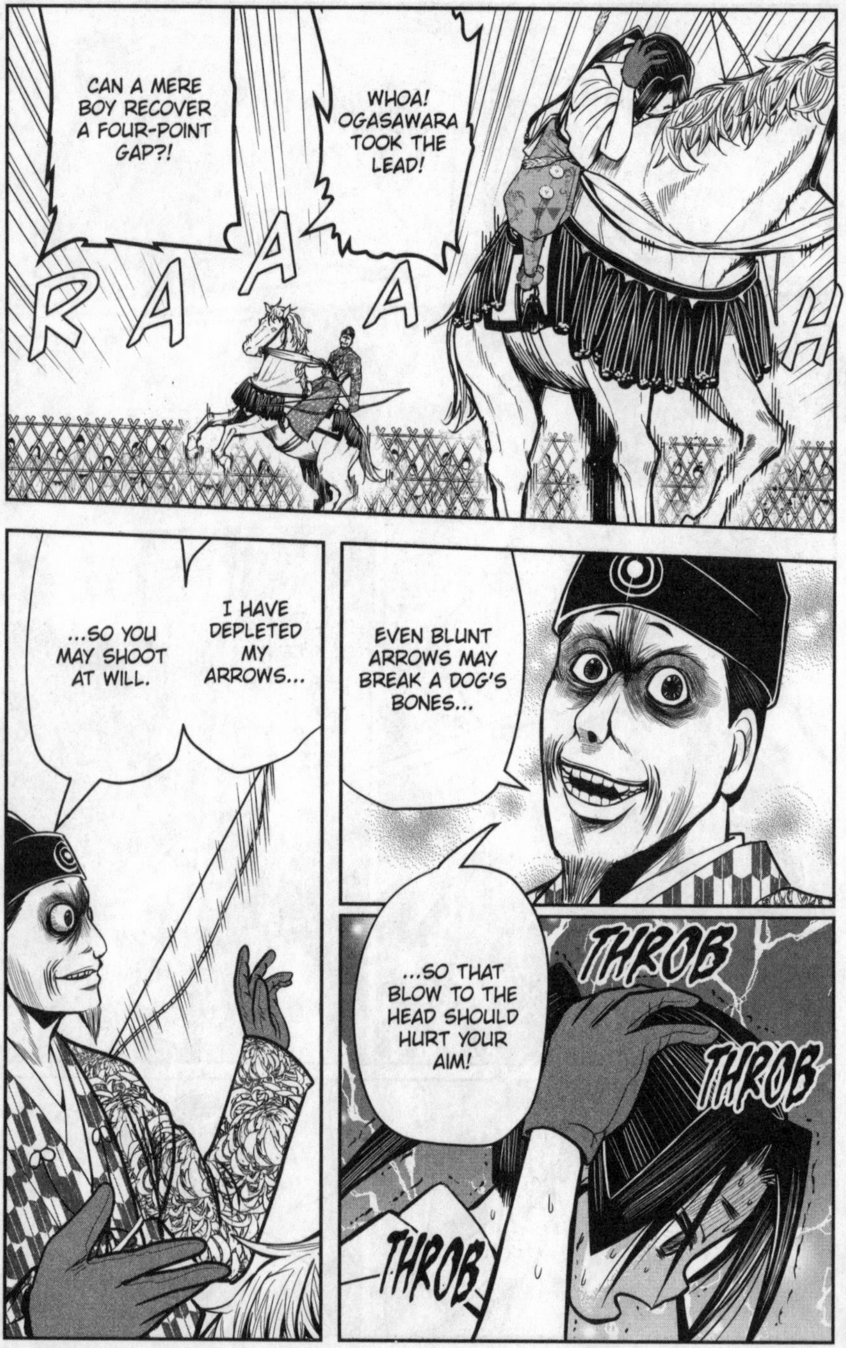
WHOA! OGASAWARA TOOK THE LEAD!
CAN A MERE BOY RECOVER A FOUR-POINT GAP?!
RAAAH
EVEN BLUNT ARROWS MAY BREAK A DOG'S BONES...
...SO THAT BLOW TO THE HEAD SHOULD HURT YOUR AIM!
THROB
THROB
THROB
I HAVE DEPLETED MY ARROWS...
...SO YOU MAY SHOOT AT WILL.

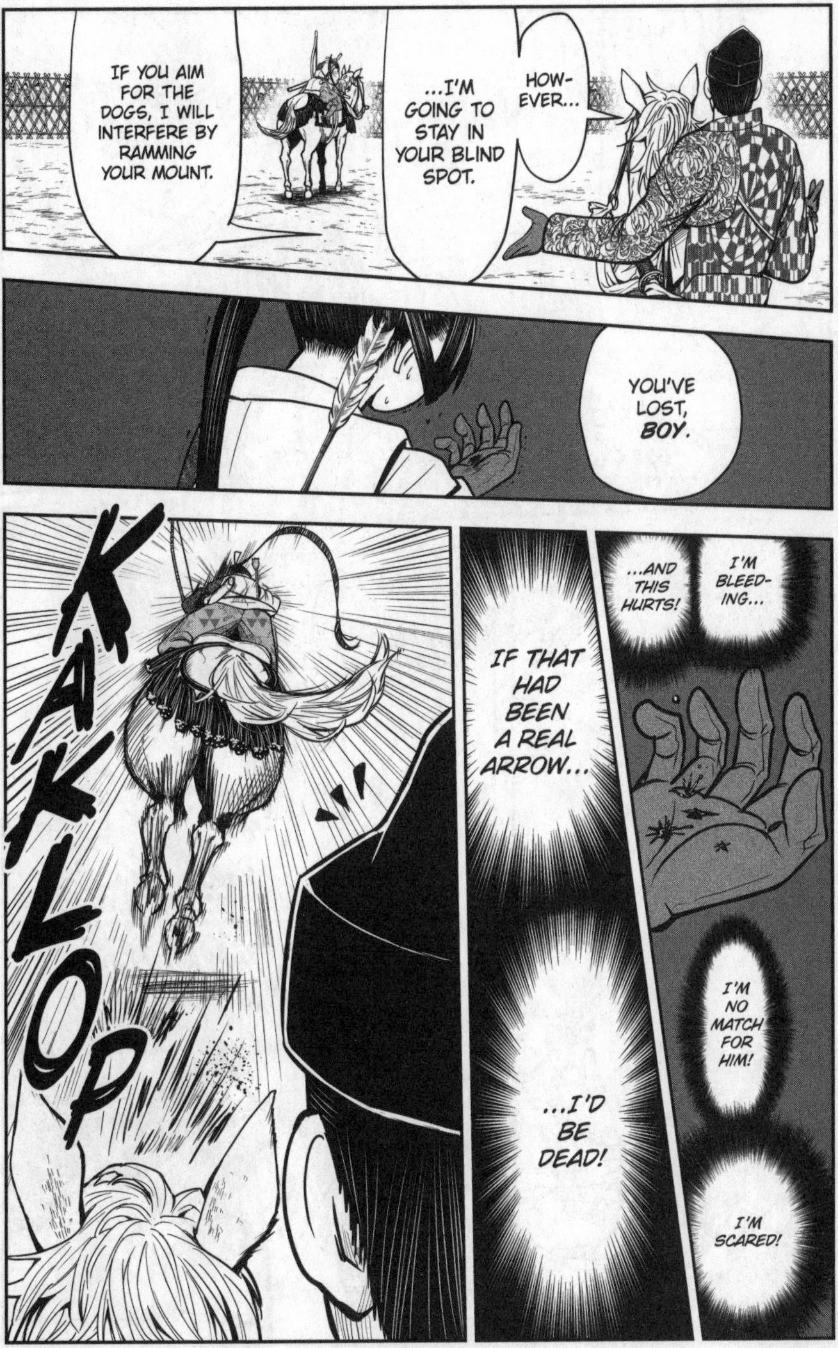
HOW-EVER...
...I'M GOING TO STAY IN YOUR BLIND SPOT.
IF YOU AIM FOR THE DOGS, I WILL INTERFERE BY RAMMING YOUR MOUNT.
YOU'VE LOST, *BOY*.
I'M BLEED-ING...
...AND THIS HURTS!
I'M NO MATCH FOR HIM!
I'M SCARED!
IF THAT HAD BEEN A REAL ARROW...
...I'D BE DEAD!
KAKLOP

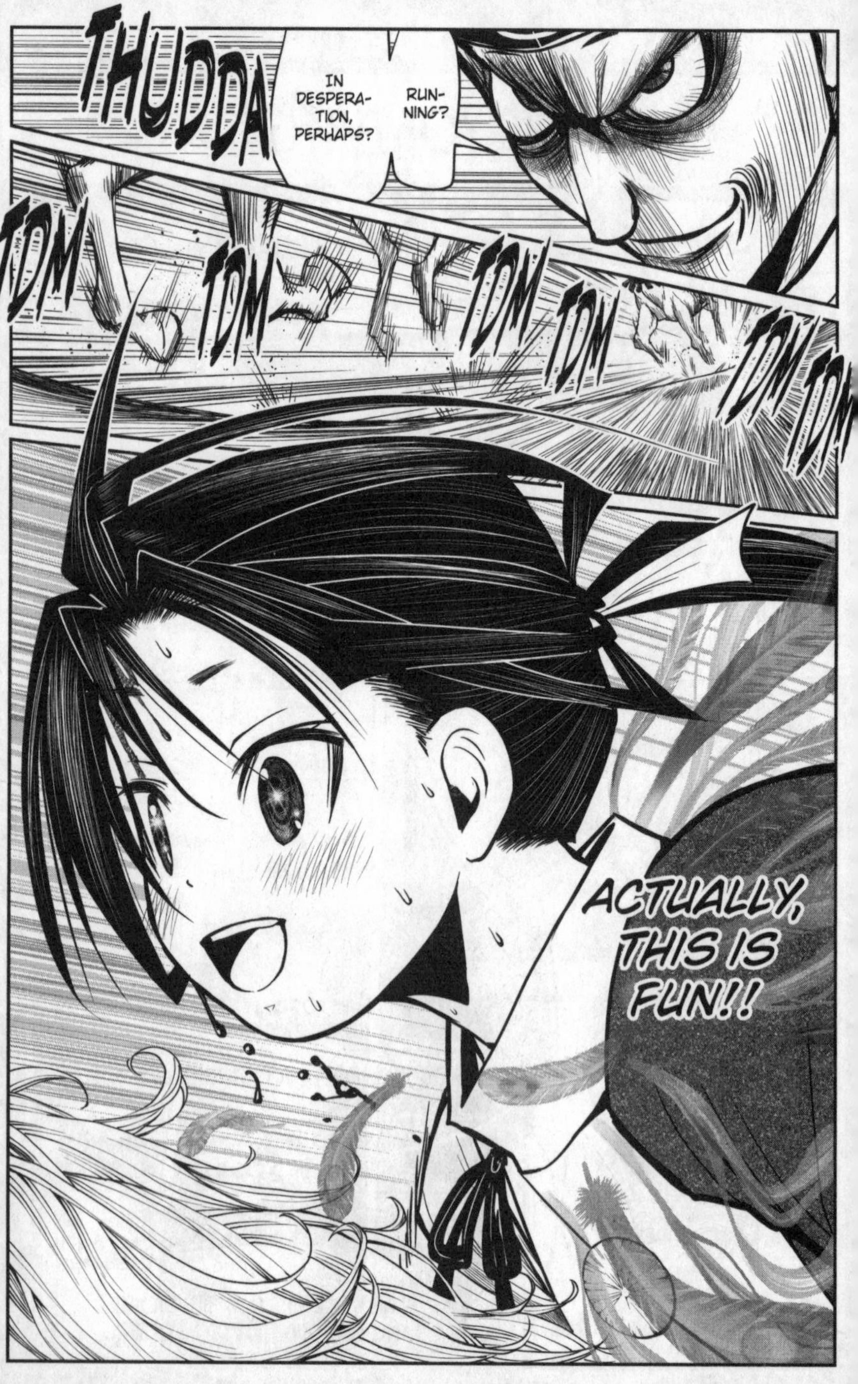
RUNNING? IN DESPERATION, PERHAPS?
THUDDA
TDM TDM TDM TDM TDM TDM TDM
ACTUALLY, THIS IS FUN!!

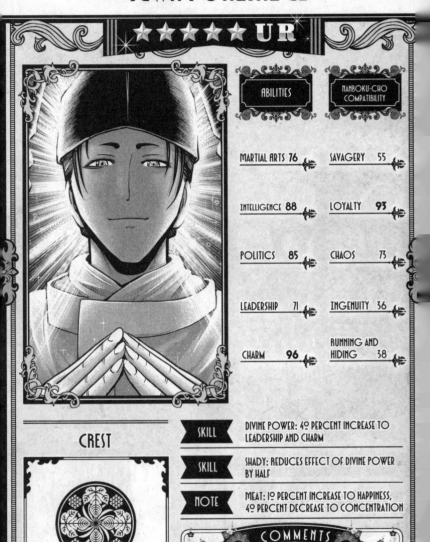

1333

SUWA YORISHIGE

★★★★★ UR

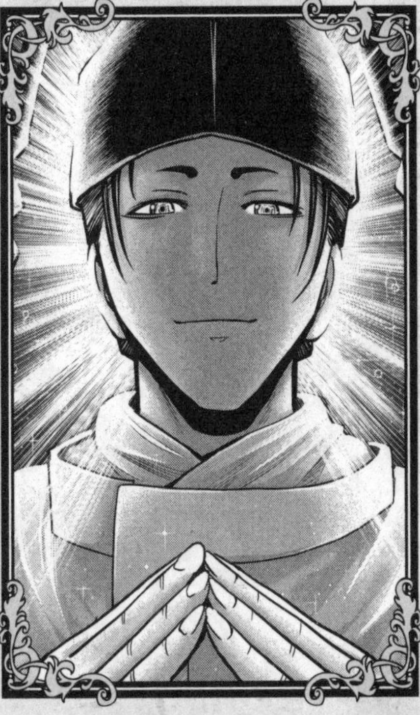

ABILITIES		NANBOKU-CHO COMPATIBILITY	
MARTIAL ARTS	76	SAVAGERY	55
INTELLIGENCE	88	LOYALTY	93
POLITICS	85	CHAOS	73
LEADERSHIP	71	INGENUITY	36
CHARM	96	RUNNING AND HIDING	38

CREST

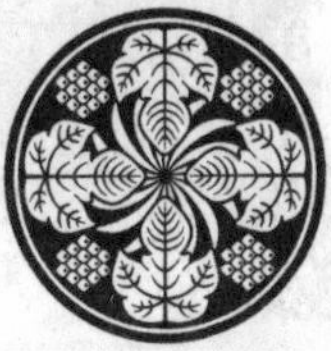

PAPER MULBERRY LEAVES AND FRUIT

SKILL DIVINE POWER: 40 PERCENT INCREASE TO LEADERSHIP AND CHARM

SKILL SHADY: REDUCES EFFECT OF DIVINE POWER BY HALF

NOTE MEAT: 10 PERCENT INCREASE TO HAPPINESS, 40 PERCENT DECREASE TO CONCENTRATION

COMMENTS

AT FIRST, EVERYONE SAYS, "RELIGION IS SUSPICIOUS" AND "THAT'S SCARY," BUT...

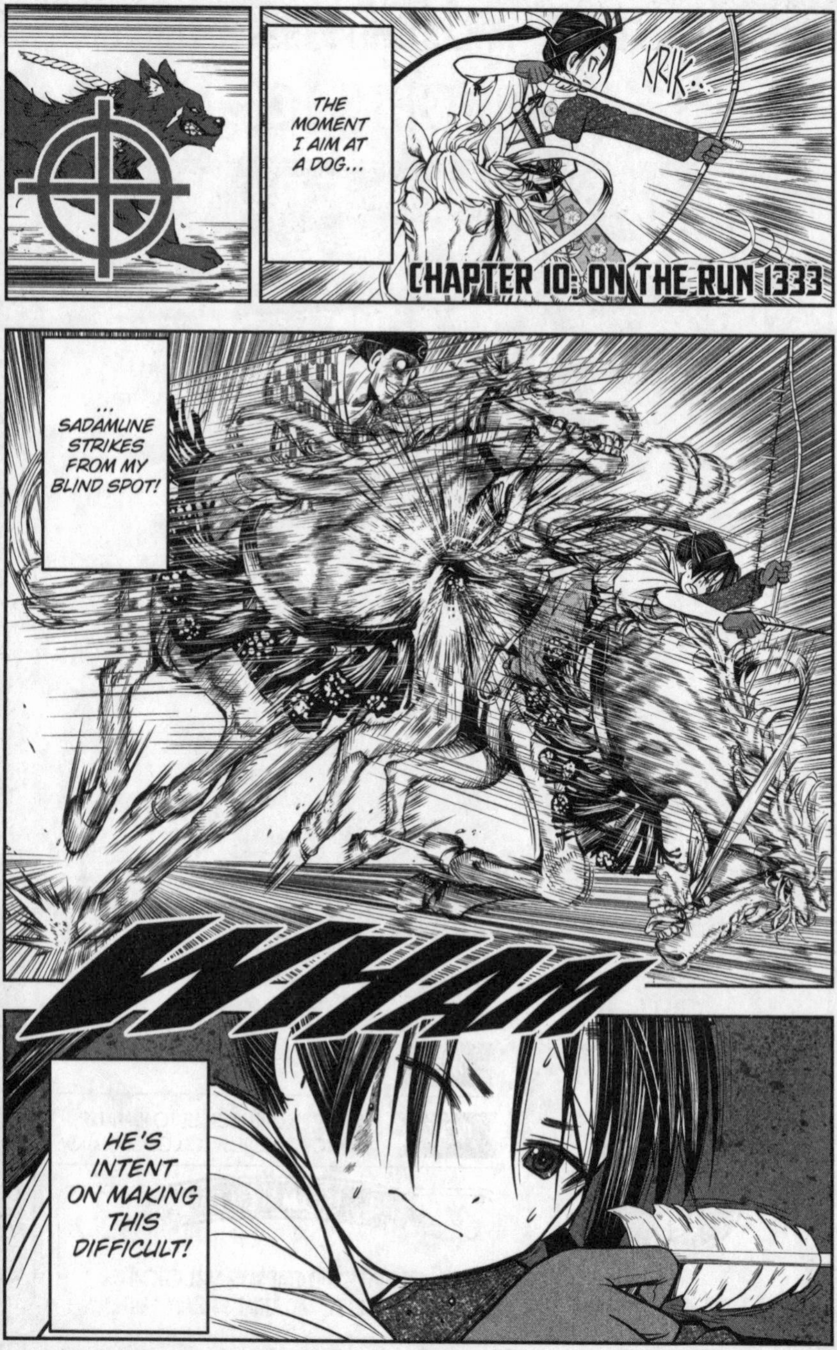
THE MOMENT I AIM AT A DOG...
KRIK...
CHAPTER 10: ON THE RUN 1333
... SADAMUNE STRIKES FROM MY BLIND SPOT!
WHAM
HE'S INTENT ON MAKING THIS DIFFICULT!

CHAPTER 10: ON THE RUN 1333

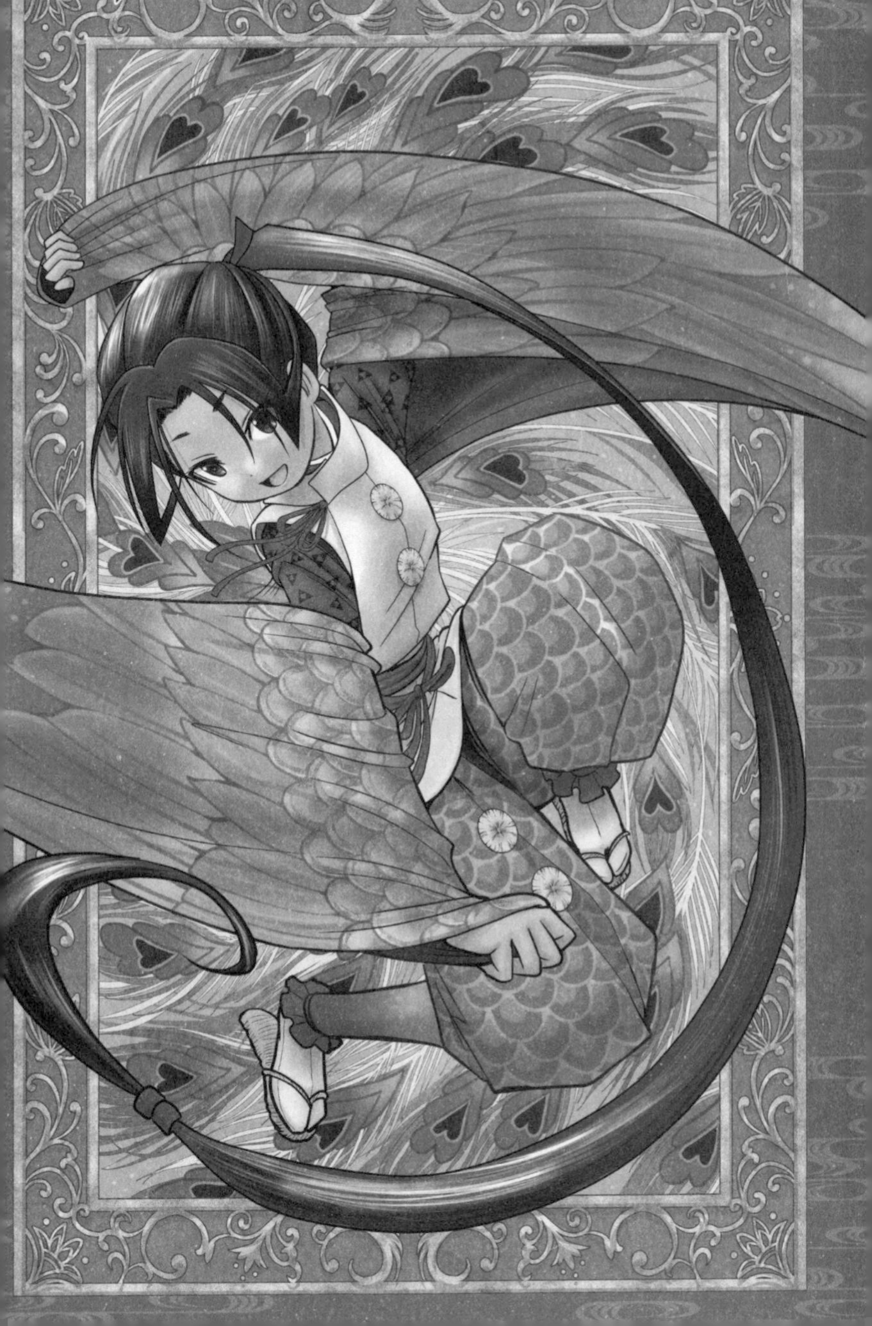

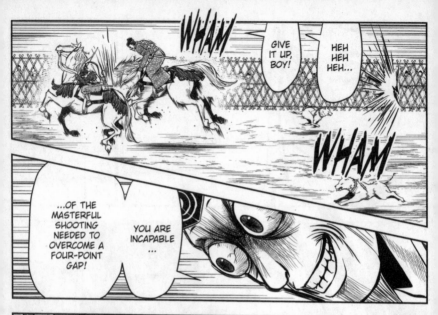

WHAM
HEH HEH HEH...
GIVE IT UP, BOY!
WHAM
YOU ARE INCAPABLE ...
...OF THE MASTERFUL SHOOTING NEEDED TO OVERCOME A FOUR-POINT GAP!
RUN, CHOJU-MARU!
YOU CANNOT BEST HIM AT MARKSMAN-SHIP...
...SO PREPARE YOUR SHOTS CAREFULLY WHILE YOU FLEE!
FWAAH

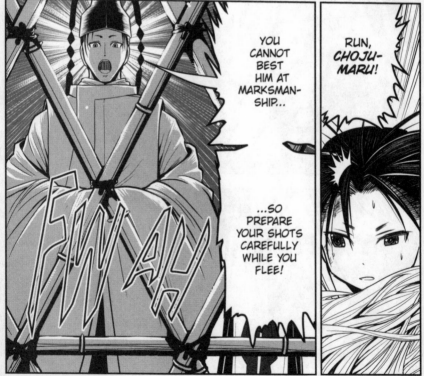

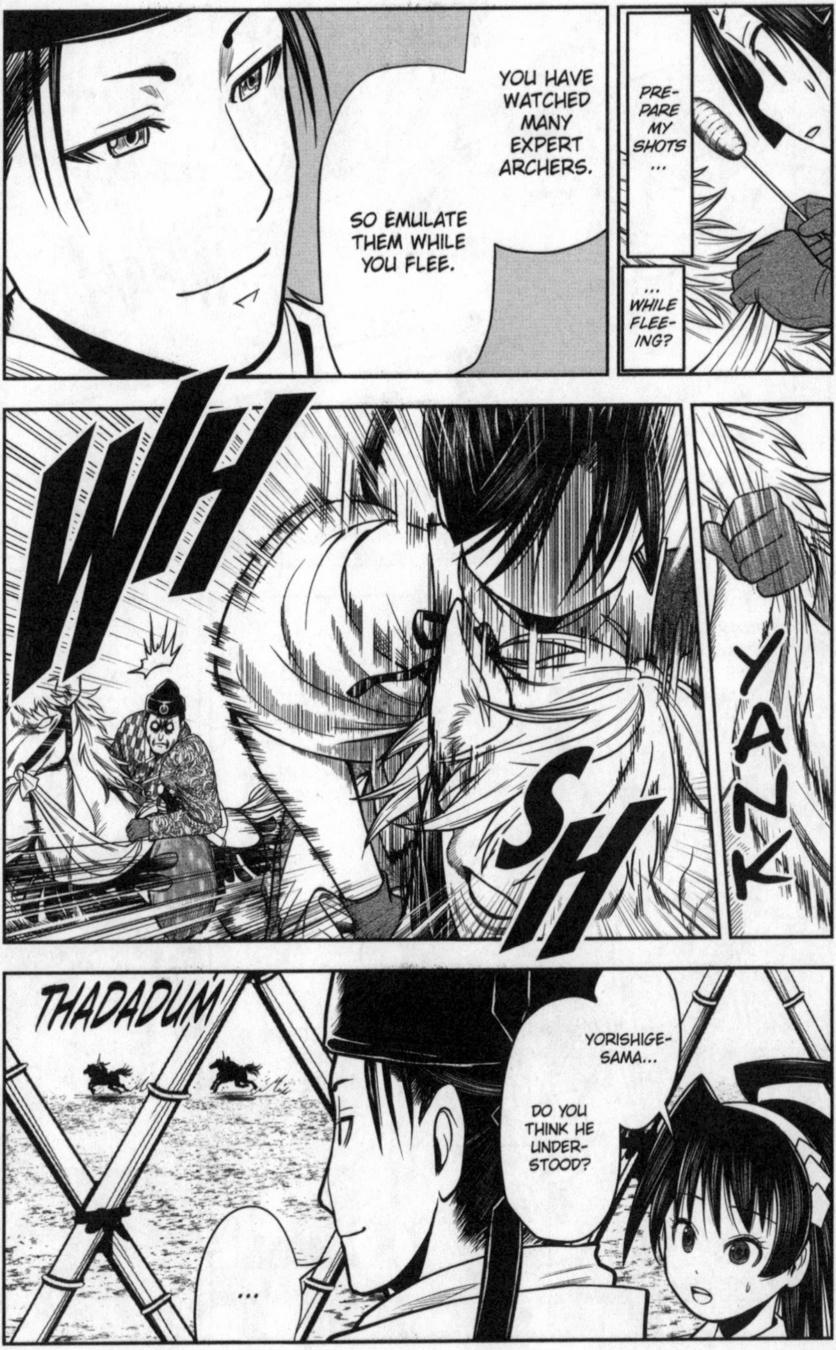
PRE-PARE MY SHOTS...
...WHILE FLEE-ING?
YOU HAVE WATCHED MANY EXPERT ARCHERS.
SO EMULATE THEM WHILE YOU FLEE.
YANK
WH
SH
THADADUM
YORISHIGE-SAMA...
DO YOU THINK HE UNDER-STOOD?
...

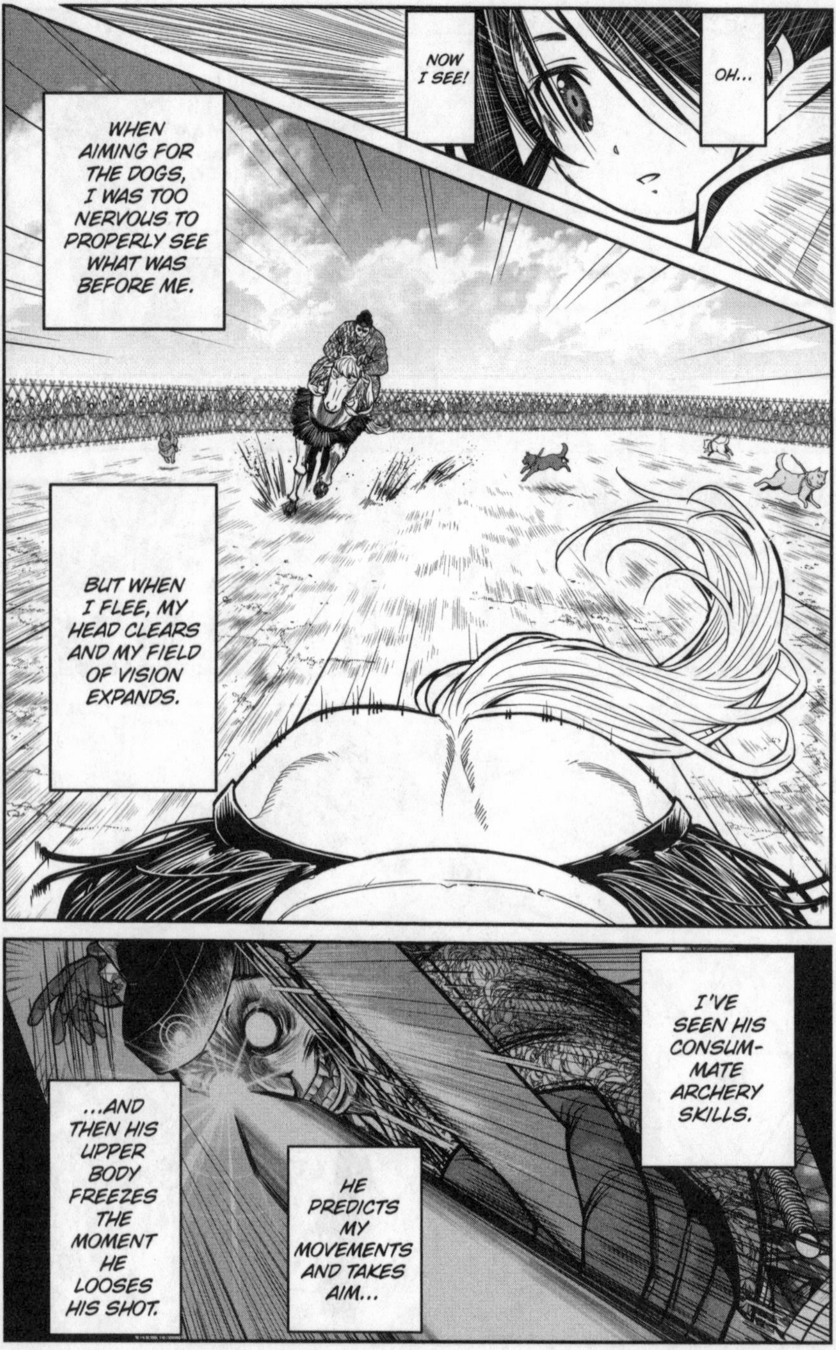
OH...
NOW I SEE!
WHEN AIMING FOR THE DOGS, I WAS TOO NERVOUS TO PROPERLY SEE WHAT WAS BEFORE ME.
BUT WHEN I FLEE, MY HEAD CLEARS AND MY FIELD OF VISION EXPANDS.
I'VE SEEN HIS CONSUM-MATE ARCHERY SKILLS.
HE PREDICTS MY MOVEMENTS AND TAKES AIM...
...AND THEN HIS UPPER BODY FREEZES THE MOMENT HE LOOSES HIS SHOT.

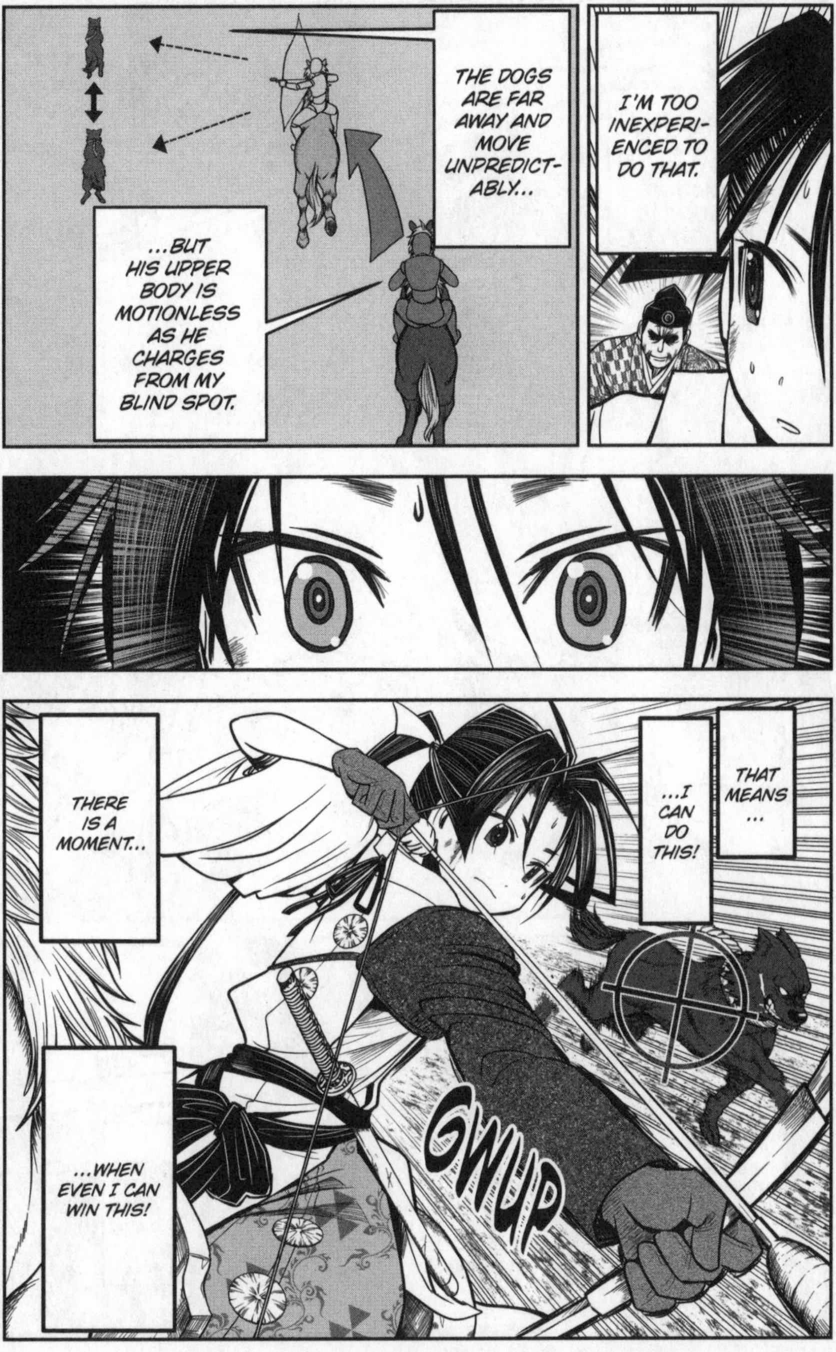
I'M TOO INEXPERIENCED TO DO THAT.
THE DOGS ARE FAR AWAY AND MOVE UNPREDICTABLY...
...BUT HIS UPPER BODY IS MOTIONLESS AS HE CHARGES FROM MY BLIND SPOT.
THAT MEANS...
...I CAN DO THIS!
THERE IS A MOMENT...
GWUP
...WHEN EVEN I CAN WIN THIS!

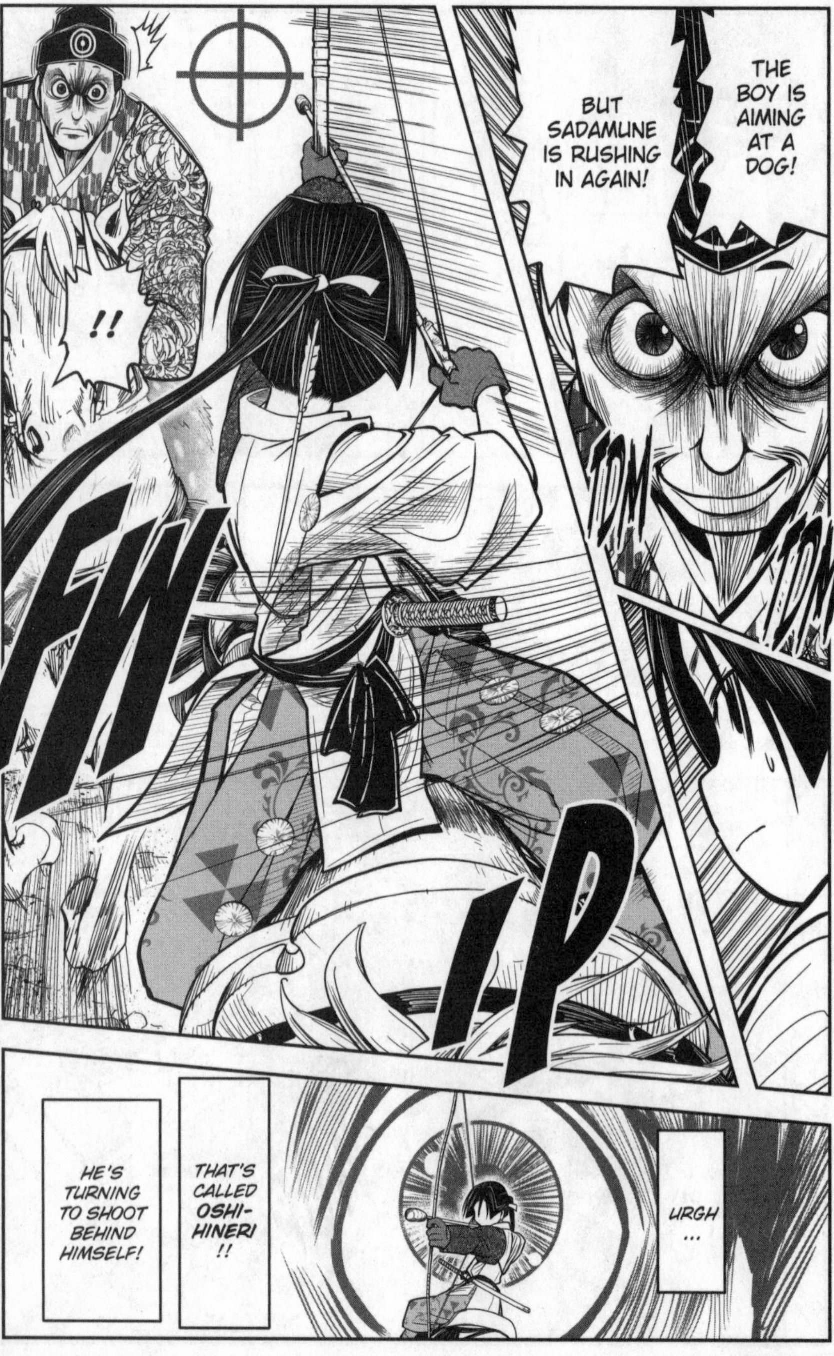
THE BOY IS AIMING AT A DOG!
BUT SADAMUNE IS RUSHING IN AGAIN!
TOM
TOM
!!
FWIP
URGH ...
THAT'S CALLED OSHI-HINERI !!
HE'S TURNING TO SHOOT BEHIND HIMSELF!

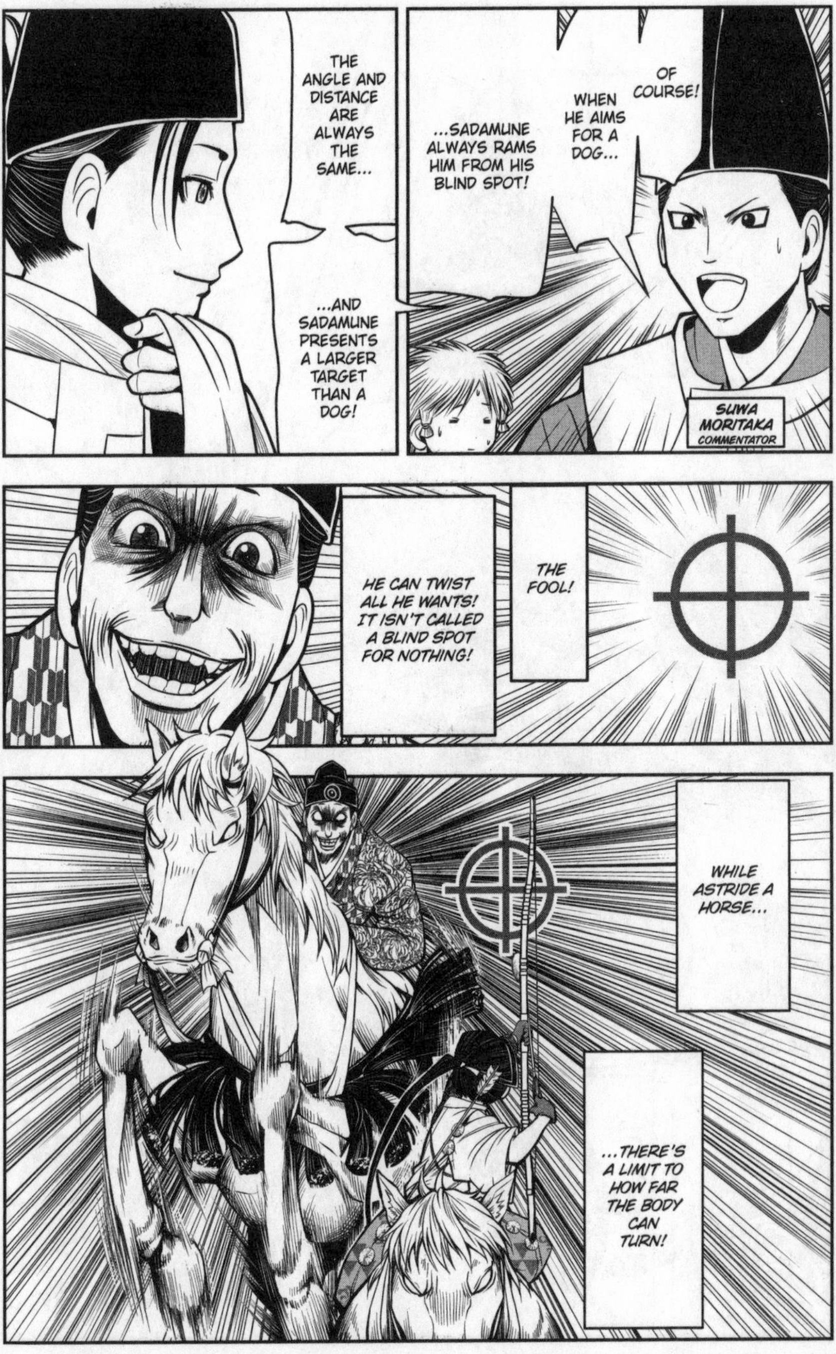
OF COURSE!
WHEN HE AIMS FOR A DOG...
...SADAMUNE ALWAYS RAMS HIM FROM HIS BLIND SPOT!
SUWA MORITAKA COMMENTATOR
THE ANGLE AND DISTANCE ARE ALWAYS THE SAME...
...AND SADAMUNE PRESENTS A LARGER TARGET THAN A DOG!
THE FOOL!
HE CAN TWIST ALL HE WANTS! IT ISN'T CALLED A BLIND SPOT FOR NOTHING!
WHILE ASTRIDE A HORSE...
...THERE'S A LIMIT TO HOW FAR THE BODY CAN TURN!

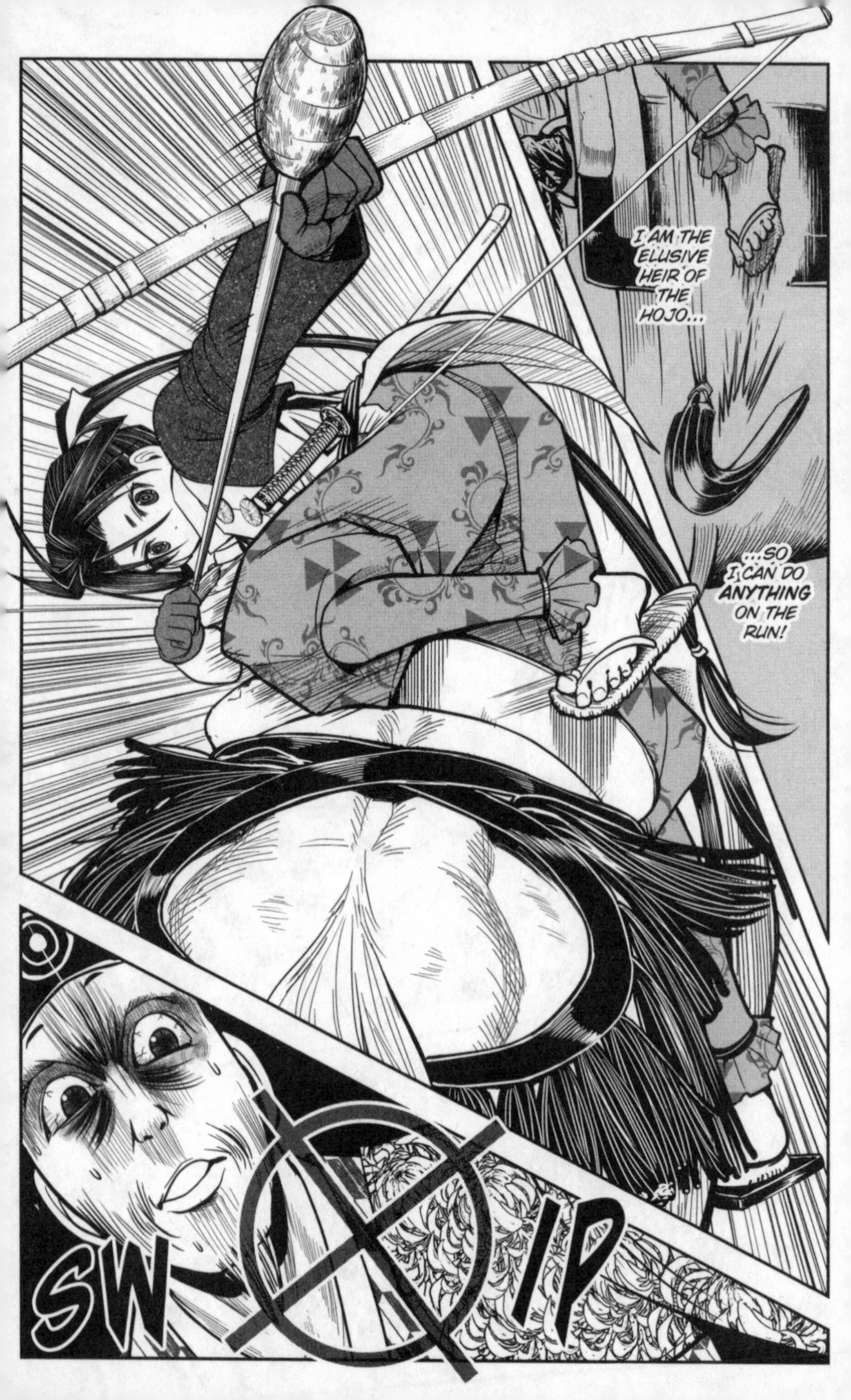
I AM THE ELUSIVE HEIR OF THE HOJO...
...SO I CAN DO ANYTHING ON THE RUN!
SWIP

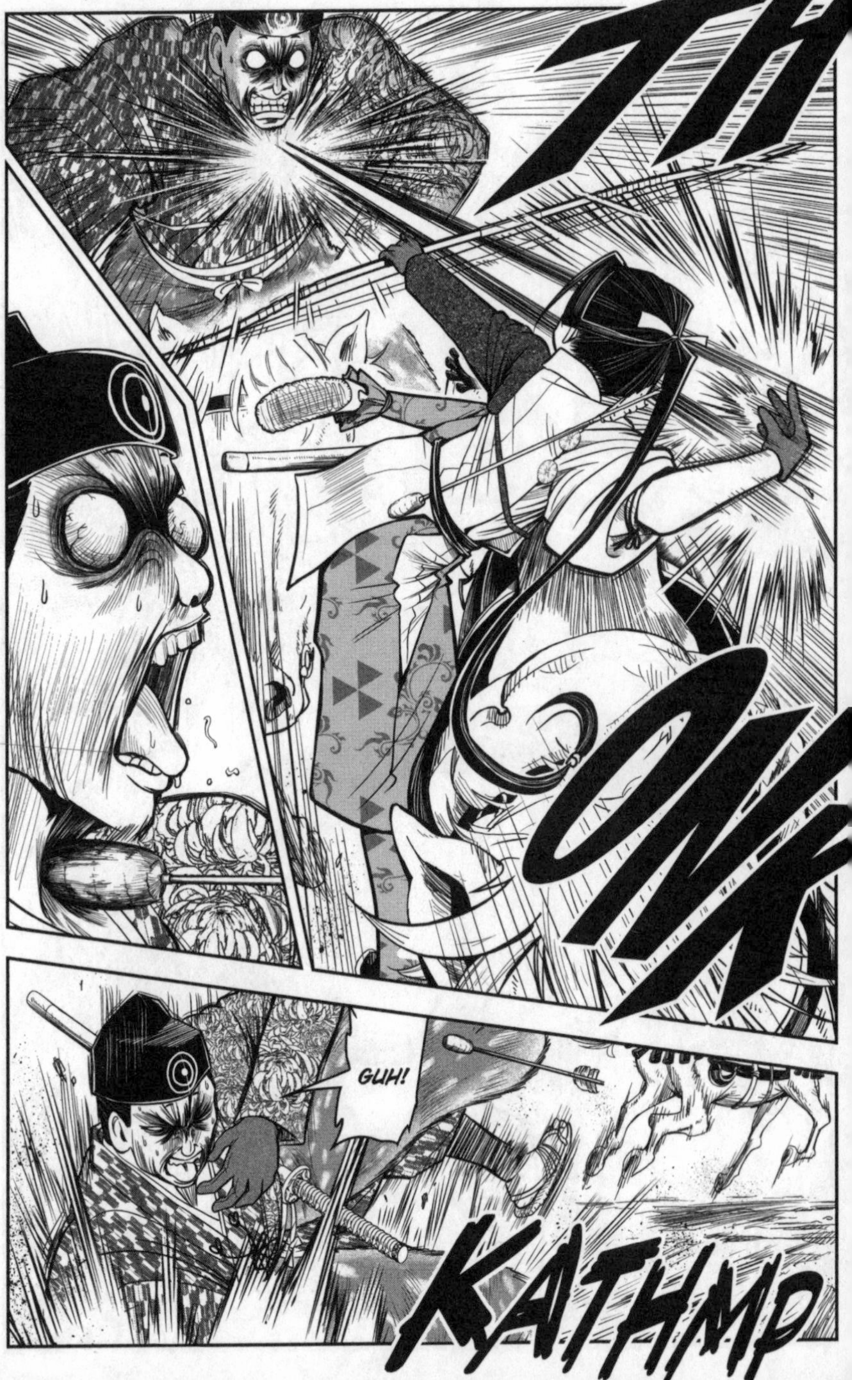
GUH!
KATHMP

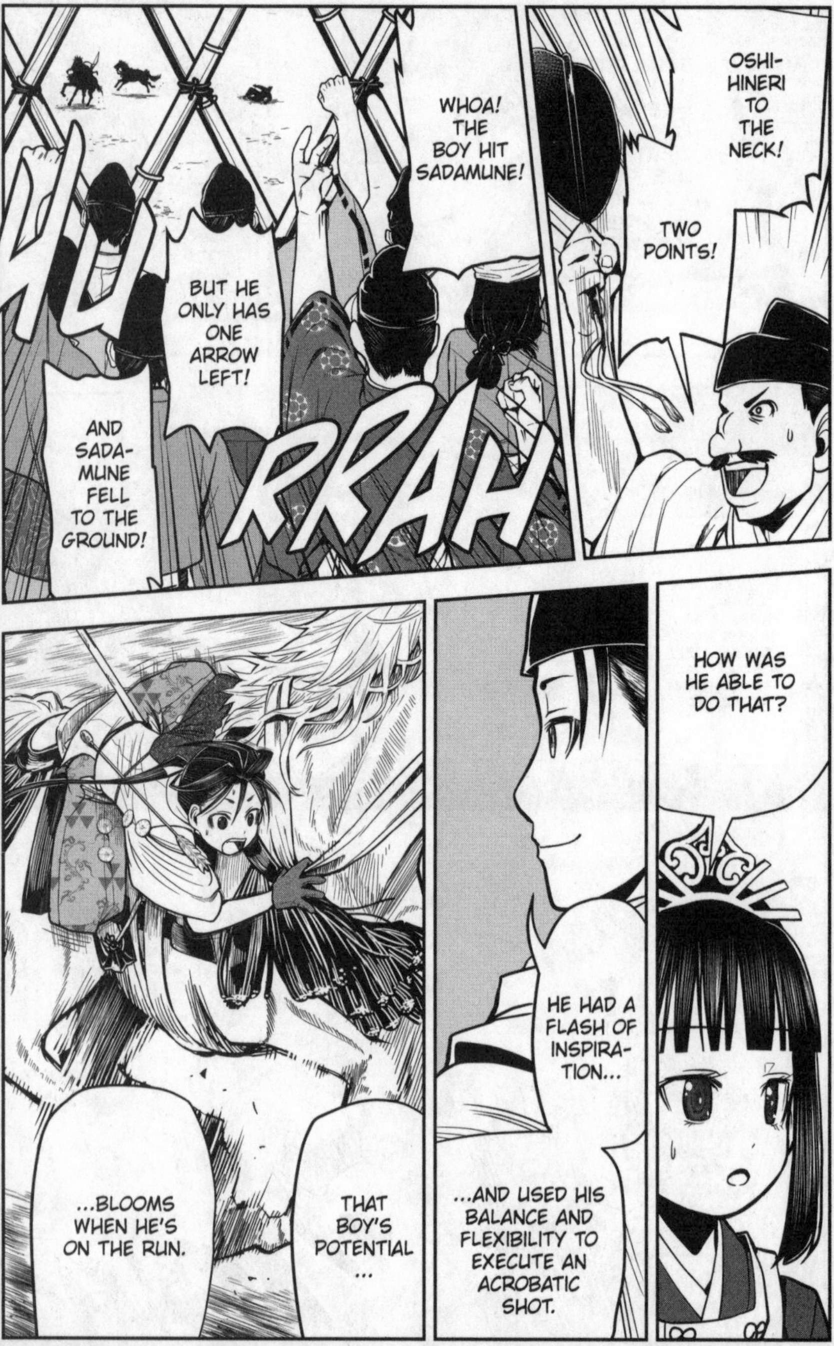
OSHI-HINERI TO THE NECK!
TWO POINTS!
WHOA! THE BOY HIT SADAMUNE!
BUT HE ONLY HAS ONE ARROW LEFT!
HU
RRAH
AND SADAMUNE FELL TO THE GROUND!
HOW WAS HE ABLE TO DO THAT?
HE HAD A FLASH OF INSPIRATION...
...AND USED HIS BALANCE AND FLEXIBILITY TO EXECUTE AN ACROBATIC SHOT.
THAT BOY'S POTENTIAL ...
...BLOOMS WHEN HE'S ON THE RUN.

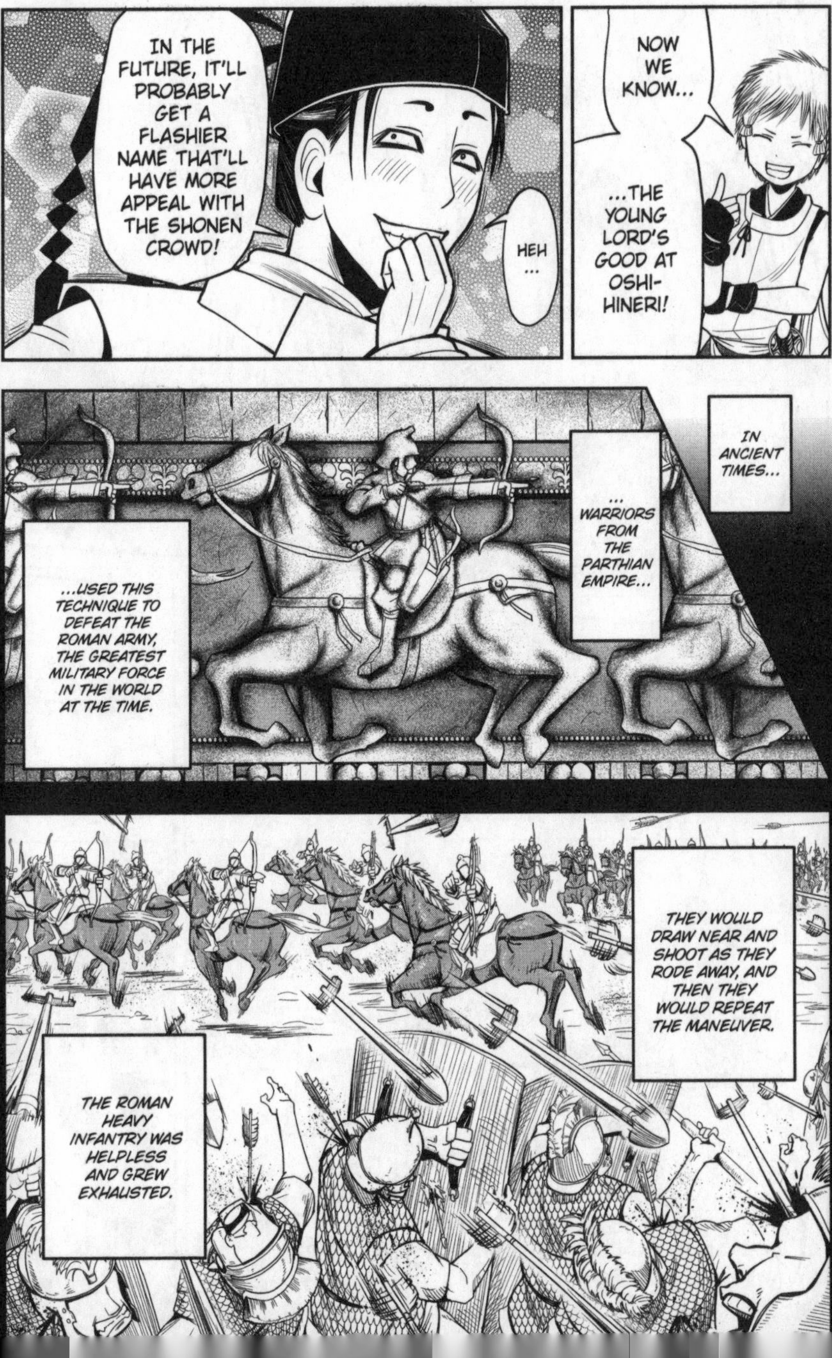
NOW WE KNOW...
...THE YOUNG LORD'S GOOD AT OSHI-HINERI!
IN THE FUTURE, IT'LL PROBABLY GET A FLASHIER NAME THAT'LL HAVE MORE APPEAL WITH THE SHONEN CROWD!
HEH ...
IN ANCIENT TIMES...
... WARRIORS FROM THE PARTHIAN EMPIRE...
...USED THIS TECHNIQUE TO DEFEAT THE ROMAN ARMY, THE GREATEST MILITARY FORCE IN THE WORLD AT THE TIME.
THEY WOULD DRAW NEAR AND SHOOT AS THEY RODE AWAY, AND THEN THEY WOULD REPEAT THE MANEUVER.
THE ROMAN HEAVY INFANTRY WAS HELPLESS AND GREW EXHAUSTED.

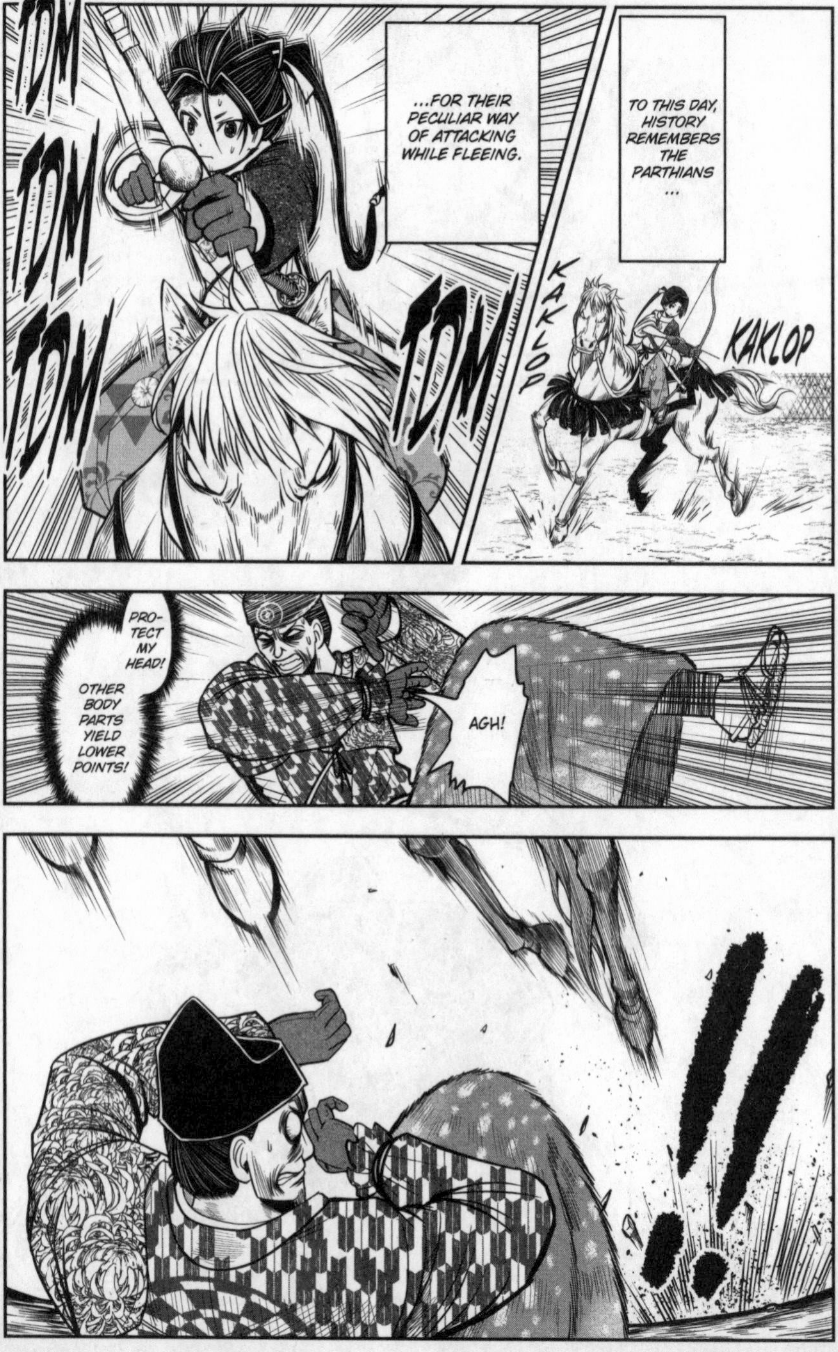

TO THIS DAY, HISTORY REMEMBERS THE PARTHIANS ...
KAKLOP
KAKLOP
...FOR THEIR PECULIAR WAY OF ATTACKING WHILE FLEEING.
TDM
TDM TDM TDM
AGH!
PROTECT MY HEAD! OTHER BODY PARTS YIELD LOWER POINTS!
!!

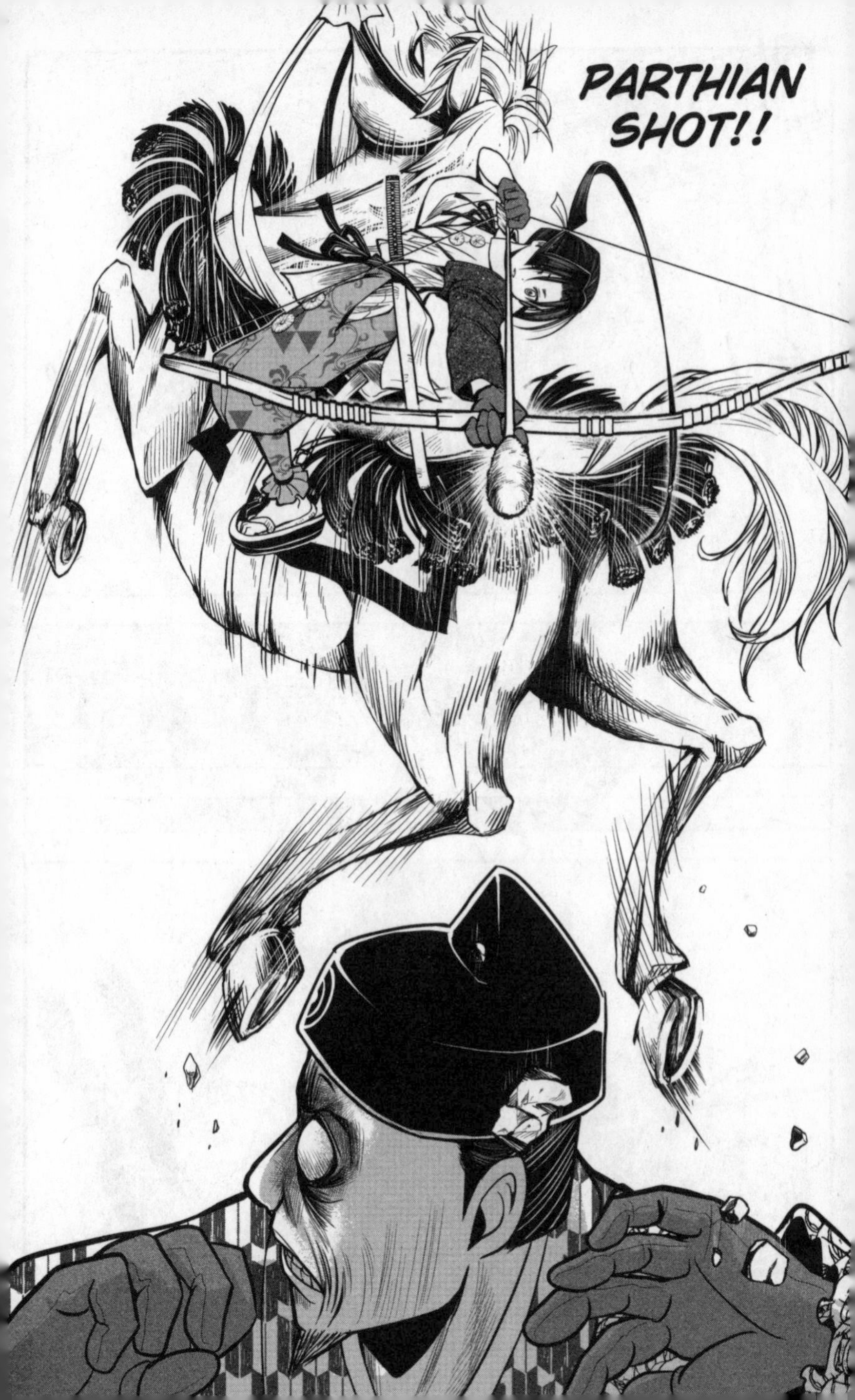
PARTHIAN SHOT!!

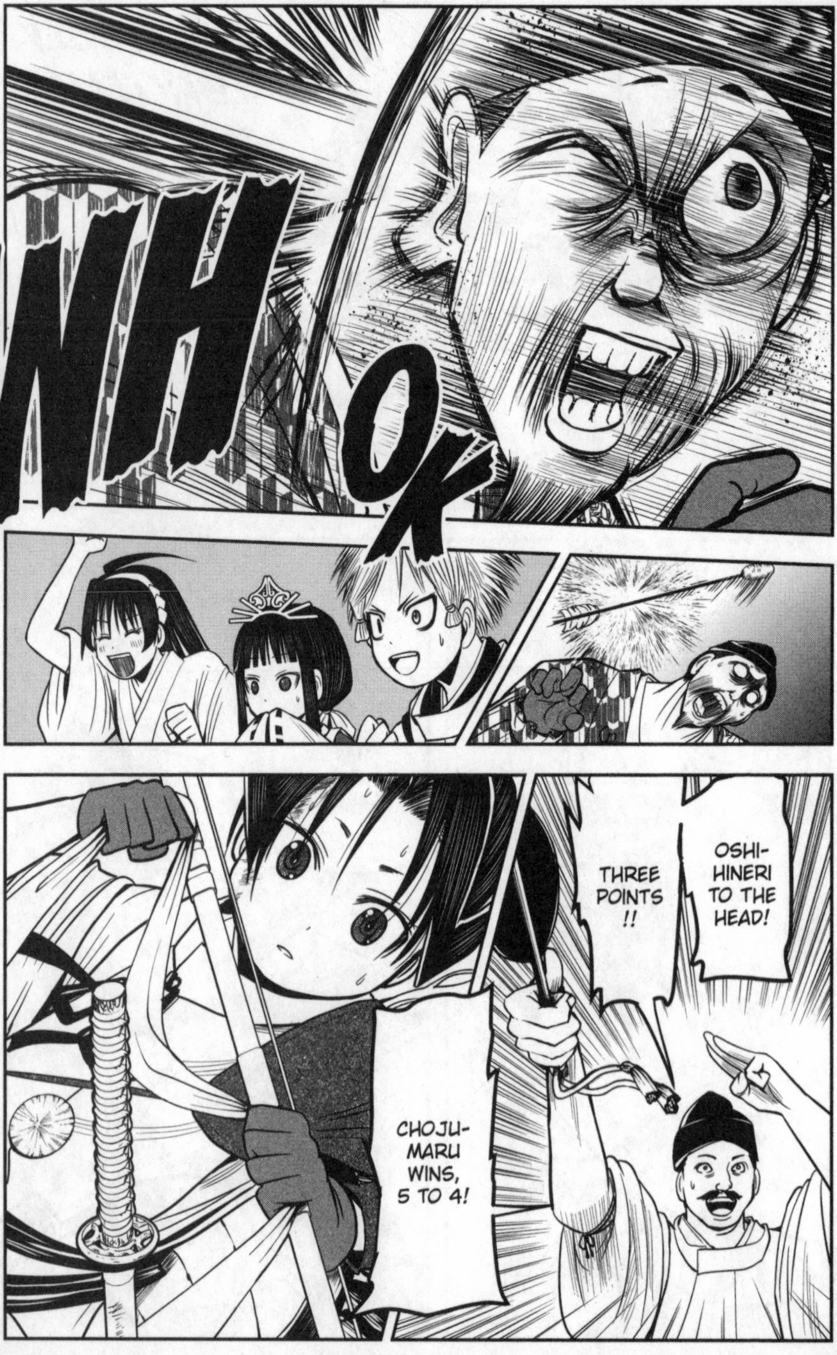
WHOK
OSHI-HINERI TO THE HEAD!
THREE POINTS!!
CHOJU-MARU WINS, 5 TO 4!

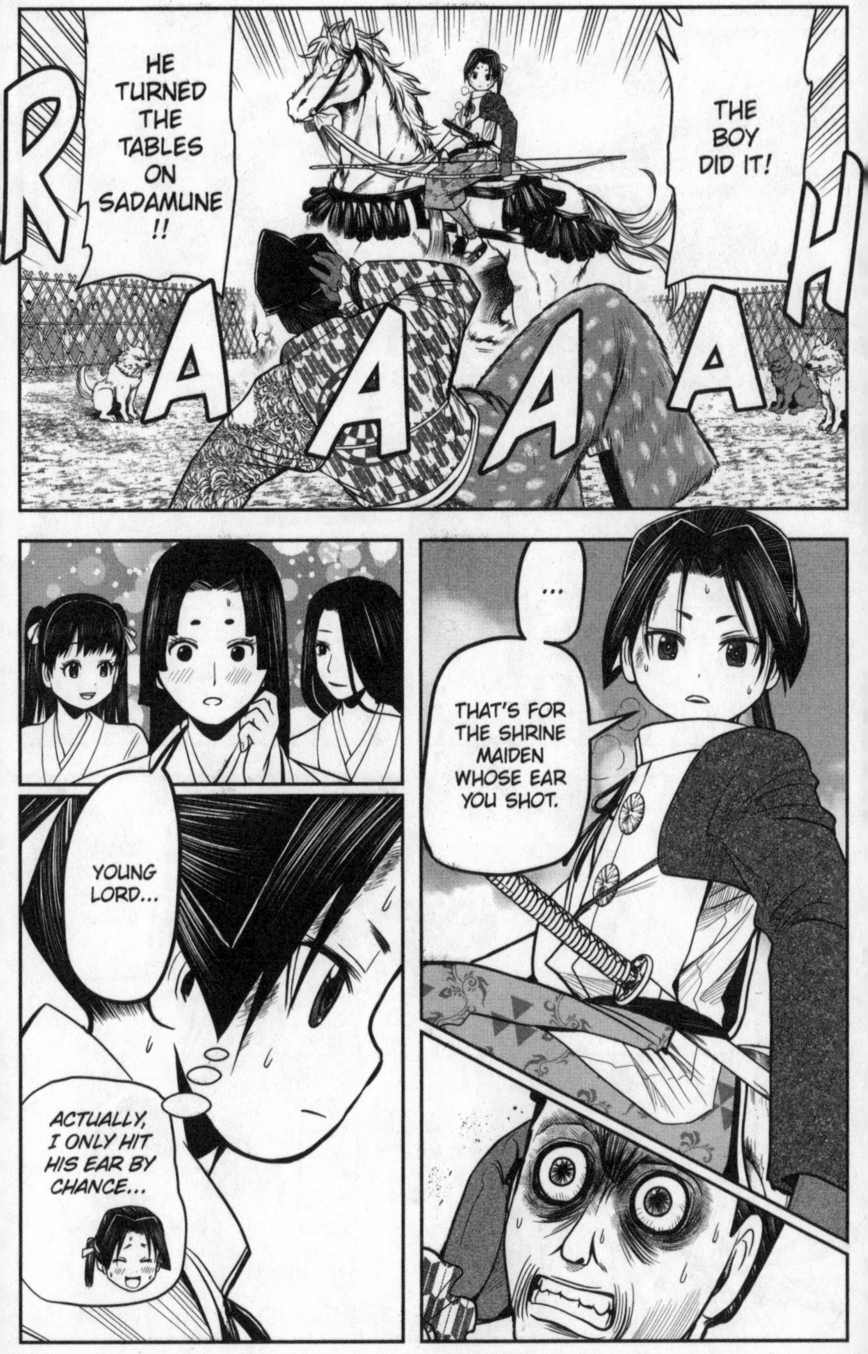
THE BOY DID IT!
HE TURNED THE TABLES ON SADAMUNE!!
RAAAAH
...
THAT'S FOR THE SHRINE MAIDEN WHOSE EAR YOU SHOT.
YOUNG LORD...
ACTUALLY, I ONLY HIT HIS EAR BY CHANCE...

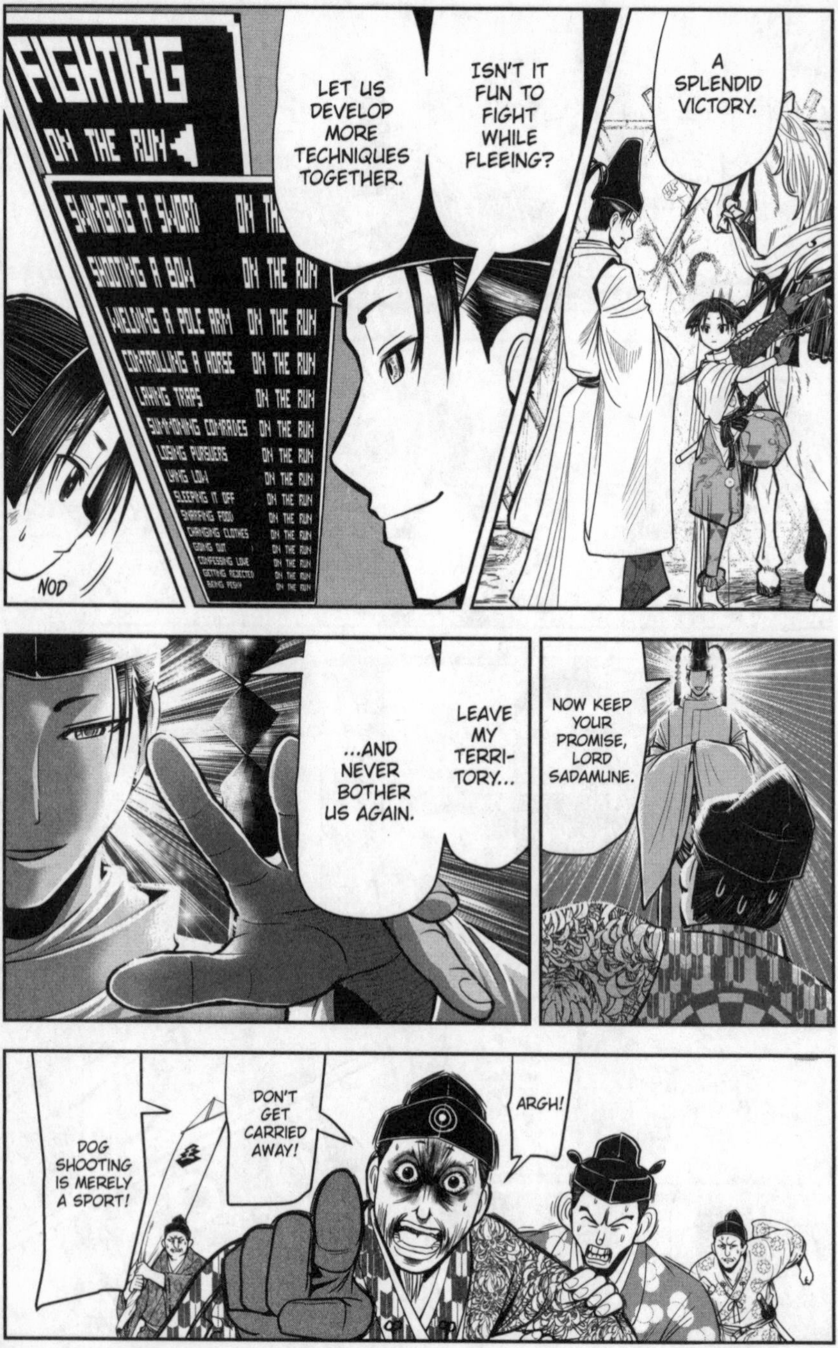
A SPLENDID VICTORY.
ISN'T IT FUN TO FIGHT WHILE FLEEING?
LET US DEVELOP MORE TECHNIQUES TOGETHER.
FIGHTING ON THE RUN
SWINGING A SWORD ON THE
SHOOTING A BOW ON THE RUN
WIELDING A POLE ARM ON THE RUN
CONTROLLING A HORSE ON THE RUN
LAYING TRAPS ON THE RUN
SUMMONING COMRADES ON THE RUN
LOSING PURSUERS ON THE RUN
LYING LOW ON THE RUN
SLEEPING IT OFF ON THE RUN
SHARING FOOD ON THE RUN
CHANGING CLOTHES ON THE RUN
GOING OUT ON THE RUN
CONFESSING LOVE ON THE RUN
GETTING REJECTED ON THE RUN
BEING PESKY ON THE RUN
NOD
NOW KEEP YOUR PROMISE, LORD SADAMUNE.
LEAVE MY TERRITORY...
...AND NEVER BOTHER US AGAIN.
ARGH!
DON'T GET CARRIED AWAY!
DOG SHOOTING IS MERELY A SPORT!

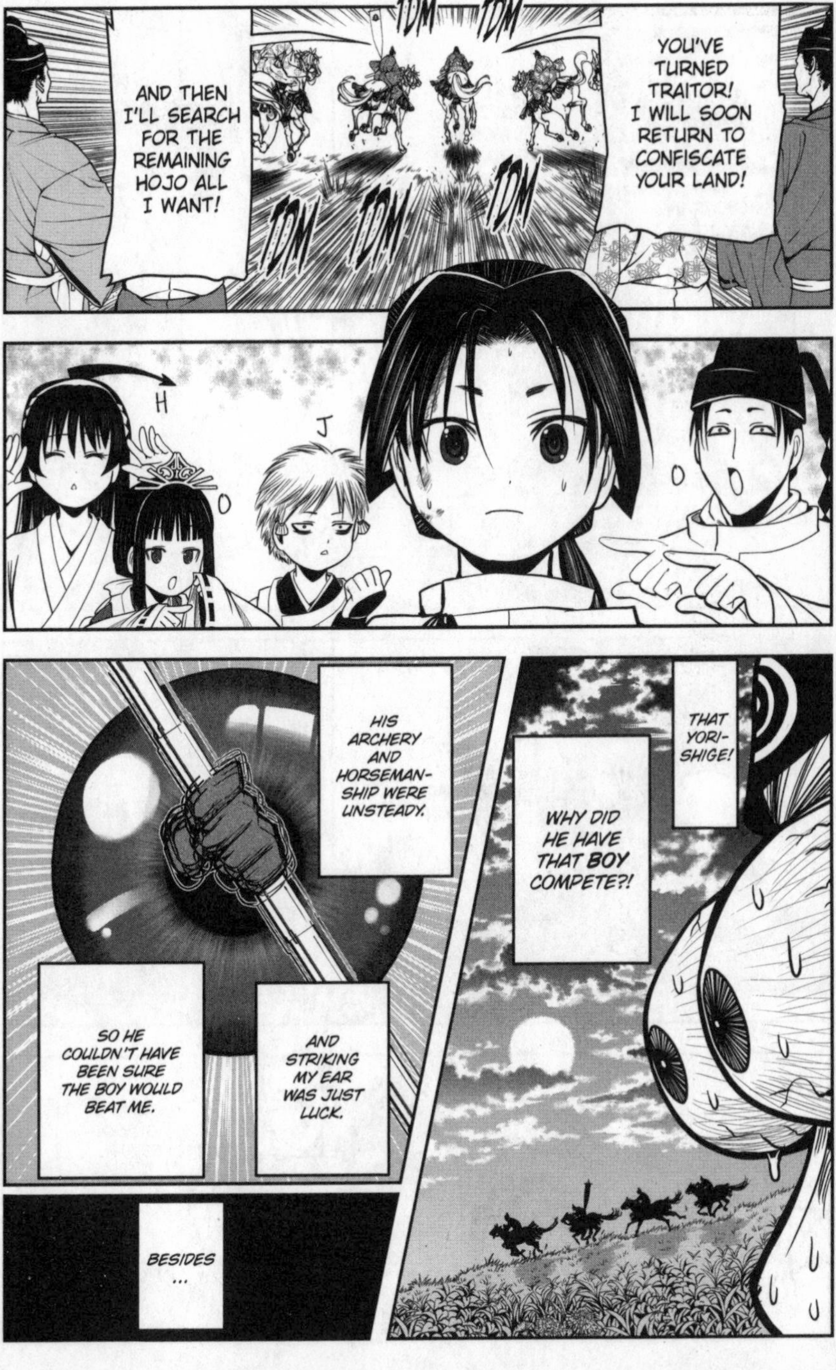
YOU'VE TURNED TRAITOR! I WILL SOON RETURN TO CONFISCATE YOUR LAND!
TDM TDM
TDM TDM TDM
AND THEN I'LL SEARCH FOR THE REMAINING HOJO ALL I WANT!
O
J
O
H
THAT YORISHIGE!
WHY DID HE HAVE THAT BOY COMPETE?!
HIS ARCHERY AND HORSEMANSHIP WERE UNSTEADY.
AND STRIKING MY EAR WAS JUST LUCK.
SO HE COULDN'T HAVE BEEN SURE THE BOY WOULD BEAT ME.
BESIDES...

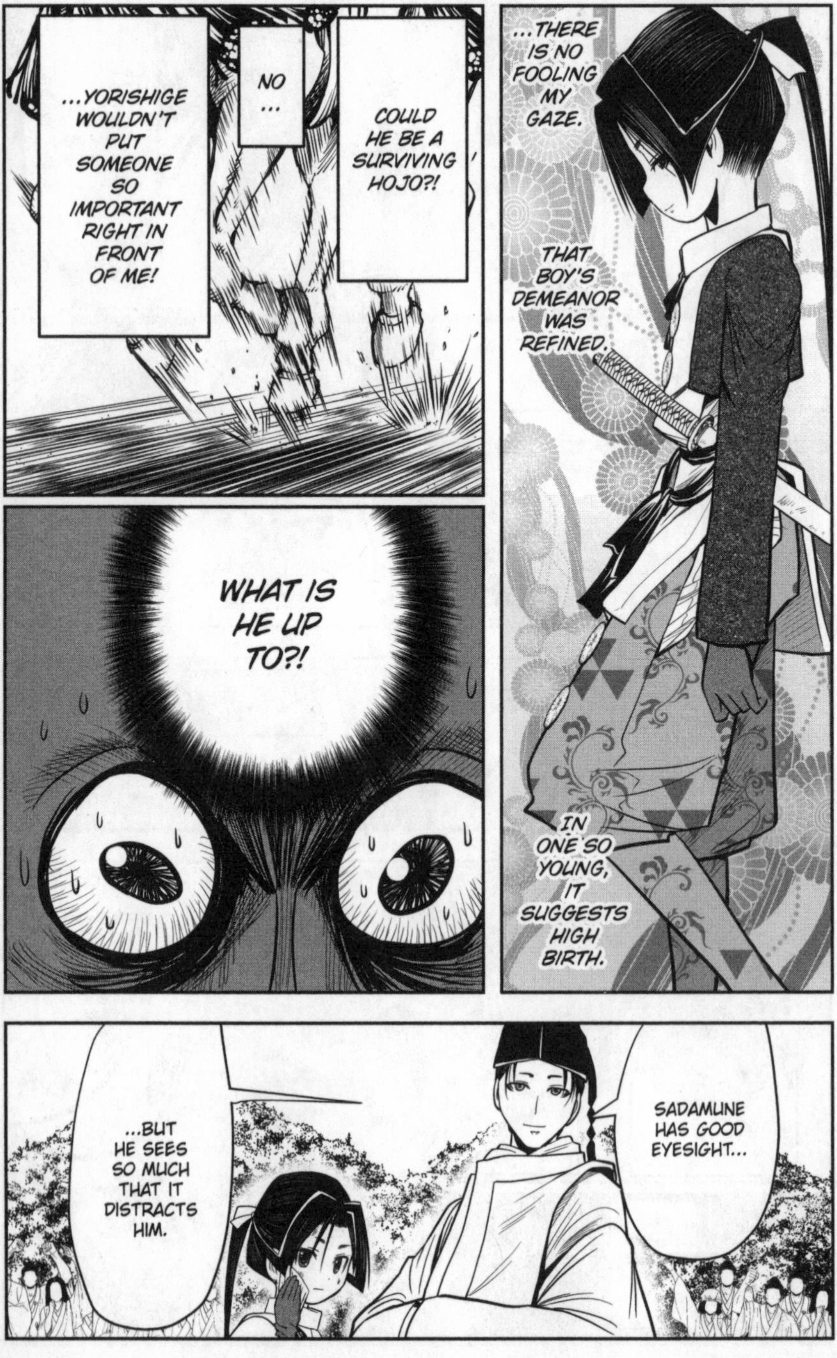
...THERE IS NO FOOLING MY GAZE.
THAT BOY'S DEMEANOR WAS REFINED.
IN ONE SO YOUNG, IT SUGGESTS HIGH BIRTH.
COULD HE BE A SURVIVING HOJO?!
NO...
...YORISHIGE WOULDN'T PUT SOMEONE SO IMPORTANT RIGHT IN FRONT OF ME!
WHAT IS HE UP TO?!
SADAMUNE HAS GOOD EYESIGHT...
...BUT HE SEES SO MUCH THAT IT DISTRACTS HIM.

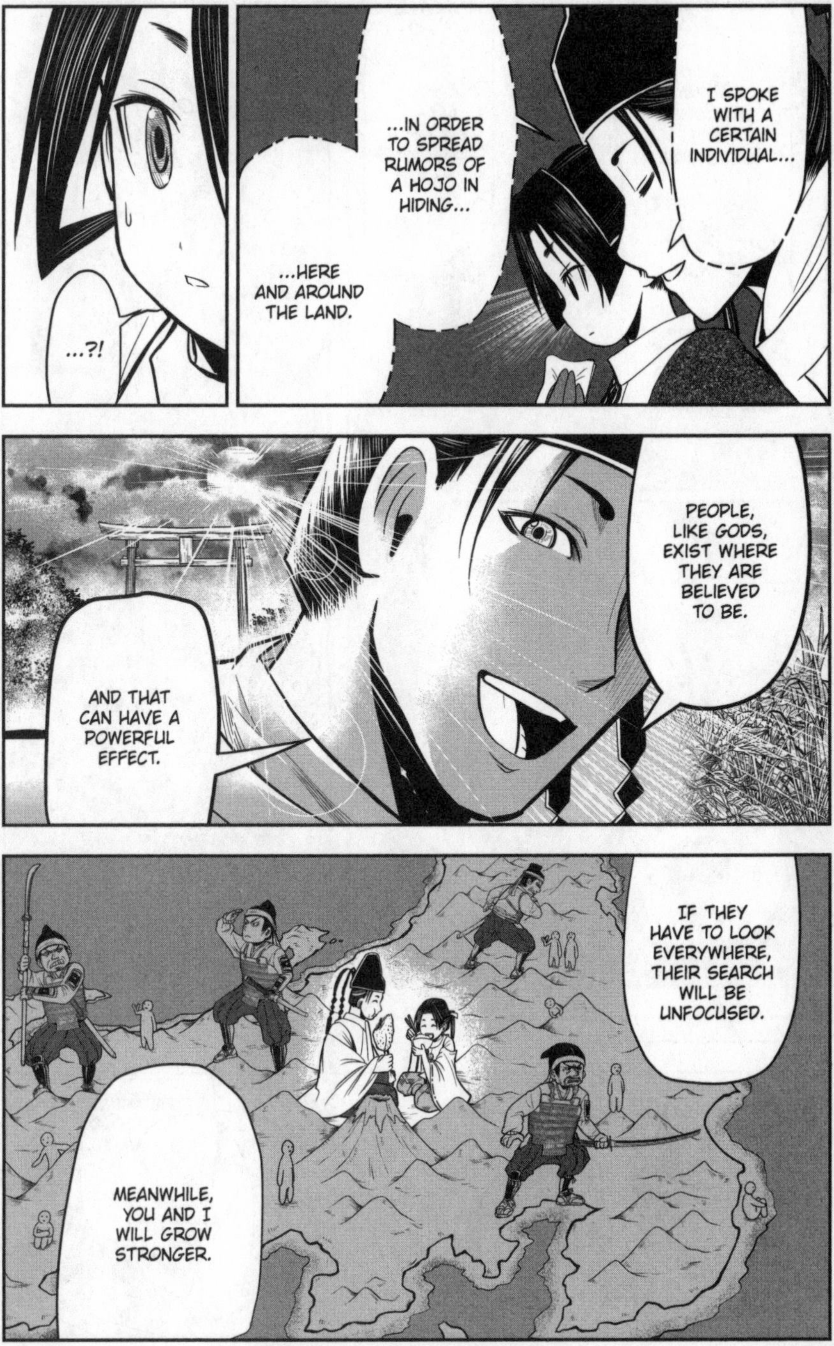
I SPOKE WITH A CERTAIN INDIVIDUAL...
...IN ORDER TO SPREAD RUMORS OF A HOJO IN HIDING...
...HERE AND AROUND THE LAND.
...?!
PEOPLE, LIKE GODS, EXIST WHERE THEY ARE BELIEVED TO BE.
AND THAT CAN HAVE A POWERFUL EFFECT.
IF THEY HAVE TO LOOK EVERYWHERE, THEIR SEARCH WILL BE UNFOCUSED.
MEANWHILE, YOU AND I WILL GROW STRONGER.

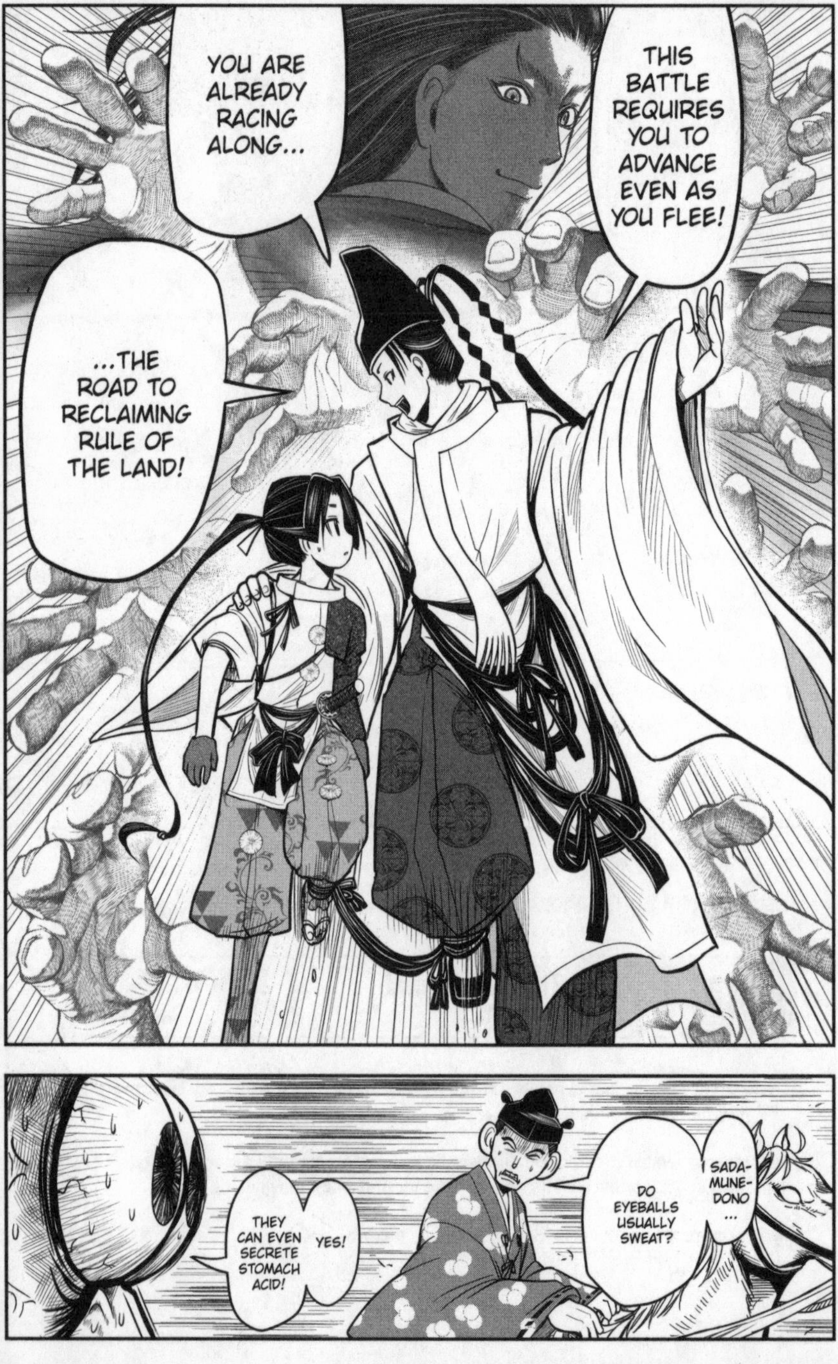
THIS BATTLE REQUIRES YOU TO ADVANCE EVEN AS YOU FLEE!
YOU ARE ALREADY RACING ALONG...
...THE ROAD TO RECLAIMING RULE OF THE LAND!
SADA-MUNE-DONO ...
DO EYEBALLS USUALLY SWEAT?
YES!
THEY CAN EVEN SECRETE STOMACH ACID!

That Misprint on the Table of Contents Comment Page at the Back of *Jump*

63 **The Elusive Youth**
YUSEI MATSUI

FAN LETTERS ENCOURAGED
ME EVEN WHEN I WASN'T IN
SERIALIZATION.
THANKS! ⟨YUSEI⟩

A difference of one kanji character made the title sound like it's for a socially aware
TV program or something...

For reasons related to too much digitization and outsourcing of editing recently,
mistakes and misprints are arising that were unthinkable in the analog days.

Some are pretty serious, but they're funny, so that's okay.

CHAPTER 11: SON OF WEALTH 1333

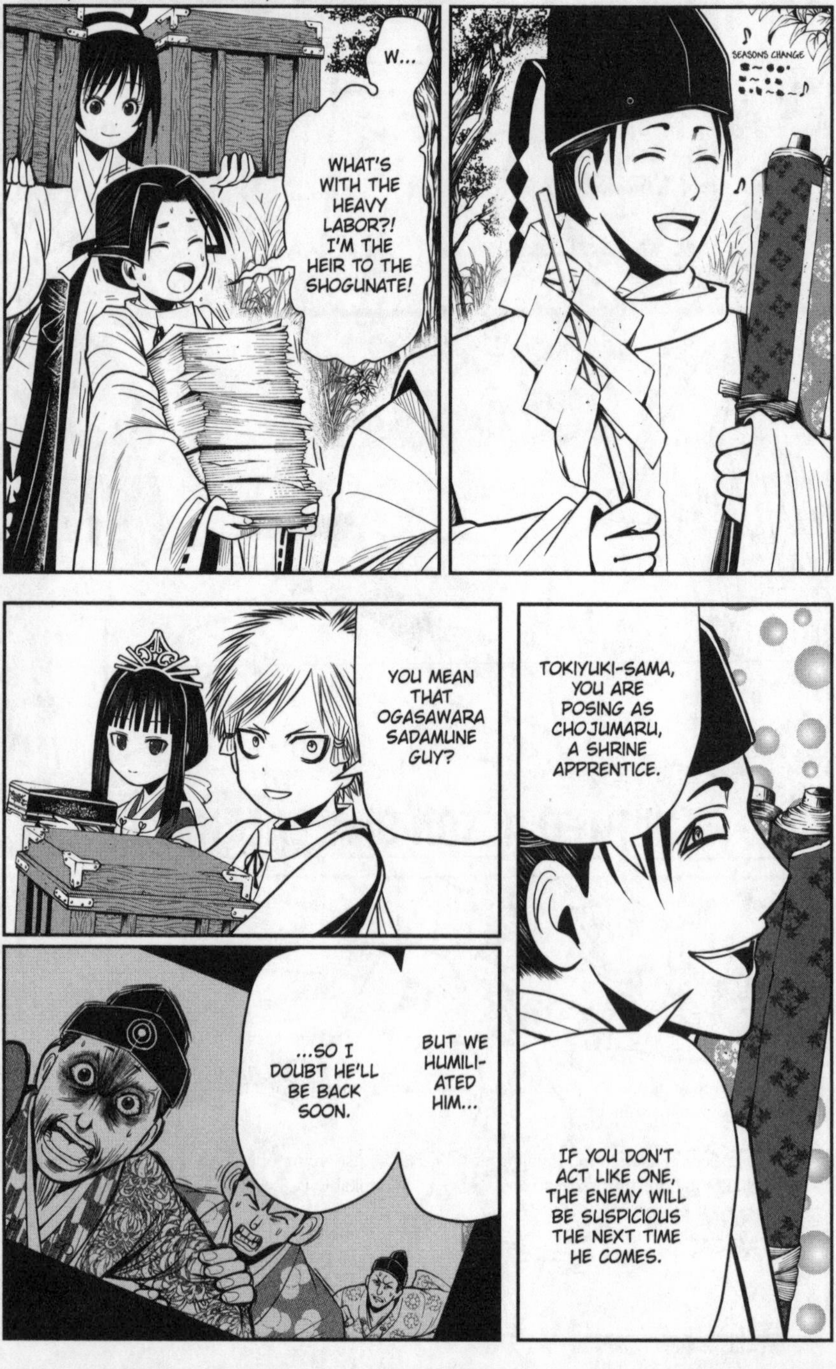
SEASONS CHANGE
W...
WHAT'S WITH THE HEAVY LABOR?! I'M THE HEIR TO THE SHOGUNATE!
TOKIYUKI-SAMA, YOU ARE POSING AS CHOJUMARU, A SHRINE APPRENTICE.
IF YOU DON'T ACT LIKE ONE, THE ENEMY WILL BE SUSPICIOUS THE NEXT TIME HE COMES.
YOU MEAN THAT OGASAWARA SADAMUNE GUY?
BUT WE HUMILI-ATED HIM...
...SO I DOUBT HE'LL BE BACK SOON.

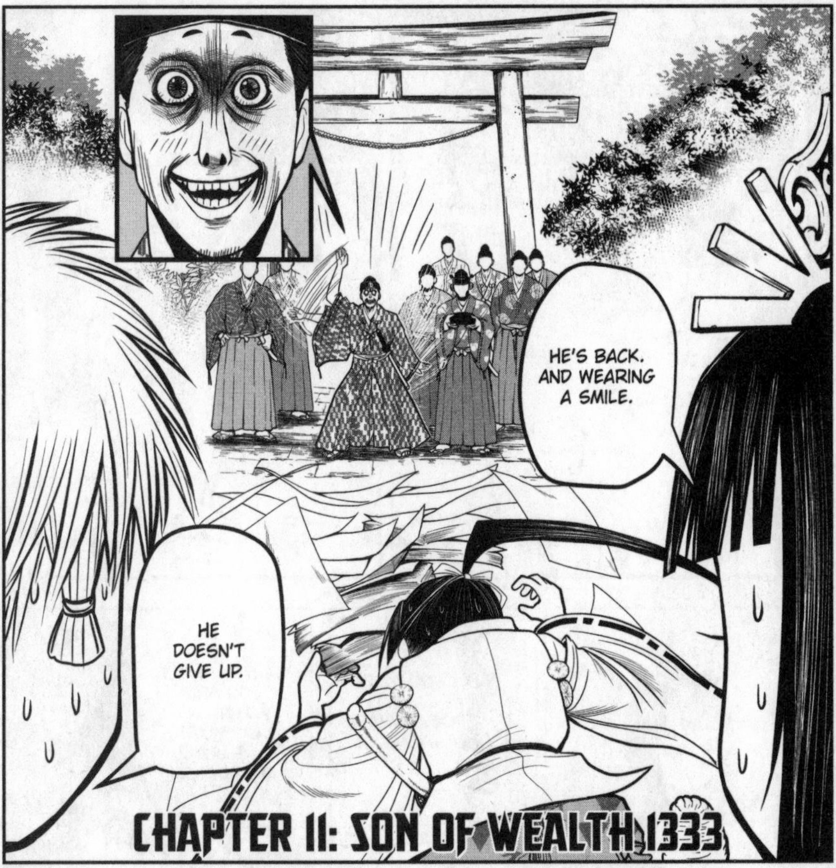
HE'S BACK. AND WEARING A SMILE.
HE DOESN'T GIVE UP.
CHAPTER 11: SON OF WEALTH 1333

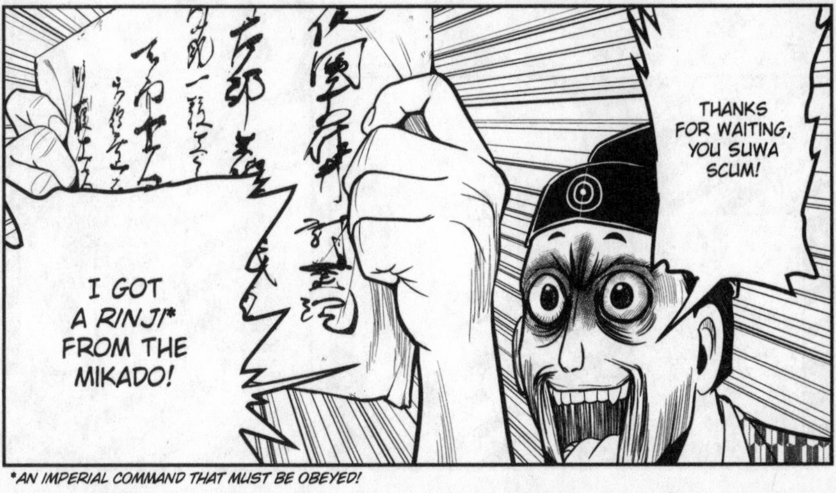
THANKS FOR WAITING, YOU SUWA SCUM!
I GOT A *RINJI** FROM THE MIKADO!

**AN IMPERIAL COMMAND THAT MUST BE OBEYED!*

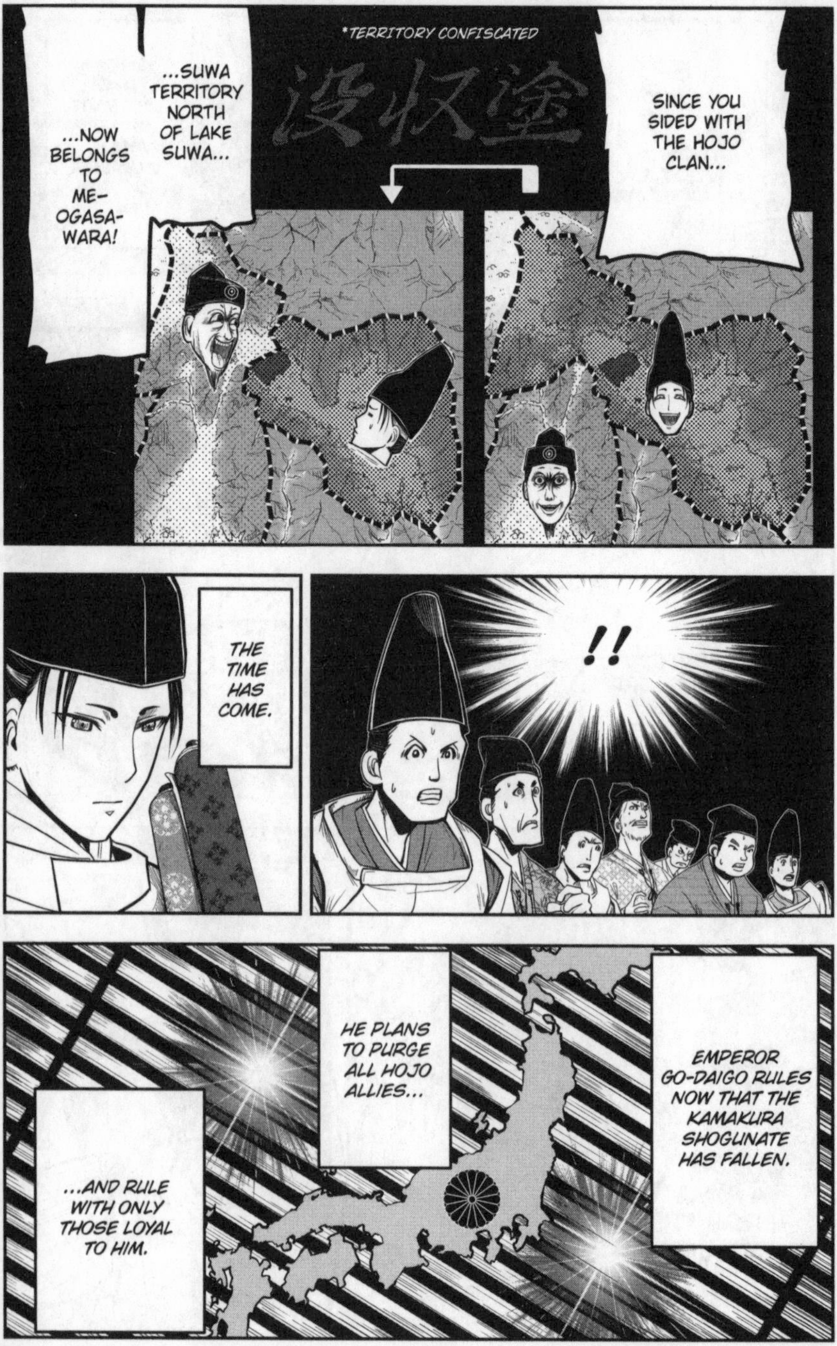
SINCE YOU SIDED WITH THE HOJO CLAN...
没収途
*TERRITORY CONFISCATED
...SUWA TERRITORY NORTH OF LAKE SUWA...
...NOW BELONGS TO ME—OGASAWARA!
!!
THE TIME HAS COME.
EMPEROR GO-DAIGO RULES NOW THAT THE KAMAKURA SHOGUNATE HAS FALLEN.
HE PLANS TO PURGE ALL HOJO ALLIES...
...AND RULE WITH ONLY THOSE LOYAL TO HIM.

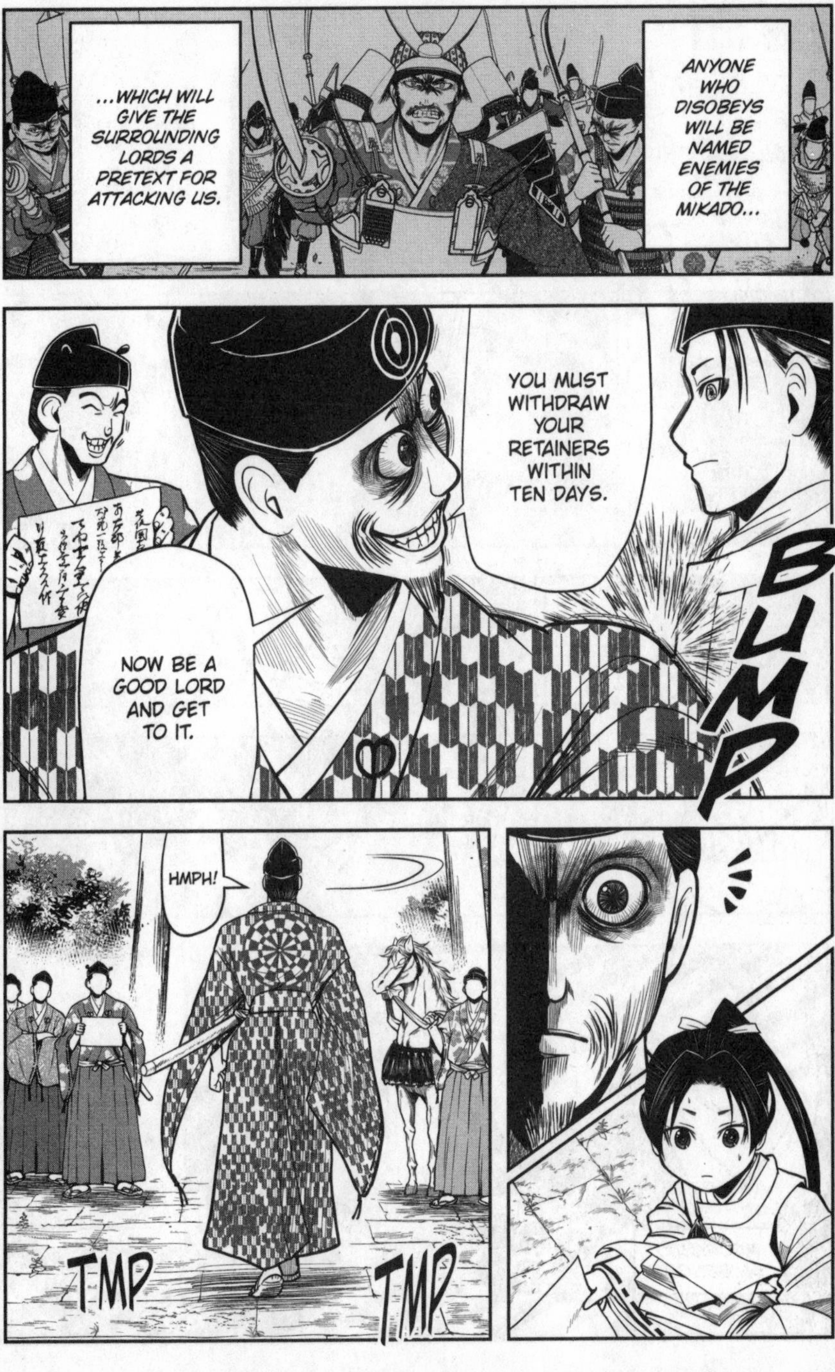
ANYONE WHO DISOBEYS WILL BE NAMED ENEMIES OF THE MIKADO...
...WHICH WILL GIVE THE SURROUNDING LORDS A PRETEXT FOR ATTACKING US.
YOU MUST WITHDRAW YOUR RETAINERS WITHIN TEN DAYS.
NOW BE A GOOD LORD AND GET TO IT.
BUMP
HMPH!
TMP
TMP

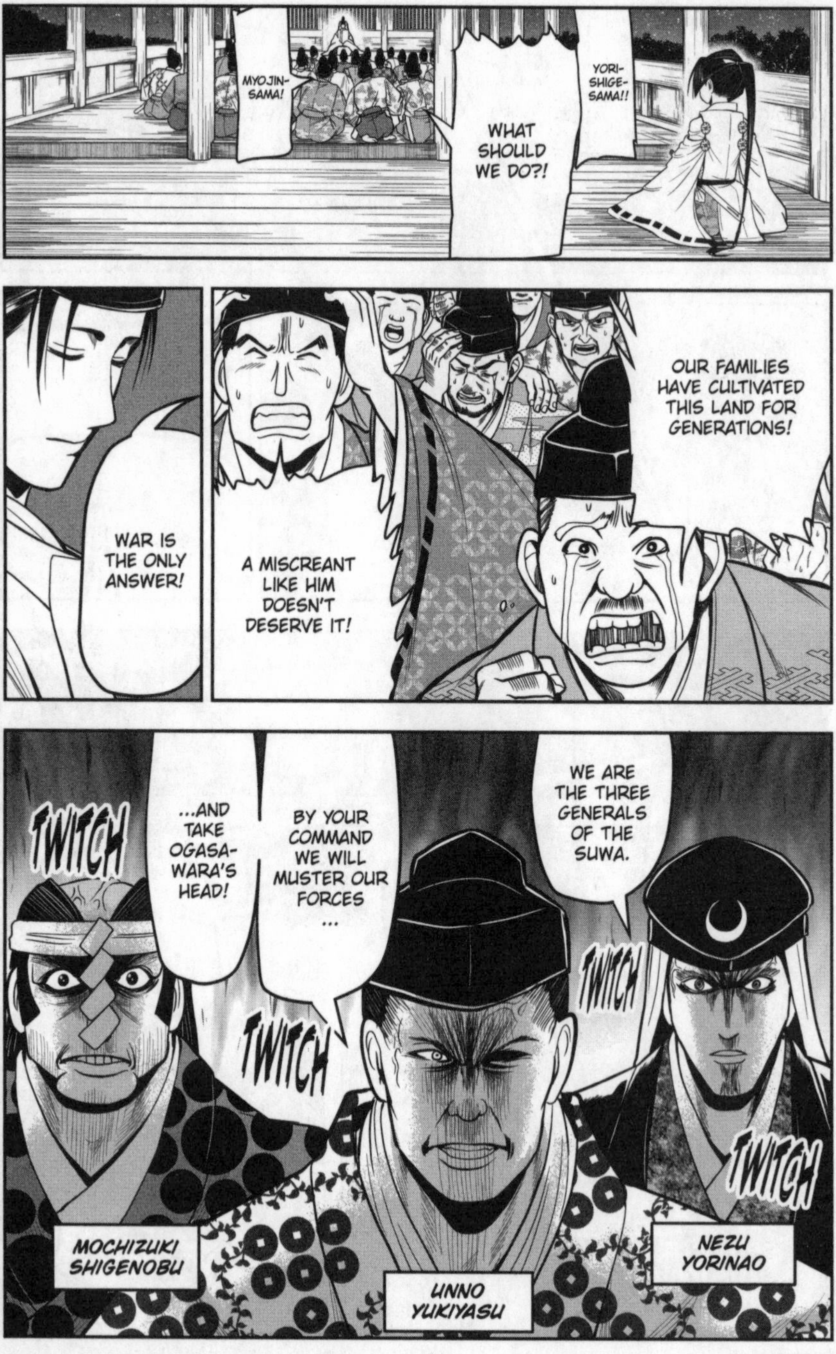
YORI-SHIGE-SAMA!!
WHAT SHOULD WE DO?!
MYOJIN-SAMA!
OUR FAMILIES HAVE CULTIVATED THIS LAND FOR GENERATIONS!
A MISCREANT LIKE HIM DOESN'T DESERVE IT!
WAR IS THE ONLY ANSWER!
WE ARE THE THREE GENERALS OF THE SUWA.
BY YOUR COMMAND WE WILL MUSTER OUR FORCES ...
...AND TAKE OGASAWARA'S HEAD!
TWITCH
TWITCH
TWITCH
TWITCH
NEZU YORINAO
UNNO YUKIYASU
MOCHIZUKI SHIGENOBU

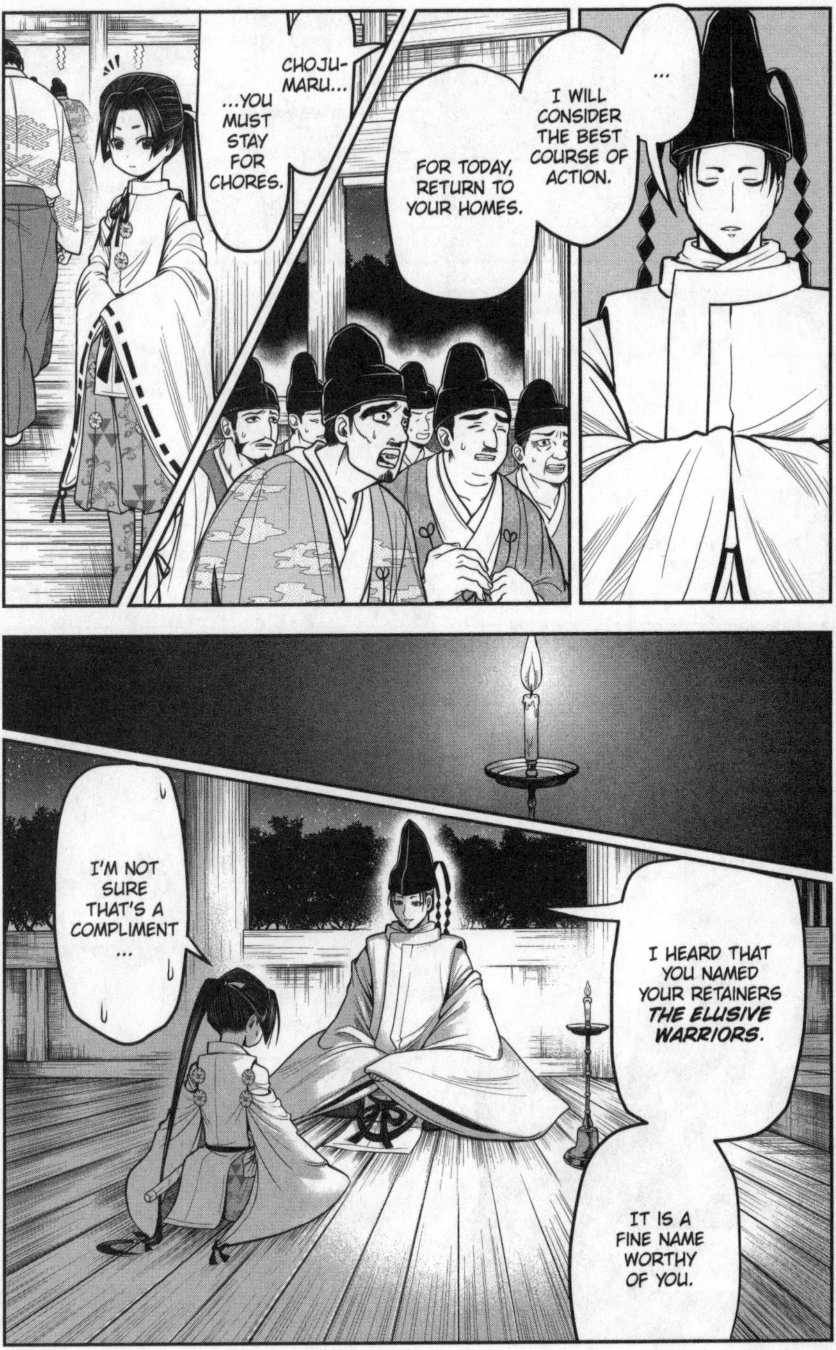
...
I WILL CONSIDER THE BEST COURSE OF ACTION.
FOR TODAY, RETURN TO YOUR HOMES.
CHOJU-MARU...
...YOU MUST STAY FOR CHORES.
I HEARD THAT YOU NAMED YOUR RETAINERS ***THE ELUSIVE WARRIORS.***
IT IS A FINE NAME WORTHY OF YOU.
I'M NOT SURE THAT'S A COMPLIMENT ...

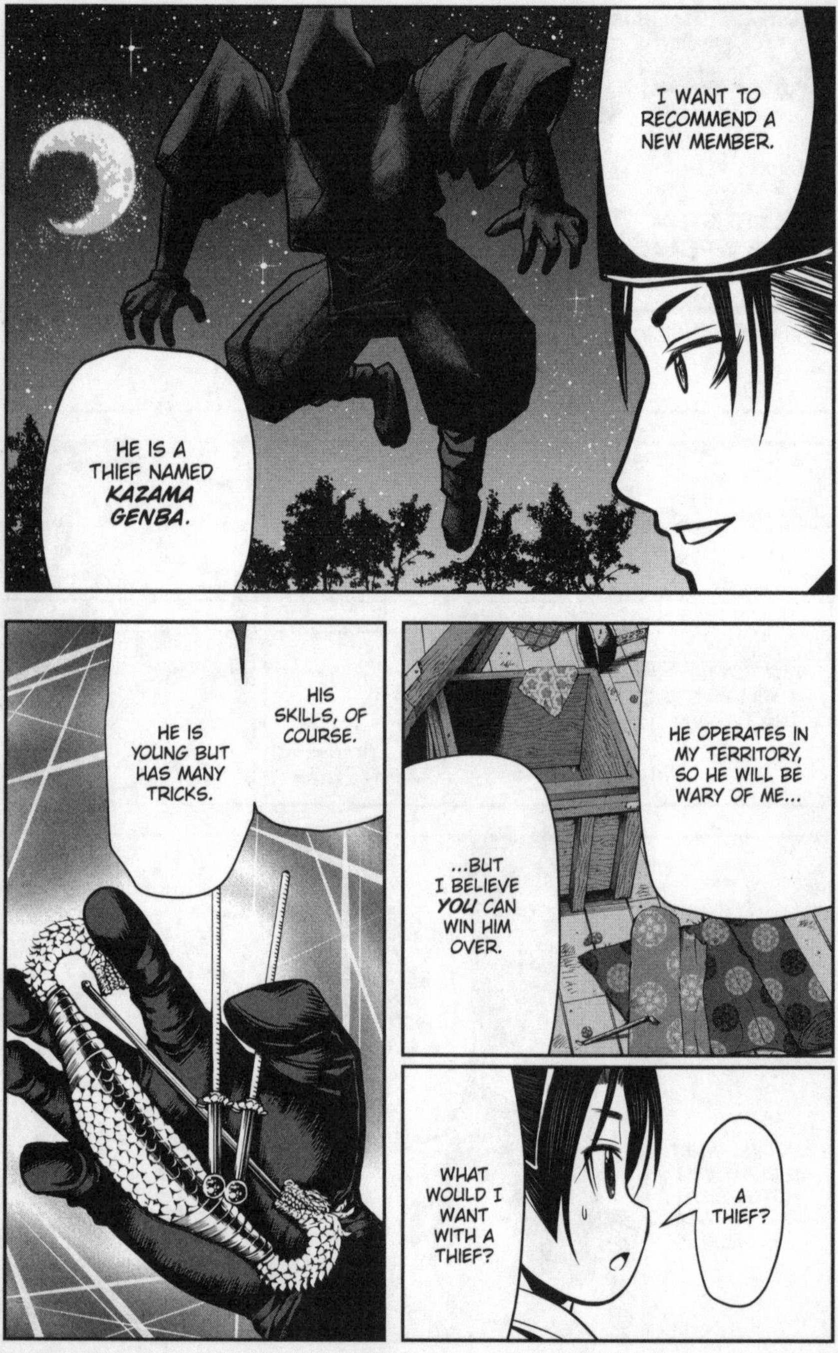
I WANT TO RECOMMEND A NEW MEMBER.
HE IS A THIEF NAMED *KAZAMA GENBA*.
HE OPERATES IN MY TERRITORY, SO HE WILL BE WARY OF ME...
...BUT I BELIEVE *YOU* CAN WIN HIM OVER.
A THIEF?
WHAT WOULD I WANT WITH A THIEF?
HIS SKILLS, OF COURSE.
HE IS YOUNG BUT HAS MANY TRICKS.

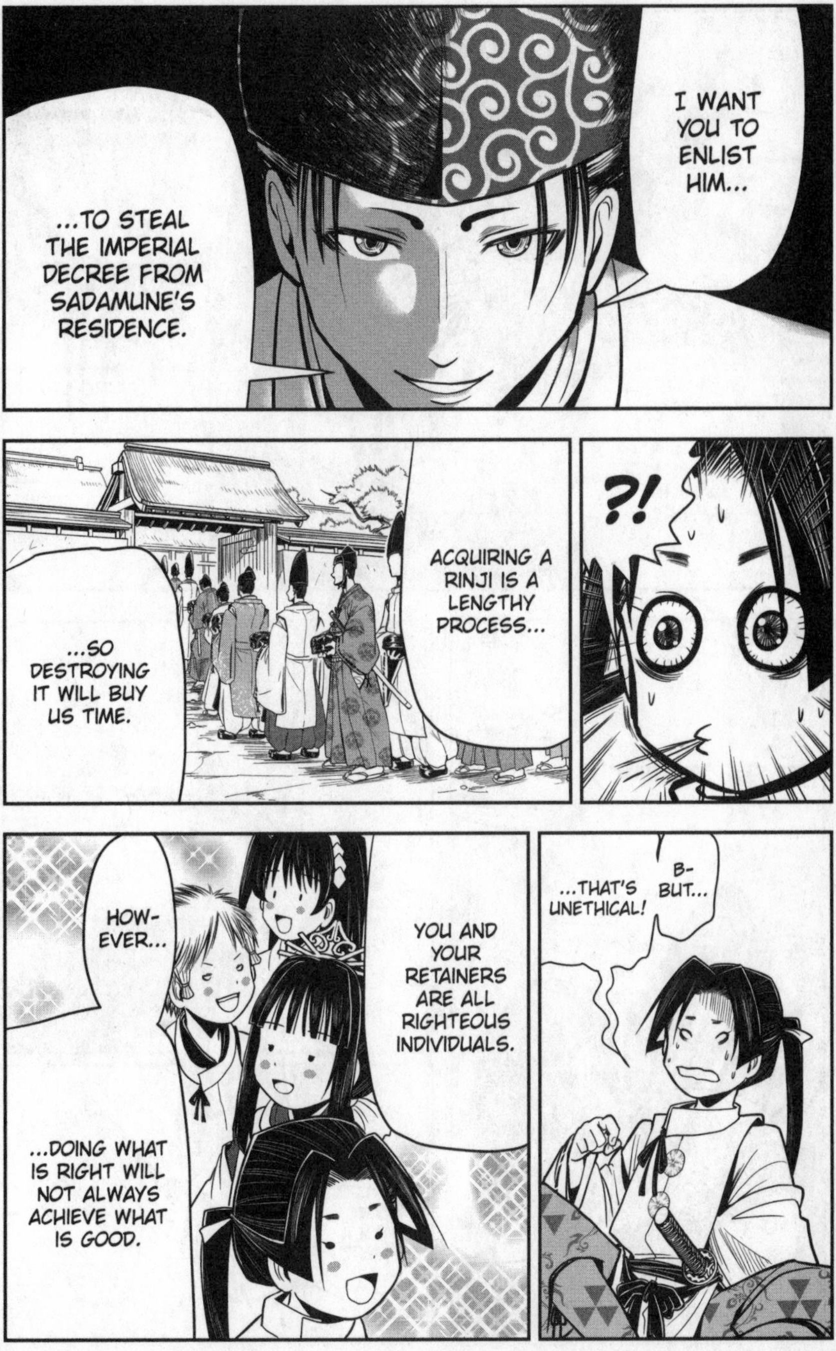
I WANT YOU TO ENLIST HIM...
...TO STEAL THE IMPERIAL DECREE FROM SADAMUNE'S RESIDENCE.
?!
ACQUIRING A RINJI IS A LENGTHY PROCESS...
...SO DESTROYING IT WILL BUY US TIME.
B- BUT...
...THAT'S UNETHICAL!
YOU AND YOUR RETAINERS ARE ALL RIGHTEOUS INDIVIDUALS.
HOW-EVER...
...DOING WHAT IS RIGHT WILL NOT ALWAYS ACHIEVE WHAT IS GOOD.

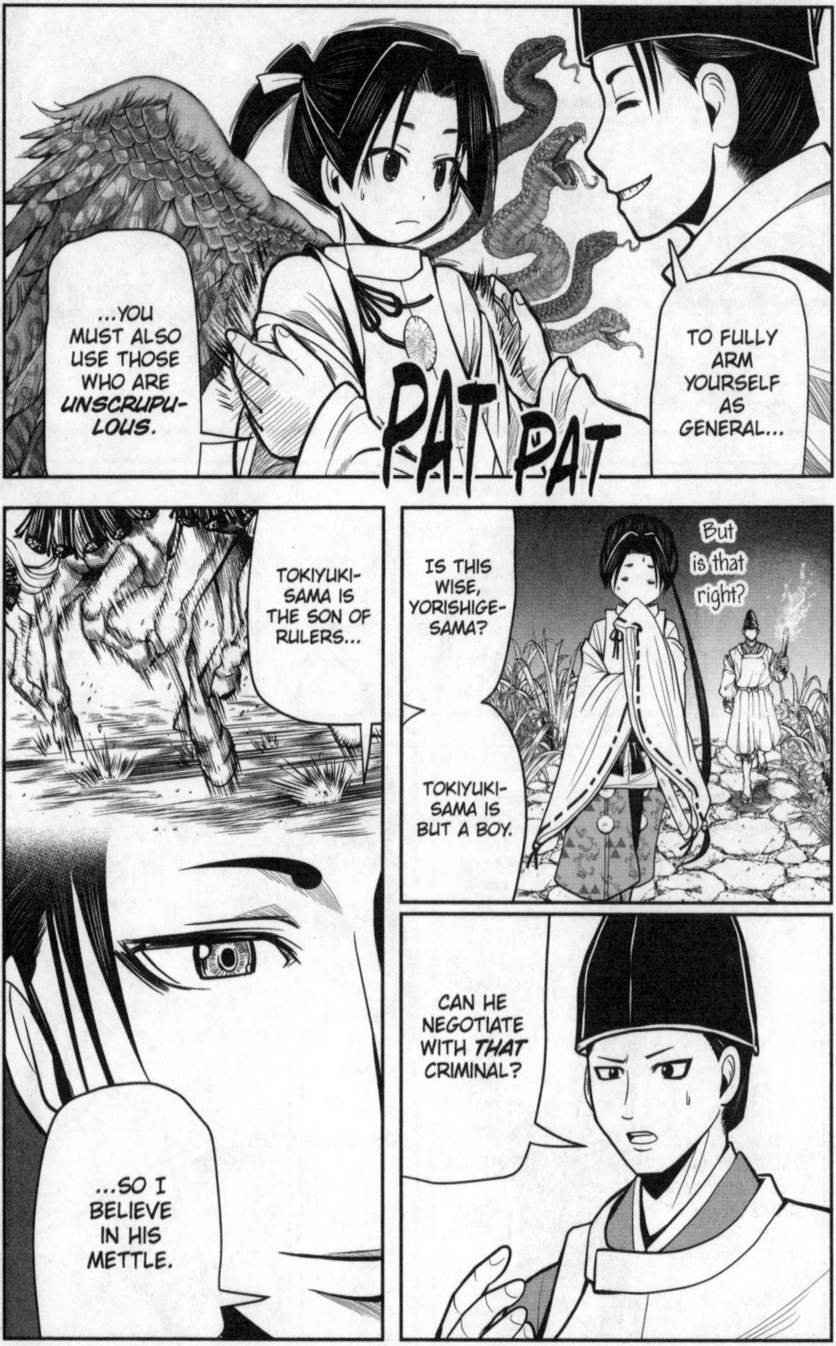

TO FULLY ARM YOURSELF AS GENERAL...
...YOU MUST ALSO USE THOSE WHO ARE *UNSCRUPULOUS*.
PAT PAT
But is that right?
IS THIS WISE, YORISHIGE-SAMA?
TOKIYUKI-SAMA IS BUT A BOY.
CAN HE NEGOTIATE WITH *THAT* CRIMINAL?
TOKIYUKI-SAMA IS THE SON OF RULERS...
...SO I BELIEVE IN HIS METTLE.

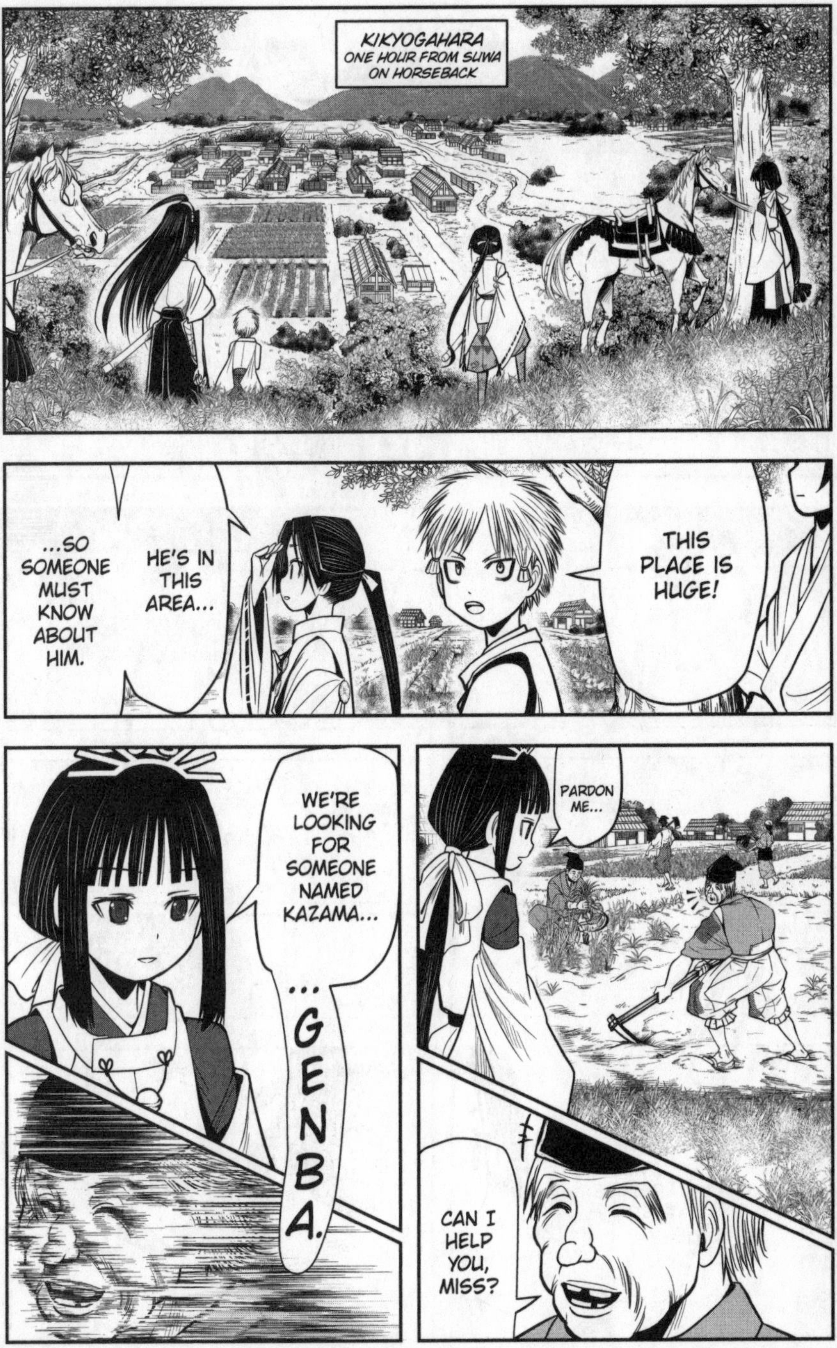
KIKYOGAHARA
ONE HOUR FROM SUWA ON HORSEBACK
THIS PLACE IS HUGE!
HE'S IN THIS AREA...
...SO SOMEONE MUST KNOW ABOUT HIM.
PARDON ME...
CAN I HELP YOU, MISS?
WE'RE LOOKING FOR SOMEONE NAMED KAZAMA...
...GENBA.

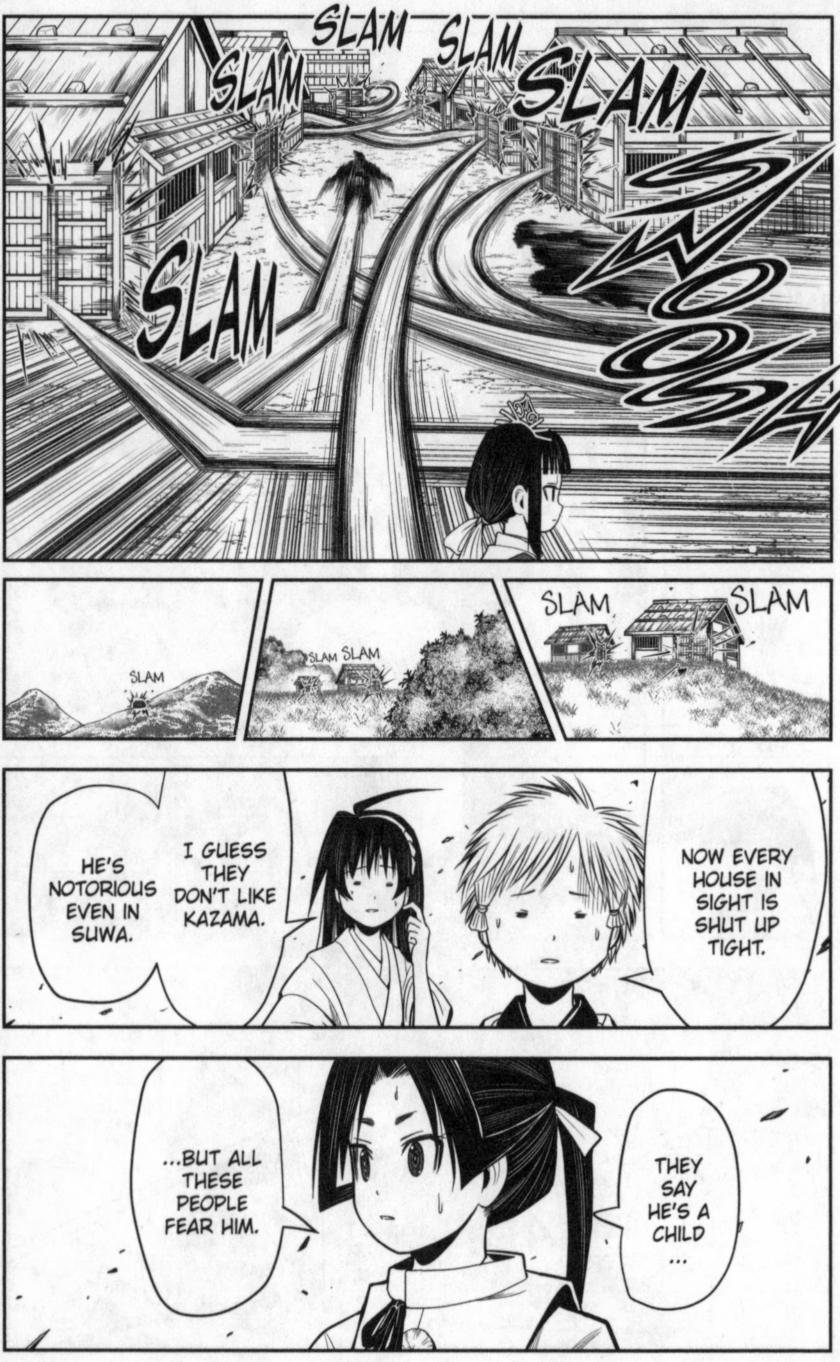
SLAM
SLAM
SLAM
SLAM
SLAM
SWOOSH
SLAM
SLAM
SLAM SLAM
SLAM
NOW EVERY HOUSE IN SIGHT IS SHUT UP TIGHT.
I GUESS THEY DON'T LIKE KAZAMA.
HE'S NOTORIOUS EVEN IN SUWA.
THEY SAY HE'S A CHILD ...
...BUT ALL THESE PEOPLE FEAR HIM.

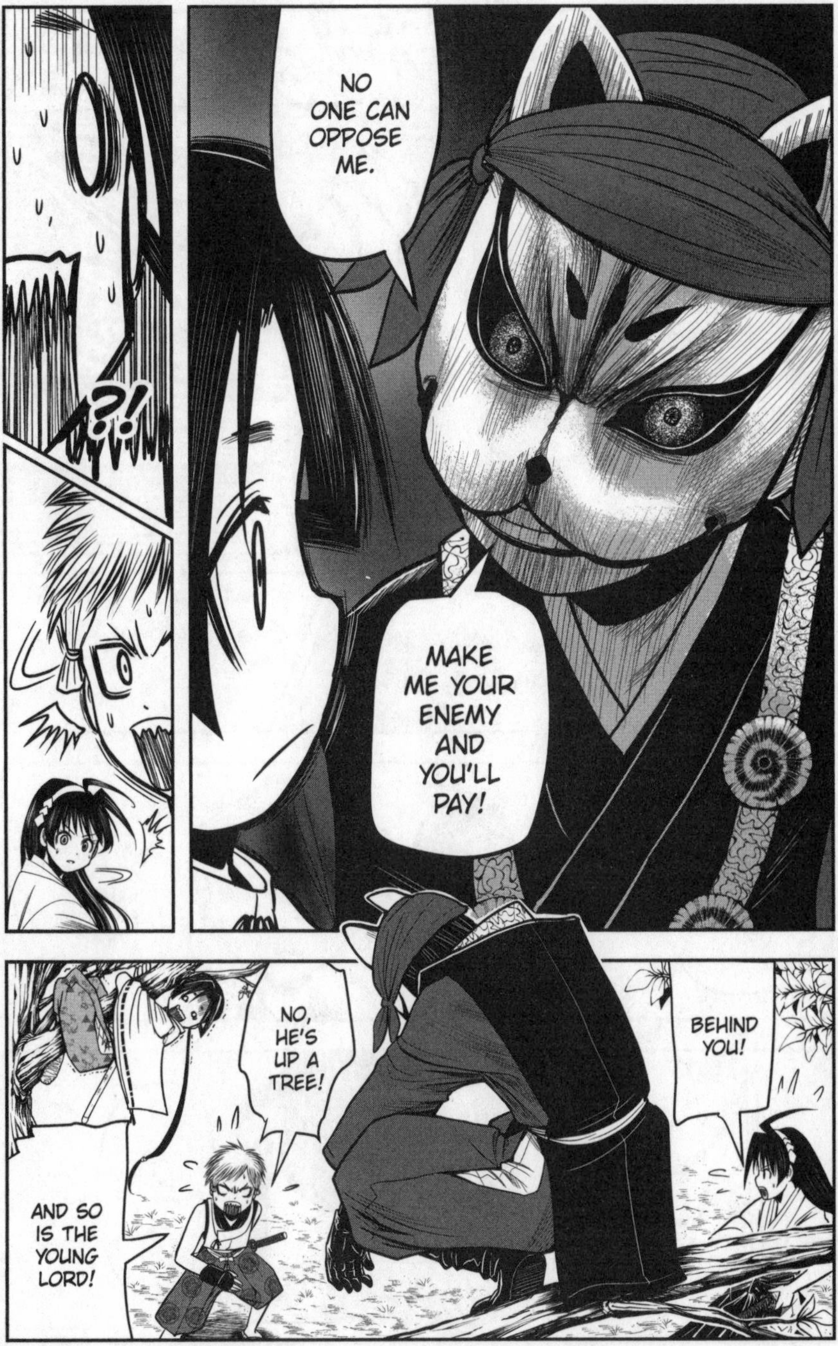
NO ONE CAN OPPOSE ME.
MAKE ME YOUR ENEMY AND YOU'LL PAY!
?!
BEHIND YOU!
NO, HE'S UP A TREE!
AND SO IS THE YOUNG LORD!

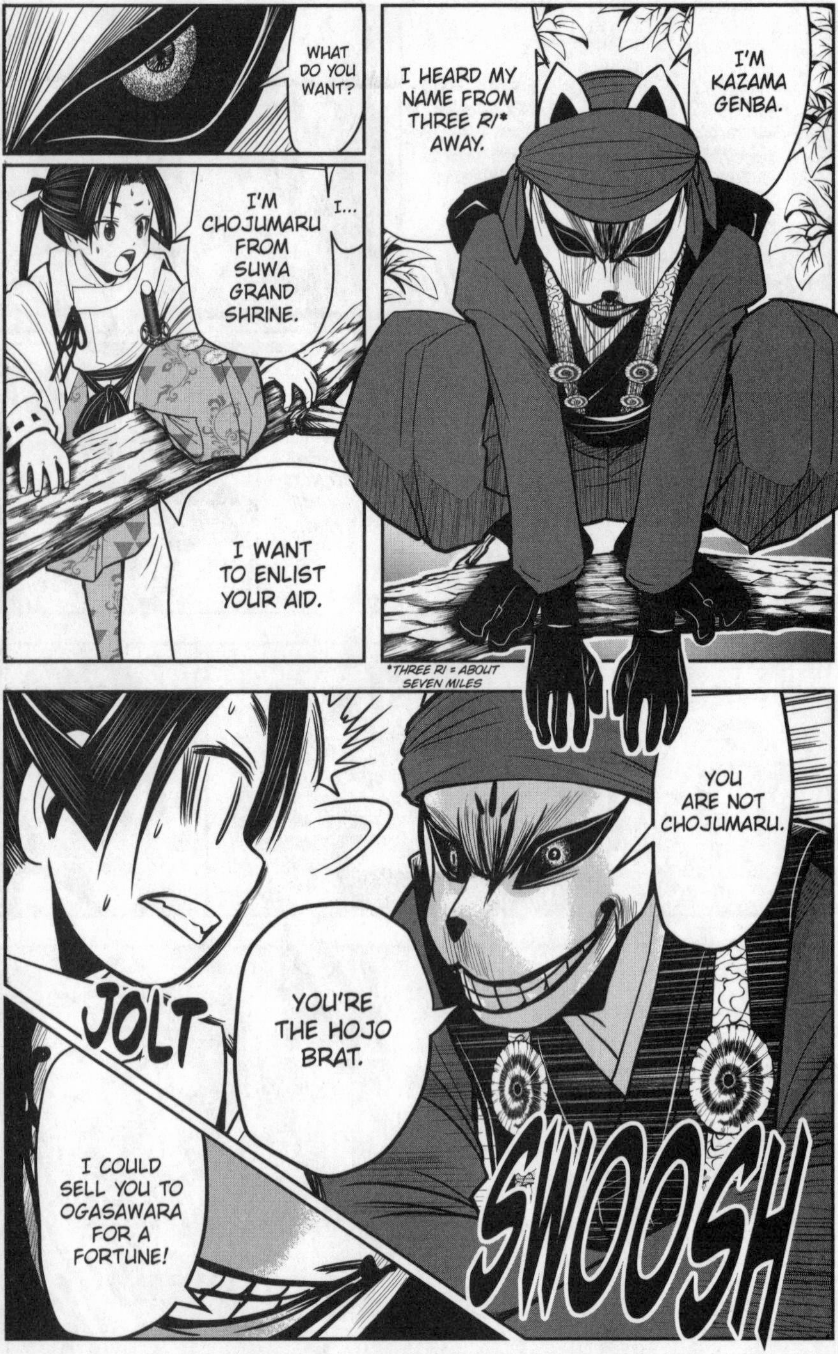
I'M KAZAMA GENBA.
I HEARD MY NAME FROM THREE RI* AWAY.
WHAT DO YOU WANT?
I...
I'M CHOJUMARU FROM SUWA GRAND SHRINE.
I WANT TO ENLIST YOUR AID.
*THREE RI = ABOUT SEVEN MILES
YOU ARE NOT CHOJUMARU.
JOLT
YOU'RE THE HOJO BRAT.
SWOOSH
I COULD SELL YOU TO OGASAWARA FOR A FORTUNE!

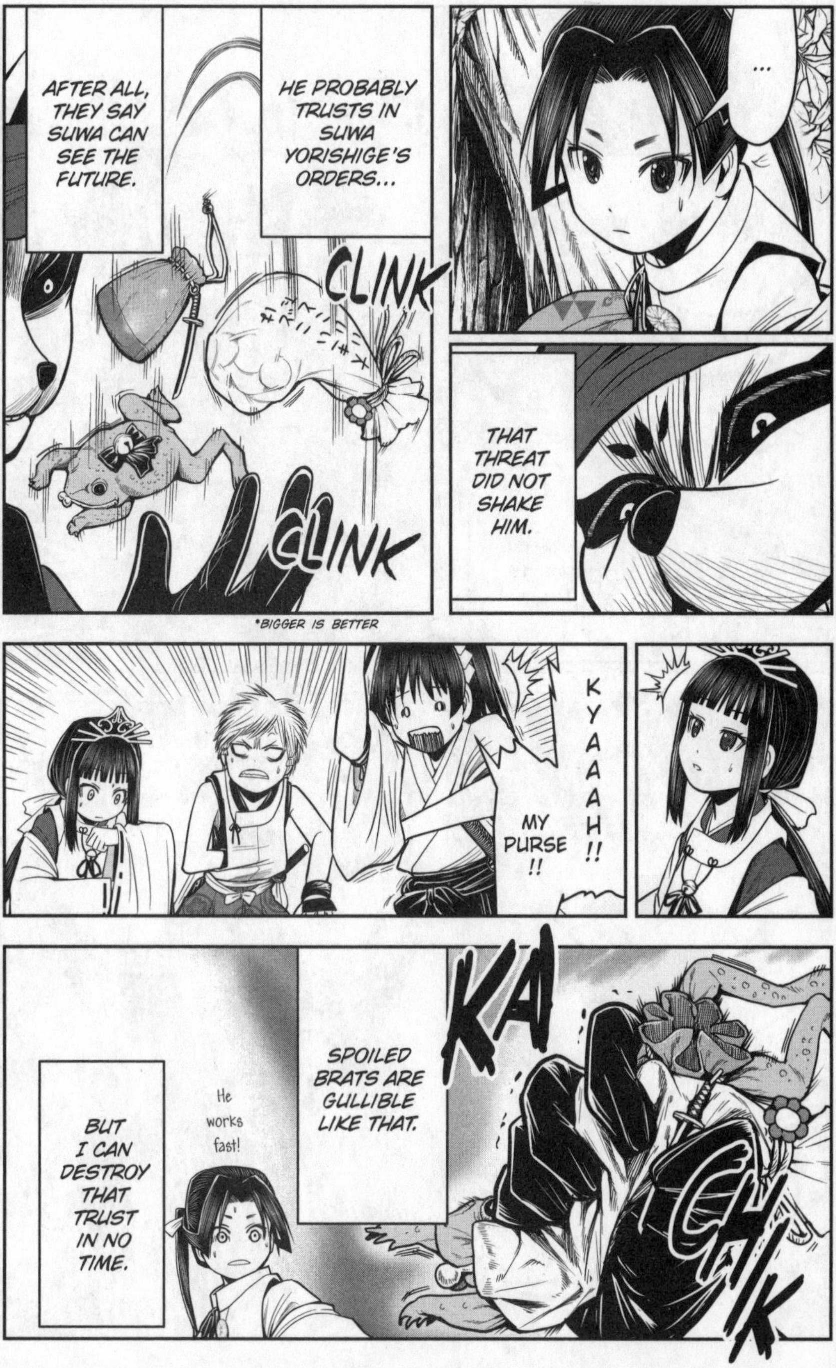
...
THAT THREAT DID NOT SHAKE HIM.
HE PROBABLY TRUSTS IN SUWA YORISHIGE'S ORDERS...
AFTER ALL, THEY SAY SUWA CAN SEE THE FUTURE.
CLINK
CLINK
*BIGGER IS BETTER
KYAAAAH!!
MY PURSE!!
KA
SPOILED BRATS ARE GULLIBLE LIKE THAT.
CHIK
He works fast!
BUT I CAN DESTROY THAT TRUST IN NO TIME.

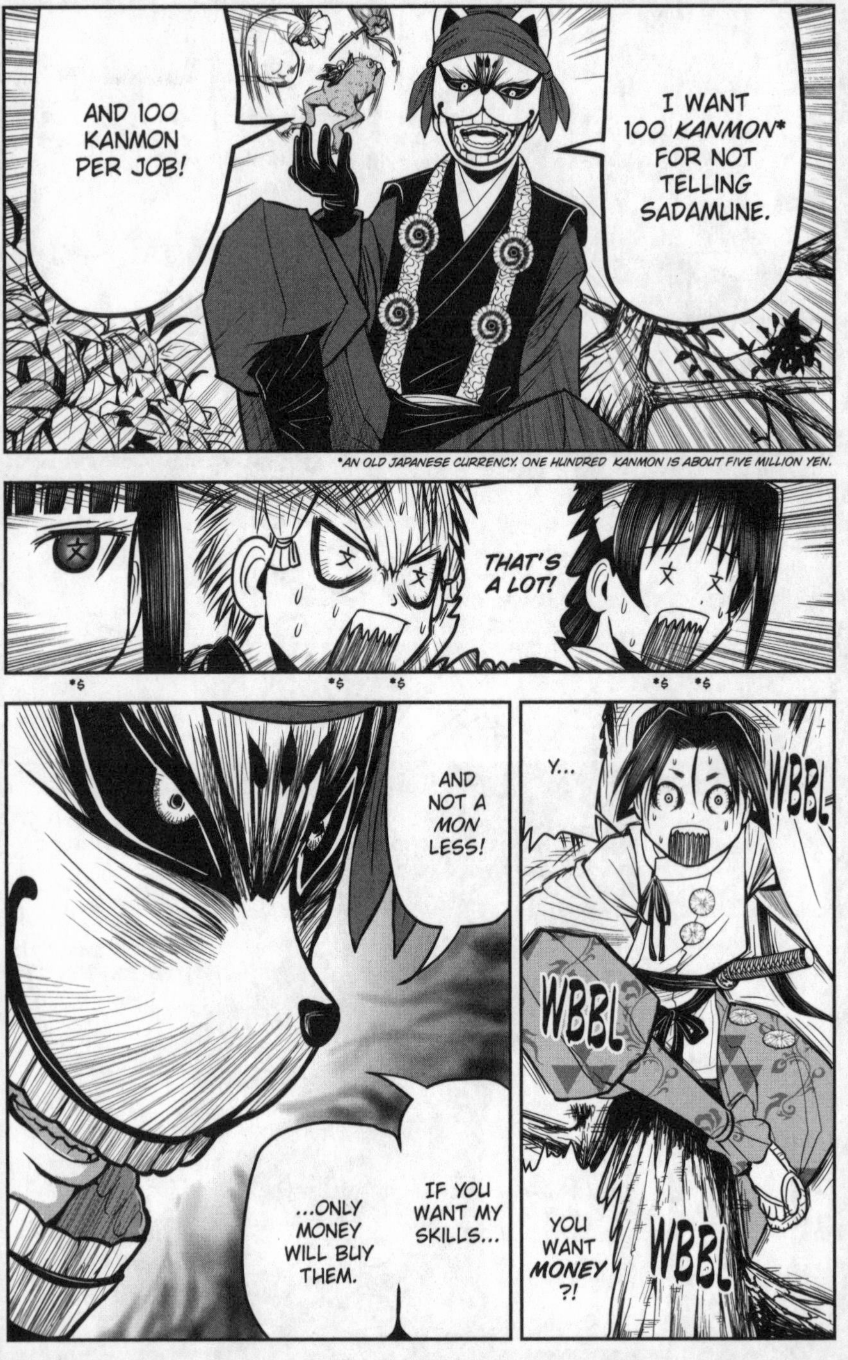
I WANT 100 *KANMON** FOR NOT TELLING SADAMUNE.
AND 100 KANMON PER JOB!
*AN OLD JAPANESE CURRENCY. ONE HUNDRED KANMON IS ABOUT FIVE MILLION YEN.
THAT'S A LOT!
WBBL
Y...
WBBL
YOU WANT *MONEY*?!
WBBL
AND NOT A *MON* LESS!
IF YOU WANT MY SKILLS...
...ONLY MONEY WILL BUY THEM.

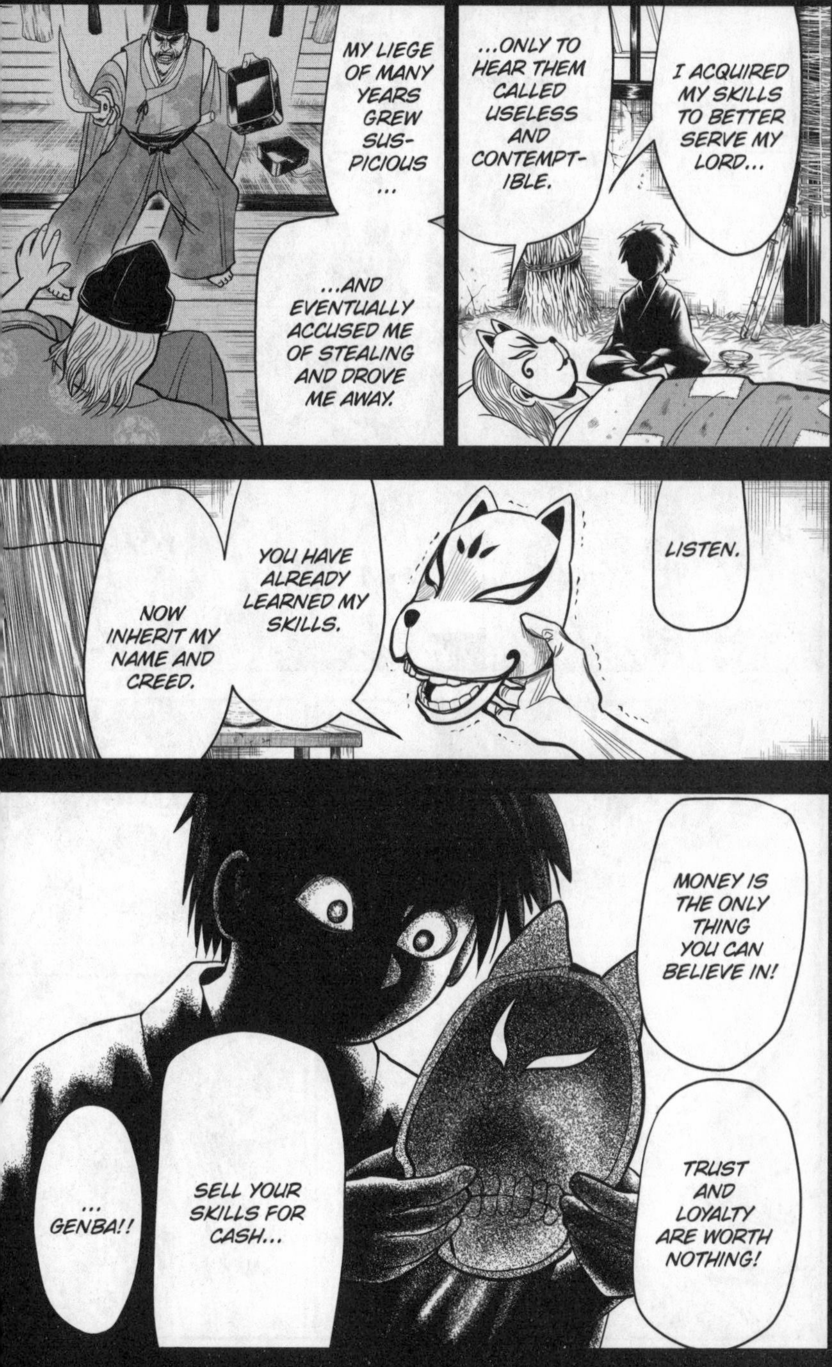
I ACQUIRED MY SKILLS TO BETTER SERVE MY LORD...
...ONLY TO HEAR THEM CALLED USELESS AND CONTEMPT-IBLE.
MY LIEGE OF MANY YEARS GREW SUS-PICIOUS...
...AND EVENTUALLY ACCUSED ME OF STEALING AND DROVE ME AWAY.
LISTEN.
YOU HAVE ALREADY LEARNED MY SKILLS.
NOW INHERIT MY NAME AND CREED.
MONEY IS THE ONLY THING YOU CAN BELIEVE IN!
TRUST AND LOYALTY ARE WORTH NOTHING!
SELL YOUR SKILLS FOR CASH...
...GENBA!!

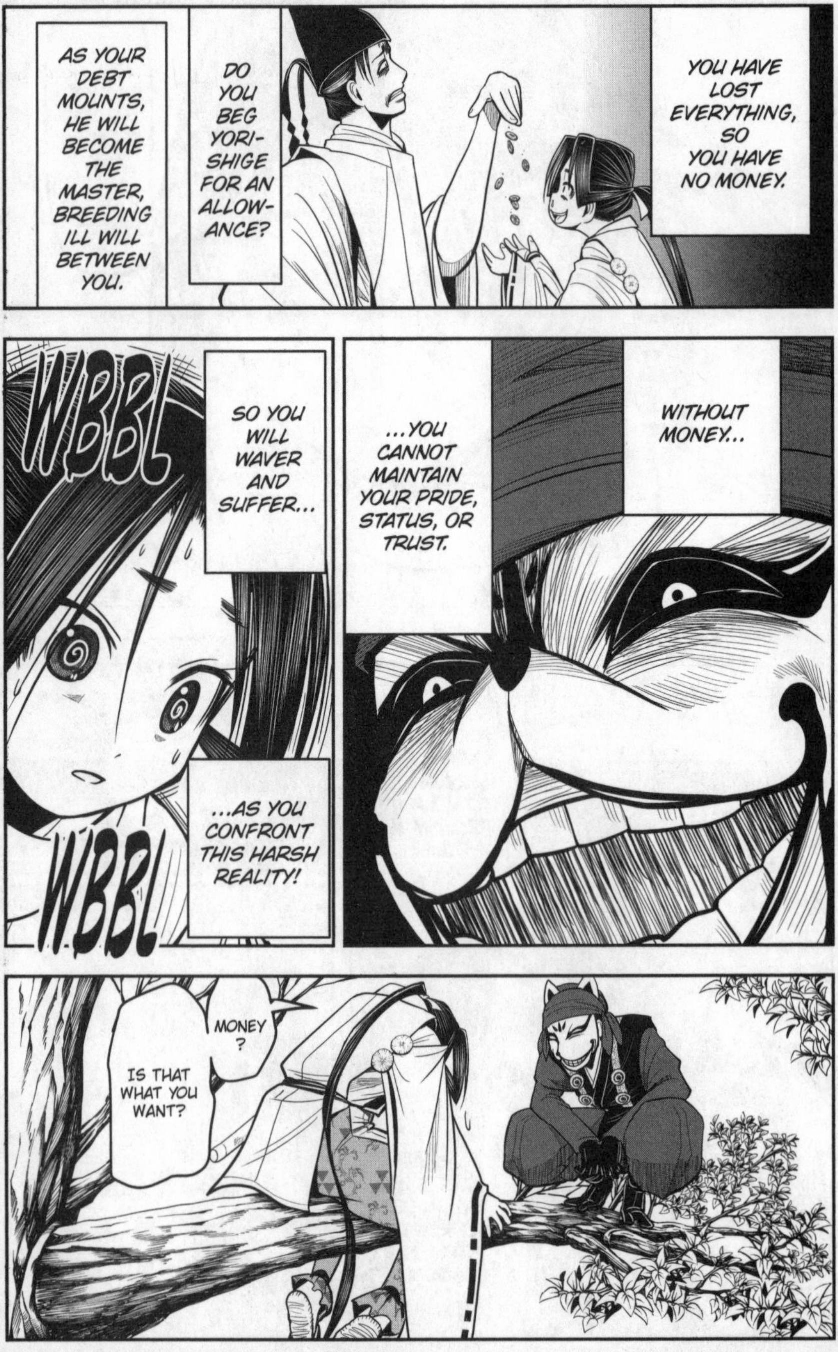
YOU HAVE LOST EVERYTHING, SO YOU HAVE NO MONEY.
DO YOU BEG YORISHIGE FOR AN ALLOWANCE?
AS YOUR DEBT MOUNTS, HE WILL BECOME THE MASTER, BREEDING ILL WILL BETWEEN YOU.
WITHOUT MONEY...
...YOU CANNOT MAINTAIN YOUR PRIDE, STATUS, OR TRUST.
WBBL
SO YOU WILL WAVER AND SUFFER...
...AS YOU CONFRONT THIS HARSH REALITY!
WBBL
MONEY?
IS THAT WHAT YOU WANT?

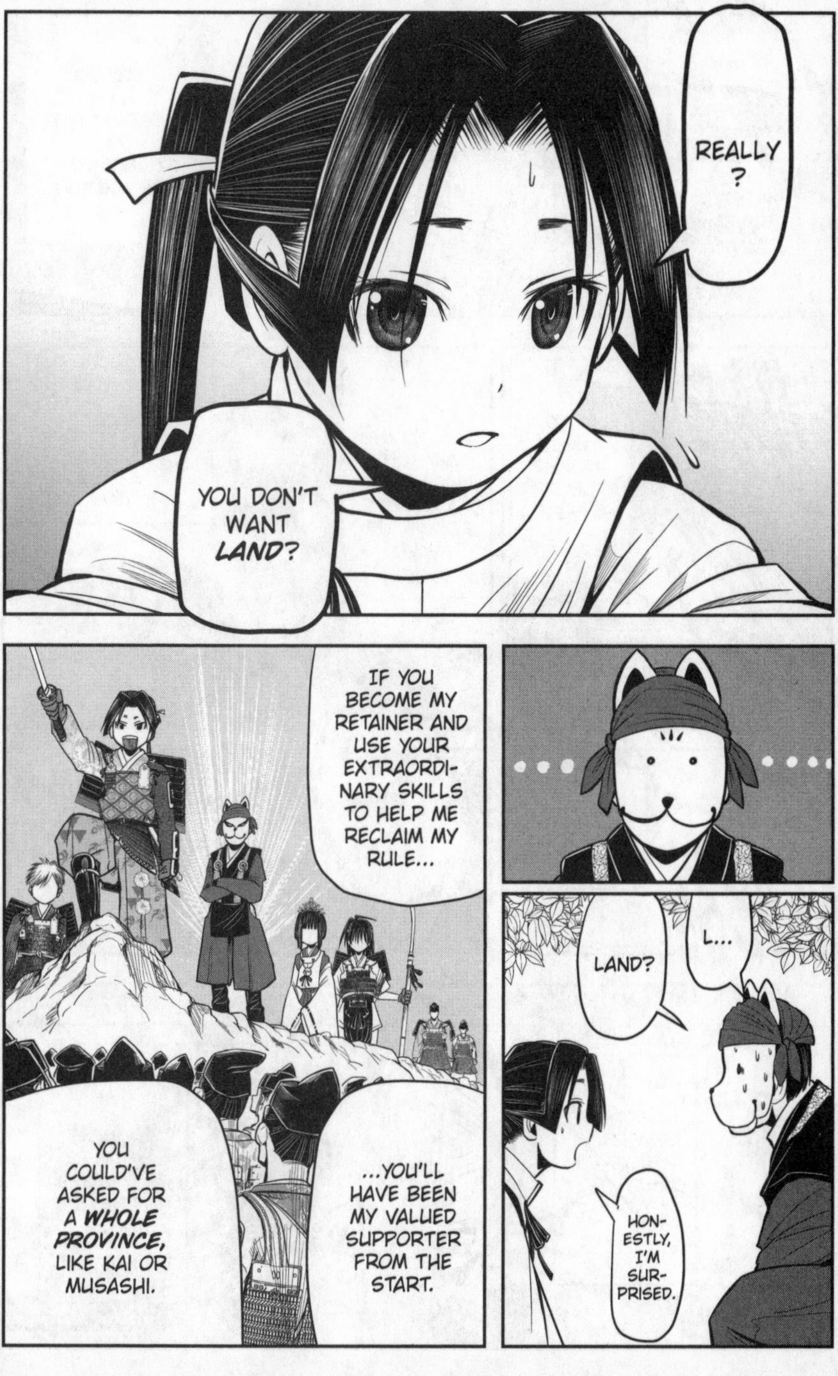
REALLY?
YOU DON'T WANT *LAND?*
L...
LAND?
HON-ESTLY, I'M SUR-PRISED.
IF YOU BECOME MY RETAINER AND USE YOUR EXTRAORDI-NARY SKILLS TO HELP ME RECLAIM MY RULE...
...YOU'LL HAVE BEEN MY VALUED SUPPORTER FROM THE START.
YOU COULD'VE ASKED FOR A *WHOLE PROVINCE,* LIKE KAI OR MUSASHI.

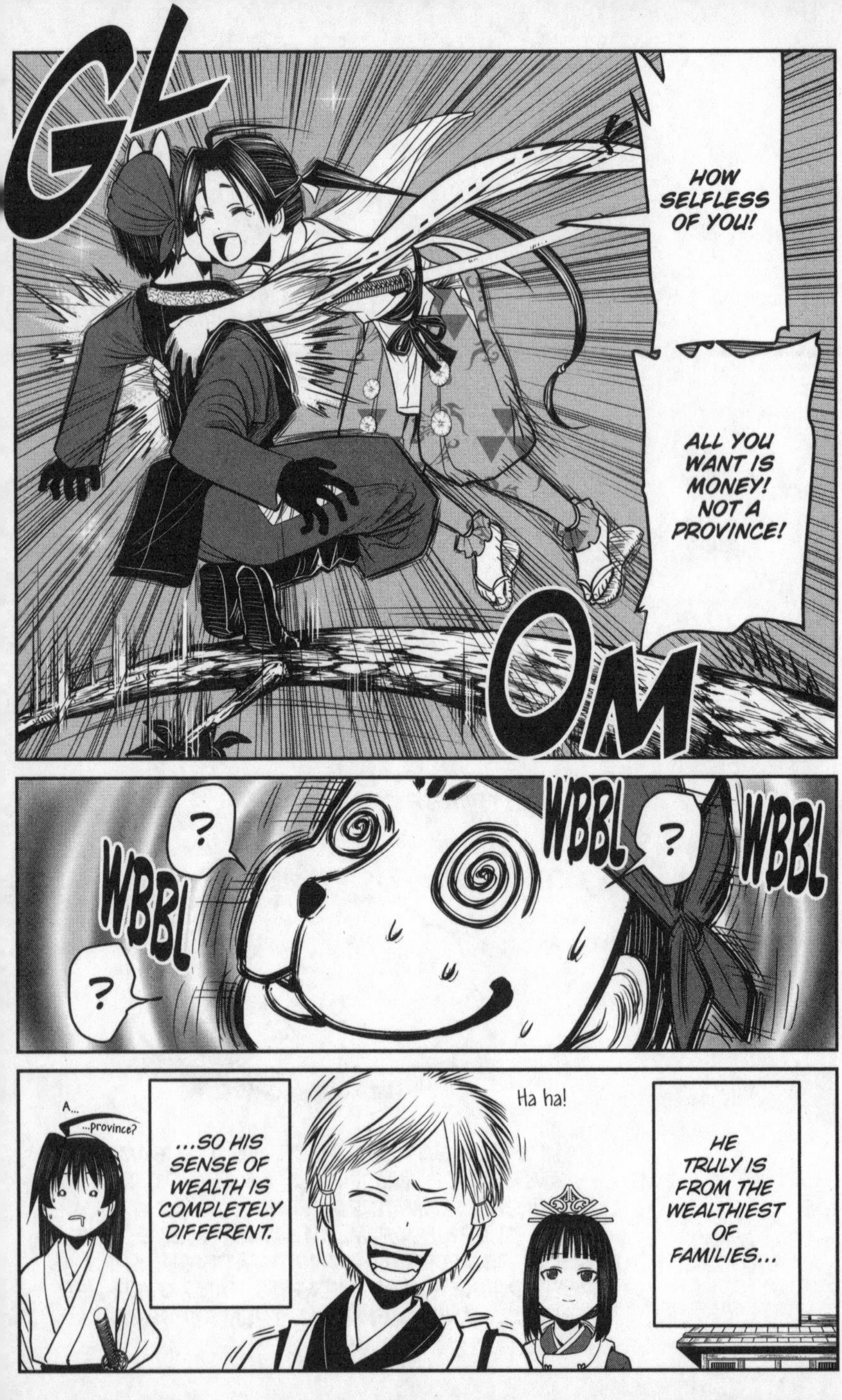
GL
HOW SELFLESS OF YOU!
ALL YOU WANT IS MONEY! NOT A PROVINCE!
OM
WBBL
?
WBBL
?
WBBL
?
HE TRULY IS FROM THE WEALTHIEST OF FAMILIES...
Ha ha!
...SO HIS SENSE OF WEALTH IS COMPLETELY DIFFERENT.
A...
...province?

AYAKO'S WALLET

*BIGGER IS BETTER

大きいことはいいことだ

IT'S BIG, BUT SHE RECEIVES THE SAME
AMOUNT OF ALLOWANCE AS THE OTHER
RETAINERS. COMPARED TO HOW MUCH IT CAN
HOLD, THERE ISN'T MUCH MONEY INSIDE. SHE
MIXES IN ROCKS SO IF BANDITS ATTACK, SHE CAN
PRETEND LIKE SHE'S GOING TO HAND OVER HER
WALLET AND THEN BEAT THEM TO DEATH.

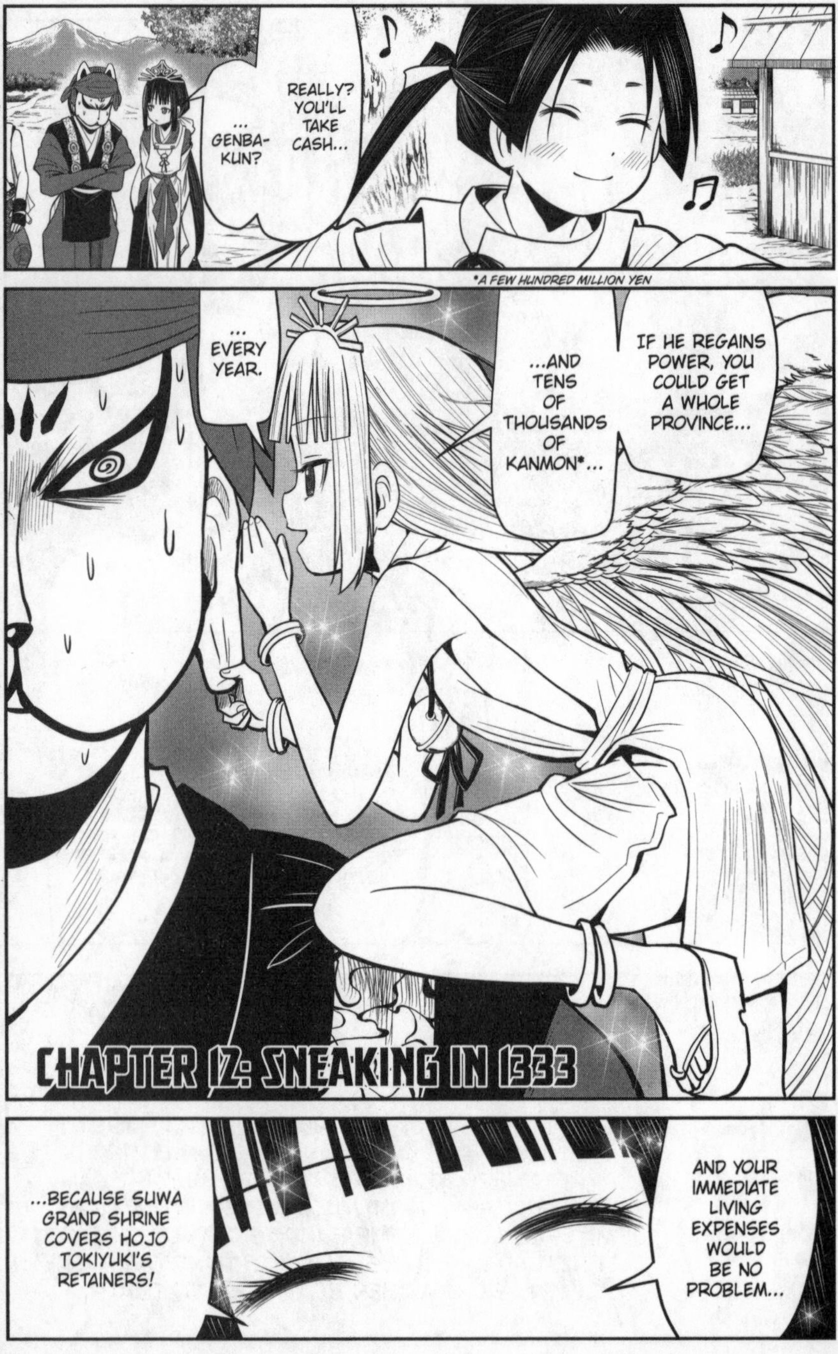
REALLY? YOU'LL TAKE CASH...
... GENBA-KUN?
IF HE REGAINS POWER, YOU COULD GET A WHOLE PROVINCE...
...AND TENS OF THOUSANDS OF KANMON*...
... EVERY YEAR.
CHAPTER 12: SNEAKING IN 1333
AND YOUR IMMEDIATE LIVING EXPENSES WOULD BE NO PROBLEM...
...BECAUSE SUWA GRAND SHRINE COVERS HOJO TOKIYUKI'S RETAINERS!

*A FEW HUNDRED MILLION YEN

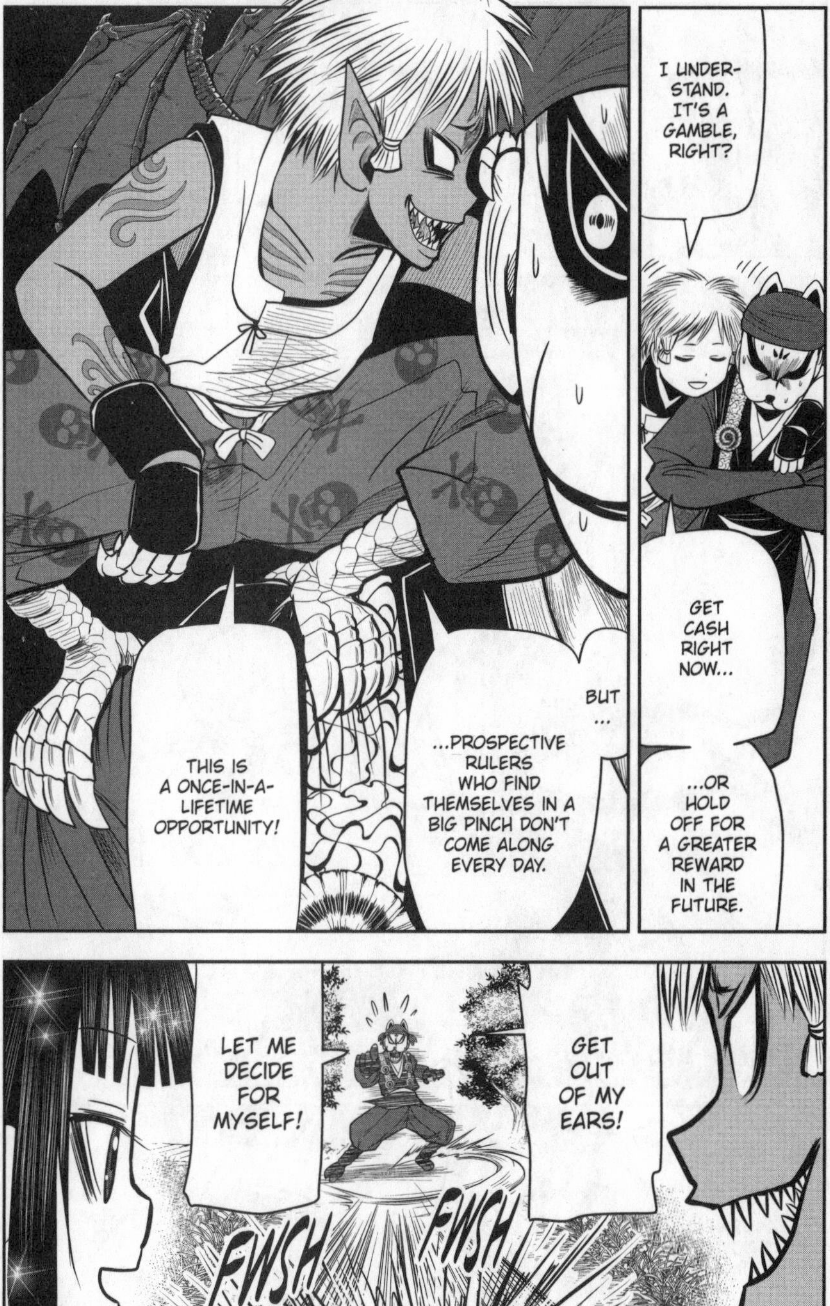
I UNDER-STAND. IT'S A GAMBLE, RIGHT?
GET CASH RIGHT NOW...
...OR HOLD OFF FOR A GREATER REWARD IN THE FUTURE.
BUT ...
...PROSPECTIVE RULERS WHO FIND THEMSELVES IN A BIG PINCH DON'T COME ALONG EVERY DAY.
THIS IS A ONCE-IN-A-LIFETIME OPPORTUNITY!
GET OUT OF MY EARS!
LET ME DECIDE FOR MYSELF!
FWSH
FWSH

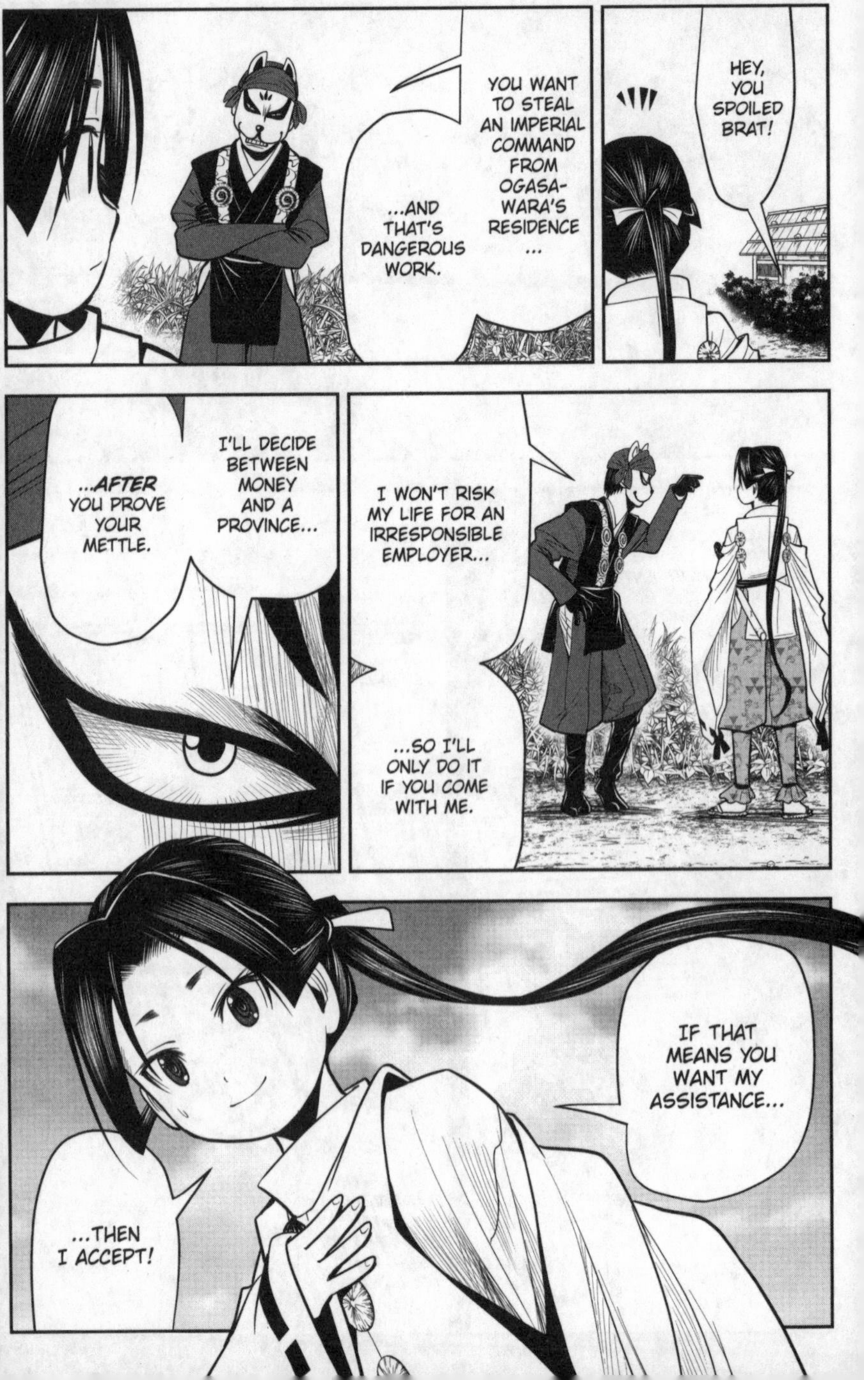
HEY, YOU SPOILED BRAT!
YOU WANT TO STEAL AN IMPERIAL COMMAND FROM OGASA-WARA'S RESIDENCE...
...AND THAT'S DANGEROUS WORK.
I WON'T RISK MY LIFE FOR AN IRRESPONSIBLE EMPLOYER...
...SO I'LL ONLY DO IT IF YOU COME WITH ME.
I'LL DECIDE BETWEEN MONEY AND A PROVINCE...
...*AFTER* YOU PROVE YOUR METTLE.
IF THAT MEANS YOU WANT MY ASSISTANCE...
...THEN I ACCEPT!

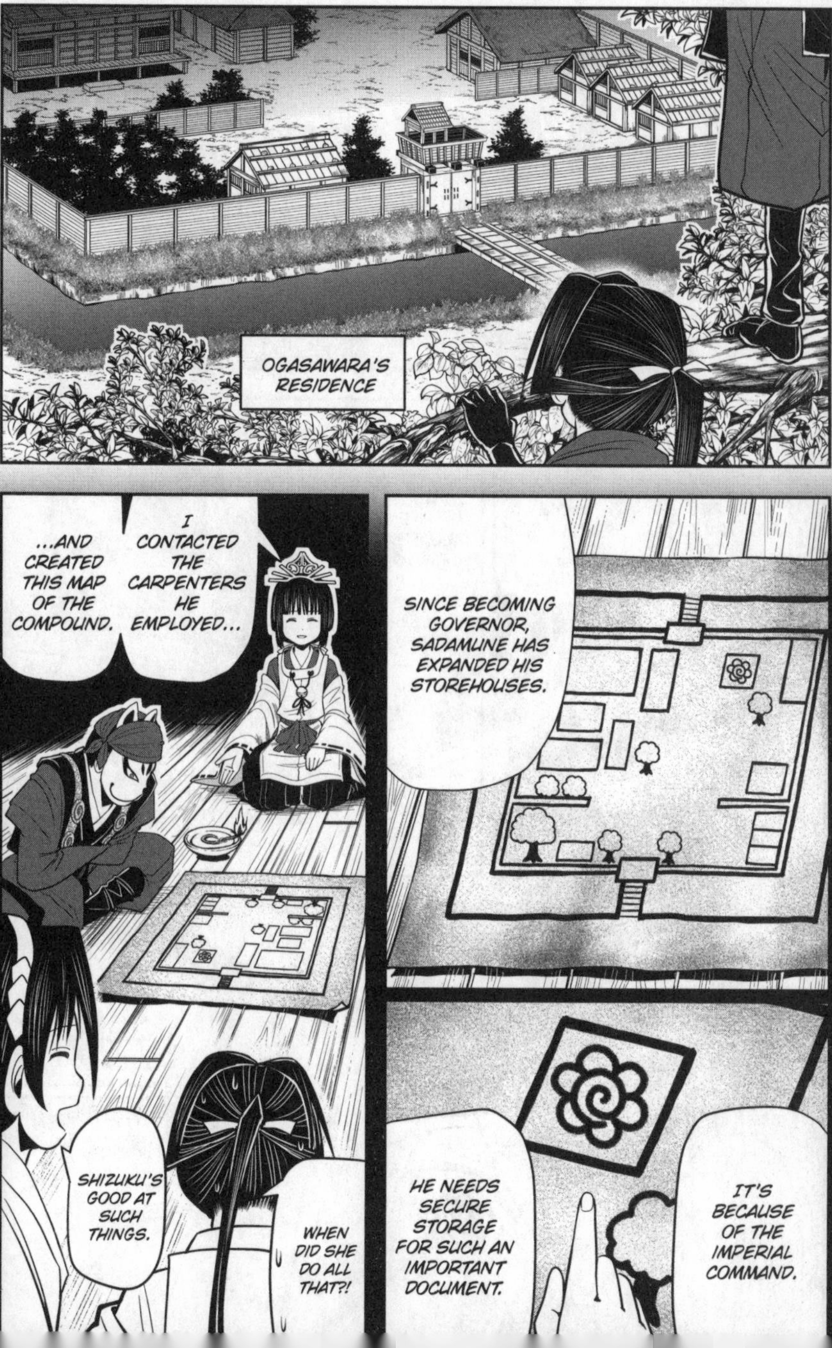
OGASAWARA'S RESIDENCE
SINCE BECOMING GOVERNOR, SADAMUNE HAS EXPANDED HIS STOREHOUSES.
IT'S BECAUSE OF THE IMPERIAL COMMAND.
HE NEEDS SECURE STORAGE FOR SUCH AN IMPORTANT DOCUMENT.
I CONTACTED THE CARPENTERS HE EMPLOYED...
...AND CREATED THIS MAP OF THE COMPOUND.
WHEN DID SHE DO ALL THAT?!
SHIZUKU'S GOOD AT SUCH THINGS.

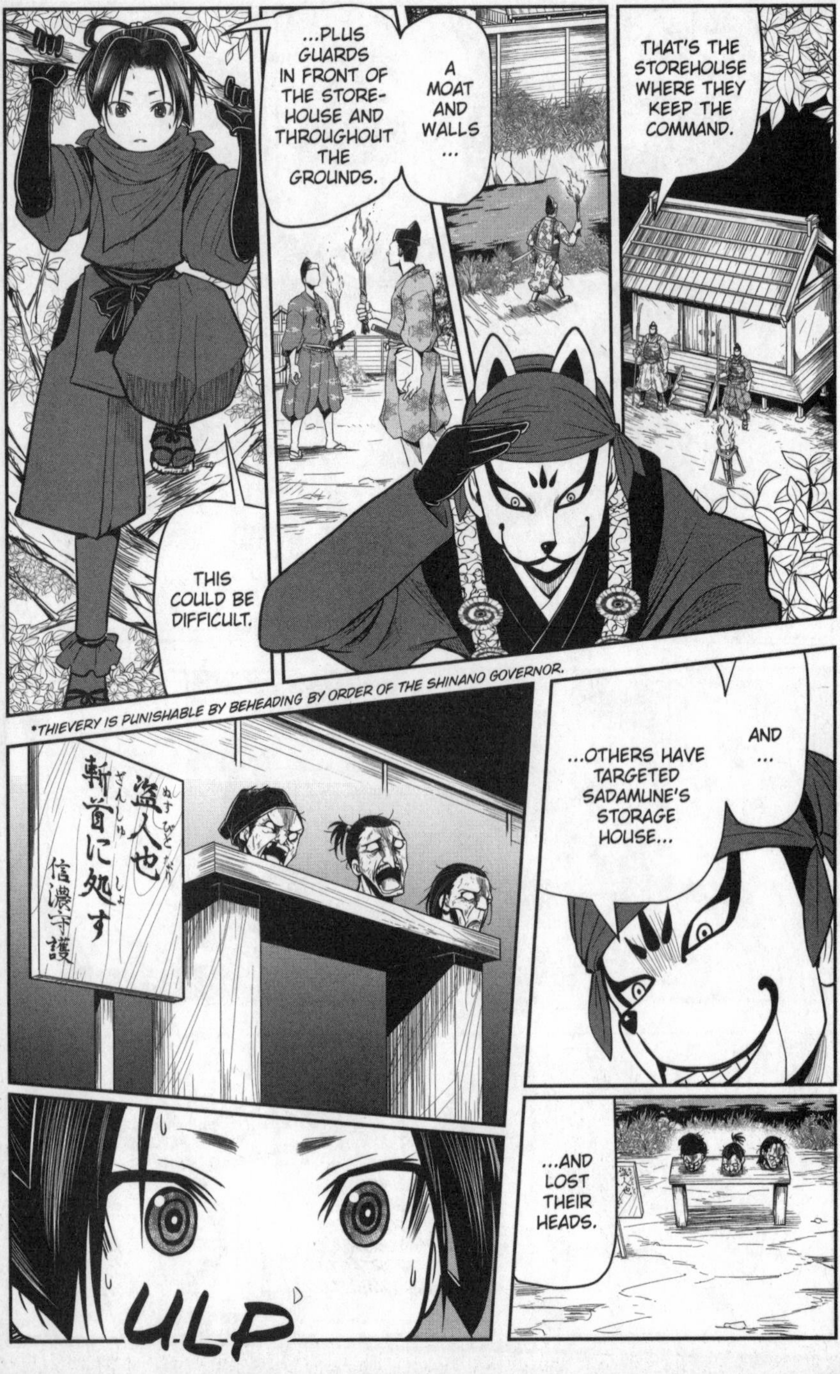
THAT'S THE STOREHOUSE WHERE THEY KEEP THE COMMAND.
A MOAT AND WALLS ...
...PLUS GUARDS IN FRONT OF THE STORE-HOUSE AND THROUGHOUT THE GROUNDS.
THIS COULD BE DIFFICULT.
AND ...
...OTHERS HAVE TARGETED SADAMUNE'S STORAGE HOUSE...
盗人也
斬首に処す
信濃守護
*THIEVERY IS PUNISHABLE BY BEHEADING BY ORDER OF THE SHINANO GOVERNOR.
...AND LOST THEIR HEADS.
U-L-P

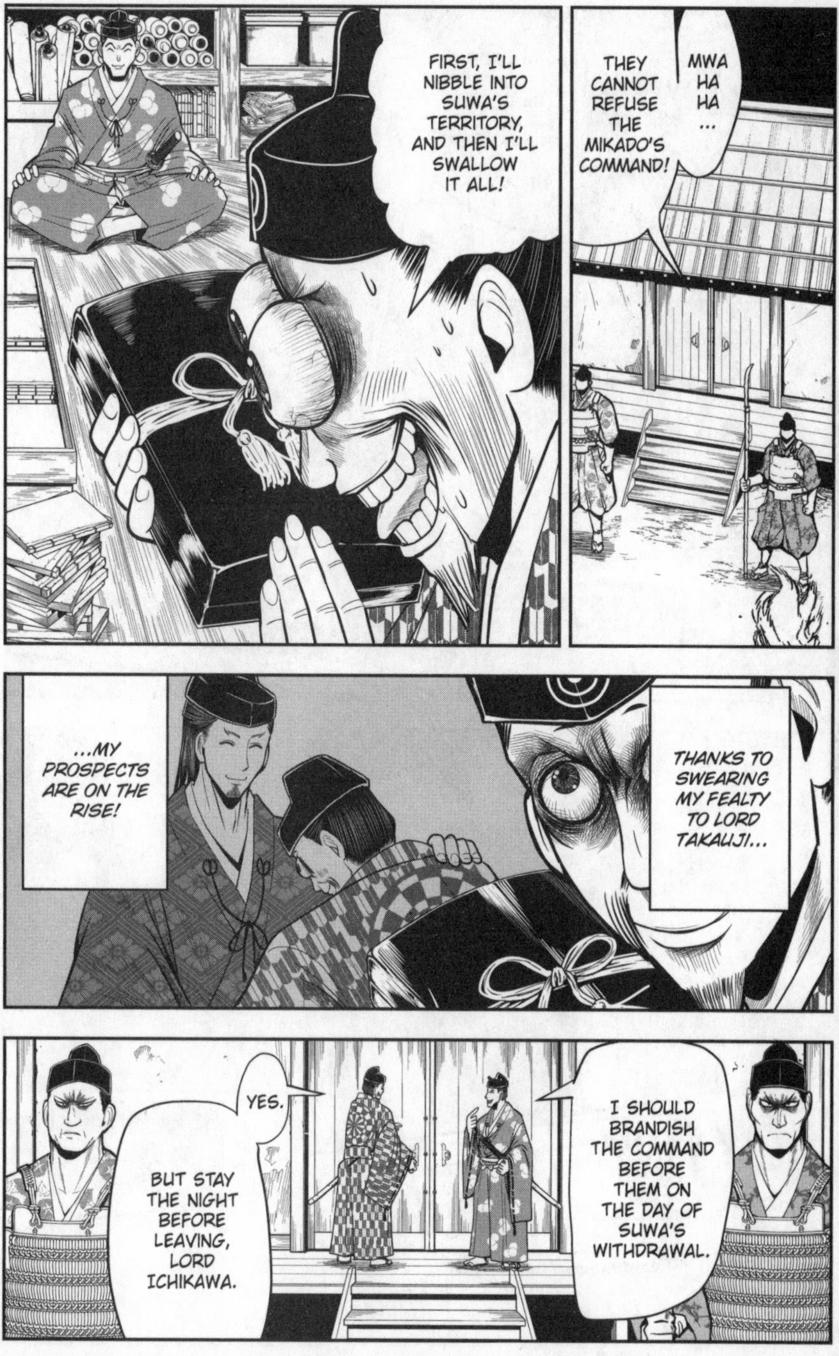

MWA HA HA...
THEY CANNOT REFUSE THE MIKADO'S COMMAND!
FIRST, I'LL NIBBLE INTO SUWA'S TERRITORY, AND THEN I'LL SWALLOW IT ALL!
THANKS TO SWEARING MY FEALTY TO LORD TAKAUJI...
...MY PROSPECTS ARE ON THE RISE!
I SHOULD BRANDISH THE COMMAND BEFORE THEM ON THE DAY OF SUWA'S WITHDRAWAL.
YES.
BUT STAY THE NIGHT BEFORE LEAVING, LORD ICHIKAWA.

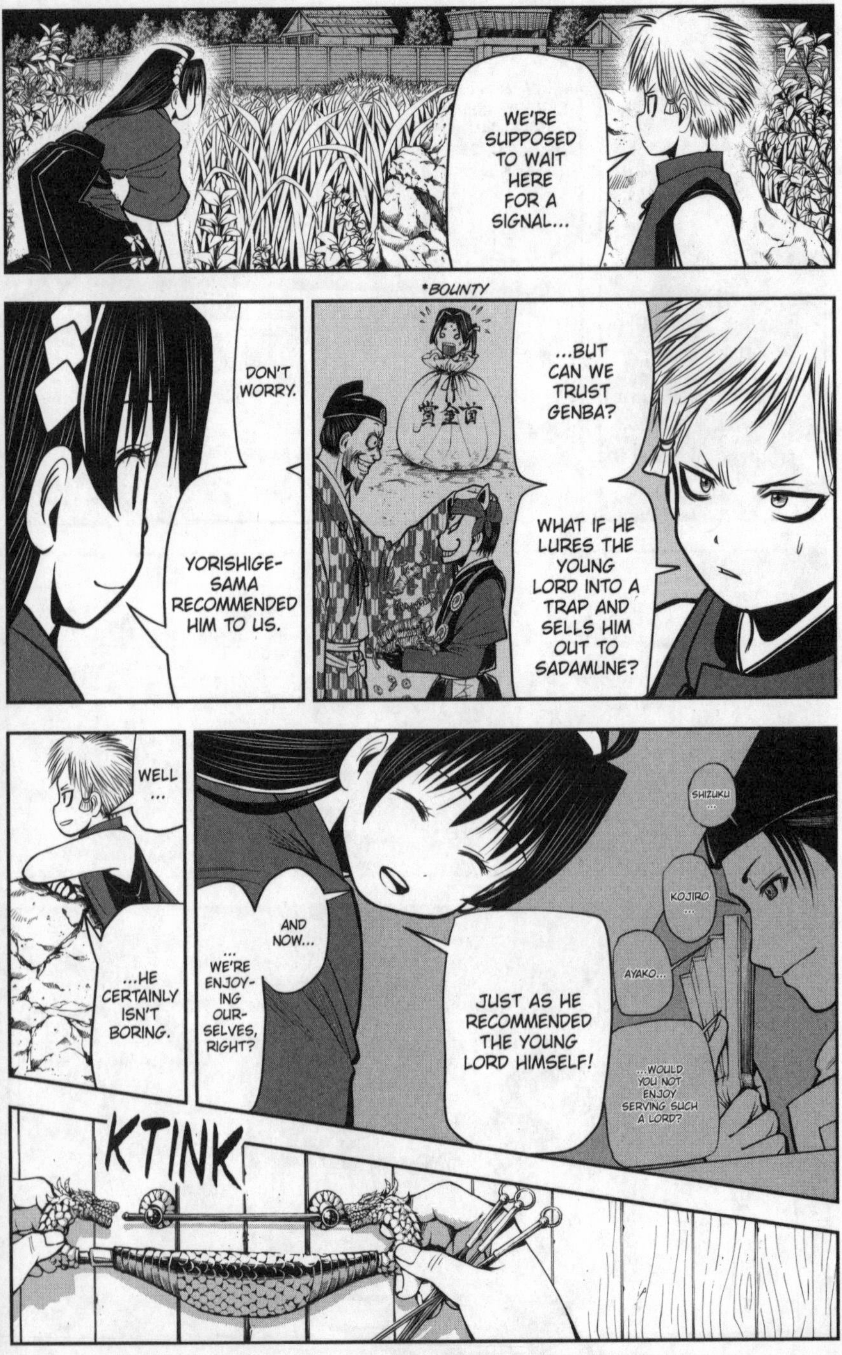
WE'RE SUPPOSED TO WAIT HERE FOR A SIGNAL...
...BUT CAN WE TRUST GENBA?
賞金首
*BOUNTY
WHAT IF HE LURES THE YOUNG LORD INTO A TRAP AND SELLS HIM OUT TO SADAMUNE?
DON'T WORRY.
YORISHIGE-SAMA RECOMMENDED HIM TO US.
SHIZUKU ...
KOJIRO ...
AYAKO...
...WOULD YOU NOT ENJOY SERVING SUCH A LORD?
JUST AS HE RECOMMENDED THE YOUNG LORD HIMSELF!
AND NOW...
...WE'RE ENJOYING OURSELVES, RIGHT?
WELL ...
...HE CERTAINLY ISN'T BORING.
KTINK

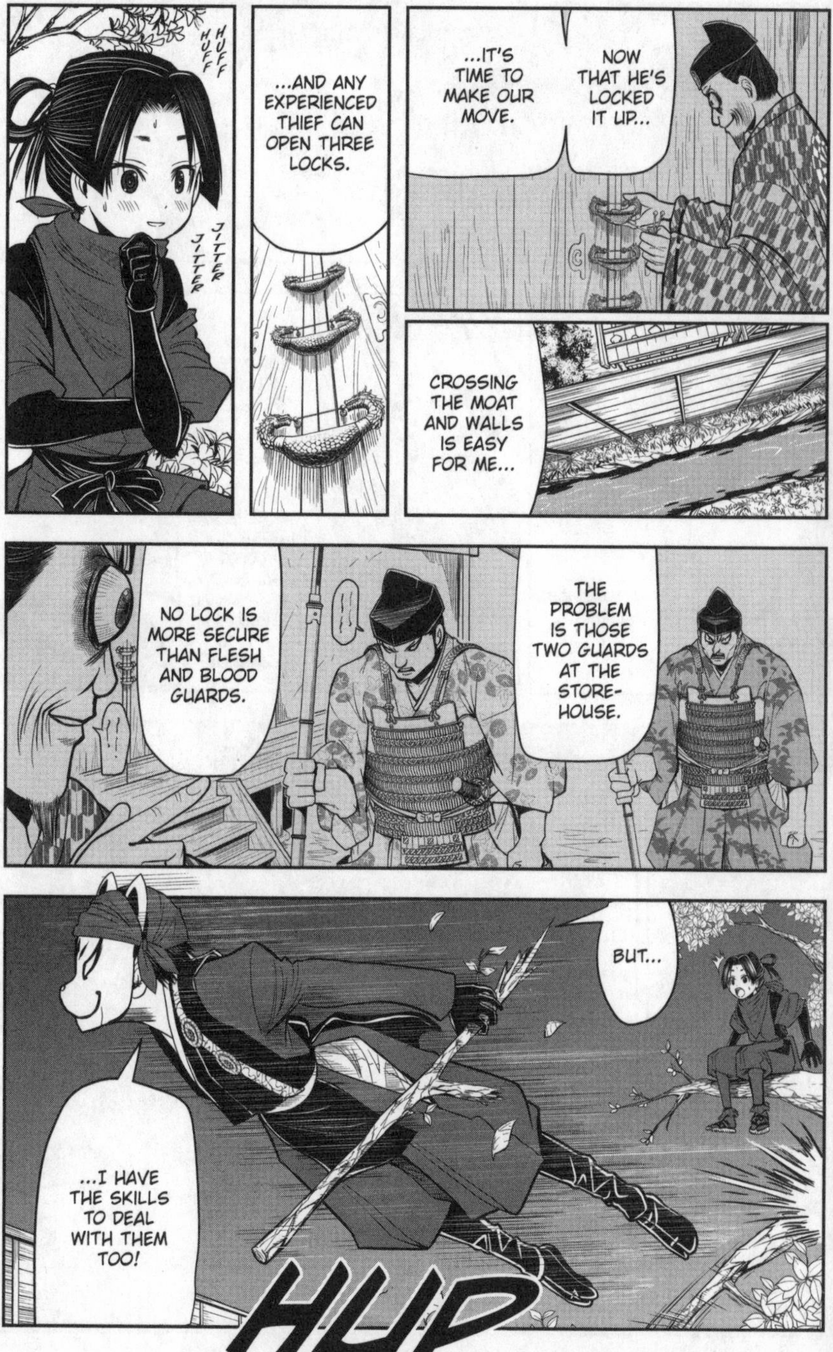
NOW THAT HE'S LOCKED IT UP...
...IT'S TIME TO MAKE OUR MOVE.
CROSSING THE MOAT AND WALLS IS EASY FOR ME...
...AND ANY EXPERIENCED THIEF CAN OPEN THREE LOCKS.
HUFF HUFF
JITTER JITTER
THE PROBLEM IS THOSE TWO GUARDS AT THE STORE-HOUSE.
!
NO LOCK IS MORE SECURE THAN FLESH AND BLOOD GUARDS.
BUT...
...I HAVE THE SKILLS TO DEAL WITH THEM TOO!
HUP

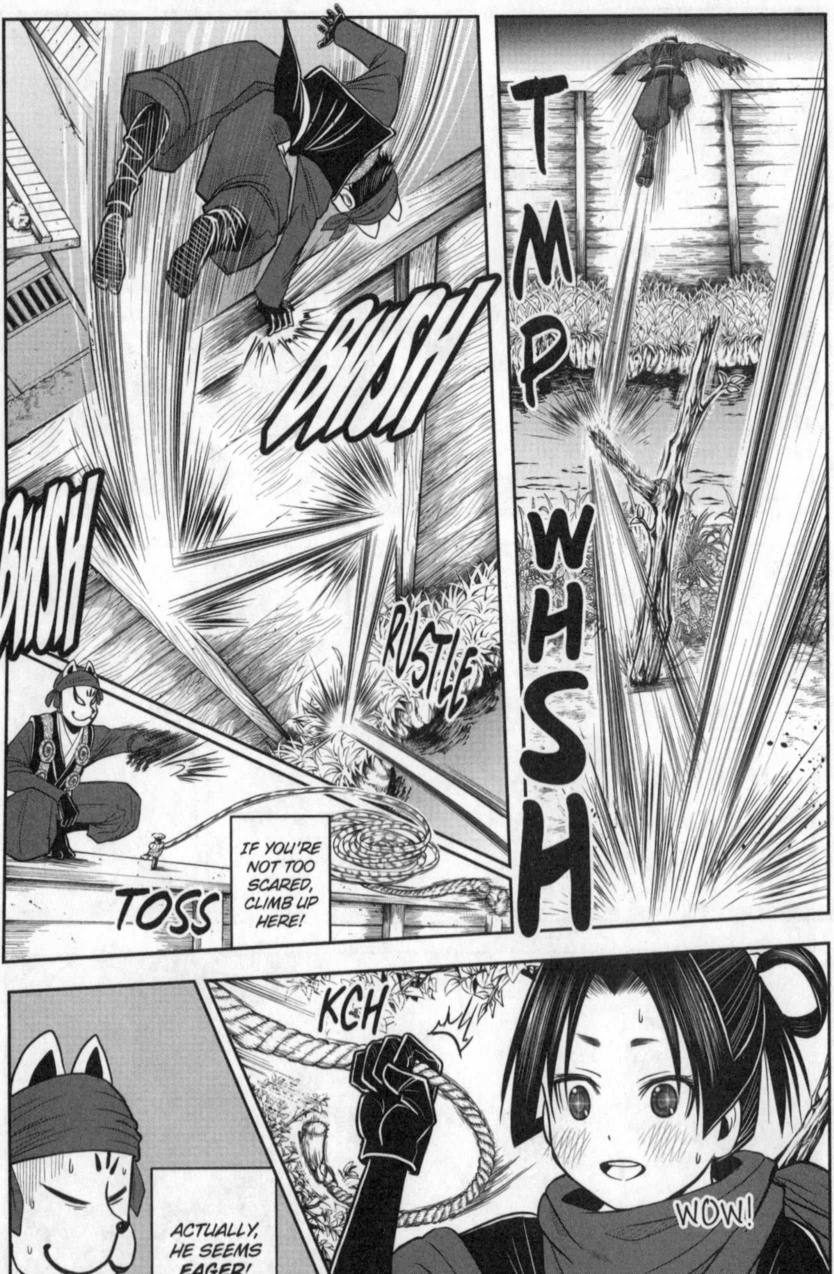
TMP
WHSH
BWSH
BWSH
RUSTLE
IF YOU'RE NOT TOO SCARED, CLIMB UP HERE!
TOSS
KCH
WOW!
ACTUALLY, HE SEEMS EAGER!

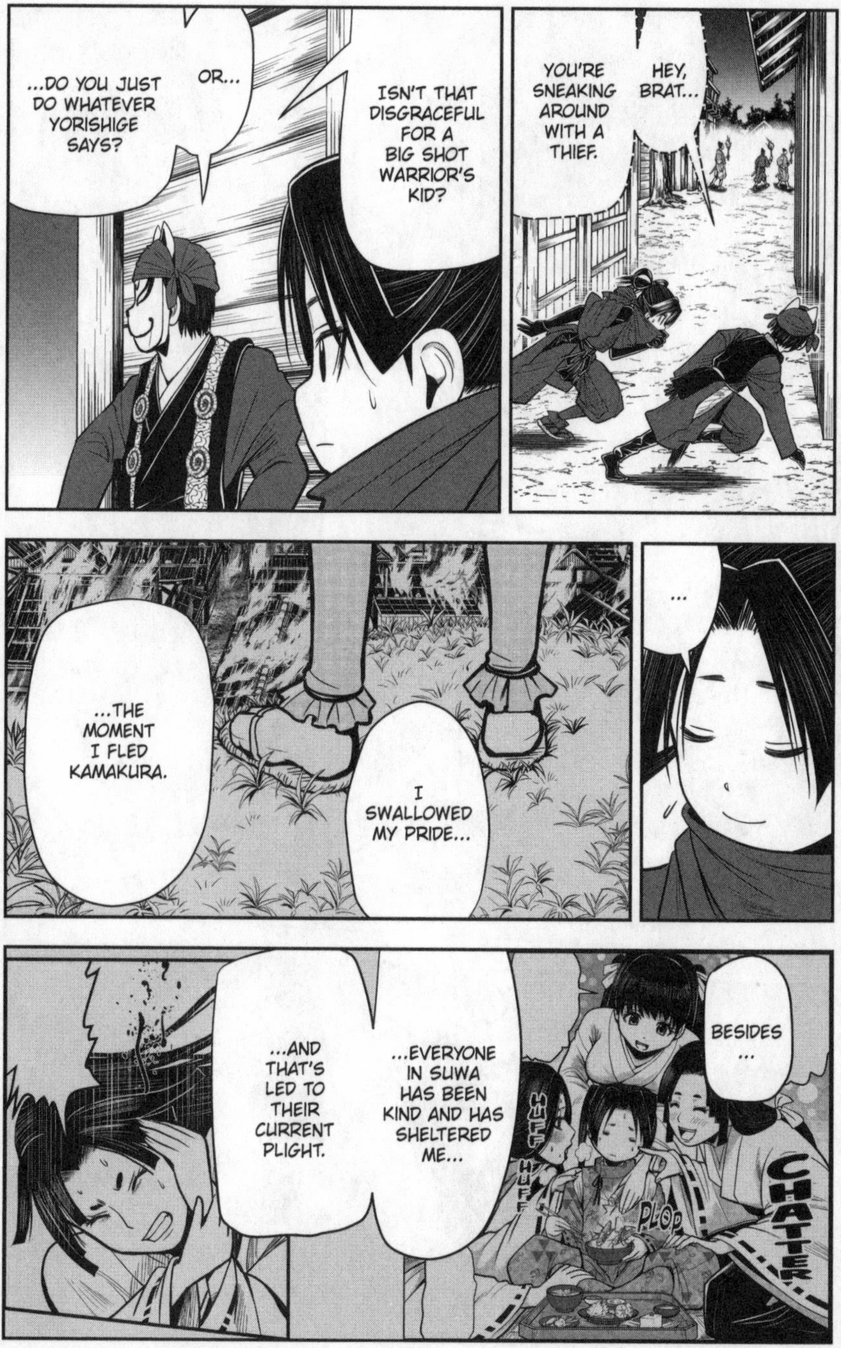
HEY, BRAT...
YOU'RE SNEAKING AROUND WITH A THIEF.
ISN'T THAT DISGRACEFUL FOR A BIG SHOT WARRIOR'S KID?
OR...
...DO YOU JUST DO WHATEVER YORISHIGE SAYS?
...
I SWALLOWED MY PRIDE...
...THE MOMENT I FLED KAMAKURA.
BESIDES ...
CHATTER
PLOP
HUFF
HUFF
...EVERYONE IN SUWA HAS BEEN KIND AND HAS SHELTERED ME...
...AND THAT'S LED TO THEIR CURRENT PLIGHT.

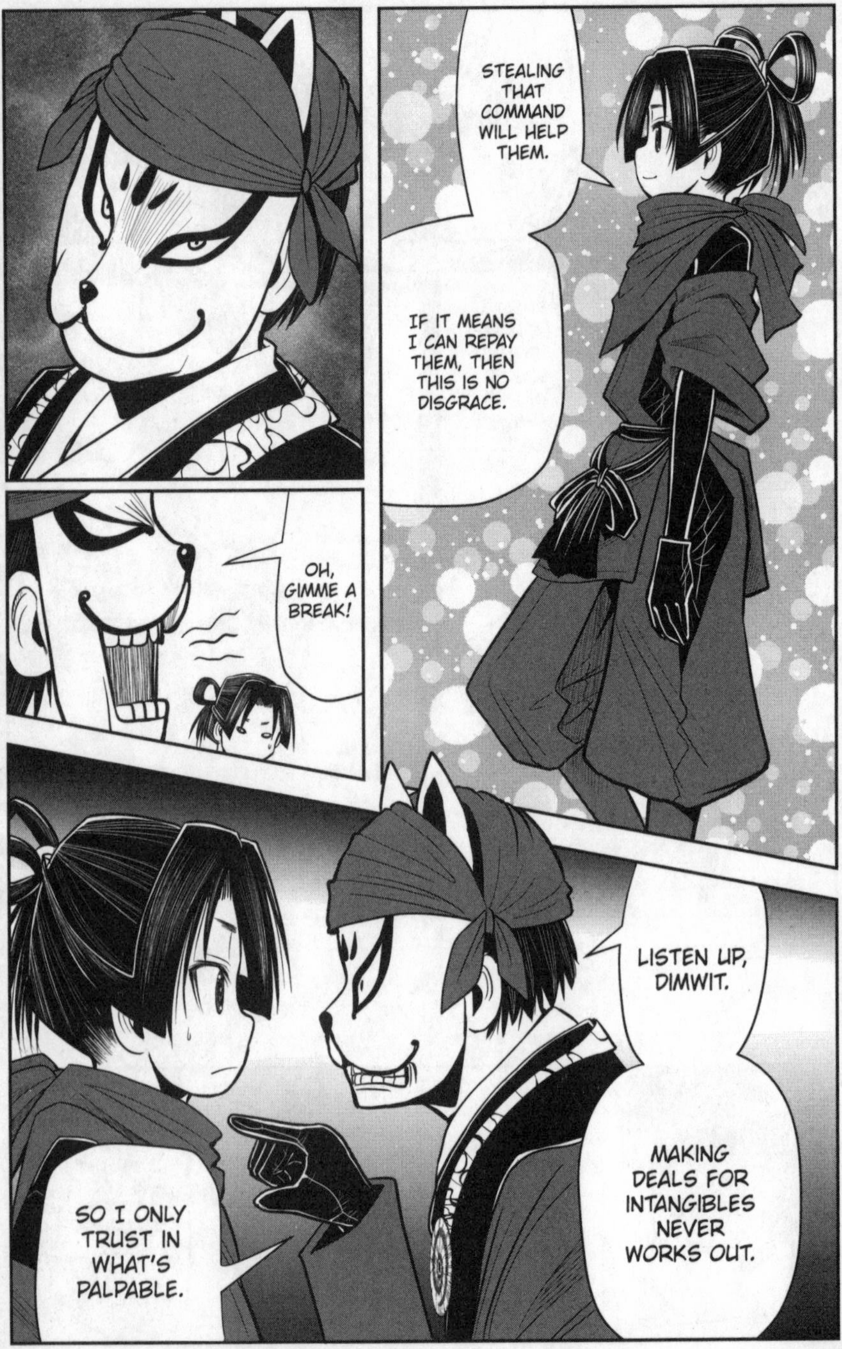
STEALING THAT COMMAND WILL HELP THEM.
IF IT MEANS I CAN REPAY THEM, THEN THIS IS NO DISGRACE.
OH, GIMME A BREAK!
LISTEN UP, DIMWIT.
MAKING DEALS FOR INTANGIBLES NEVER WORKS OUT.
SO I ONLY TRUST IN WHAT'S PALPABLE.

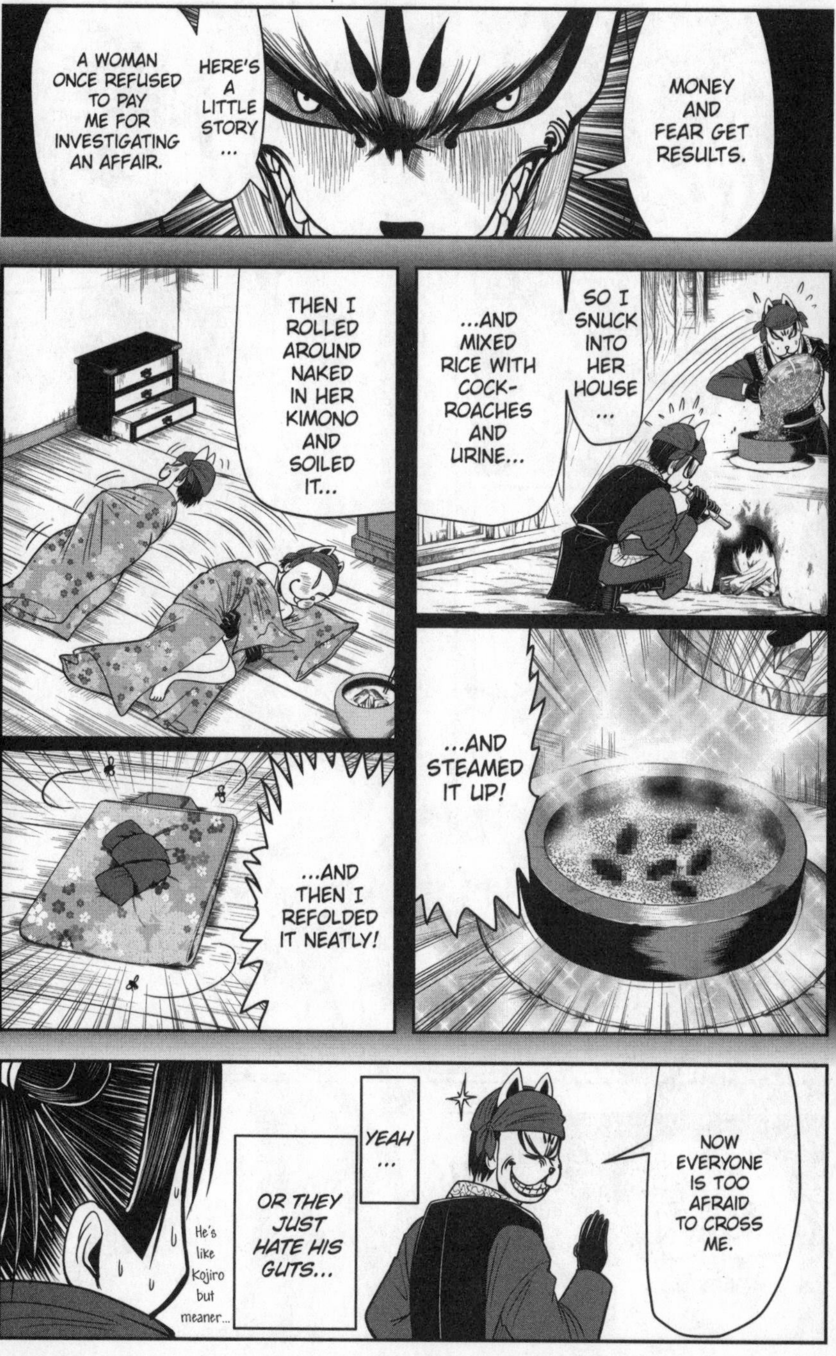
MONEY AND FEAR GET RESULTS.
HERE'S A LITTLE STORY...
A WOMAN ONCE REFUSED TO PAY ME FOR INVESTIGATING AN AFFAIR.
SO I SNUCK INTO HER HOUSE...
...AND MIXED RICE WITH COCK-ROACHES AND URINE...
...AND STEAMED IT UP!
THEN I ROLLED AROUND NAKED IN HER KIMONO AND SOILED IT...
...AND THEN I REFOLDED IT NEATLY!
NOW EVERYONE IS TOO AFRAID TO CROSS ME.
YEAH...
OR THEY JUST HATE HIS GUTS...
He's like Kojiro but meaner...

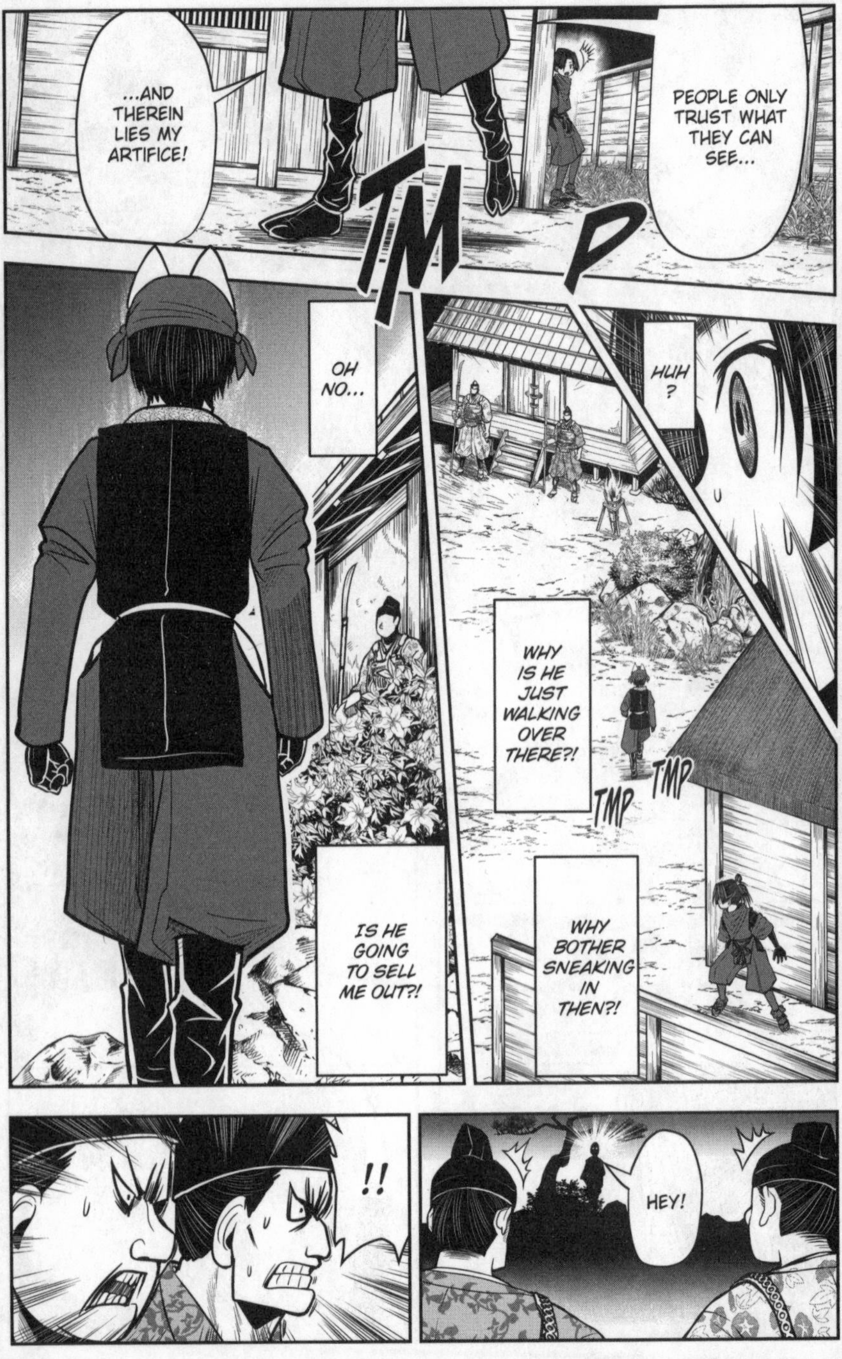
PEOPLE ONLY TRUST WHAT THEY CAN SEE...
TMP
...AND THEREIN LIES MY ARTIFICE!
HUH?
OH NO...
WHY IS HE JUST WALKING OVER THERE?!
TMP
TMP
WHY BOTHER SNEAKING IN THEN?!
IS HE GOING TO SELL ME OUT?!
HEY!
!!

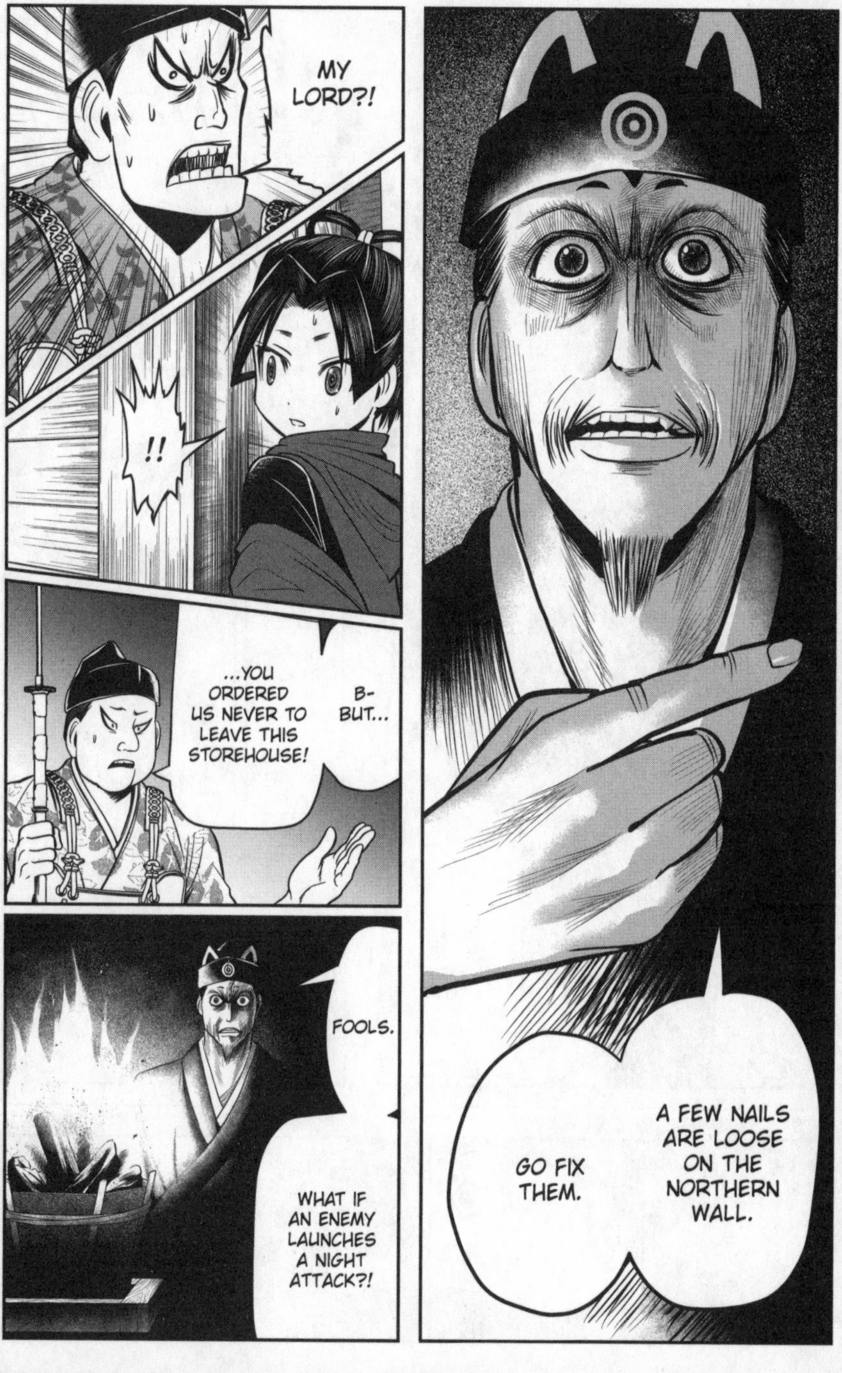
A FEW NAILS ARE LOOSE ON THE NORTHERN WALL.
GO FIX THEM.
MY LORD?!
!!
B-BUT...
...YOU ORDERED US NEVER TO LEAVE THIS STOREHOUSE!
FOOLS.
WHAT IF AN ENEMY LAUNCHES A NIGHT ATTACK?!

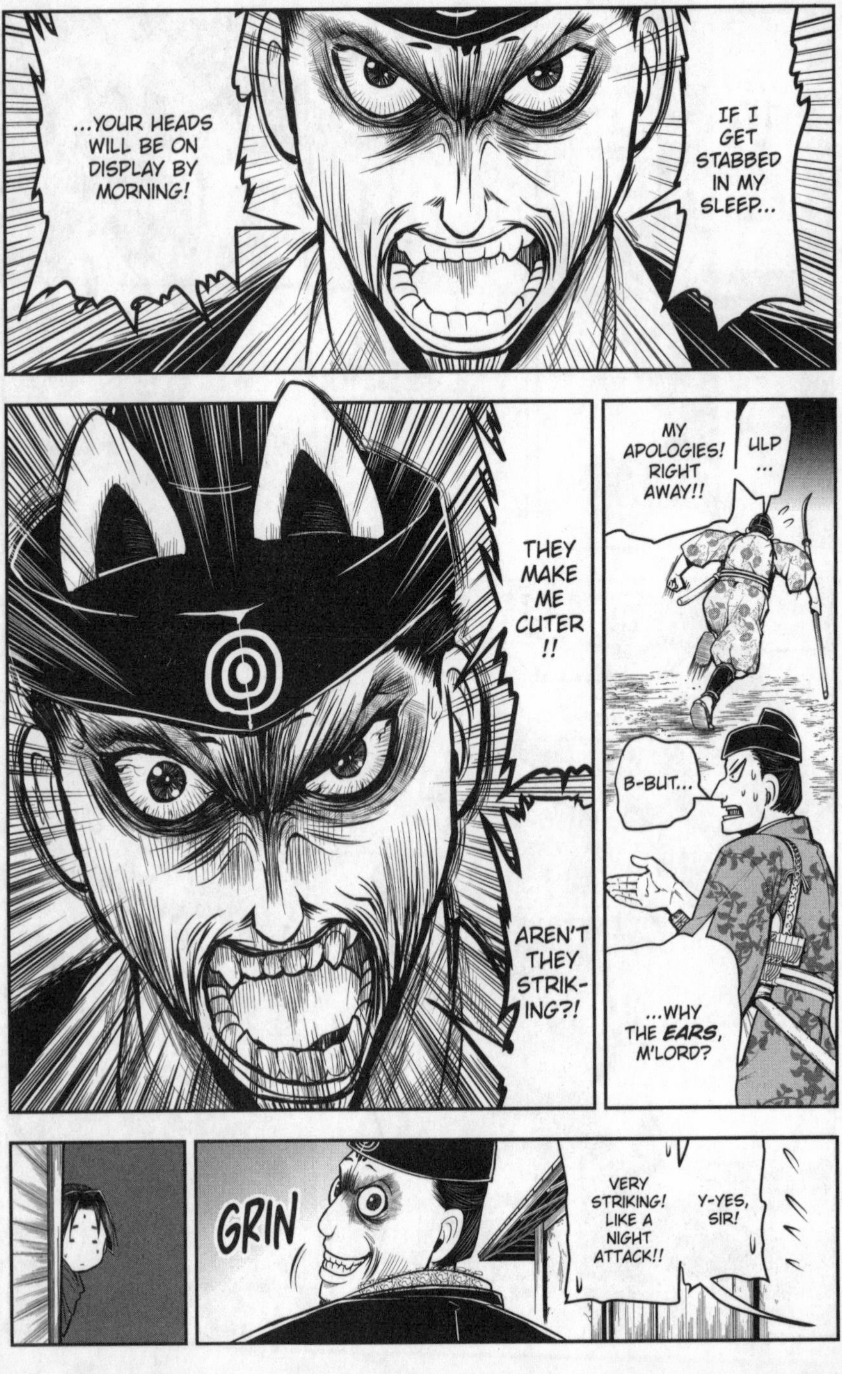
IF I GET STABBED IN MY SLEEP...
...YOUR HEADS WILL BE ON DISPLAY BY MORNING!
ULP ...
MY APOLOGIES! RIGHT AWAY!!
B-BUT...
...WHY THE EARS, M'LORD?
THEY MAKE ME CUTER!!
AREN'T THEY STRIK-ING?!
Y-YES, SIR!
VERY STRIKING! LIKE A NIGHT ATTACK!!
GRIN

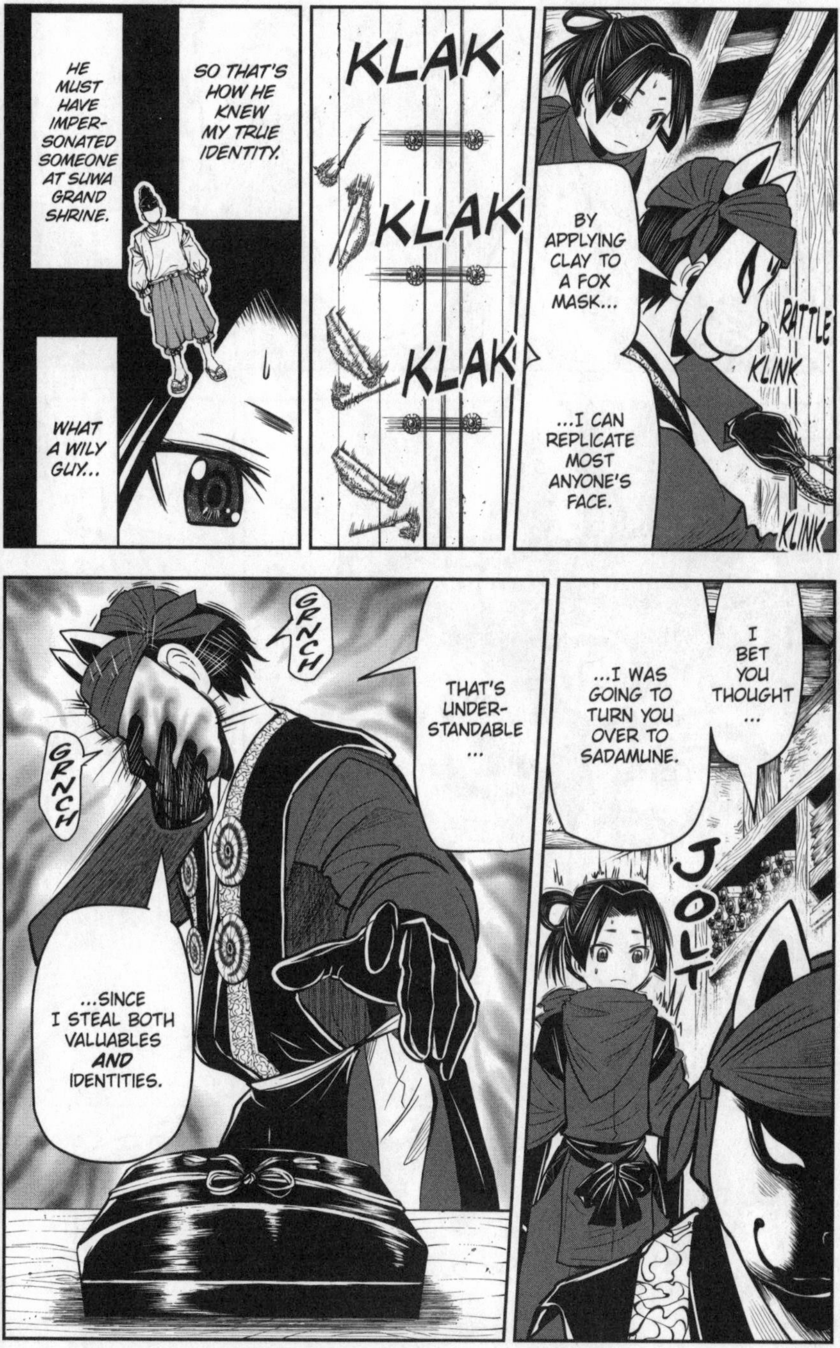
BY APPLYING CLAY TO A FOX MASK...
...I CAN REPLICATE MOST ANYONE'S FACE.
RATTLE
KLINK
KLINK
KLAK
KLAK
KLAK
SO THAT'S HOW HE KNEW MY TRUE IDENTITY.
HE MUST HAVE IMPER-SONATED SOMEONE AT SUWA GRAND SHRINE.
WHAT A WILY GUY...
I BET YOU THOUGHT...
...I WAS GOING TO TURN YOU OVER TO SADAMUNE.
JOLT
THAT'S UNDER-STANDABLE...
GRNCH
GRNCH
...SINCE I STEAL BOTH VALUABLES **AND** IDENTITIES.

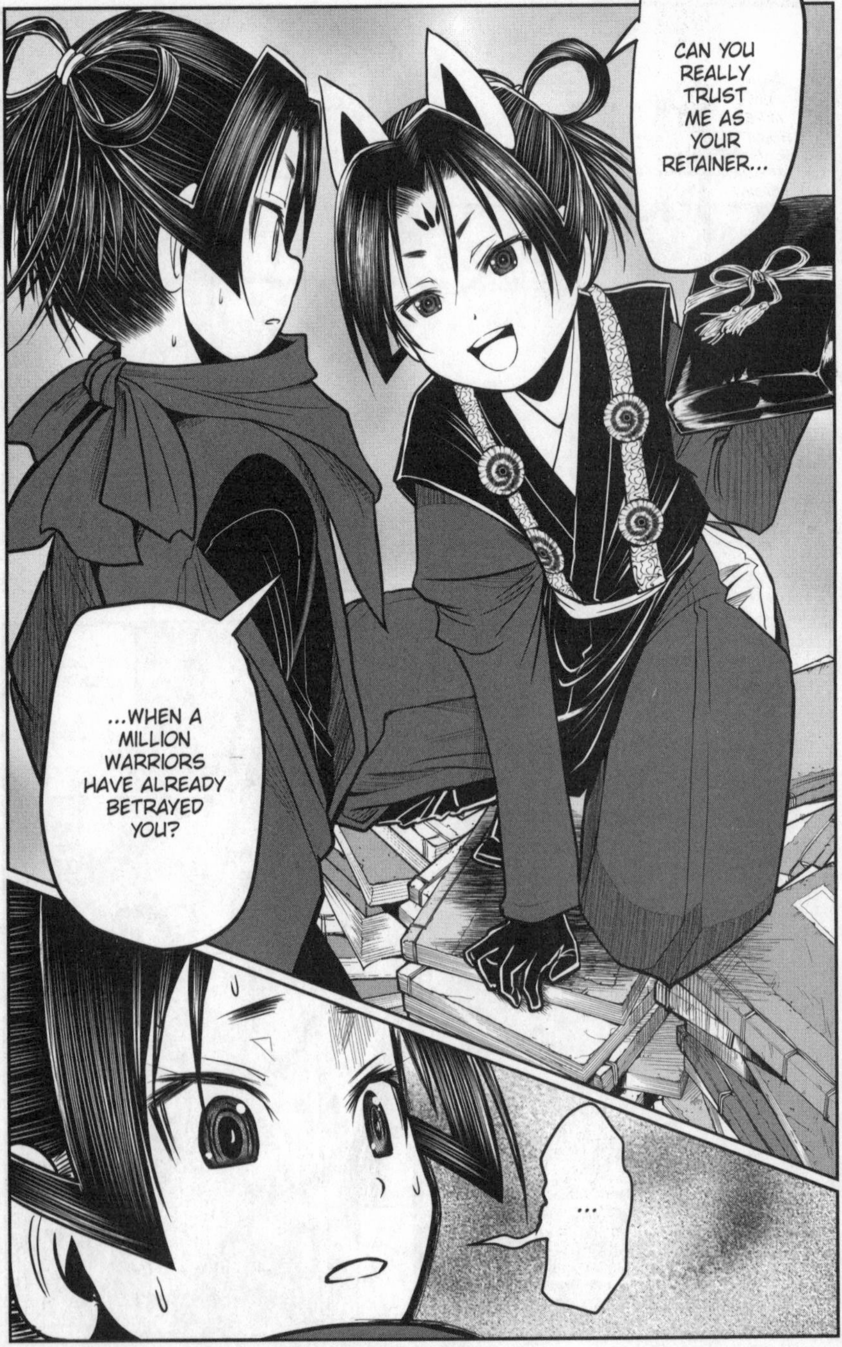
CAN YOU REALLY TRUST ME AS YOUR RETAINER...
...WHEN A MILLION WARRIORS HAVE ALREADY BETRAYED YOU?
...

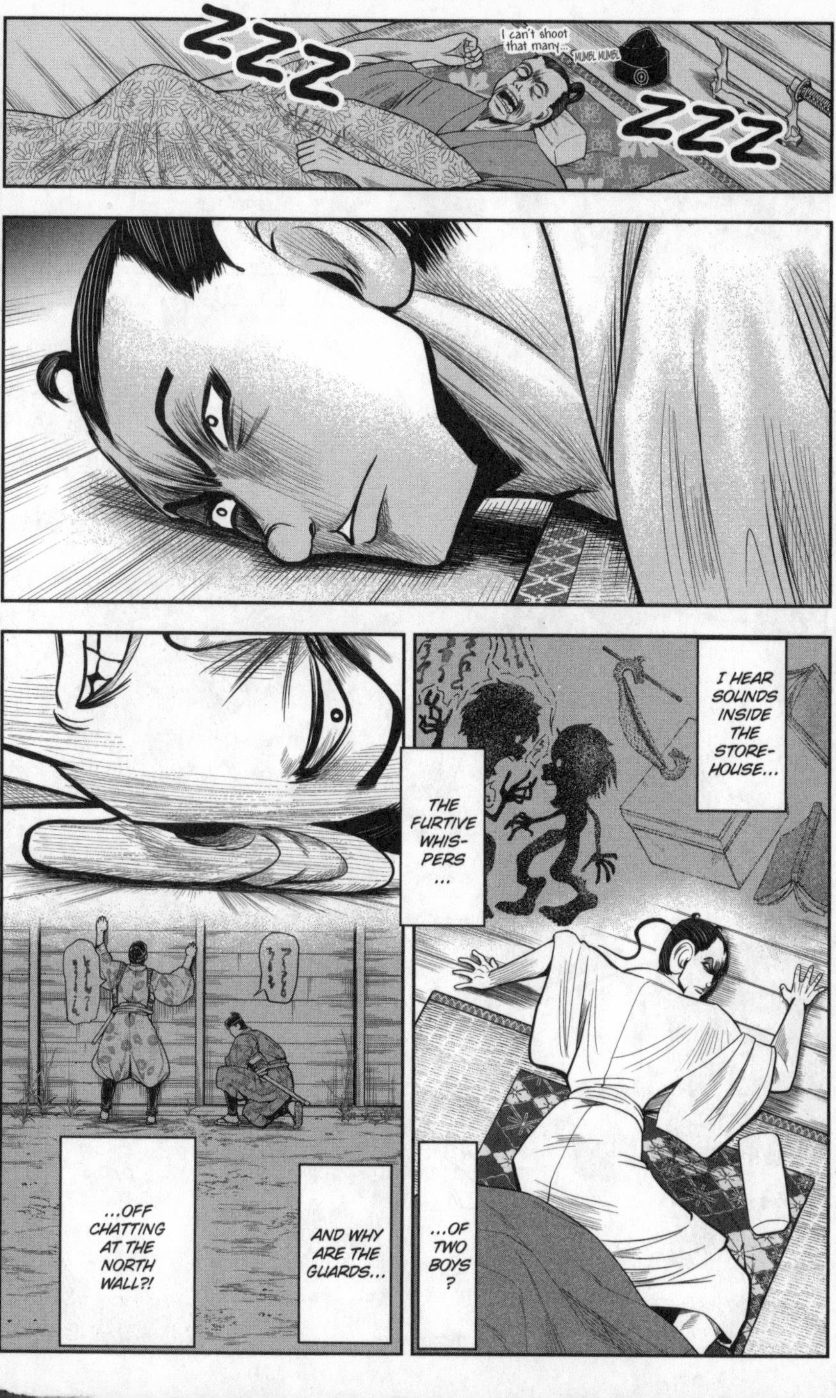
ZZZ
I can't shoot that many...
MUMBL MUMBL
ZZZ
I HEAR SOUNDS INSIDE THE STORE-HOUSE...
THE FURTIVE WHISPERS...
...OF TWO BOYS?
AND WHY ARE THE GUARDS...
...OFF CHATTING AT THE NORTH WALL?!

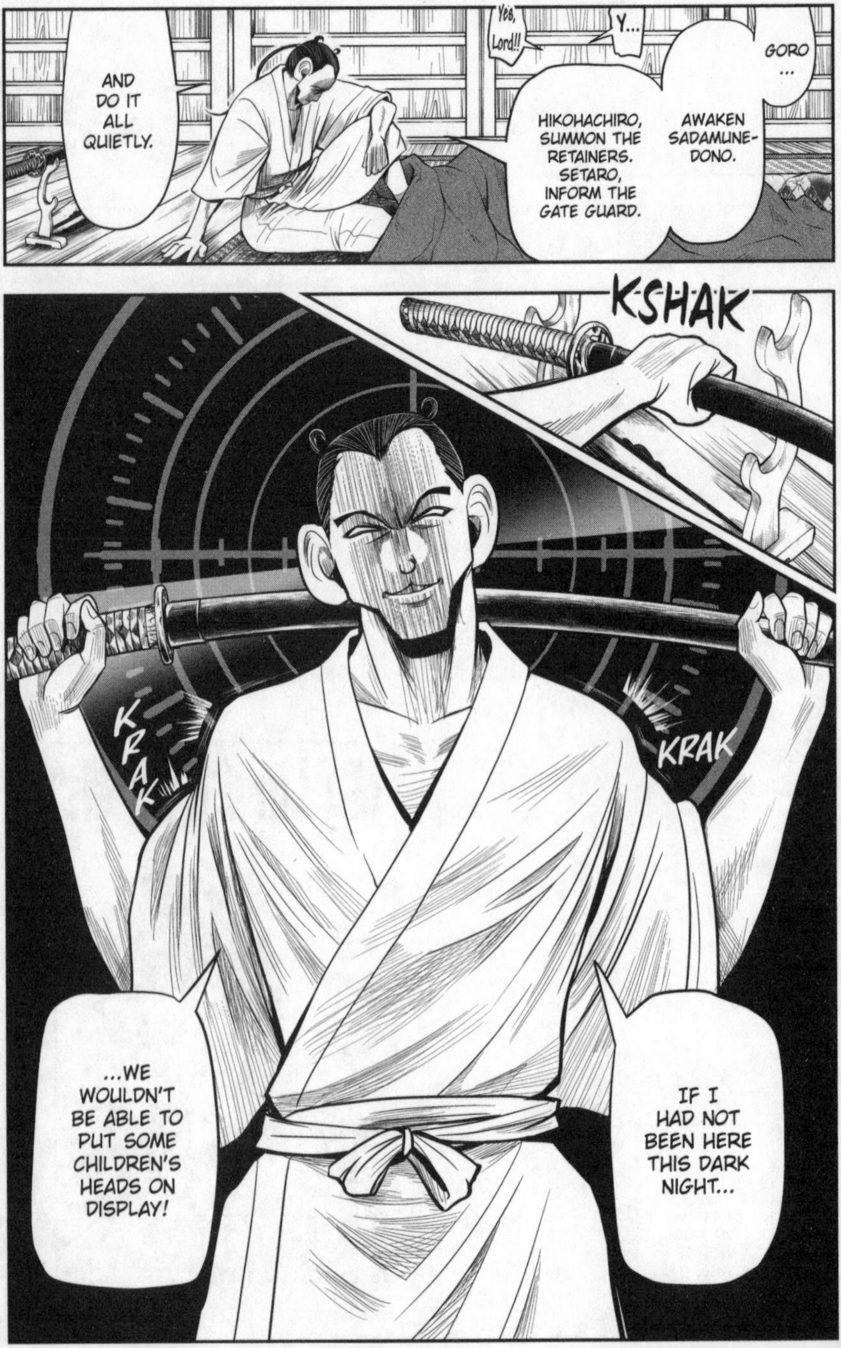
GORO ...
AWAKEN SADAMUNE-DONO.
Y...
HIKOHACHIRO, SUMMON THE RETAINERS. SETARO, INFORM THE GATE GUARD.
Yes, Lord!!
AND DO IT ALL QUIETLY.
KSHAK
KRAK
KRAK
IF I HAD NOT BEEN HERE THIS DARK NIGHT...
...WE WOULDN'T BE ABLE TO PUT SOME CHILDREN'S HEADS ON DISPLAY!

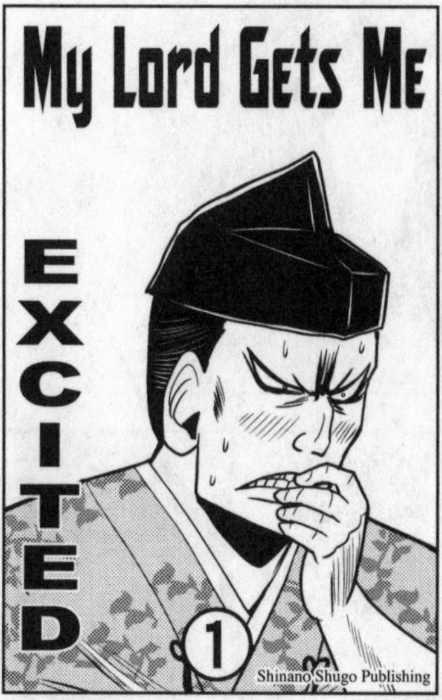
My Lord Gets Me
EXCITED
1
Shinano Shugo Publishing

CHAPTER 13: INFERNAL EARS 1333

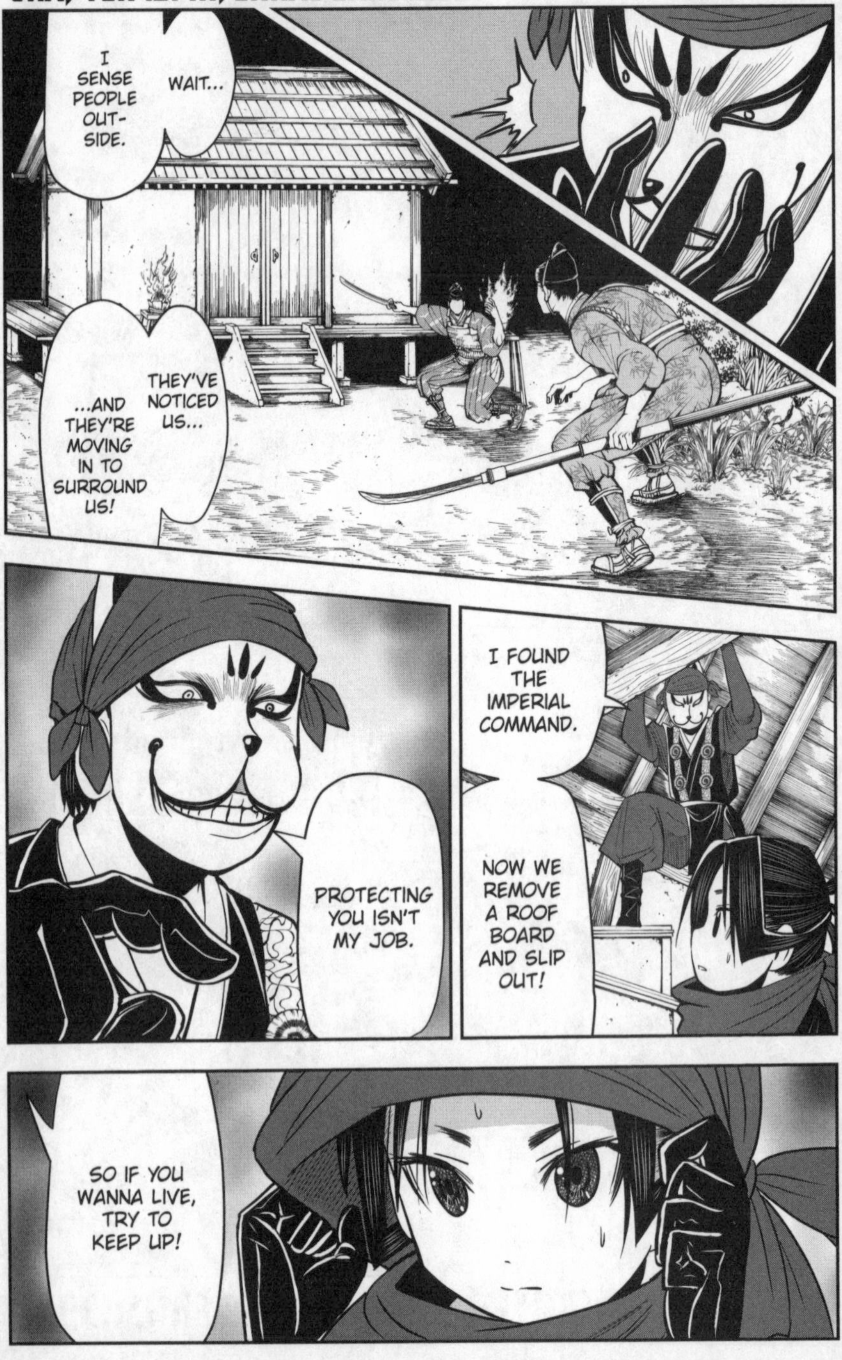
WAIT...
I SENSE PEOPLE OUT-SIDE.
THEY'VE NOTICED US...
...AND THEY'RE MOVING IN TO SURROUND US!
I FOUND THE IMPERIAL COMMAND.
NOW WE REMOVE A ROOF BOARD AND SLIP OUT!
PROTECTING YOU ISN'T MY JOB.
SO IF YOU WANNA LIVE, TRY TO KEEP UP!

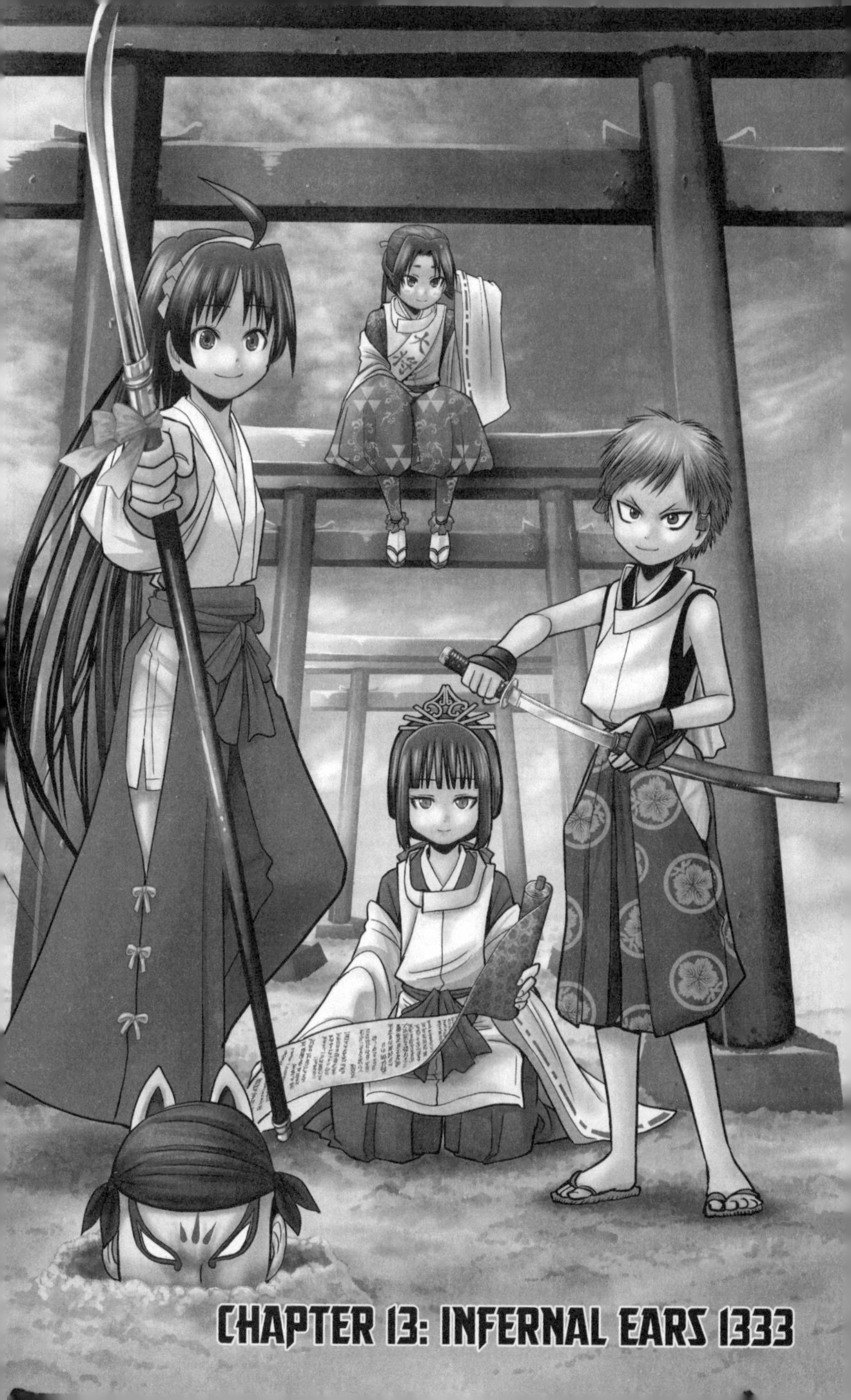
CHAPTER 13: INFERNAL EARS 1333

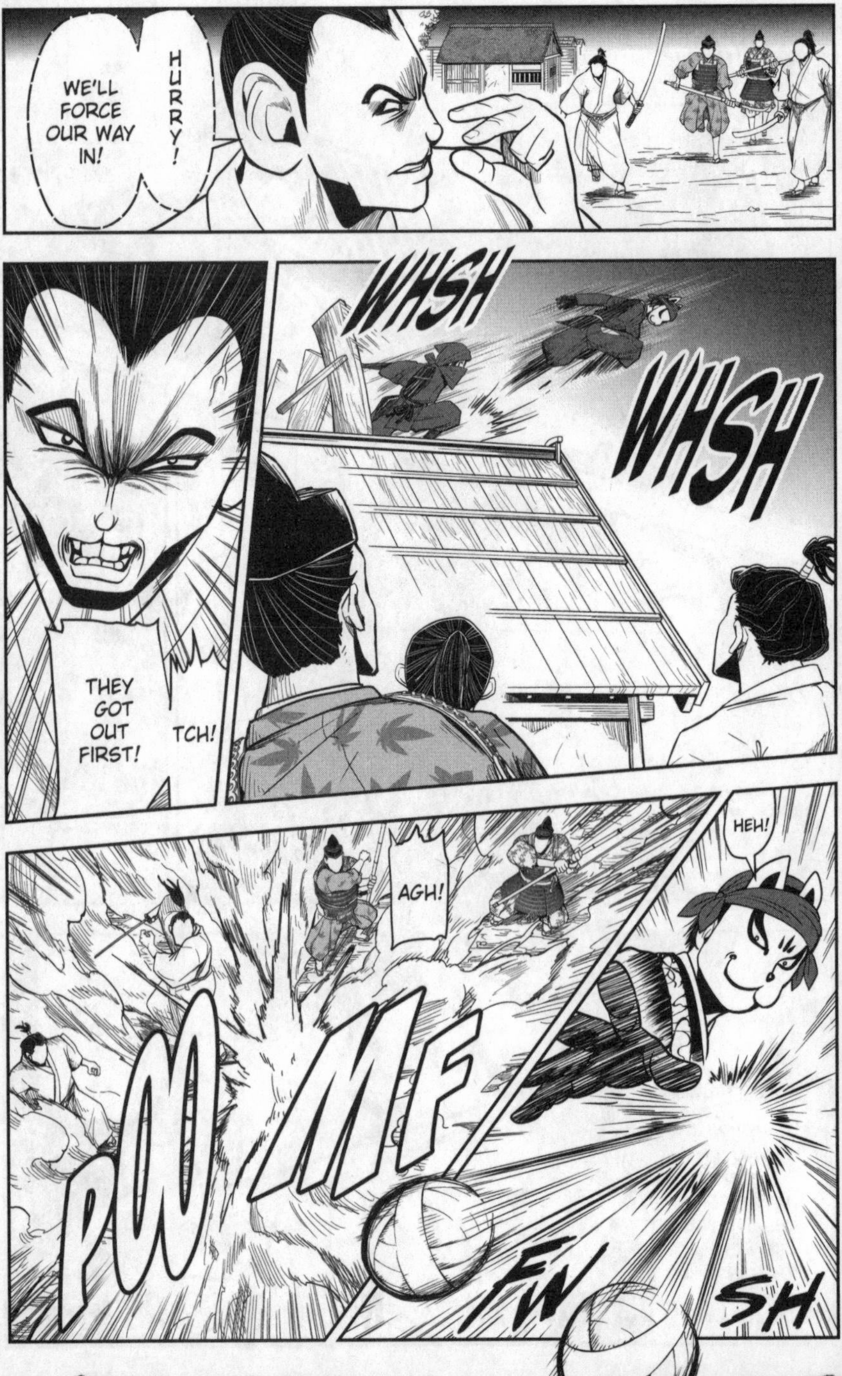
HURRY!
WE'LL FORCE OUR WAY IN!
WHSH
WHSH
TCH!
THEY GOT OUT FIRST!
HEH!
FW
SH
AGH!
POOMF

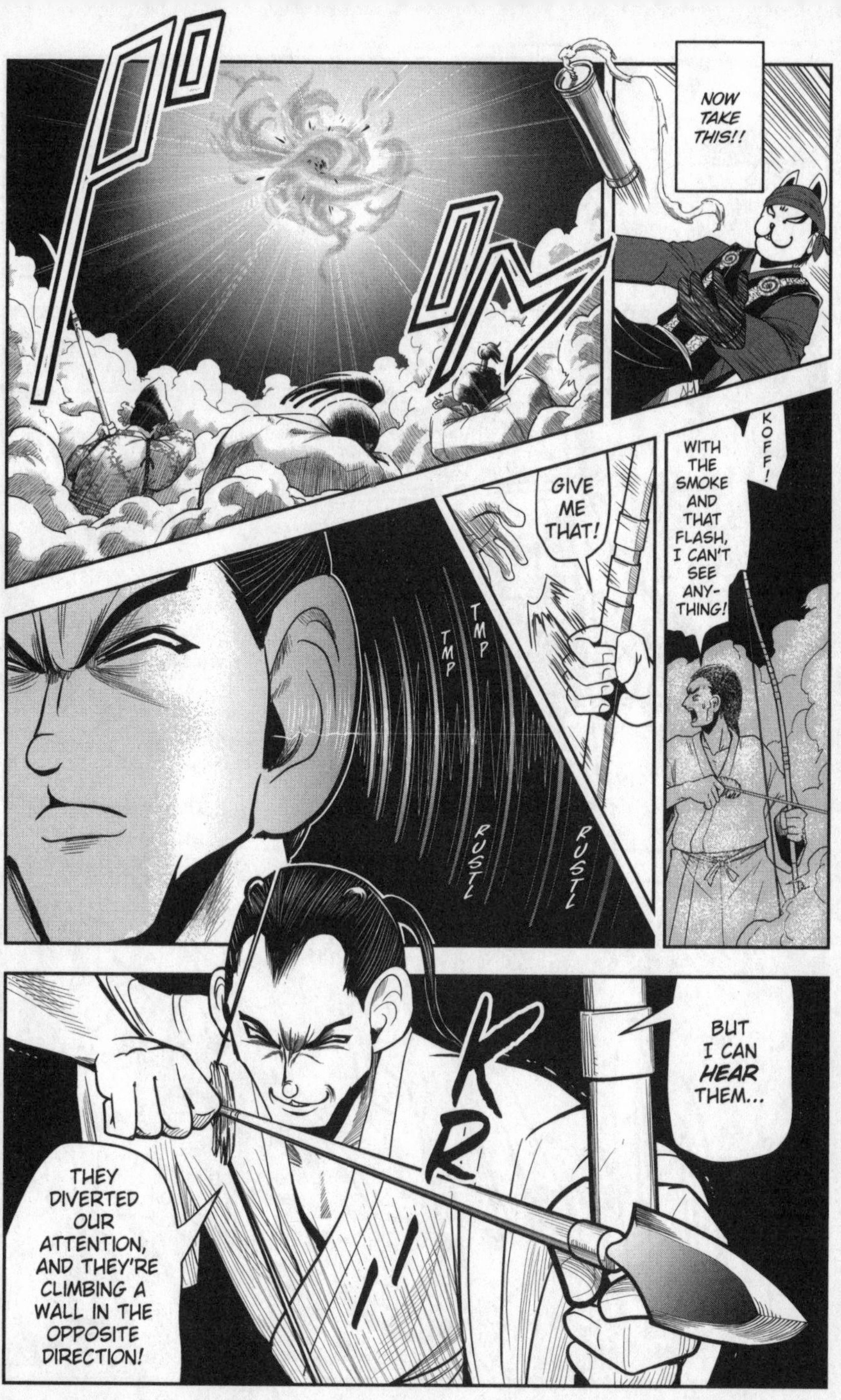

NOW TAKE THIS!!
POM
KOFF!
WITH THE SMOKE AND THAT FLASH, I CAN'T SEE ANY-THING!
GIVE ME THAT!
TMP TMP
RUSTL RUSTL
BUT I CAN *HEAR* THEM...
KR!!
THEY DIVERTED OUR ATTENTION, AND THEY'RE CLIMBING A WALL IN THE OPPOSITE DIRECTION!

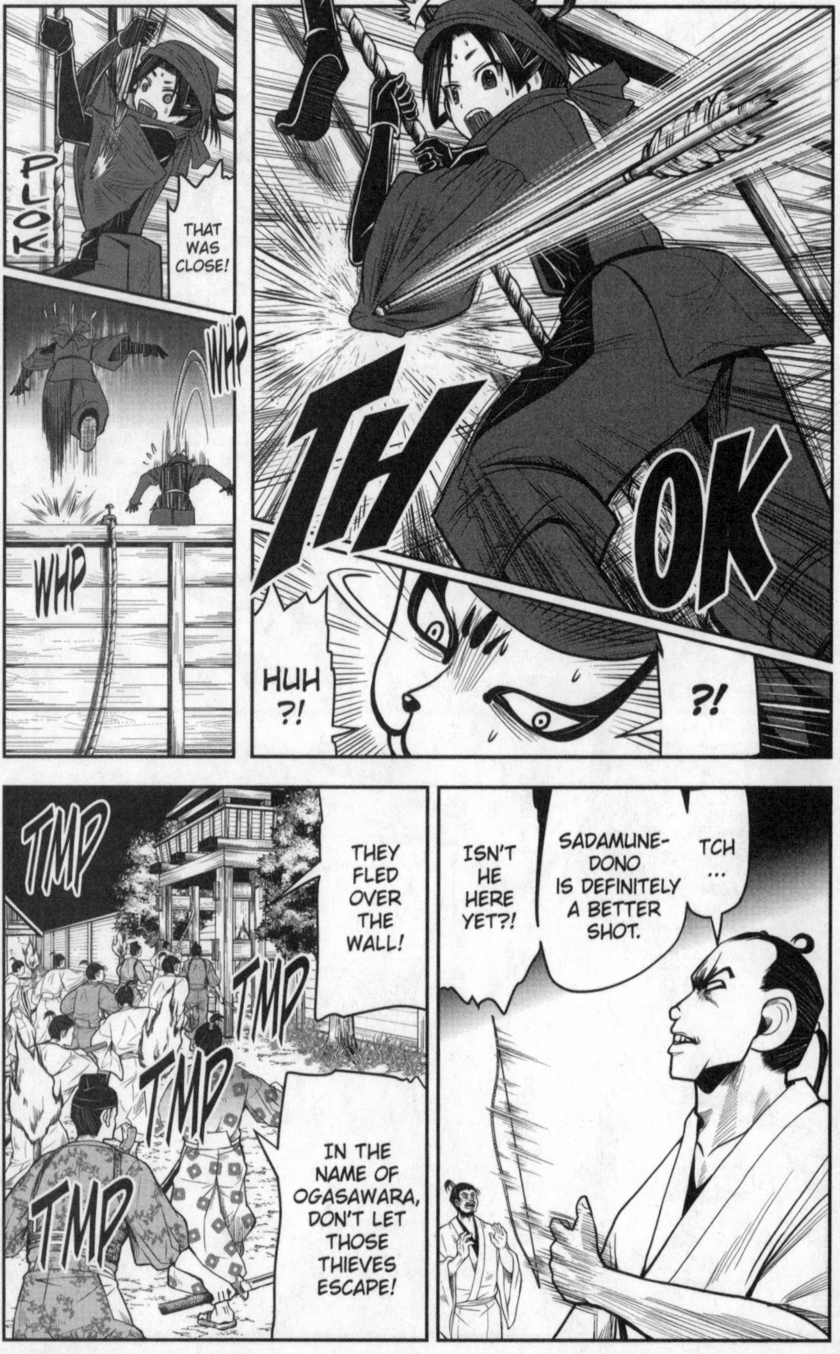
THOK
?!
HUH ?!
PLOK
THAT WAS CLOSE!
WHP
WHP
TCH ...
SADAMUNE-DONO IS DEFINITELY A BETTER SHOT.
ISN'T HE HERE YET?!
THEY FLED OVER THE WALL!
TMP
TMP
TMP
TMP
IN THE NAME OF OGASAWARA, DON'T LET THOSE THIEVES ESCAPE!

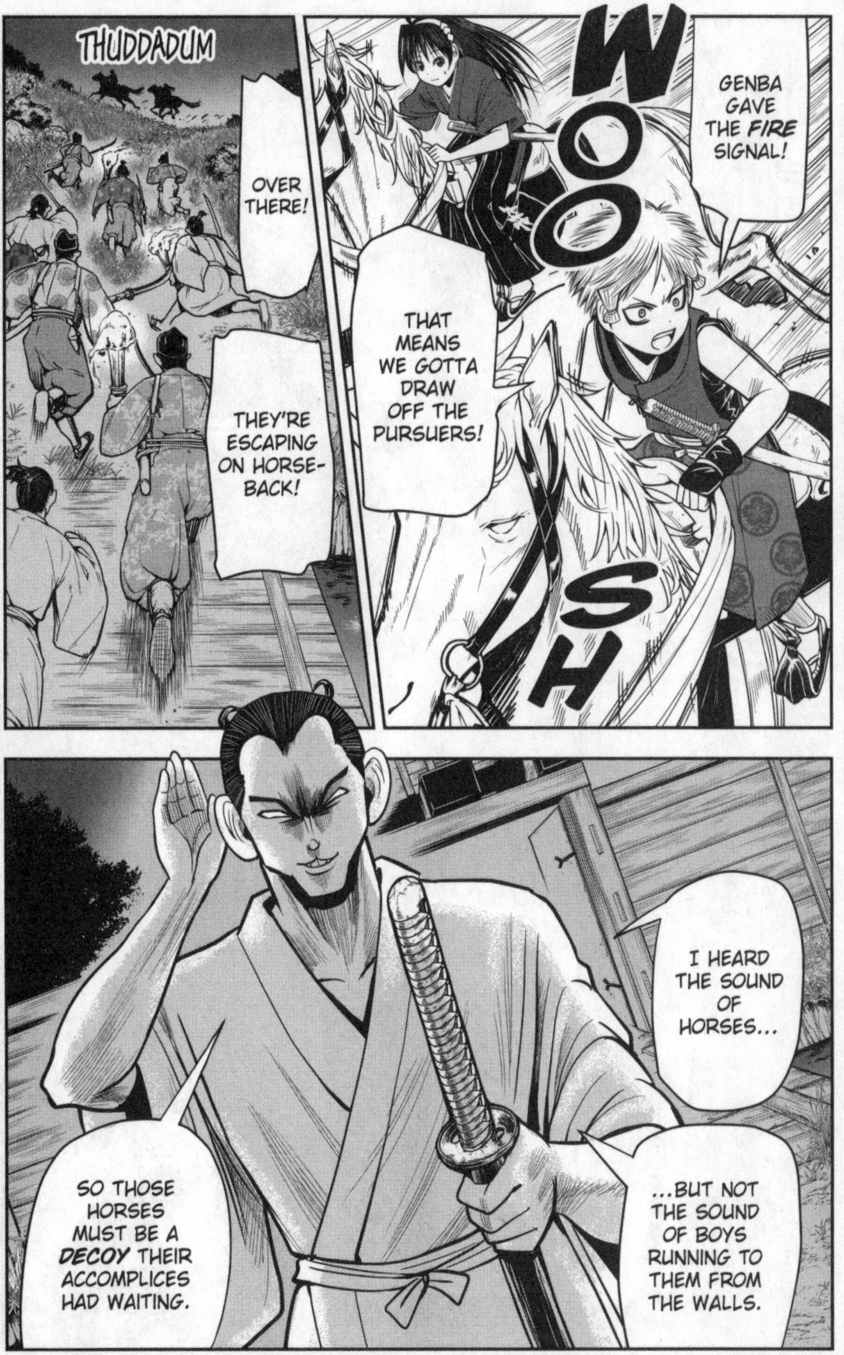
GENBA GAVE THE *FIRE* SIGNAL!
WOOO
THAT MEANS WE GOTTA DRAW OFF THE PURSUERS!
SH
THUDDADUM
OVER THERE!
THEY'RE ESCAPING ON HORSE-BACK!
I HEARD THE SOUND OF HORSES...
...BUT NOT THE SOUND OF BOYS RUNNING TO THEM FROM THE WALLS.
SO THOSE HORSES MUST BE A *DECOY* THEIR ACCOMPLICES HAD WAITING.

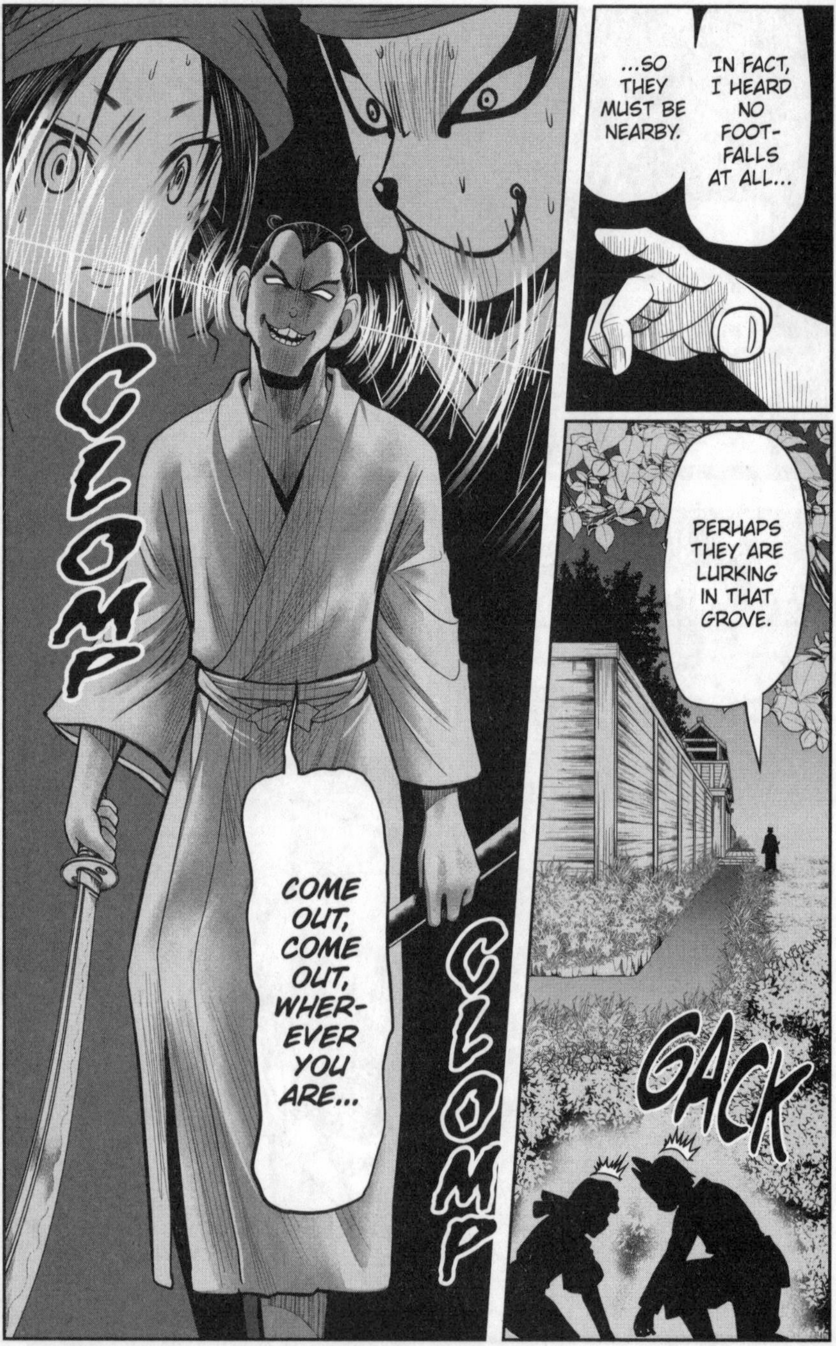
IN FACT, I HEARD NO FOOTFALLS AT ALL...
...SO THEY MUST BE NEARBY.
PERHAPS THEY ARE LURKING IN THAT GROVE.
GACK
CLOMP
COME OUT, COME OUT, WHEREVER YOU ARE...
CLOMP

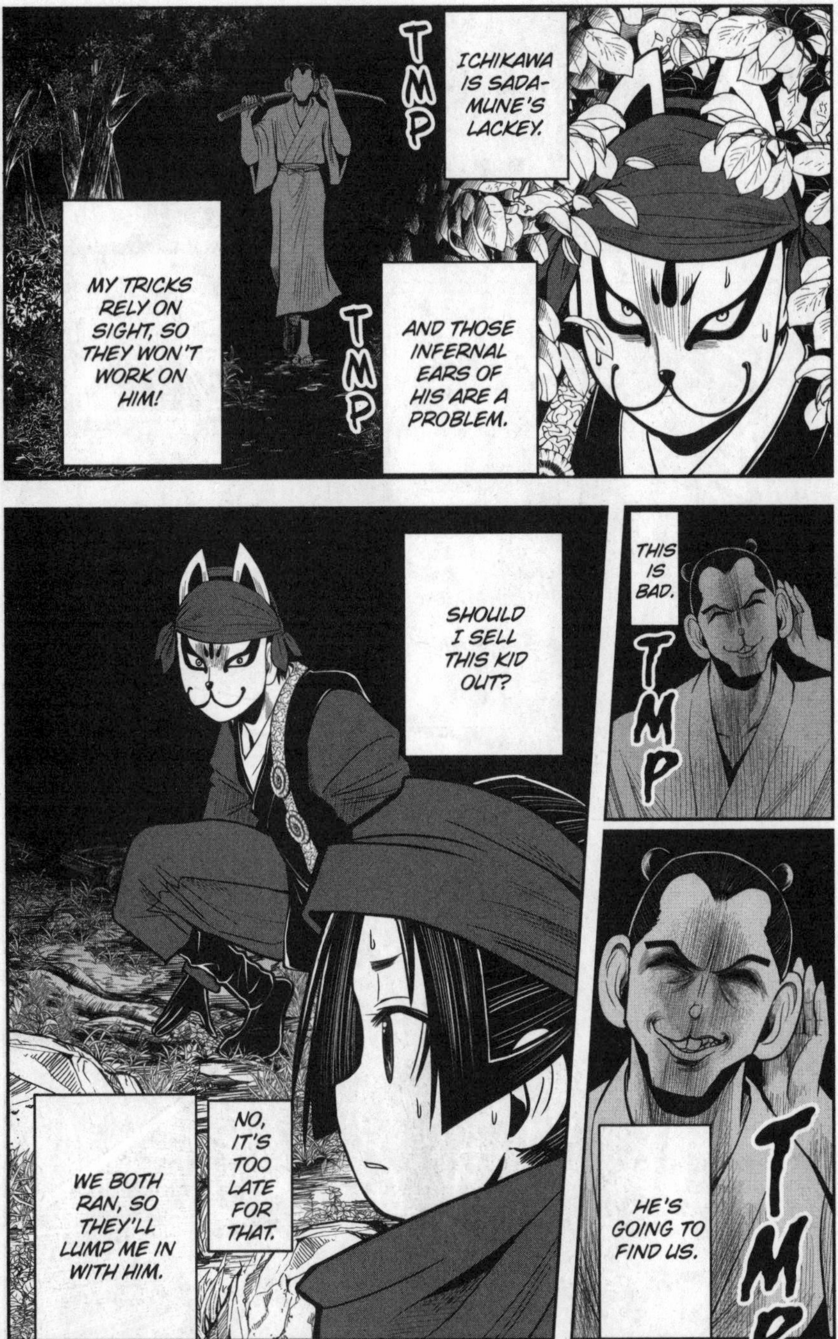
ICHIKAWA IS SADAMUNE'S LACKEY.
TMP
AND THOSE INFERNAL EARS OF HIS ARE A PROBLEM.
TMP
MY TRICKS RELY ON SIGHT, SO THEY WON'T WORK ON HIM!
THIS IS BAD.
TMP
HE'S GOING TO FIND US.
TMP
SHOULD I SELL THIS KID OUT?
NO, IT'S TOO LATE FOR THAT.
WE BOTH RAN, SO THEY'LL LUMP ME IN WITH HIM.

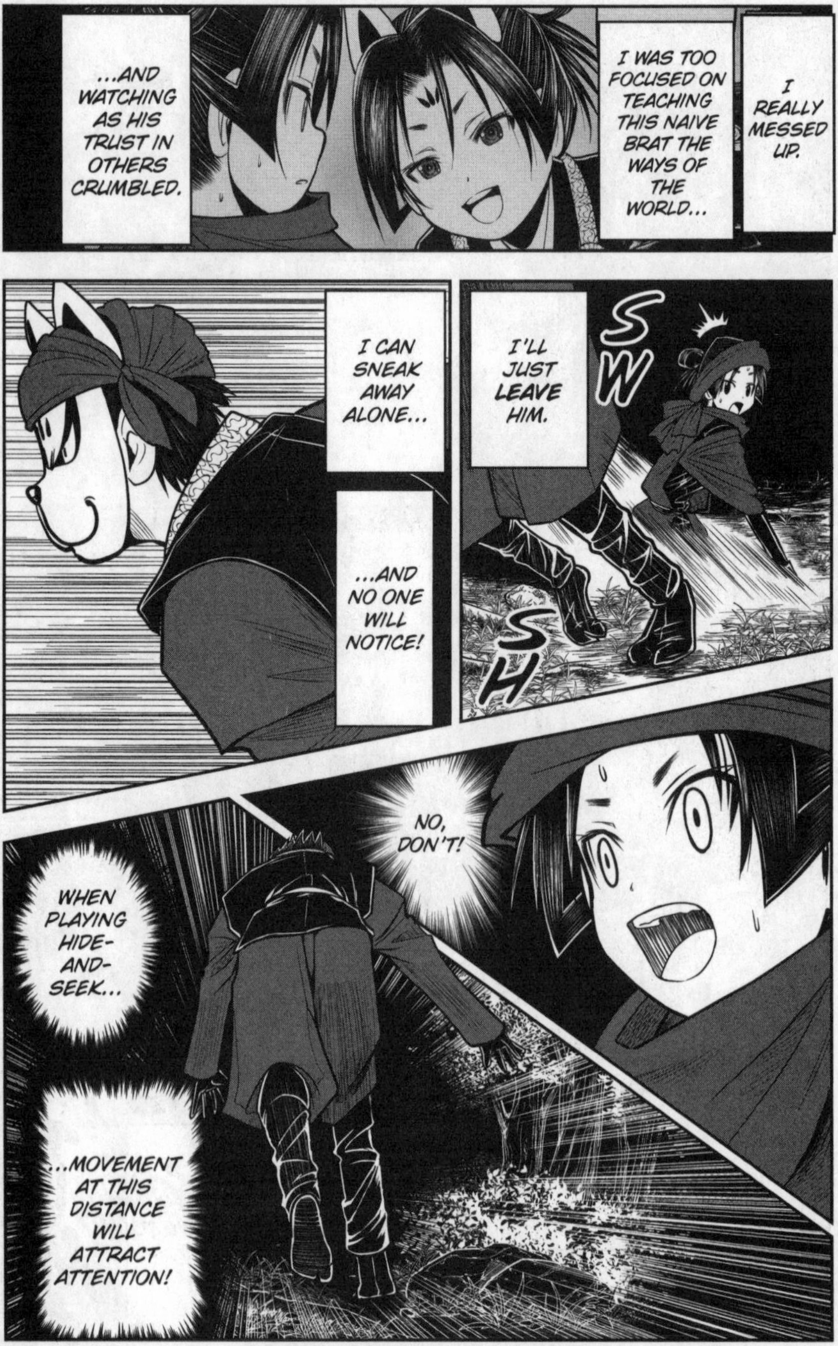
I REALLY MESSED UP.
I WAS TOO FOCUSED ON TEACHING THIS NAIVE BRAT THE WAYS OF THE WORLD...
...AND WATCHING AS HIS TRUST IN OTHERS CRUMBLED.
I'LL JUST LEAVE HIM.
SW
SH
I CAN SNEAK AWAY ALONE...
...AND NO ONE WILL NOTICE!
NO, DON'T!
WHEN PLAYING HIDE-AND-SEEK...
...MOVEMENT AT THIS DISTANCE WILL ATTRACT ATTENTION!

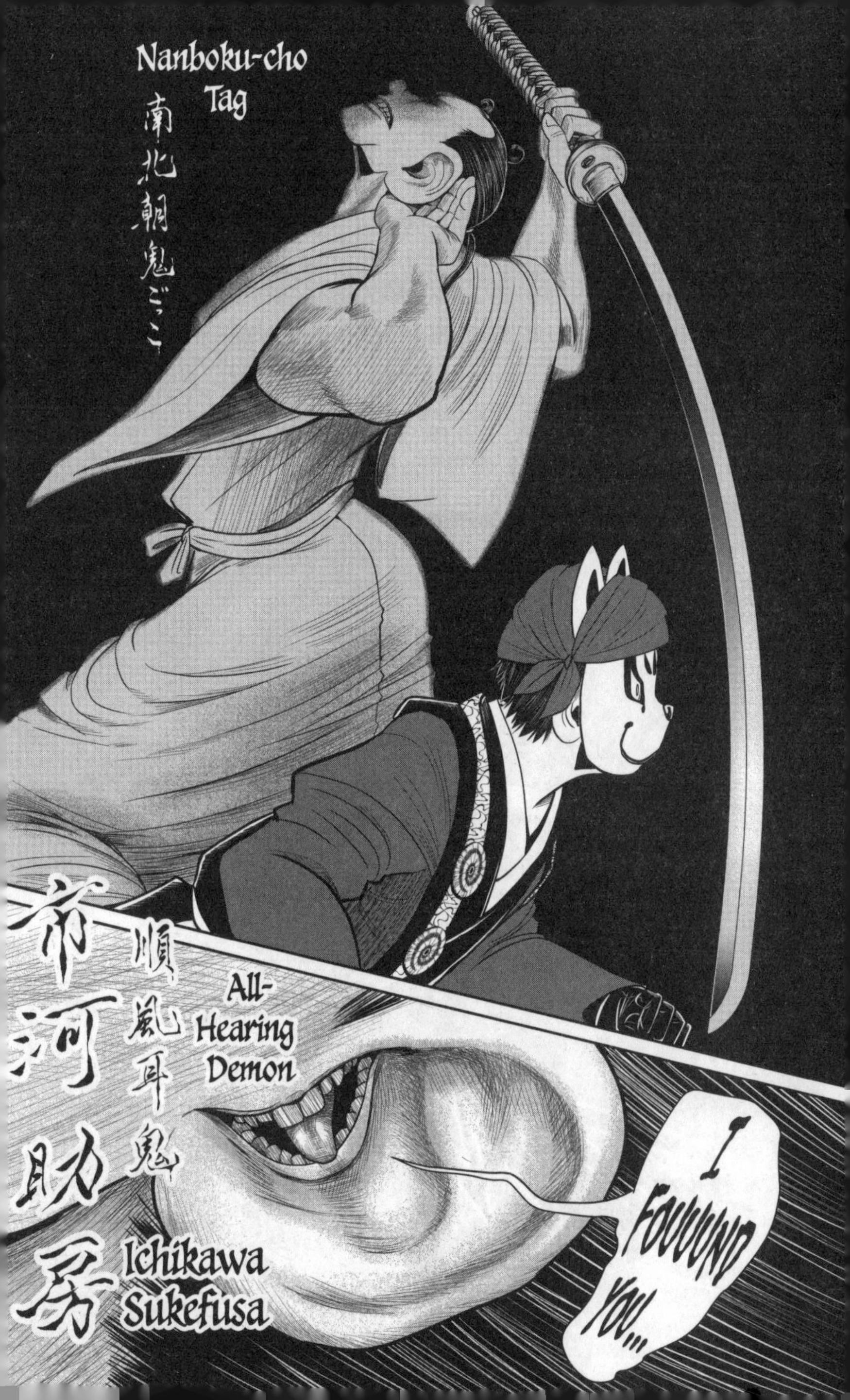
Nanboku-cho Tag
南北朝鬼ごっこ
I FOUUUND YOU...
All-Hearing Demon
順風耳鬼
Ichikawa Sukefusa
市河助房

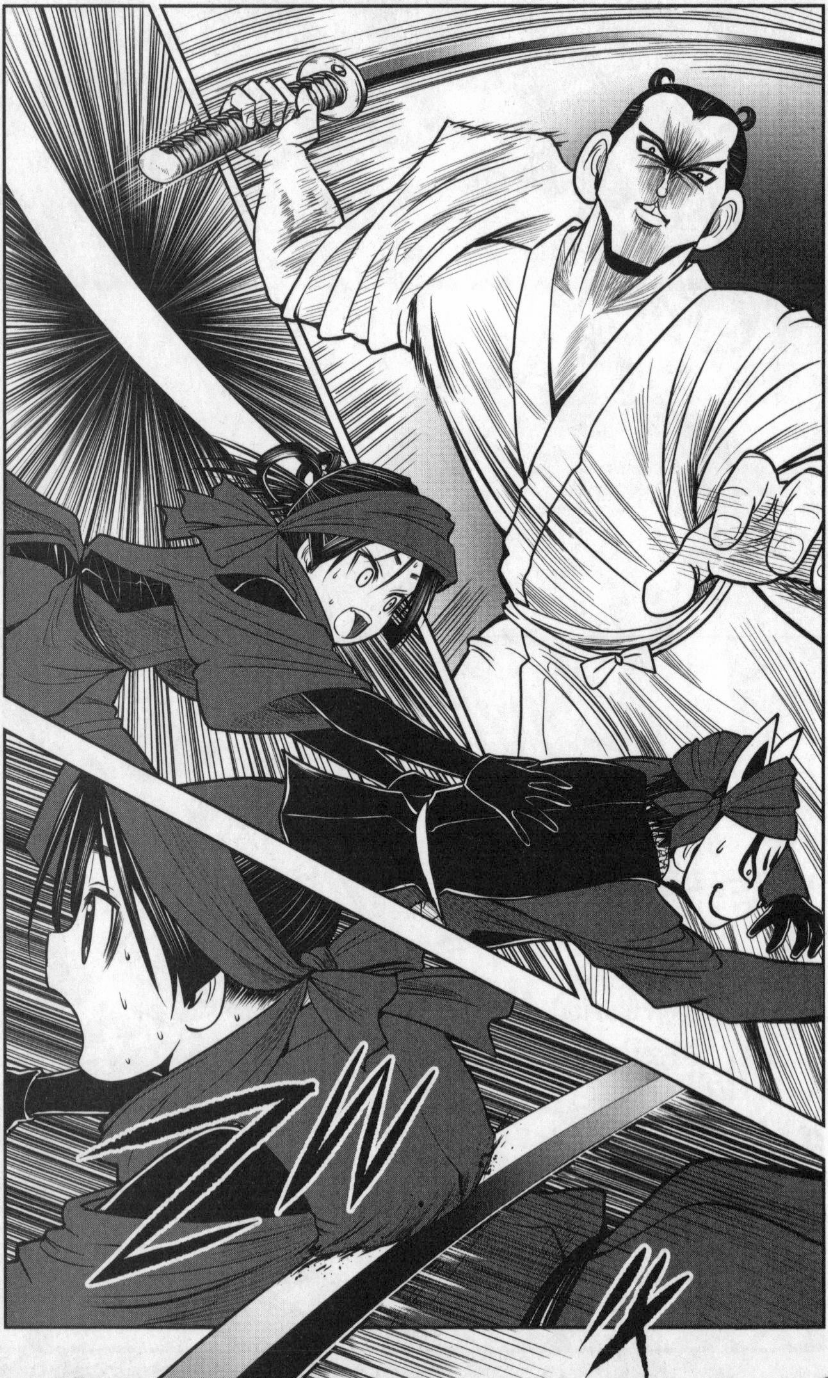
ZWN
NK

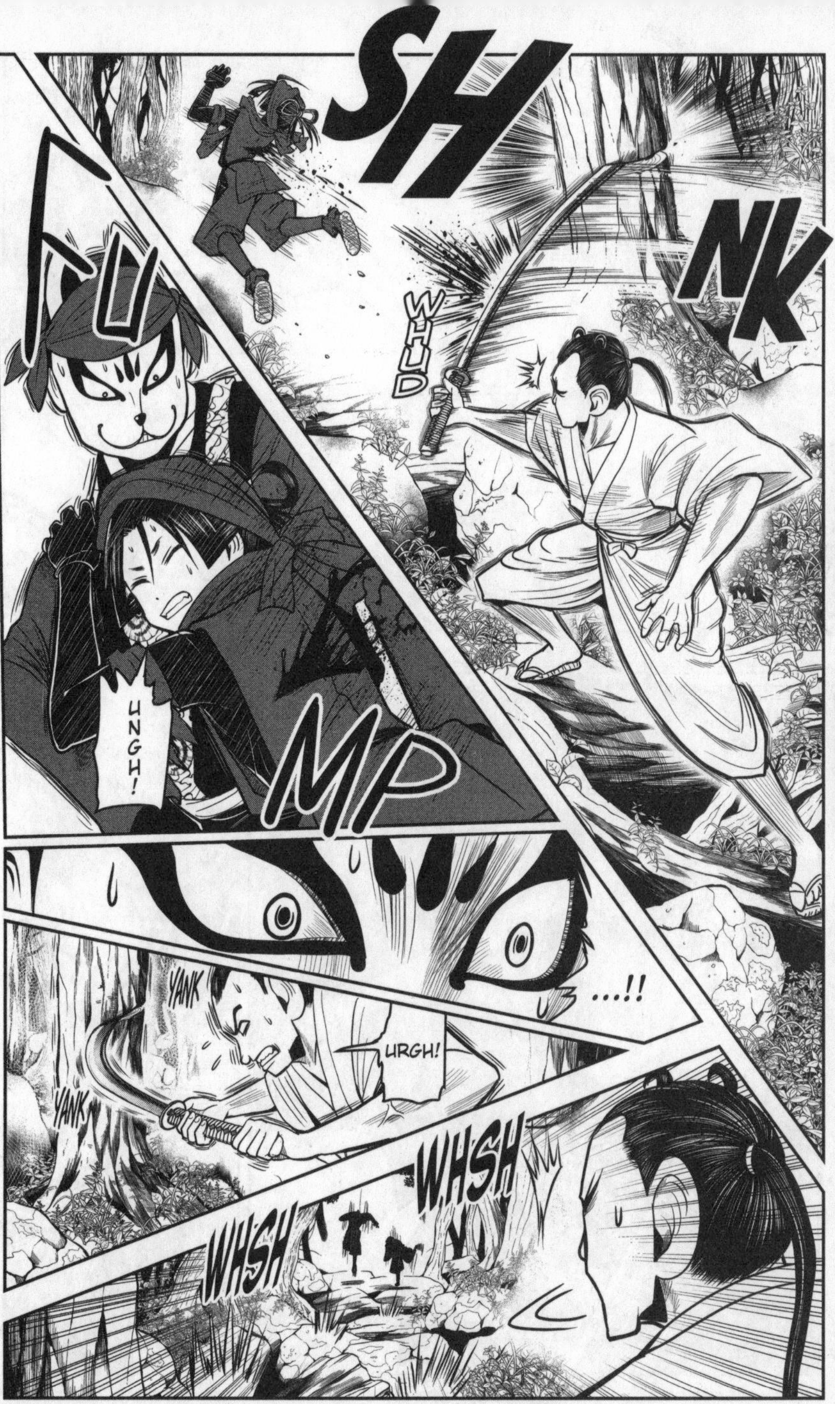

SH
NK
WHUD
FU
UNGH!
MP
...!!
YANK
URGH!
YANK
WHSH
WHSH

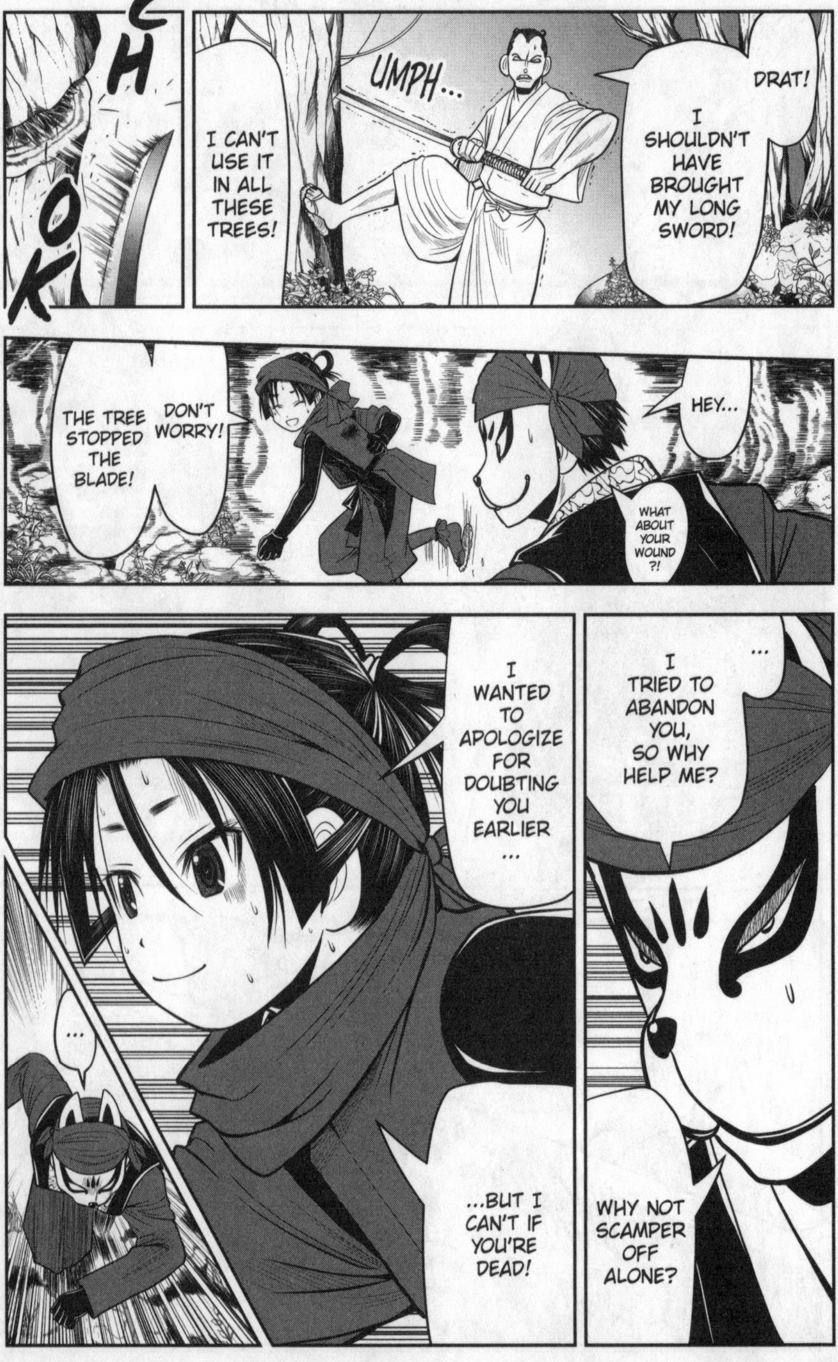
DRAT!
I SHOULDN'T HAVE BROUGHT MY LONG SWORD!
UMPH...
I CAN'T USE IT IN ALL THESE TREES!
CHOK
HEY...
WHAT ABOUT YOUR WOUND?!
DON'T WORRY!
THE TREE STOPPED THE BLADE!
...
I TRIED TO ABANDON YOU, SO WHY HELP ME?
WHY NOT SCAMPER OFF ALONE?
I WANTED TO APOLOGIZE FOR DOUBTING YOU EARLIER ...
...BUT I CAN'T IF YOU'RE DEAD!
...

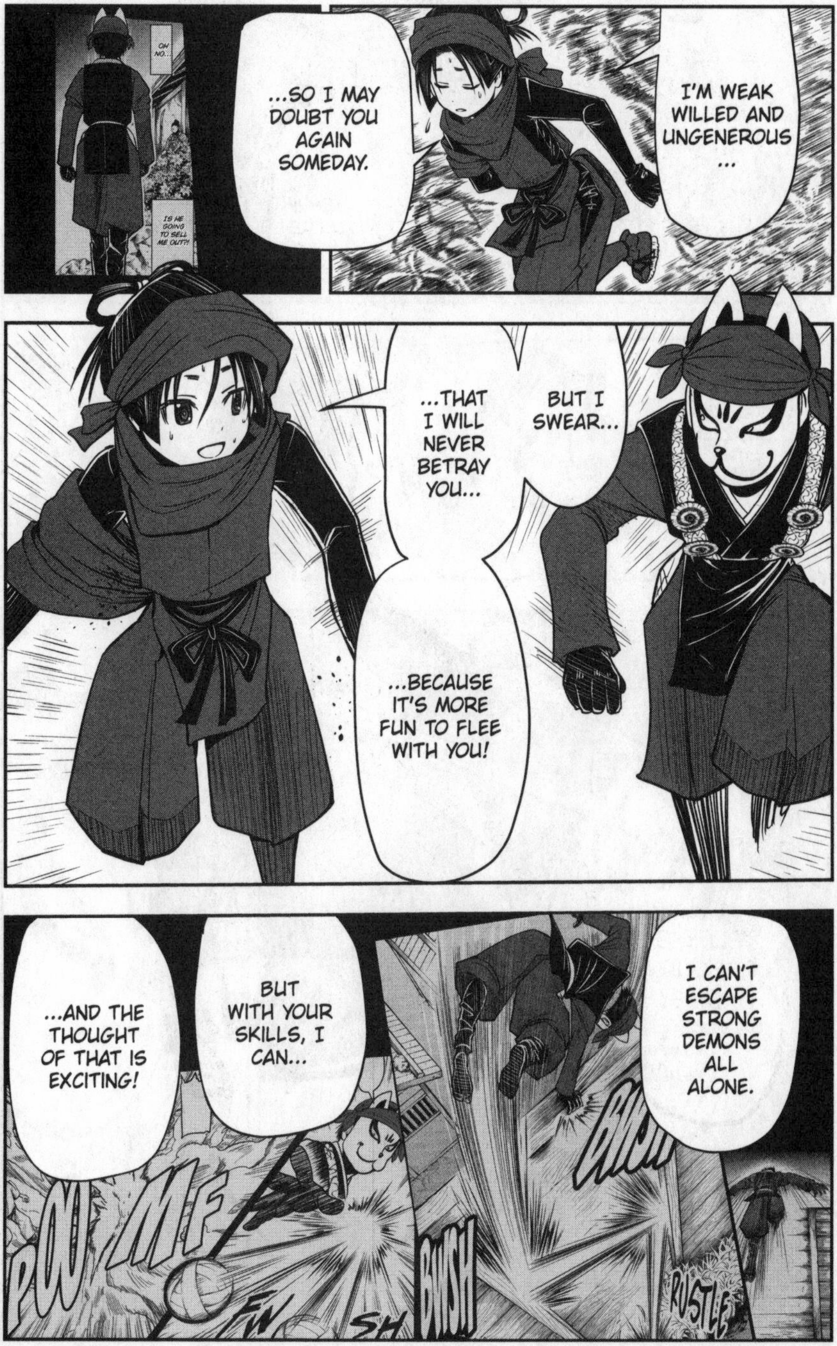
I'M WEAK WILLED AND UNGENEROUS ...
...SO I MAY DOUBT YOU AGAIN SOMEDAY.
OH NO...
IS HE GOING TO SELL ME OUT?!
BUT I SWEAR...
...THAT I WILL NEVER BETRAY YOU...
...BECAUSE IT'S MORE FUN TO FLEE WITH YOU!
I CAN'T ESCAPE STRONG DEMONS ALL ALONE.
RUSTLE
BWISH
BUT WITH YOUR SKILLS, I CAN...
...AND THE THOUGHT OF THAT IS EXCITING!
SH
FW

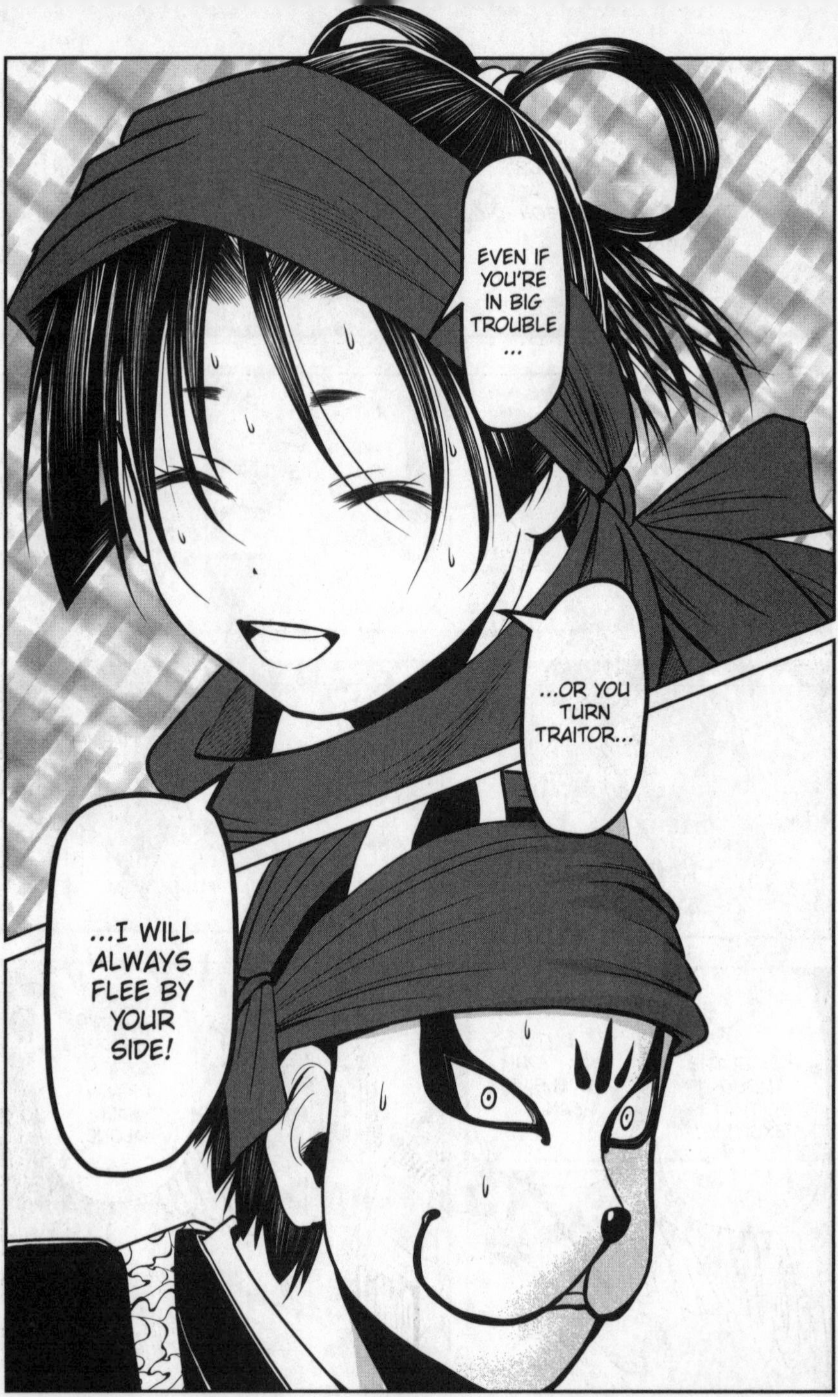
EVEN IF YOU'RE IN BIG TROUBLE ...
...OR YOU TURN TRAITOR...
...I WILL ALWAYS FLEE BY YOUR SIDE!

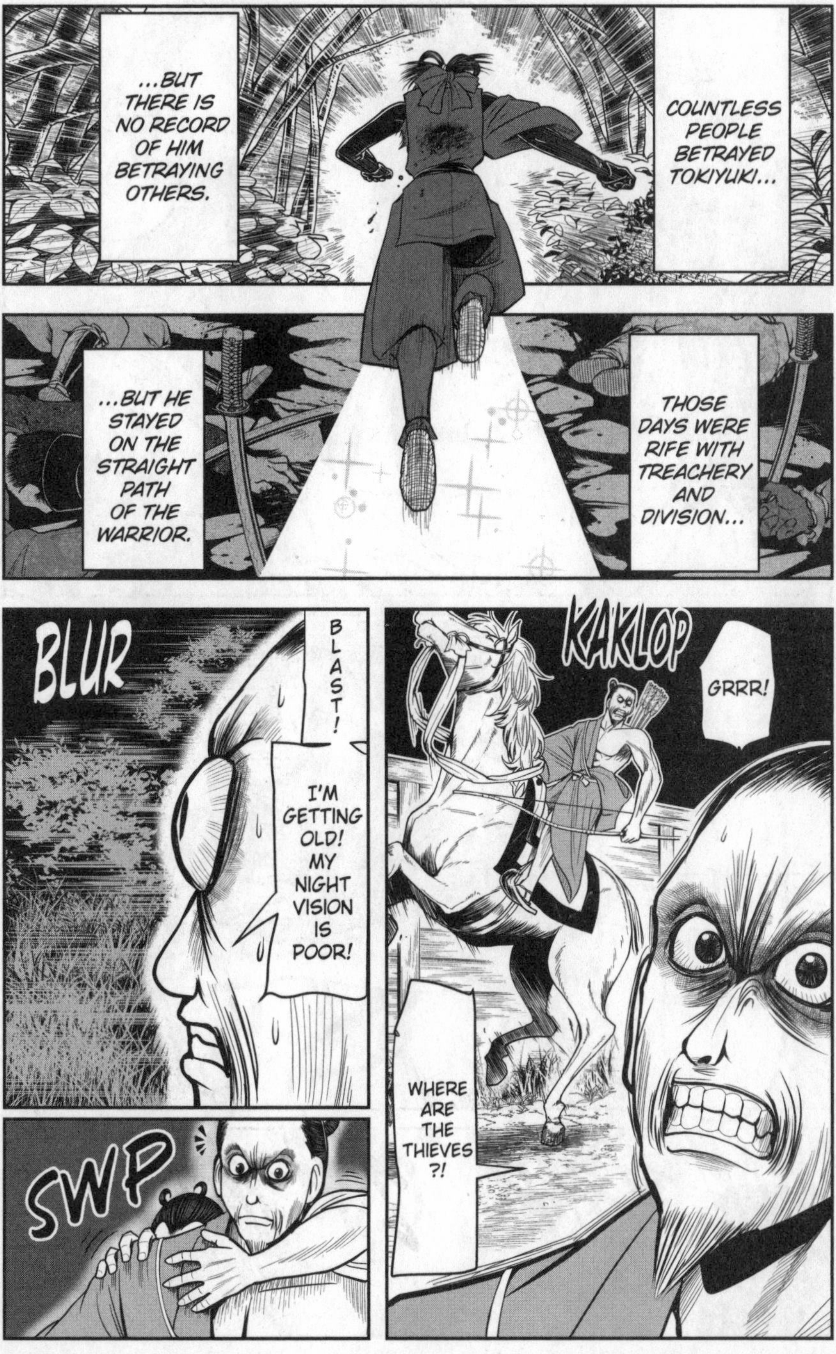
COUNTLESS PEOPLE BETRAYED TOKIYUKI...
...BUT THERE IS NO RECORD OF HIM BETRAYING OTHERS.
THOSE DAYS WERE RIFE WITH TREACHERY AND DIVISION...
...BUT HE STAYED ON THE STRAIGHT PATH OF THE WARRIOR.
KAKLOP
GRRR!
WHERE ARE THE THIEVES?!
BLUR
BLAST!
I'M GETTING OLD! MY NIGHT VISION IS POOR!
SWP

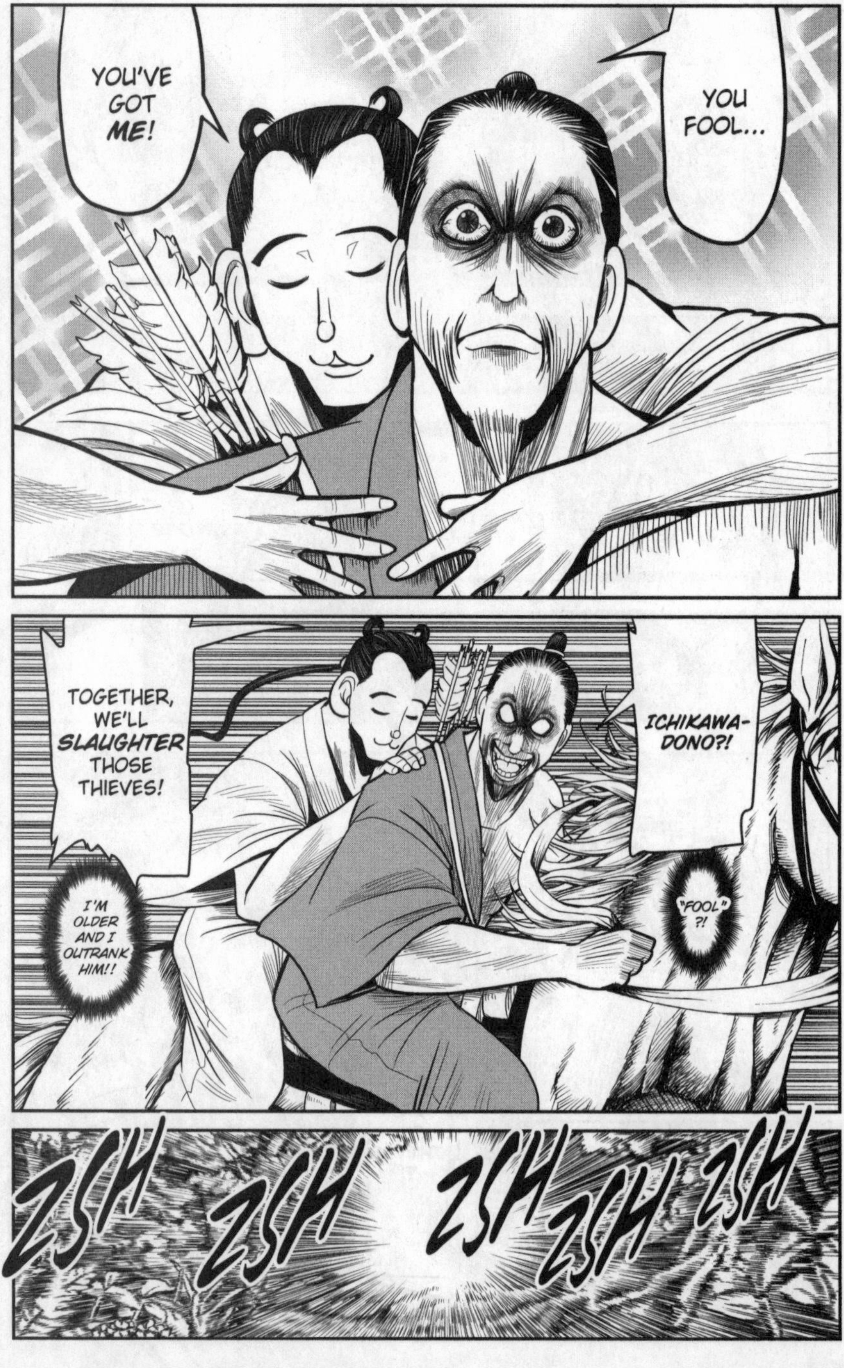
YOU FOOL...
YOU'VE GOT **ME**!
ICHIKAWA-DONO?!
"FOOL" ?!
TOGETHER, WE'LL **SLAUGHTER** THOSE THIEVES!
I'M OLDER AND I OUTRANK HIM!!
ZSH ZSH ZSH ZSH ZSH ZSH

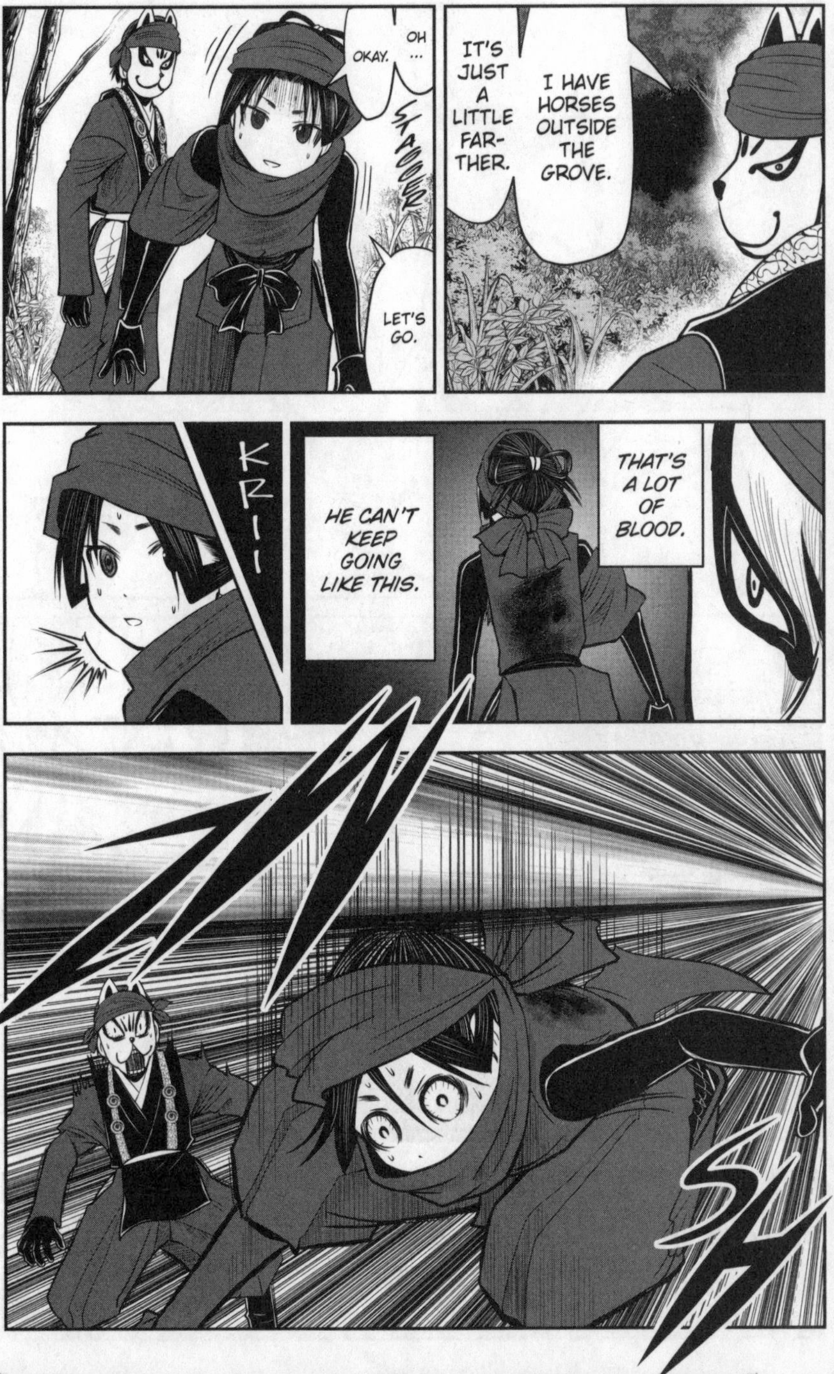
I HAVE HORSES OUTSIDE THE GROVE.
IT'S JUST A LITTLE FAR- THER.
OH ...
OKAY.
STAGGER
LET'S GO.
THAT'S A LOT OF BLOOD.
HE CAN'T KEEP GOING LIKE THIS.
KRII

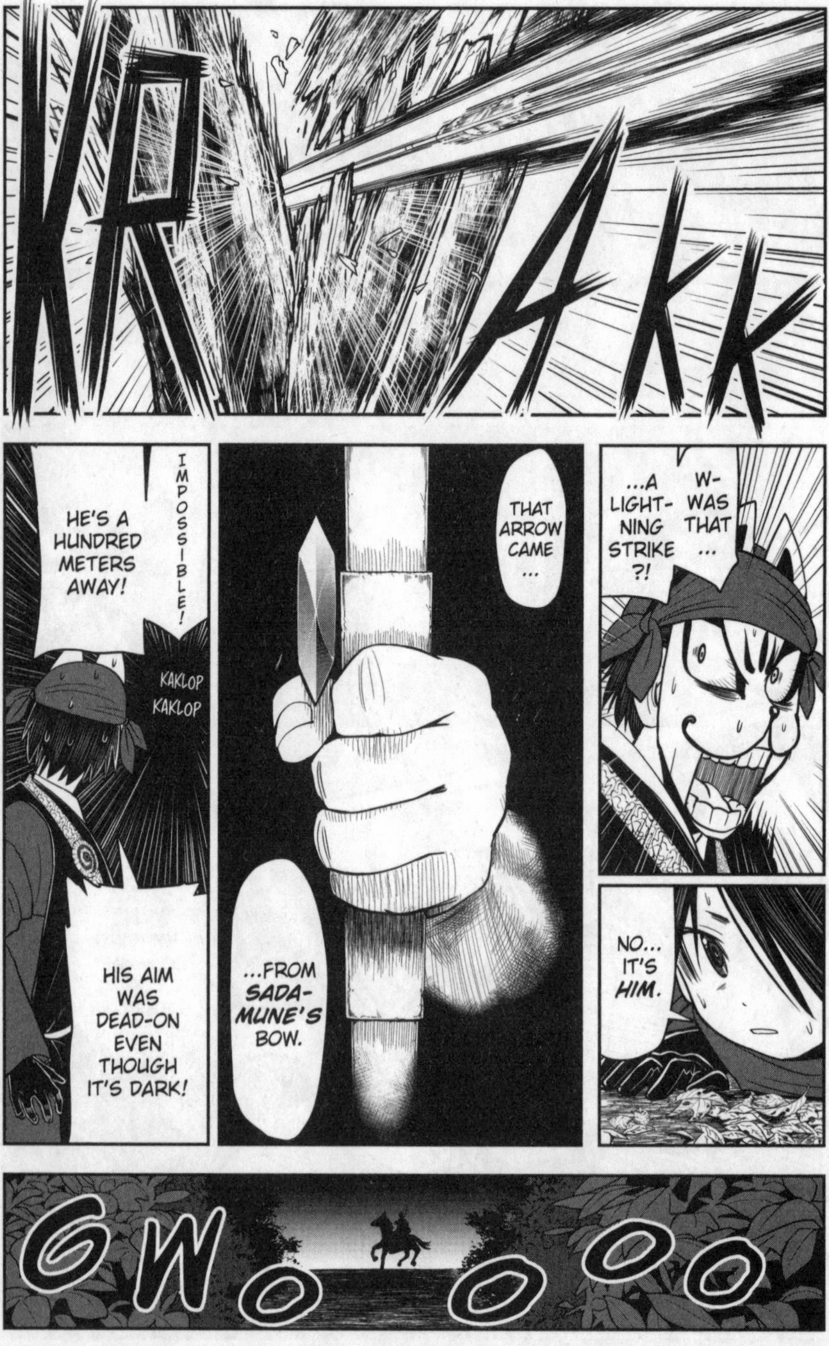
KRAKAKK
W-WAS THAT...
...A LIGHTNING STRIKE?!
NO... IT'S HIM.
THAT ARROW CAME...
...FROM SADAMUNE'S BOW.
IMPOSSIBLE!
HE'S A HUNDRED METERS AWAY!
KAKLOP KAKLOP
HIS AIM WAS DEAD-ON EVEN THOUGH IT'S DARK!
GWOOOOO

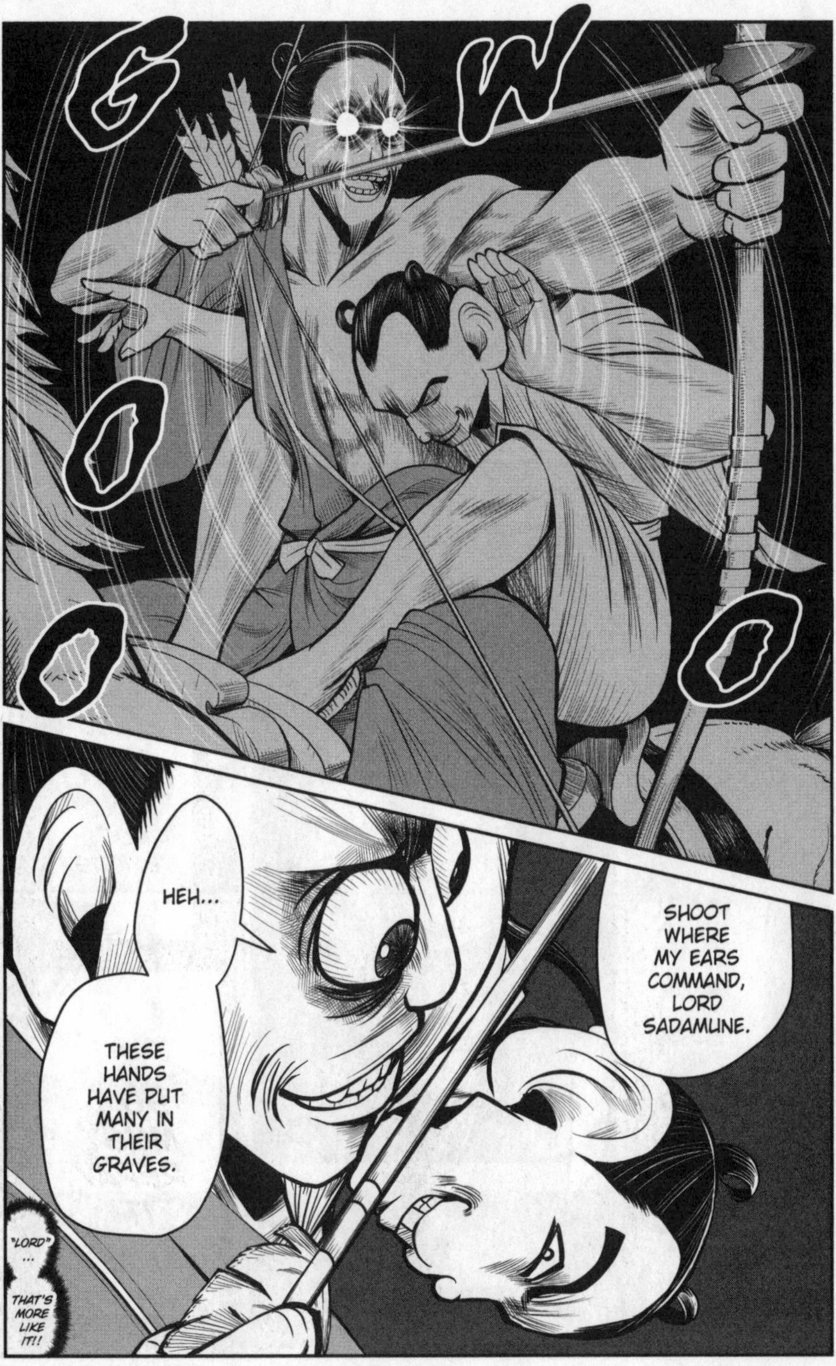
GWOOO
SHOOT WHERE MY EARS COMMAND, LORD SADAMUNE.
HEH...
THESE HANDS HAVE PUT MANY IN THEIR GRAVES.
"LORD"...
THAT'S MORE LIKE IT!!

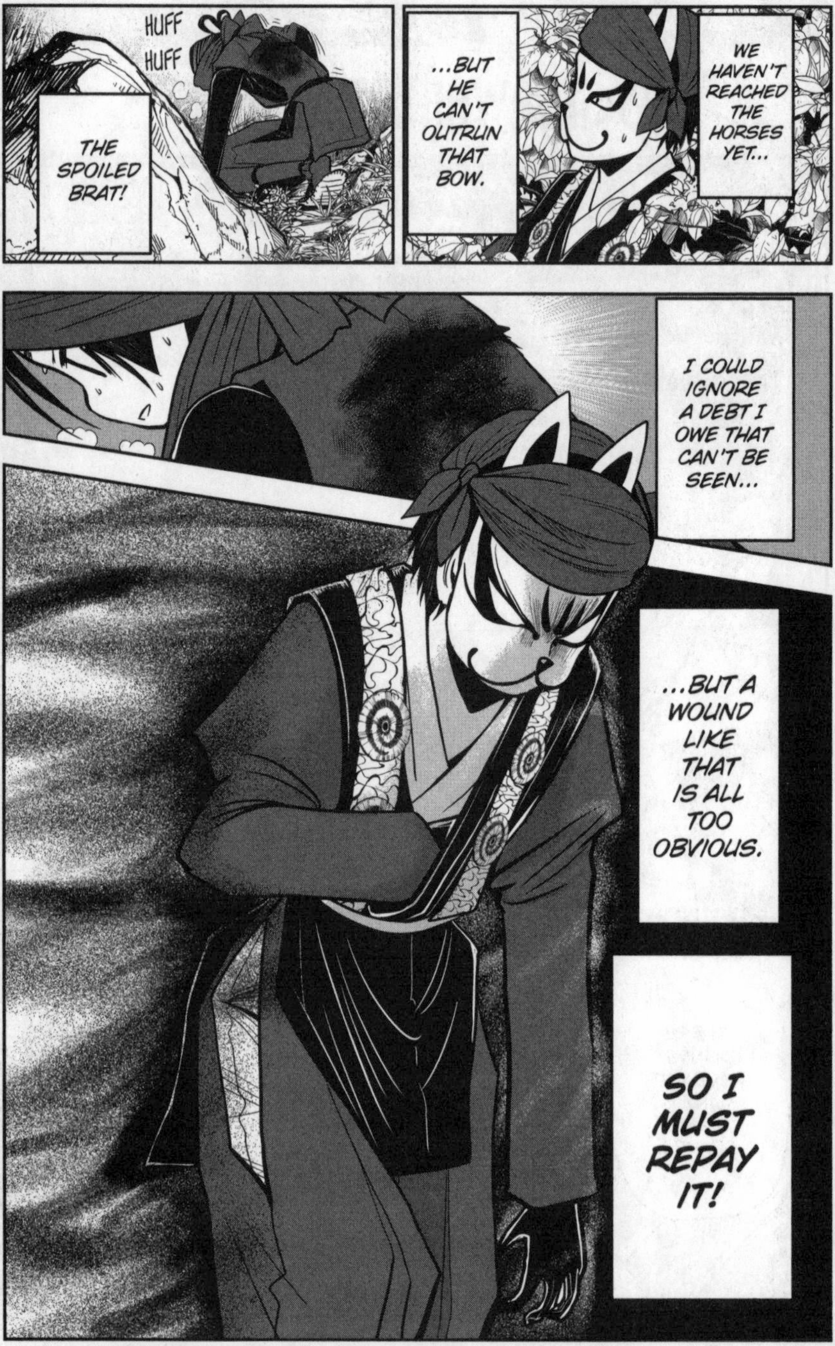
WE HAVEN'T REACHED THE HORSES YET...
...BUT HE CAN'T OUTRUN THAT BOW.
HUFF
HUFF
THE SPOILED BRAT!
I COULD IGNORE A DEBT I OWE THAT CAN'T BE SEEN...
...BUT A WOUND LIKE THAT IS ALL TOO OBVIOUS.
SO I MUST REPAY IT!

1333

OGASAWARA SADAMUNE

★★★★ SSR

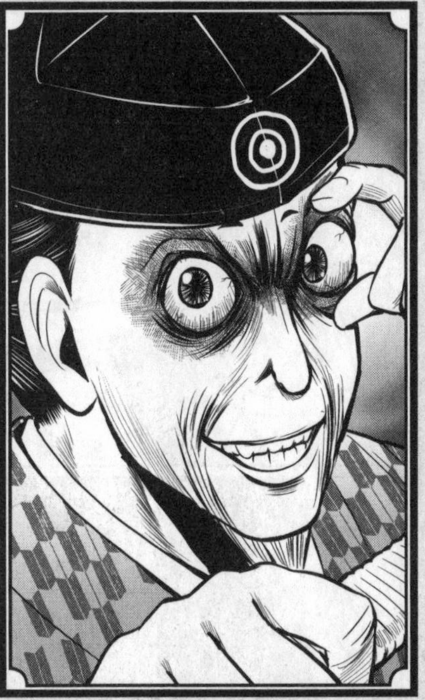

ABILITIES		NANBOKU-CHO COMPATIBILITY	
MARTIAL ART	90	SAVAGERY	87
INTELLIGENCE	73	LOYALTY	72
POLITICS	67	CHAOS	64
LEADERSHIP	69	INGENUITY	53
CHARM	80	RUNNING AND HIDING	41

CREST

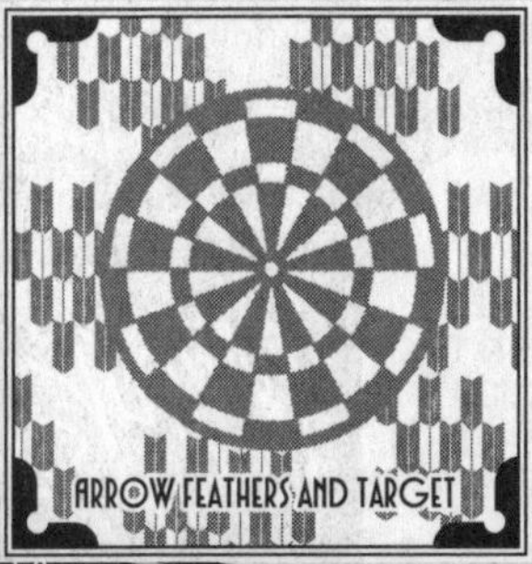

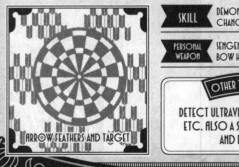

ARROW FEATHERS AND TARGET

SKILL OGASAWARA'S BOW: 35 PERCENT INCREASE TO MARTIAL ARTS AND HIT CHANCE

SKILL DEMONIC EYESIGHT: 20 PERCENT INCREASE TO HIT CHANCE , 10 PERCENT INCREASE TO OBSERVATION

PERSONAL WEAPON SENGEN: HIS STRONG-DRAW, BAMBOO-SHEATHED BOW HAS A 15 PERCENT RANGE INCREASE

OTHER THINGS HIS EYES CAN DO

DETECT ULTRAVIOLET LIGHT AND EARTHQUAKES, ETC. ALSO A SMALL DEGREE OF RESPIRATION AND EXTERNAL DIGESTION.

CHAPTER 14: COMMAND 1333

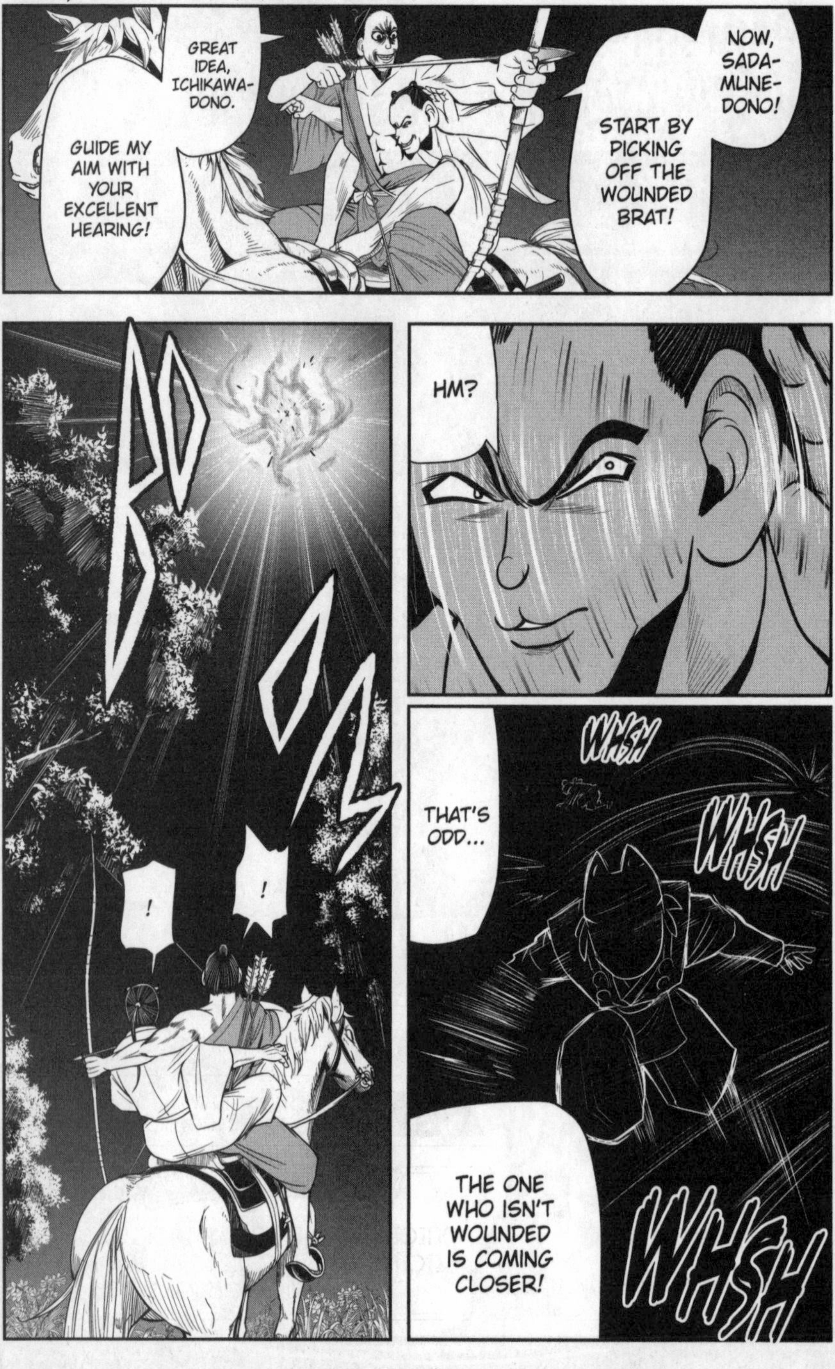

NOW, SADAMUNE-DONO!
START BY PICKING OFF THE WOUNDED BRAT!
GREAT IDEA, ICHIKAWA-DONO.
GUIDE MY AIM WITH YOUR EXCELLENT HEARING!
HM?
WHSH
WHSH
THAT'S ODD...
THE ONE WHO ISN'T WOUNDED IS COMING CLOSER!
WHSH
BOOM
!
!

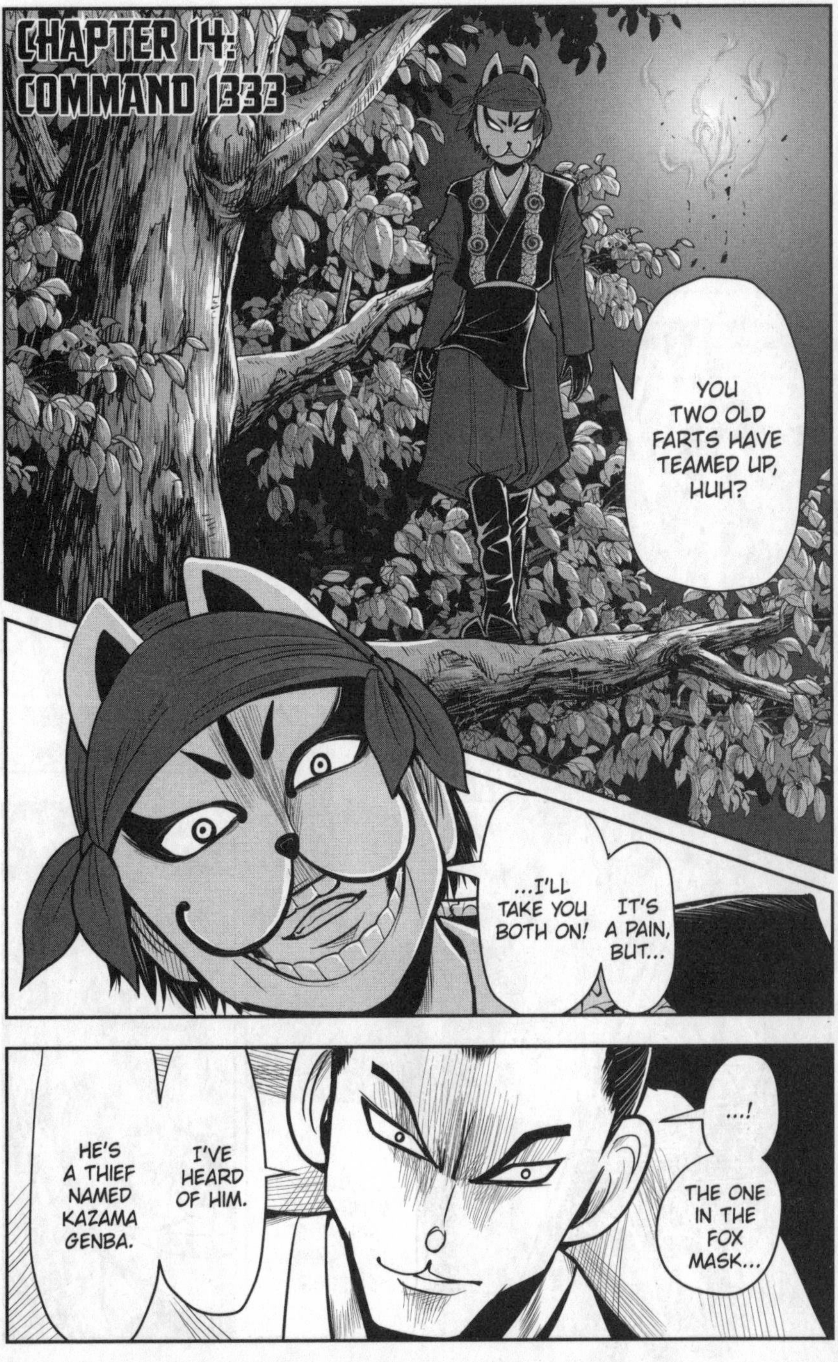
CHAPTER 14: COMMAND 1333
YOU TWO OLD FARTS HAVE TEAMED UP, HUH?
IT'S A PAIN, BUT...
...I'LL TAKE YOU BOTH ON!
...!
THE ONE IN THE FOX MASK...
I'VE HEARD OF HIM.
HE'S A THIEF NAMED KAZAMA GENBA.

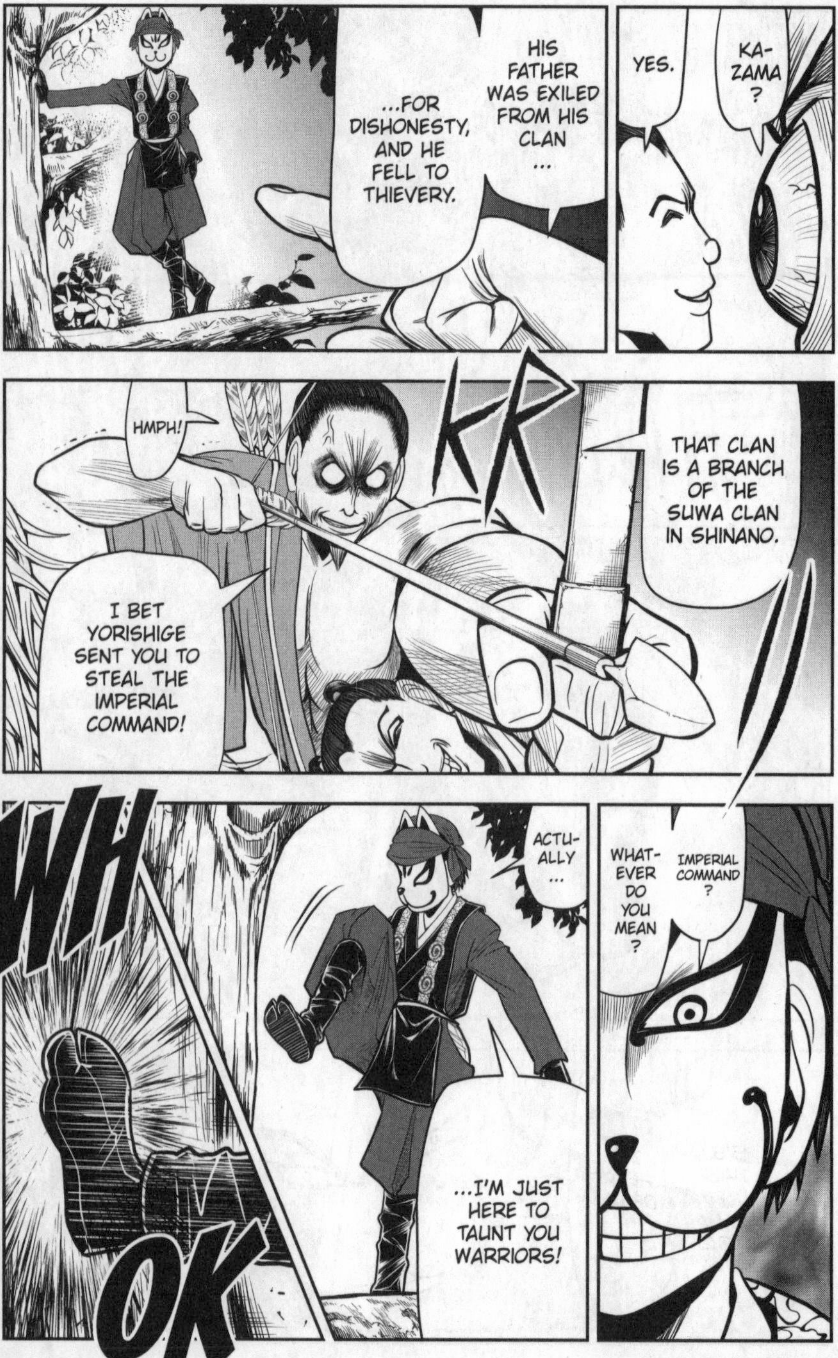
KA-ZAMA?
YES.
HIS FATHER WAS EXILED FROM HIS CLAN...
...FOR DISHONESTY, AND HE FELL TO THIEVERY.
THAT CLAN IS A BRANCH OF THE SUWA CLAN IN SHINANO.
KR
HMPH!
I BET YORISHIGE SENT YOU TO STEAL THE IMPERIAL COMMAND!
IMPERIAL COMMAND?
WHAT-EVER DO YOU MEAN?
ACTU-ALLY...
WH
...I'M JUST HERE TO TAUNT YOU WARRIORS!
OK

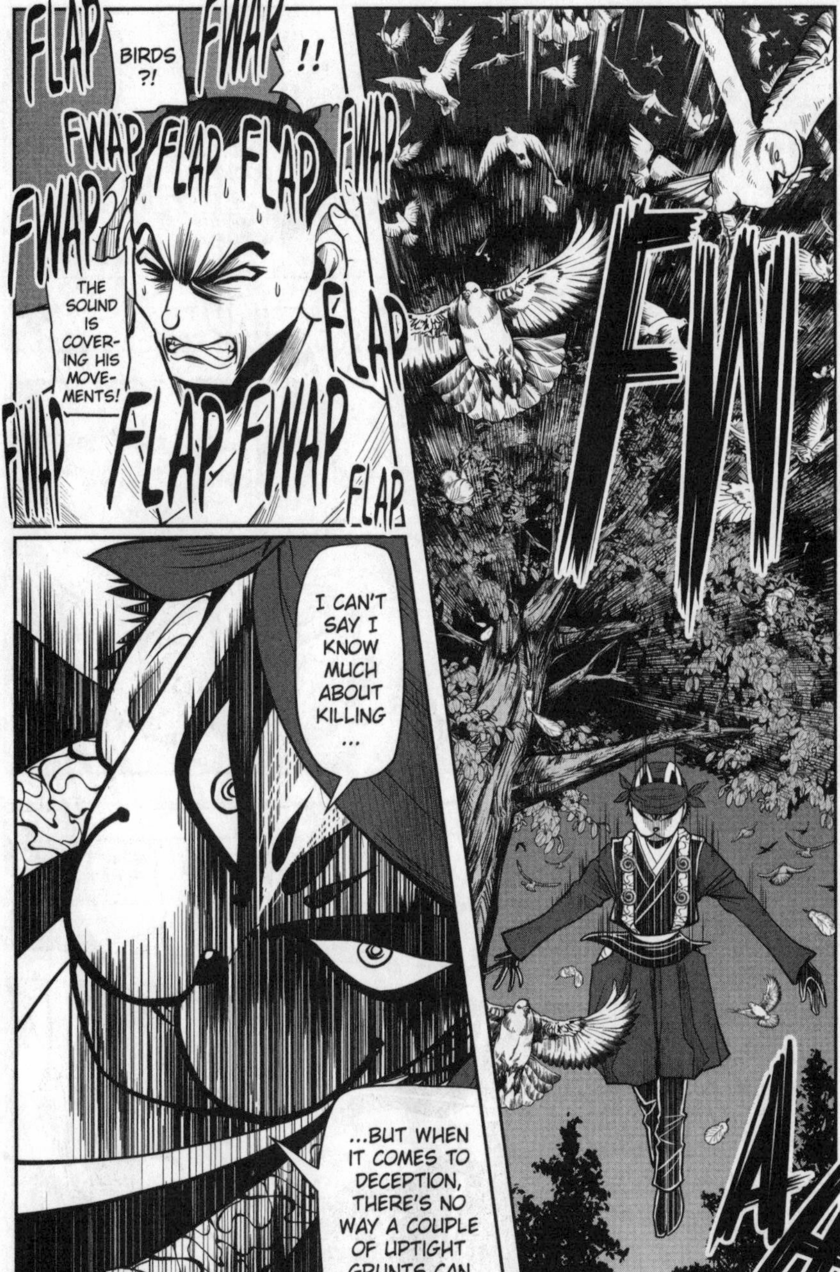
FWN
AH
FLAP
BIRDS ?!
FWAP
!!
FWAP FLAP FLAP FWAP
FWAP
THE SOUND IS COVERING HIS MOVEMENTS!
FLAP
FWAP FLAP FWAP FLAP
I CAN'T SAY I KNOW MUCH ABOUT KILLING ...
...BUT WHEN IT COMES TO DECEPTION, THERE'S NO WAY A COUPLE OF UPTIGHT GRUNTS CAN BEAT ME!

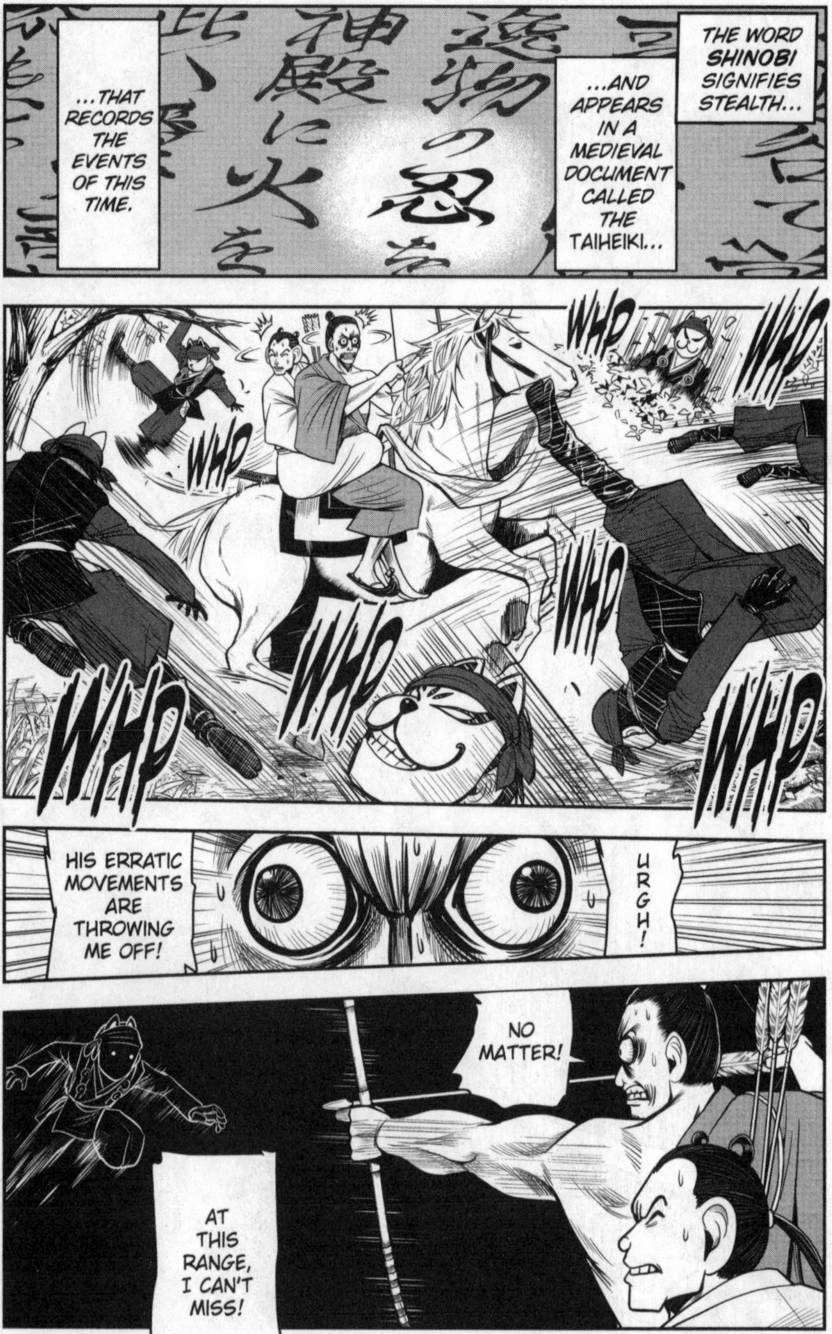
THE WORD SHINOBI SIGNIFIES STEALTH...
...AND APPEARS IN A MEDIEVAL DOCUMENT CALLED THE TAIHEIKI...
...THAT RECORDS THE EVENTS OF THIS TIME.
WHP
WHP
WHP
WHP
WHP
WHP
WHP
URGH!
HIS ERRATIC MOVEMENTS ARE THROWING ME OFF!
NO MATTER!
AT THIS RANGE, I CAN'T MISS!

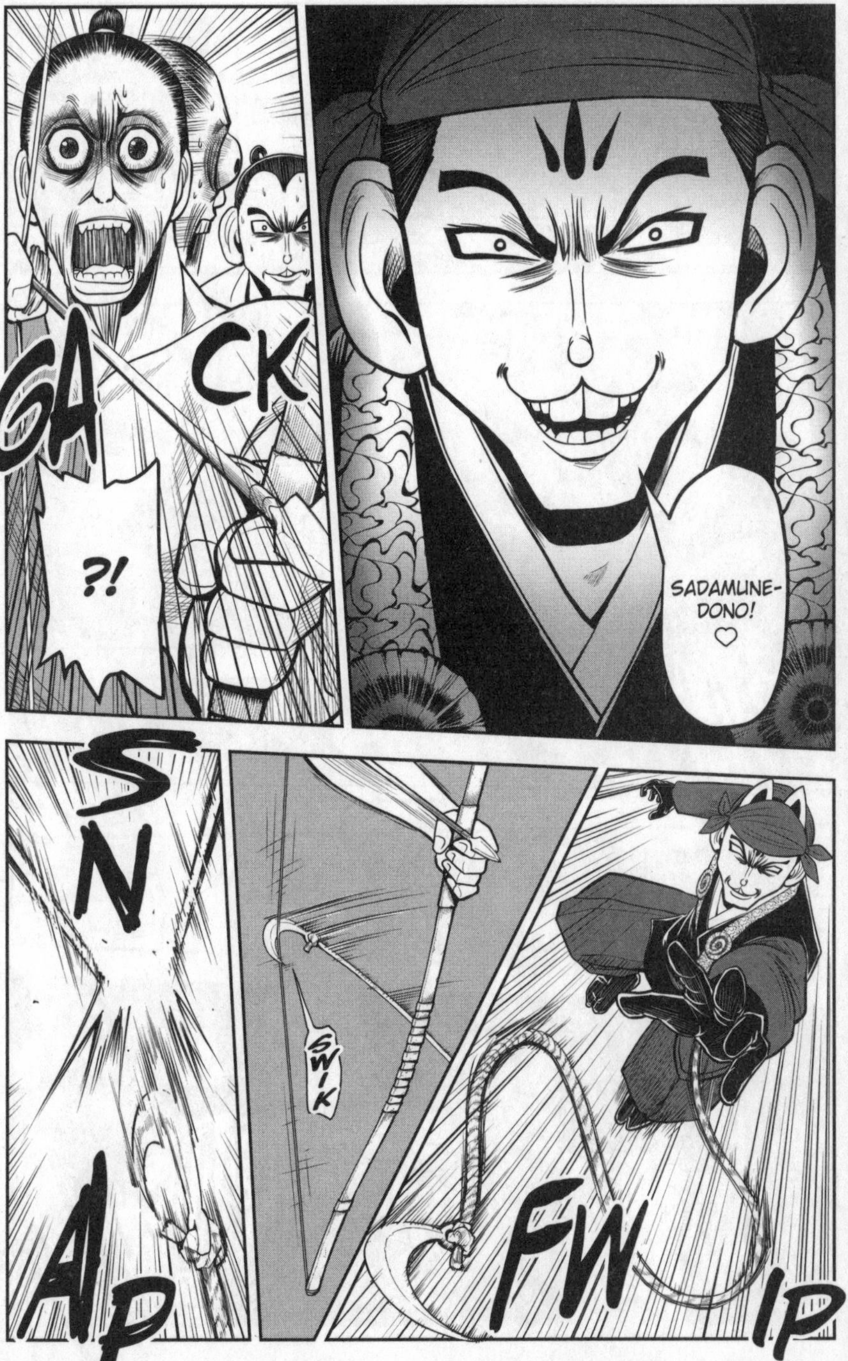
SADAMUNE-DONO! ♥
GACK
?!
FWIP
SWIK
SNAP

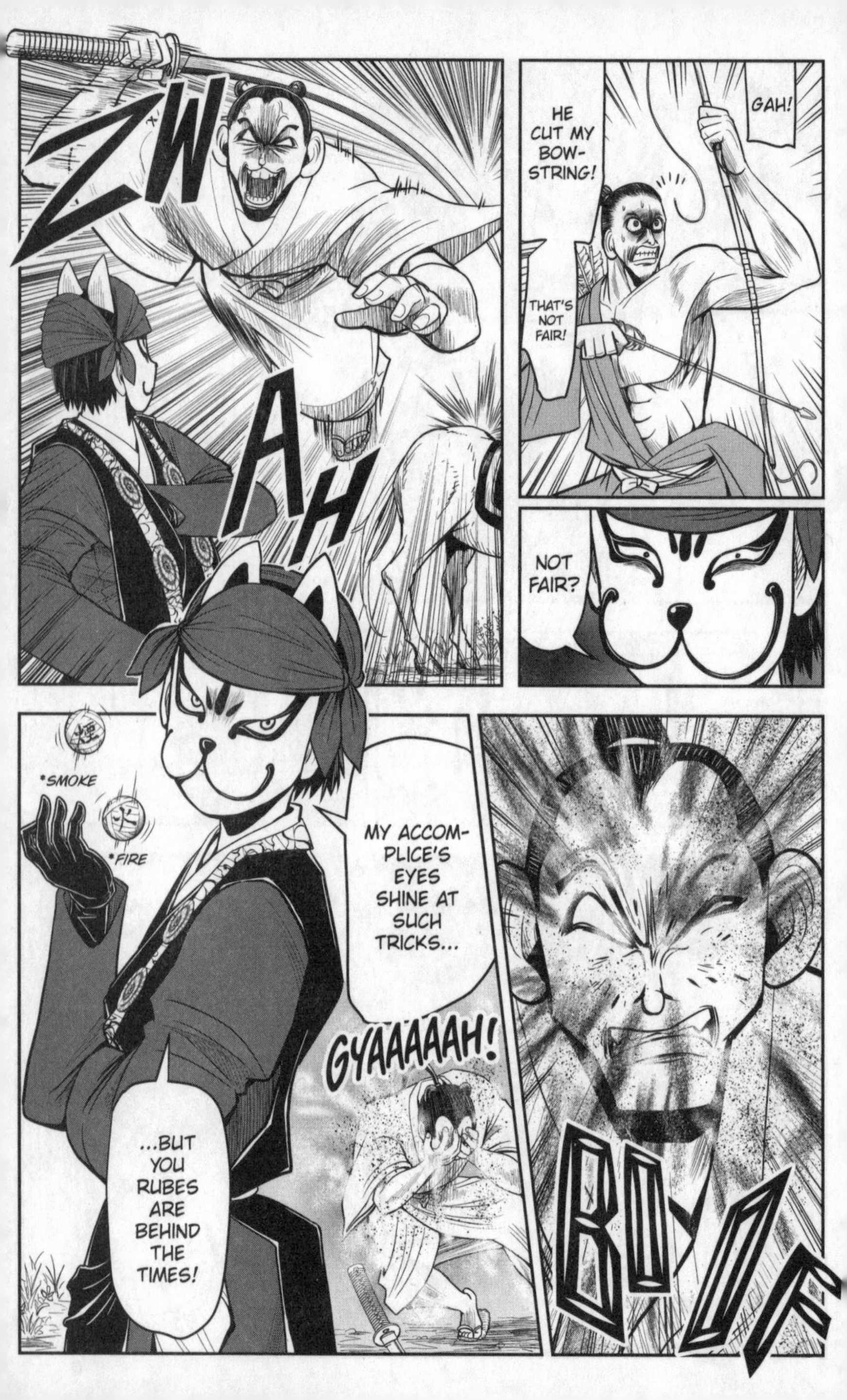
GAH!
HE CUT MY BOW-STRING!
THAT'S NOT FAIR!
NOT FAIR?
ZWAH
BOOF
MY ACCOMPLICE'S EYES SHINE AT SUCH TRICKS...
*SMOKE
*FIRE
GYAAAAAH!
...BUT YOU RUBES ARE BEHIND THE TIMES!

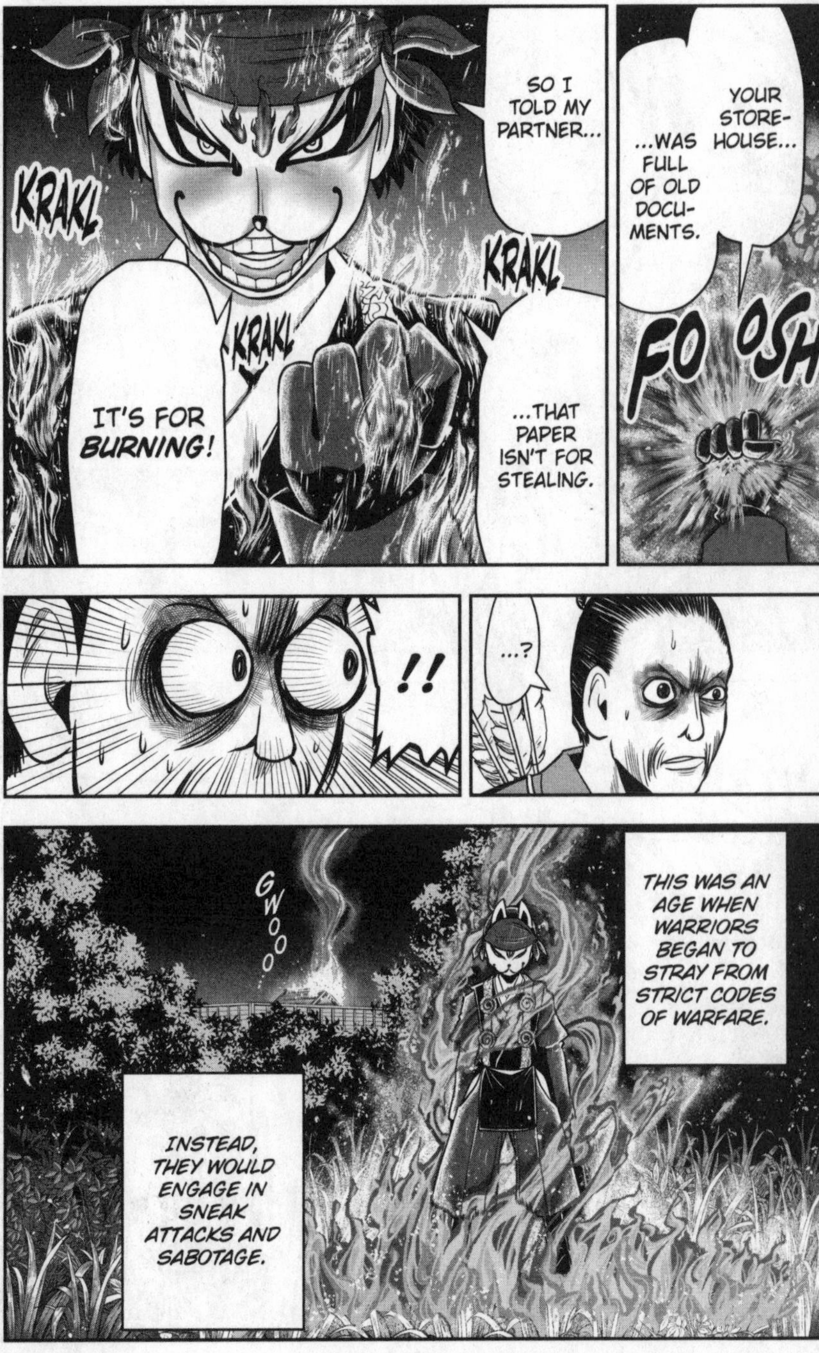
YOUR STOREHOUSE...
...WAS FULL OF OLD DOCUMENTS.
FOOSH
SO I TOLD MY PARTNER...
KRAKL
KRAKL
KRAKL
...THAT PAPER ISN'T FOR STEALING.
IT'S FOR *BURNING*!
...?
!!
THIS WAS AN AGE WHEN WARRIORS BEGAN TO STRAY FROM STRICT CODES OF WARFARE.
GWOOO...
INSTEAD, THEY WOULD ENGAGE IN SNEAK ATTACKS AND SABOTAGE.

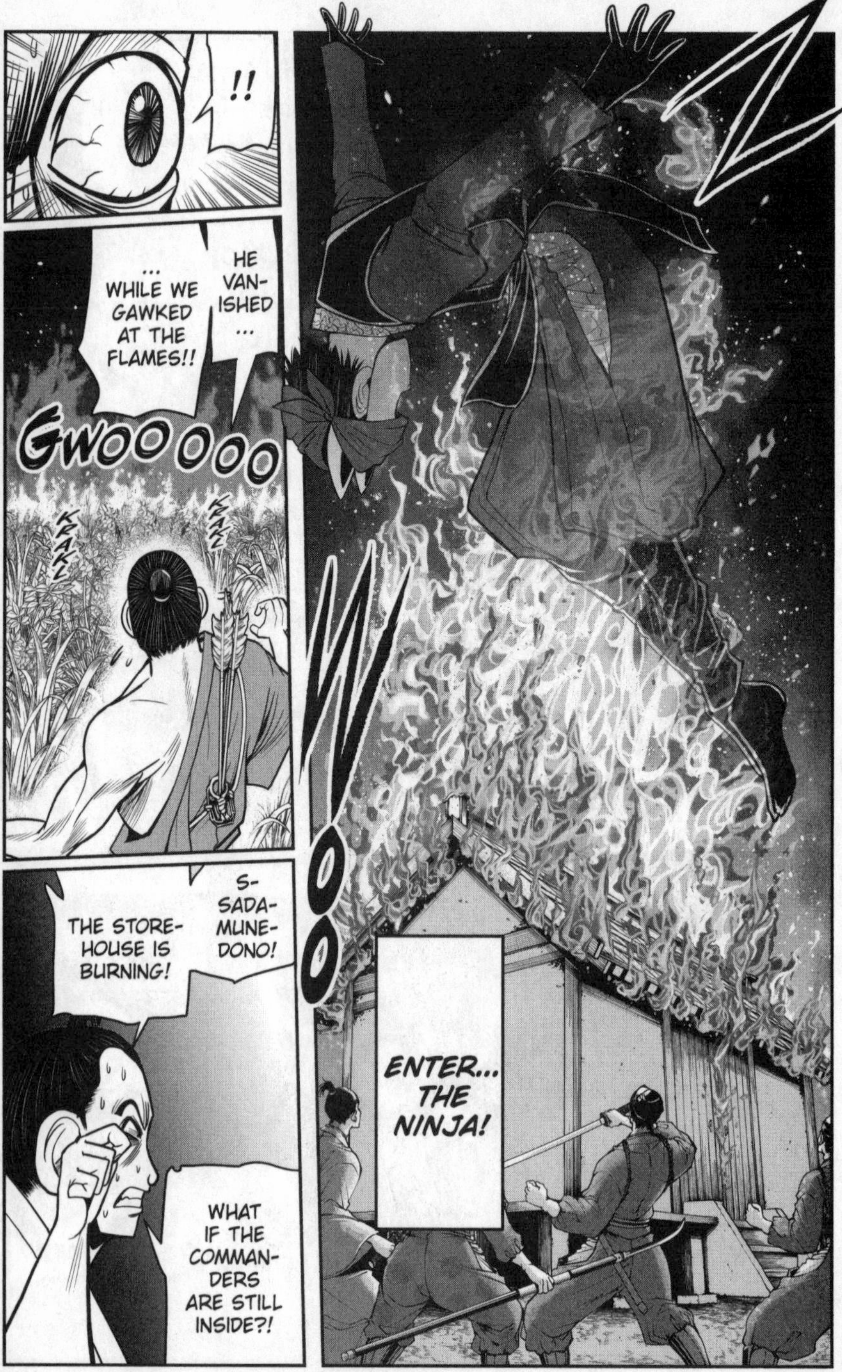
WOOO
ENTER... THE NINJA!
!!
HE VANISHED...
...WHILE WE GAWKED AT THE FLAMES!!
GWOOOOOO
KRAK
KRAK
S-SADAMUNE-DONO!
THE STOREHOUSE IS BURNING!
WHAT IF THE COMMANDERS ARE STILL INSIDE?!

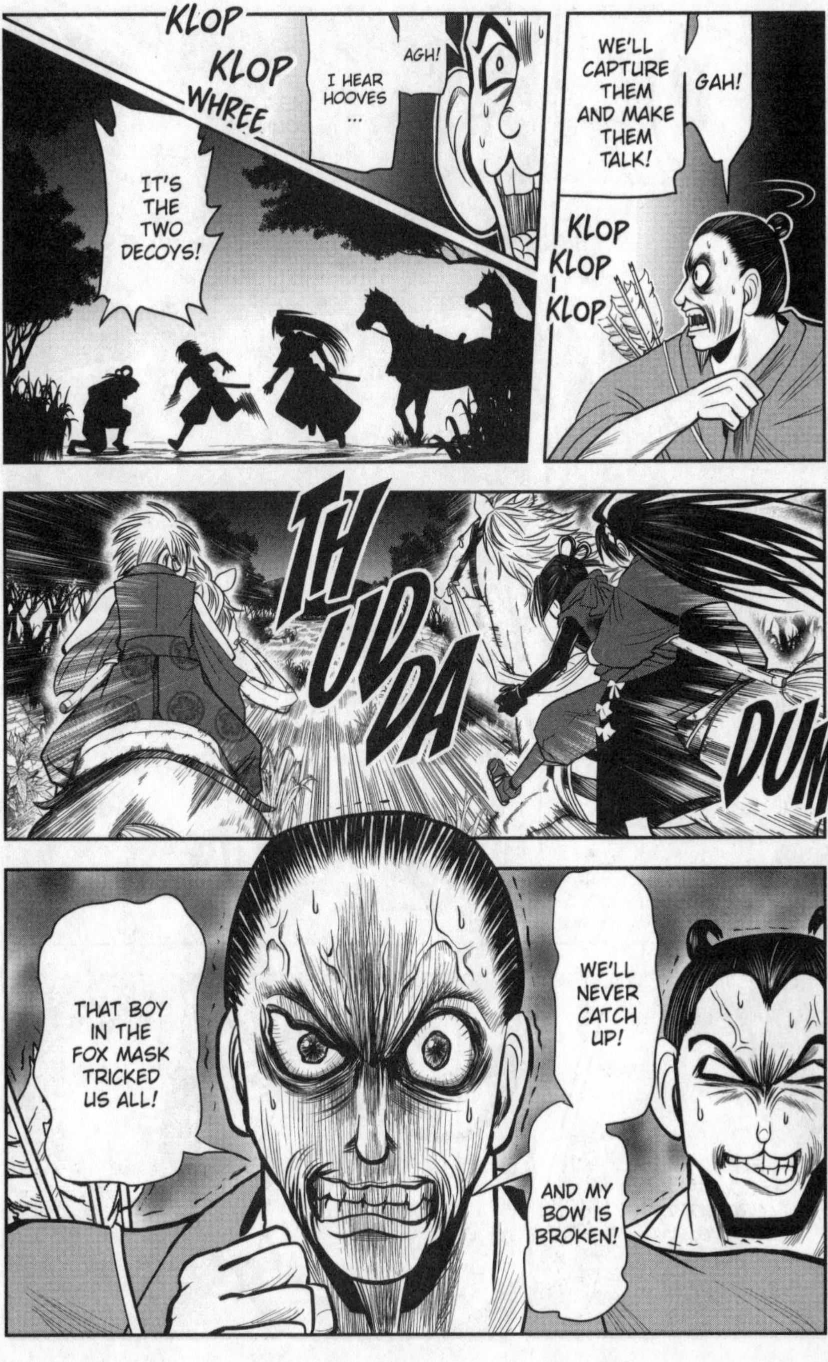
GAH!
WE'LL CAPTURE THEM AND MAKE THEM TALK!
KLOP KLOP KLOP
AGH!
I HEAR HOOVES ...
KLOP KLOP WHREE
IT'S THE TWO DECOYS!
DUM
THUDDA
WE'LL NEVER CATCH UP!
AND MY BOW IS BROKEN!
THAT BOY IN THE FOX MASK TRICKED US ALL!

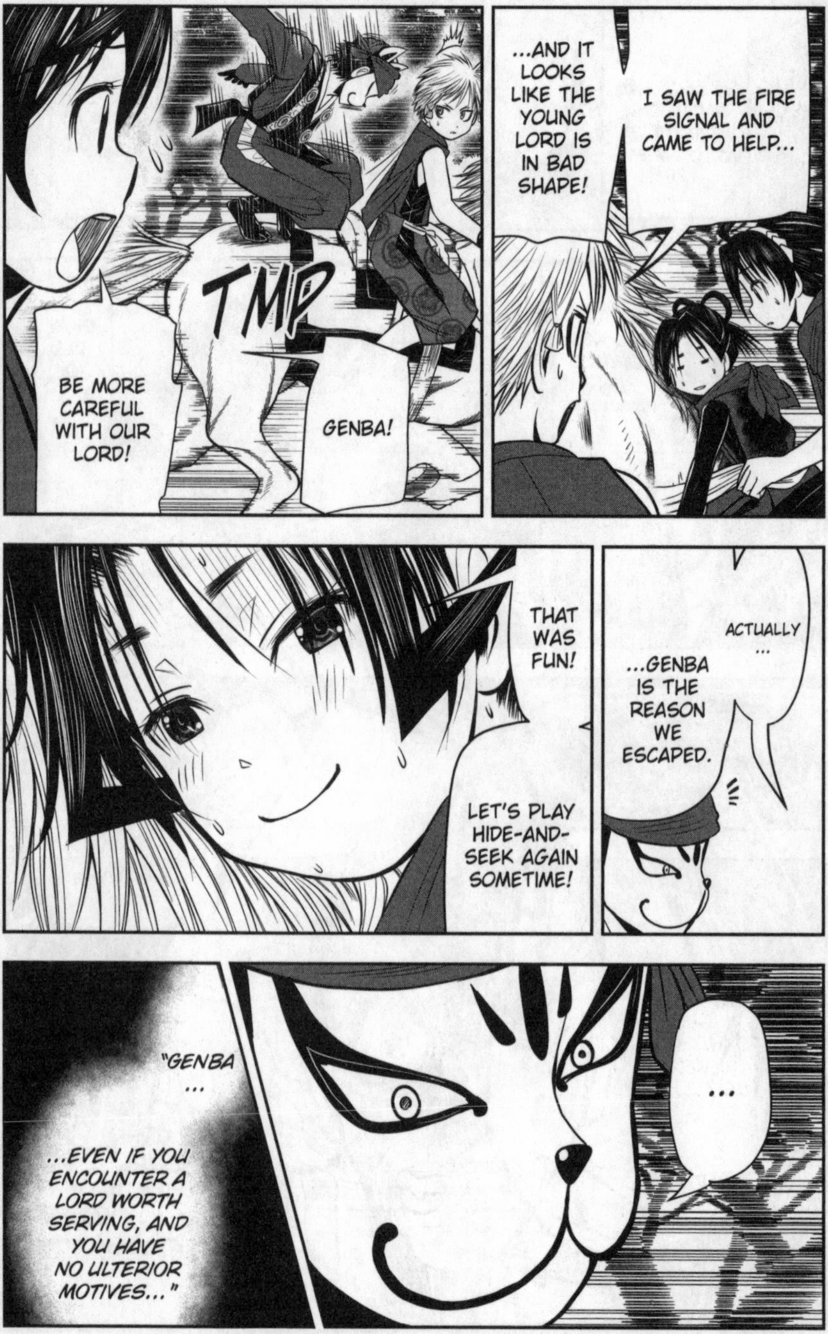
I SAW THE FIRE SIGNAL AND CAME TO HELP...
...AND IT LOOKS LIKE THE YOUNG LORD IS IN BAD SHAPE!
TMP
GENBA!
BE MORE CAREFUL WITH OUR LORD!
ACTUALLY...
...GENBA IS THE REASON WE ESCAPED.
THAT WAS FUN!
LET'S PLAY HIDE-AND-SEEK AGAIN SOMETIME!
...
"GENBA...
...EVEN IF YOU ENCOUNTER A LORD WORTH SERVING, AND YOU HAVE NO ULTERIOR MOTIVES..."

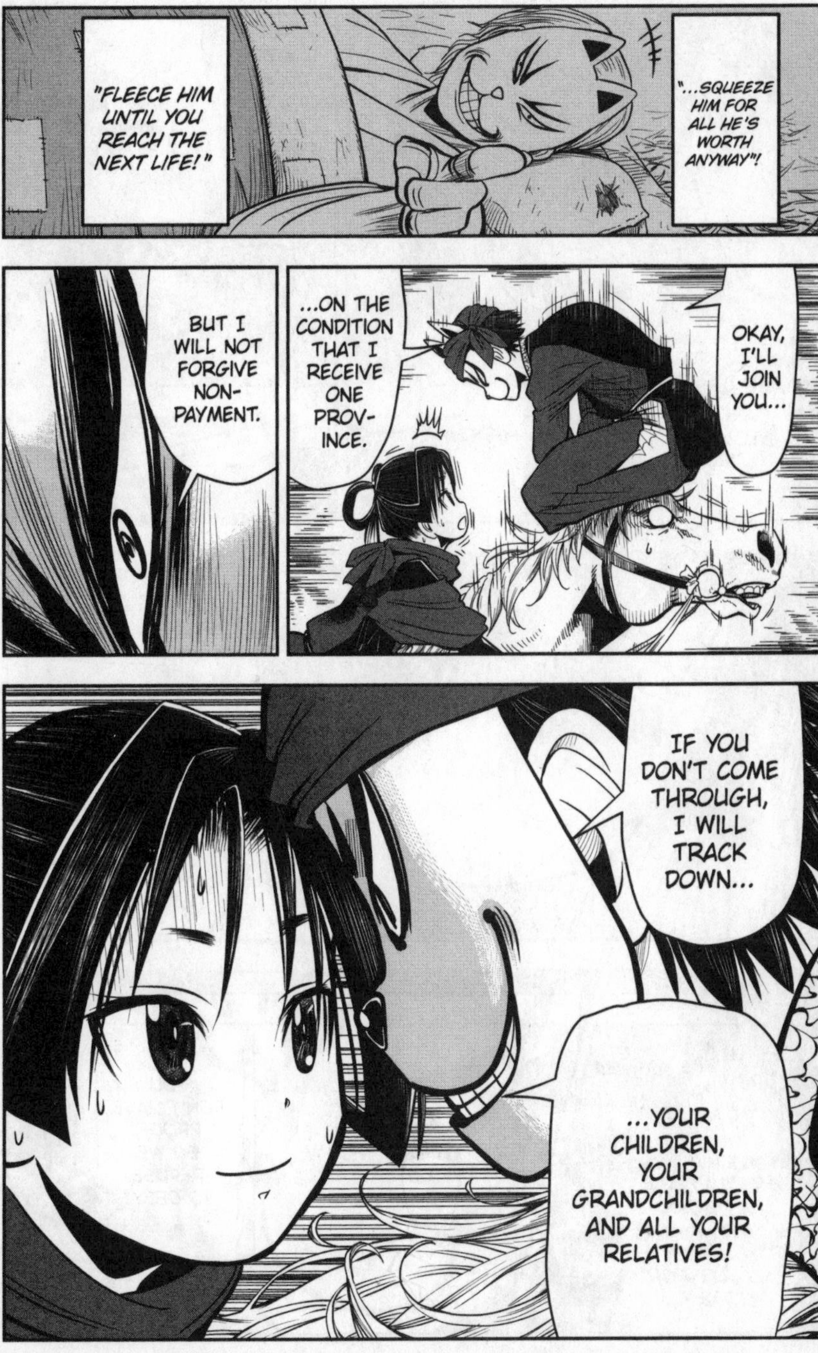
"...SQUEEZE HIM FOR ALL HE'S WORTH ANYWAY"!
"FLEECE HIM UNTIL YOU REACH THE NEXT LIFE!"
OKAY, I'LL JOIN YOU...
...ON THE CONDITION THAT I RECEIVE ONE PROVINCE.
BUT I WILL NOT FORGIVE NON-PAYMENT.
IF YOU DON'T COME THROUGH, I WILL TRACK DOWN...
...YOUR CHILDREN, YOUR GRANDCHILDREN, AND ALL YOUR RELATIVES!

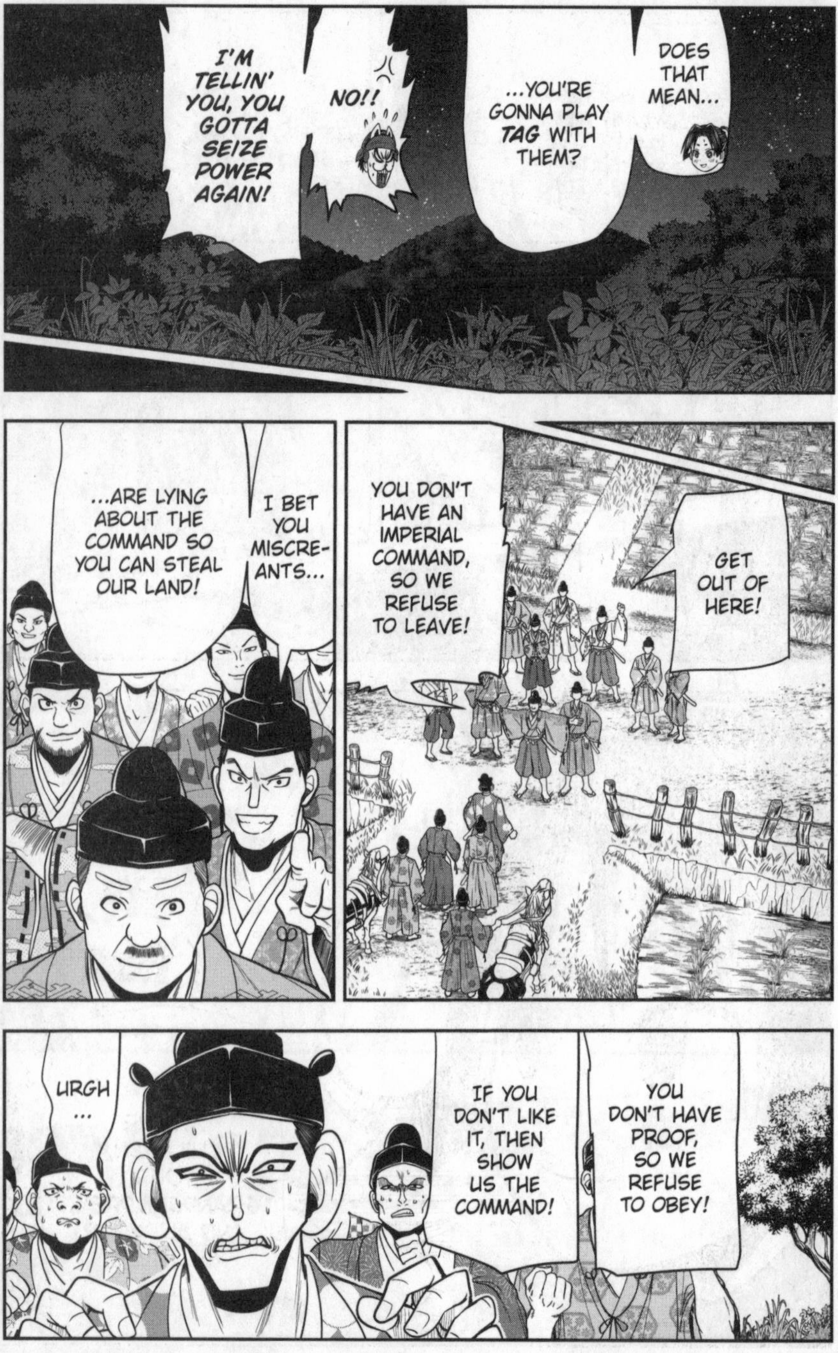
DOES THAT MEAN...
...YOU'RE GONNA PLAY TAG WITH THEM?
NO!!
I'M TELLIN' YOU, YOU GOTTA SEIZE POWER AGAIN!
GET OUT OF HERE!
YOU DON'T HAVE AN IMPERIAL COMMAND, SO WE REFUSE TO LEAVE!
I BET YOU MISCRE-ANTS...
...ARE LYING ABOUT THE COMMAND SO YOU CAN STEAL OUR LAND!
YOU DON'T HAVE PROOF, SO WE REFUSE TO OBEY!
IF YOU DON'T LIKE IT, THEN SHOW US THE COMMAND!
URGH ...

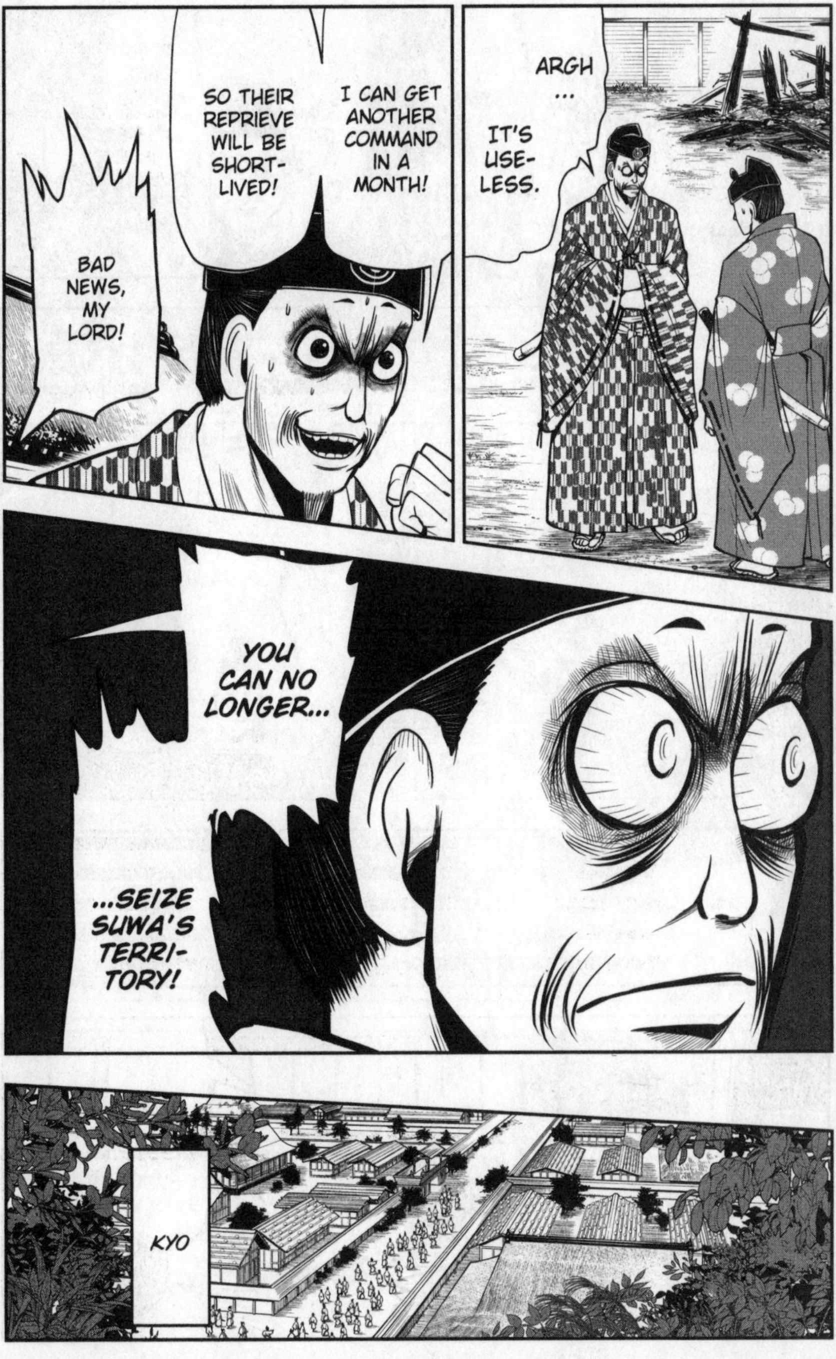
ARGH ...
IT'S USE-LESS.
I CAN GET ANOTHER COMMAND IN A MONTH!
SO THEIR REPRIEVE WILL BE SHORT-LIVED!
BAD NEWS, MY LORD!
YOU CAN NO LONGER...
...SEIZE SUWA'S TERRI-TORY!
KYO

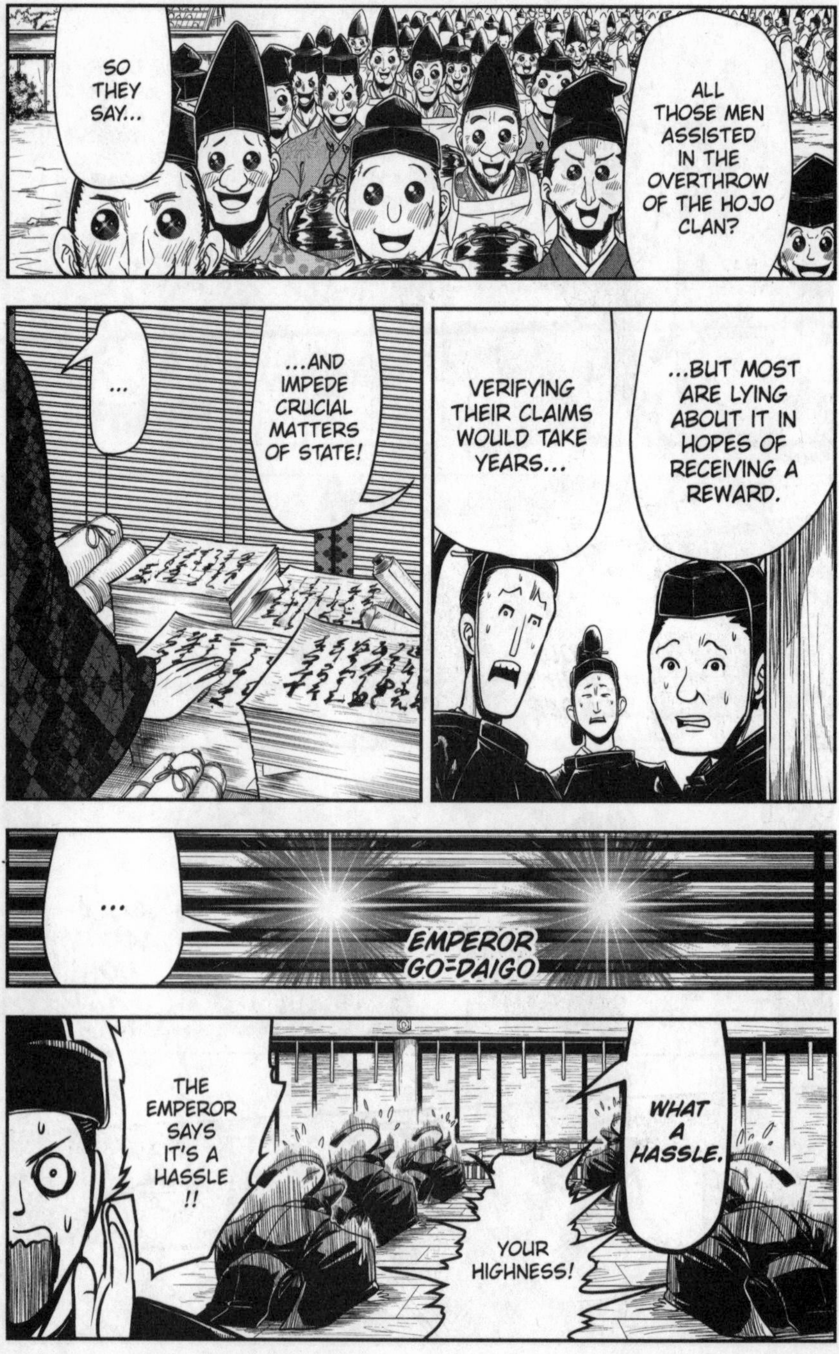
ALL THOSE MEN ASSISTED IN THE OVERTHROW OF THE HOJO CLAN?
SO THEY SAY...
...BUT MOST ARE LYING ABOUT IT IN HOPES OF RECEIVING A REWARD.
VERIFYING THEIR CLAIMS WOULD TAKE YEARS...
...AND IMPEDE CRUCIAL MATTERS OF STATE!
...
EMPEROR GO-DAIGO
...
WHAT A HASSLE.
YOUR HIGHNESS!
THE EMPEROR SAYS IT'S A HASSLE!!

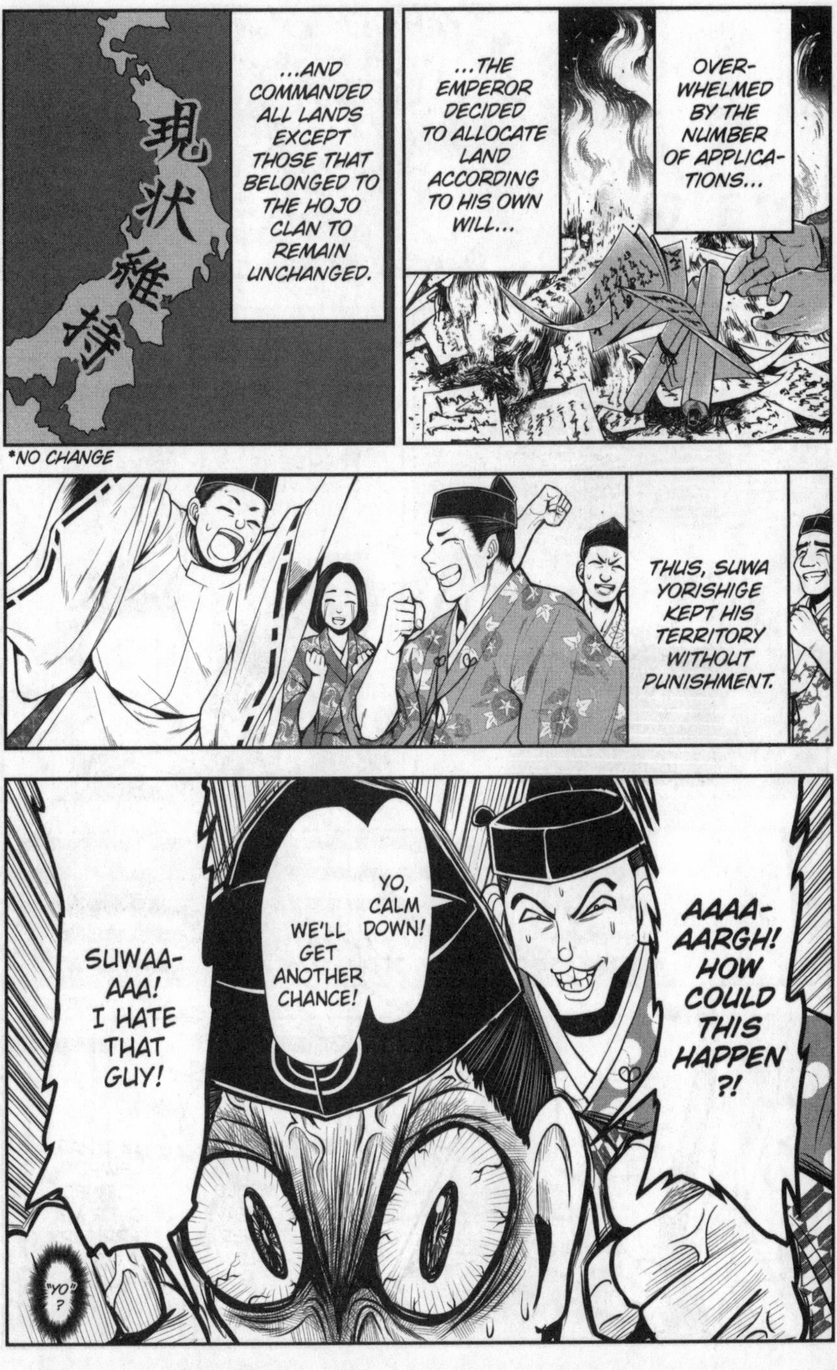
OVER-WHELMED BY THE NUMBER OF APPLICA-TIONS...
...THE EMPEROR DECIDED TO ALLOCATE LAND ACCORDING TO HIS OWN WILL...
...AND COMMANDED ALL LANDS EXCEPT THOSE THAT BELONGED TO THE HOJO CLAN TO REMAIN UNCHANGED.
現状維持
*NO CHANGE
THUS, SUWA YORISHIGE KEPT HIS TERRITORY WITHOUT PUNISHMENT.
AAAA-AARGH! HOW COULD THIS HAPPEN?!
YO, CALM DOWN!
WE'LL GET ANOTHER CHANCE!
SUWAA-AAA! I HATE THAT GUY!
"YO"?

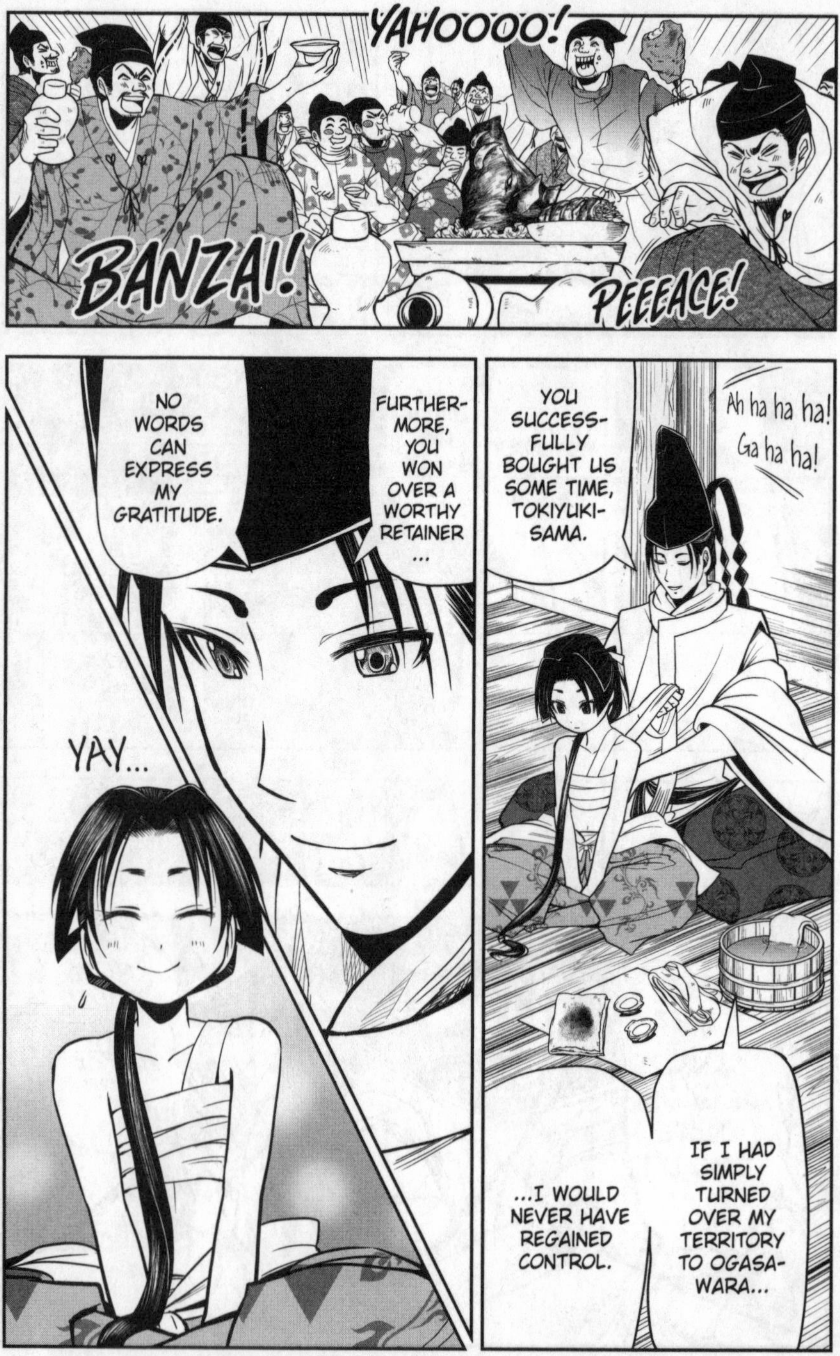
YAHOOOO!
PEEEACE!
BANZAI!
YOU SUCCESS-FULLY BOUGHT US SOME TIME, TOKIYUKI-SAMA.
Ah ha ha ha!
Ga ha ha!
IF I HAD SIMPLY TURNED OVER MY TERRITORY TO OGASA-WARA...
...I WOULD NEVER HAVE REGAINED CONTROL.
FURTHER-MORE, YOU WON OVER A WORTHY RETAINER...
NO WORDS CAN EXPRESS MY GRATITUDE.
YAY...

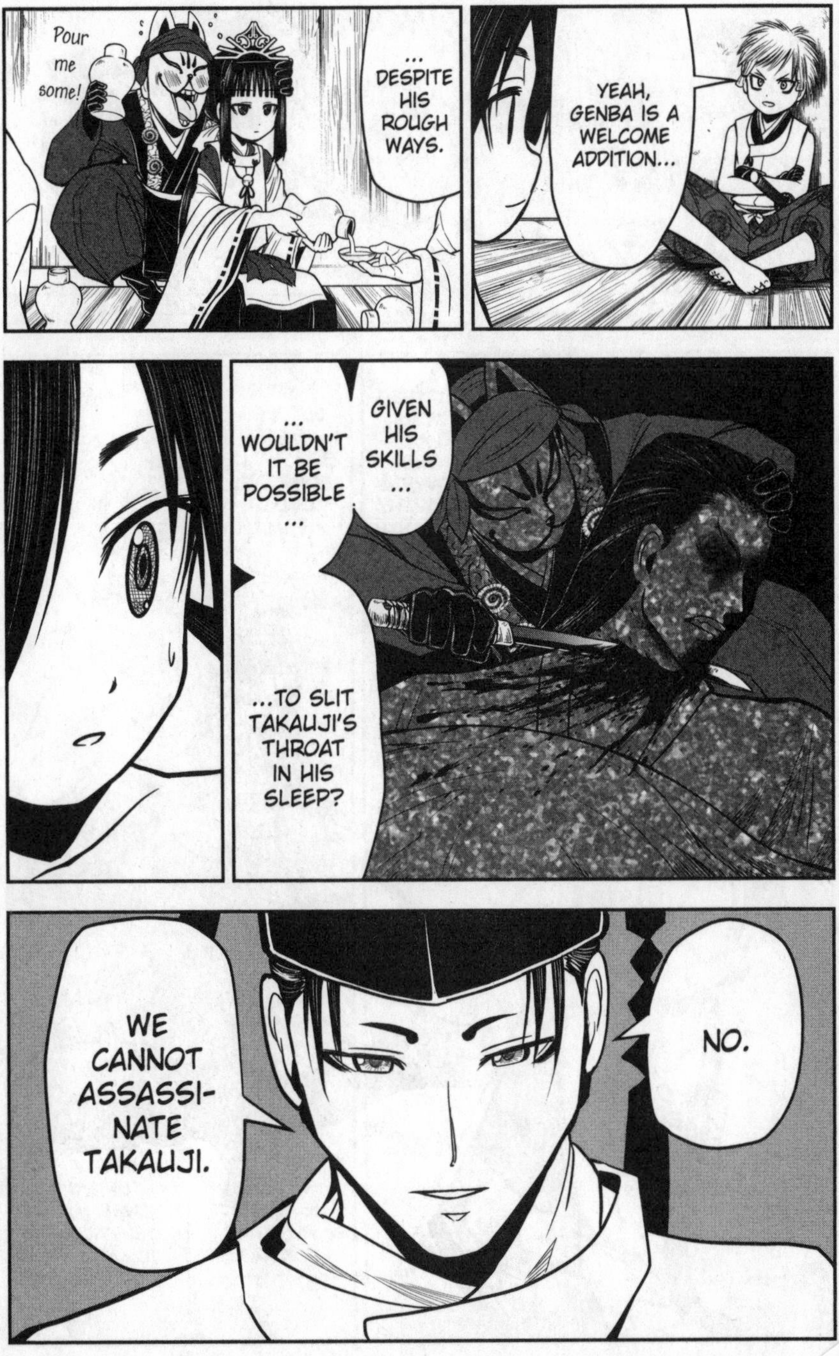
YEAH, GENBA IS A WELCOME ADDITION...
... DESPITE HIS ROUGH WAYS.
Pour me some!
GIVEN HIS SKILLS ...
... WOULDN'T IT BE POSSIBLE ...
...TO SLIT TAKAUJI'S THROAT IN HIS SLEEP?
NO.
WE CANNOT ASSASSI-NATE TAKAUJI.

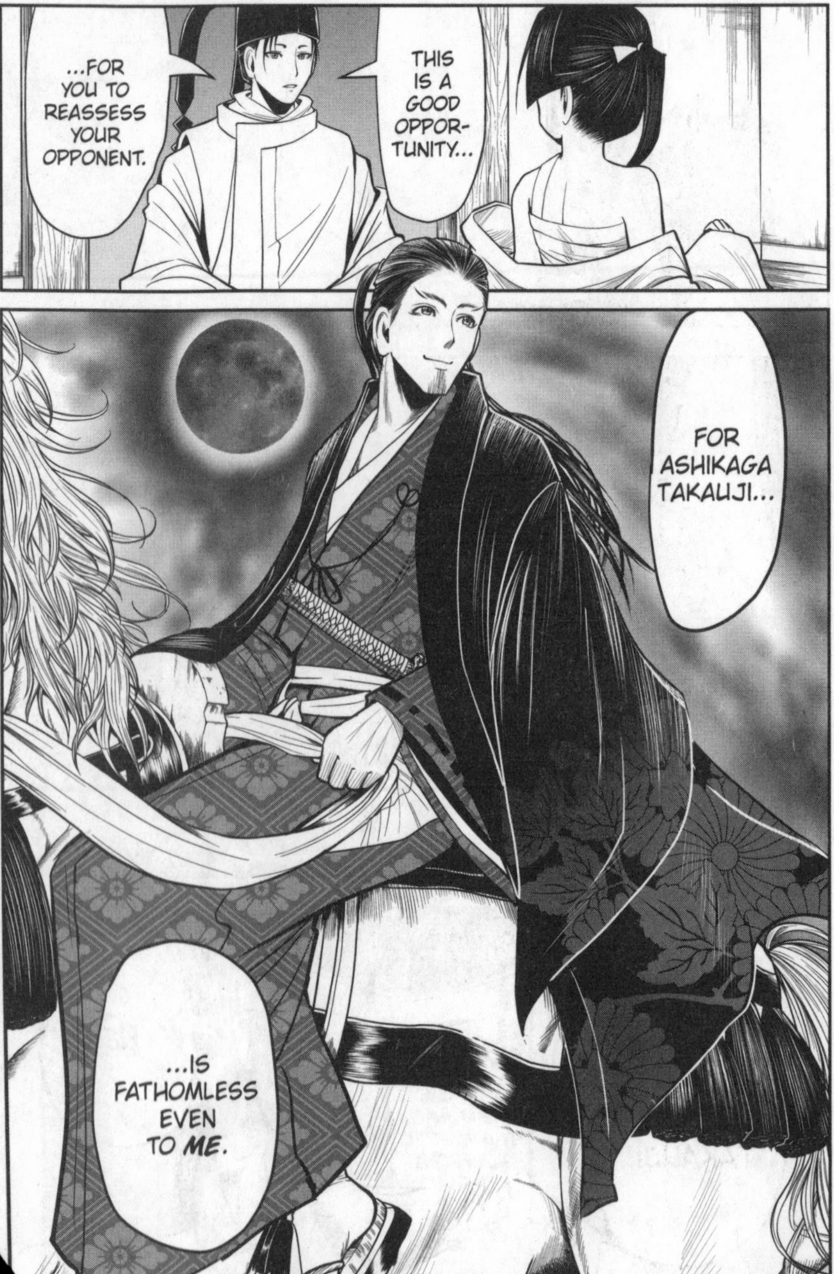
THIS IS A GOOD OPPORTUNITY...
...FOR YOU TO REASSESS YOUR OPPONENT.
FOR ASHIKAGA TAKAUJI...
...IS FATHOMLESS EVEN TO *ME*.

Really Laying It On

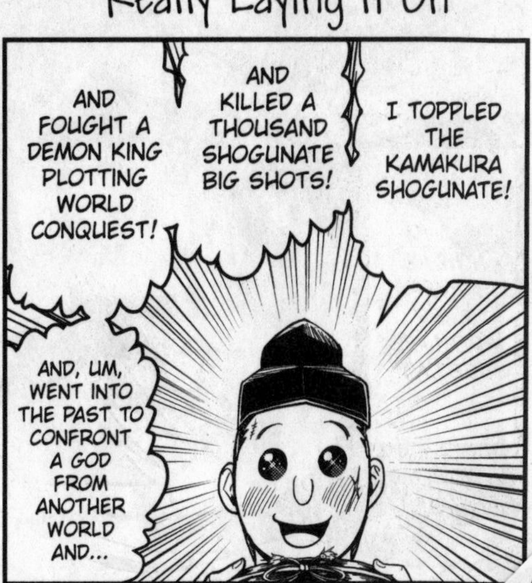
I TOPPLED THE KAMAKURA SHOGUNATE!
AND KILLED A THOUSAND SHOGUNATE BIG SHOTS!
AND FOUGHT A DEMON KING PLOTTING WORLD CONQUEST!
AND, UM, WENT INTO THE PAST TO CONFRONT A GOD FROM ANOTHER WORLD AND...

CHAPTER 15: TAKAUJI 1333

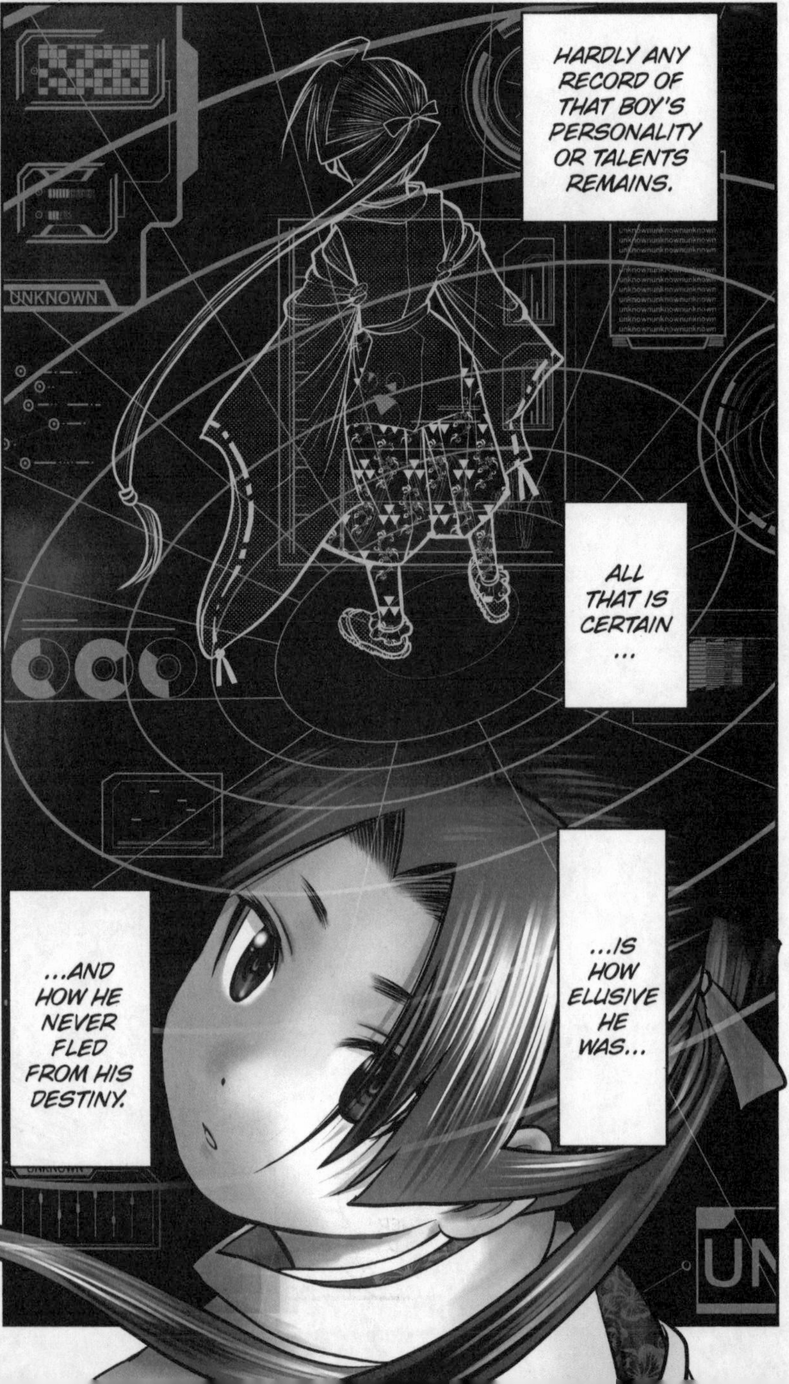

HARDLY ANY RECORD OF THAT BOY'S PERSONALITY OR TALENTS REMAINS.
UNKNOWN
ALL THAT IS CERTAIN ...
...IS HOW ELUSIVE HE WAS...
...AND HOW HE NEVER FLED FROM HIS DESTINY.

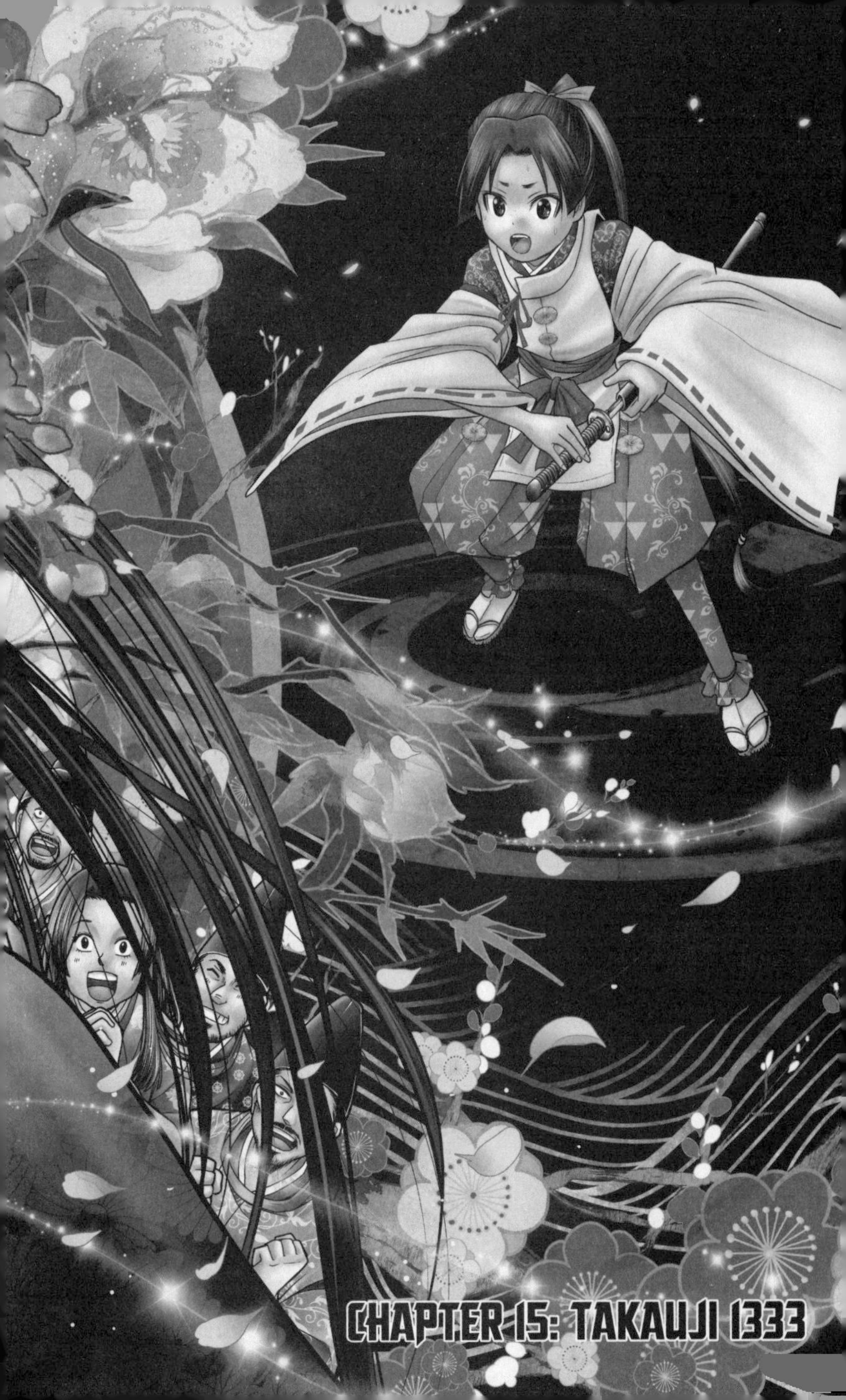
CHAPTER 15: TAKAUJI 1333

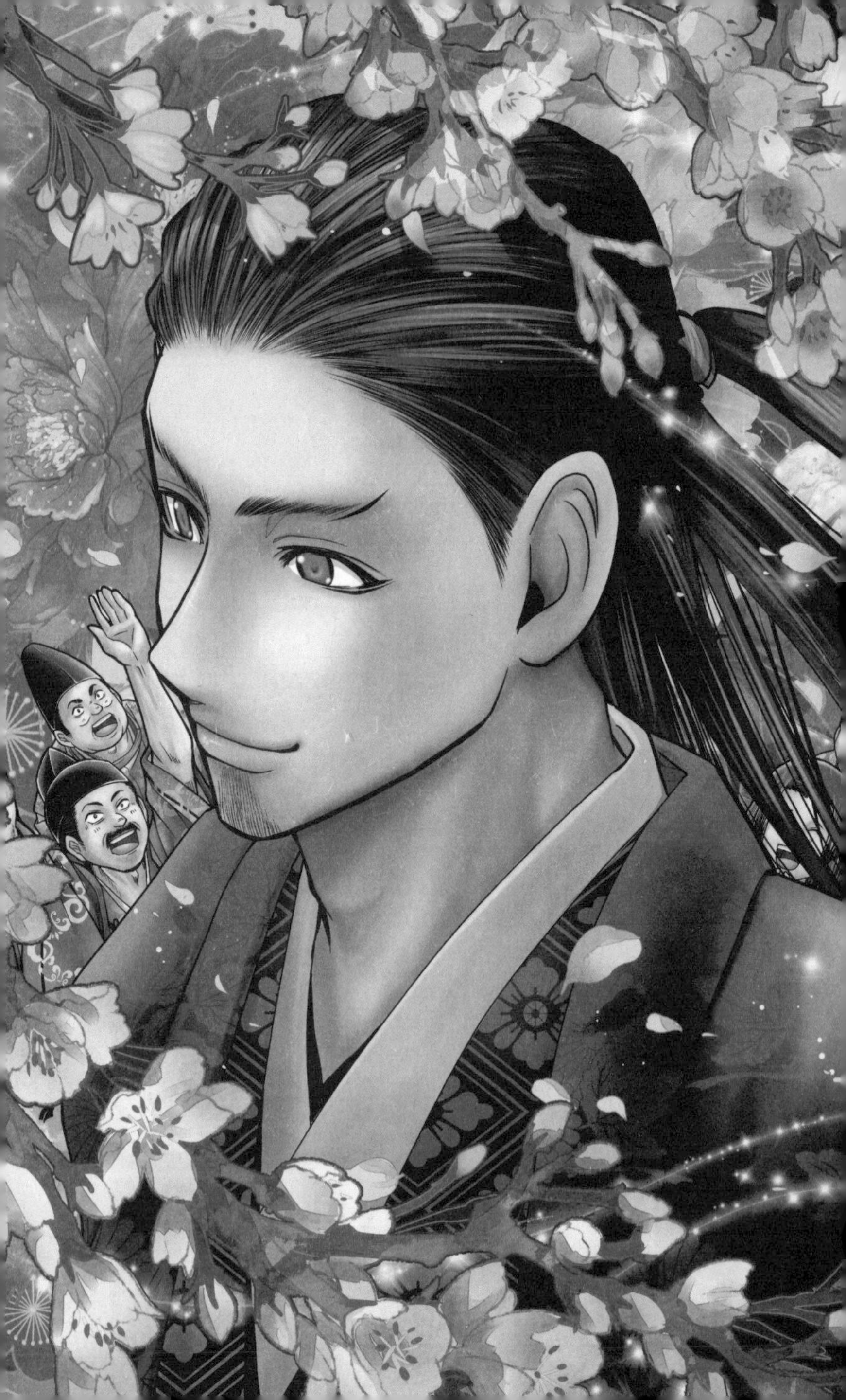

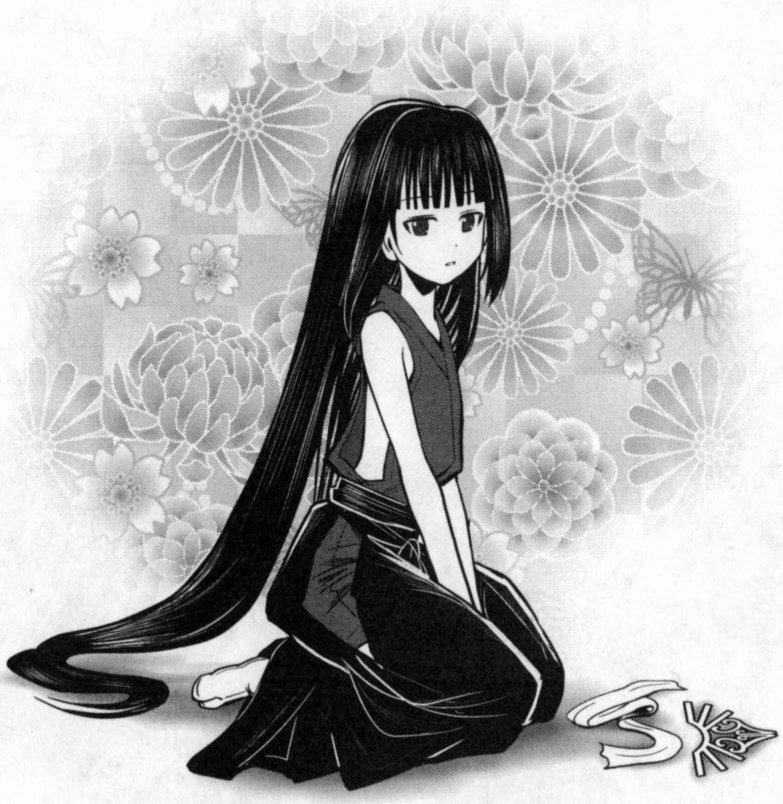

THE ELUSIVE SAMURAI

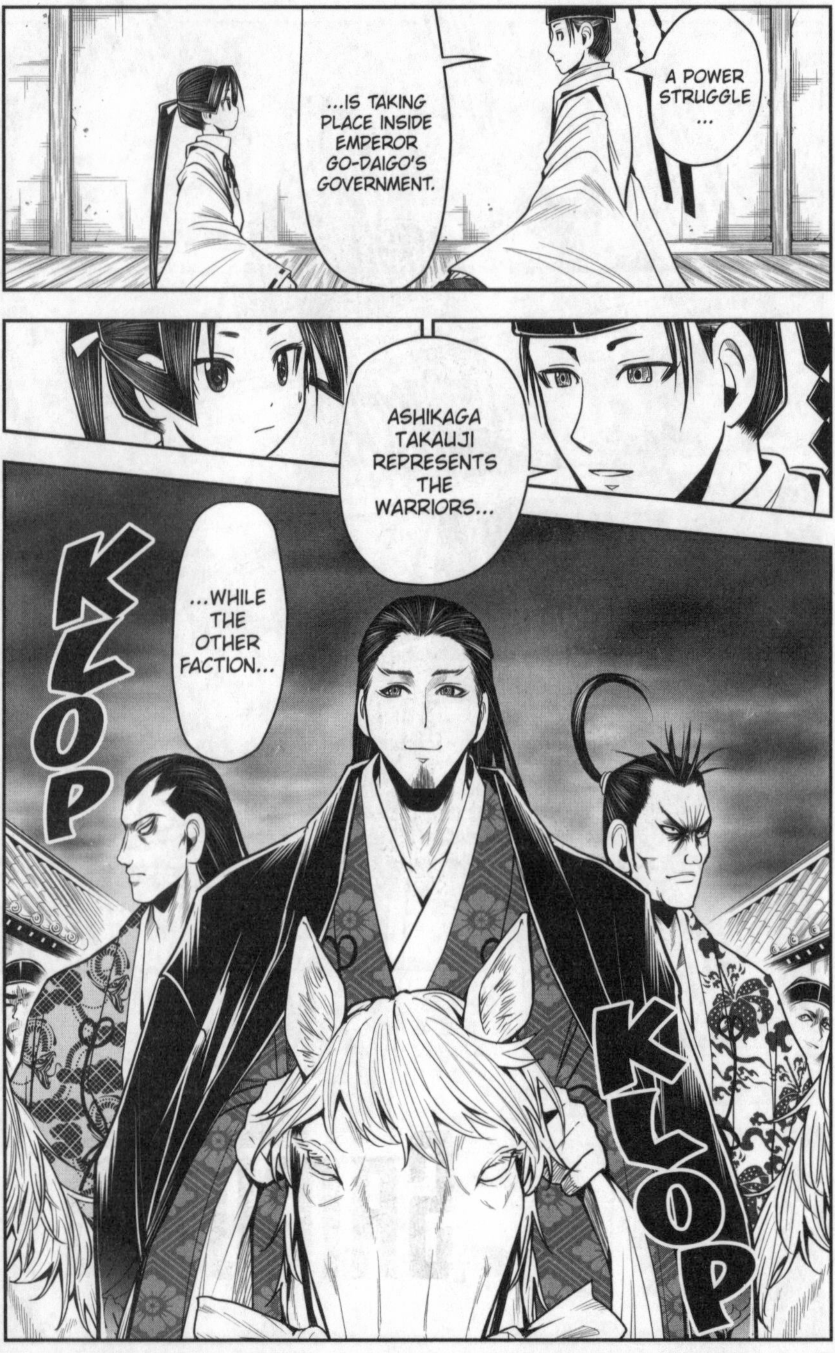
A POWER STRUGGLE ...
...IS TAKING PLACE INSIDE EMPEROR GO-DAIGO'S GOVERNMENT.
ASHIKAGA TAKAUJI REPRESENTS THE WARRIORS...
...WHILE THE OTHER FACTION...
KLOP
KLOP

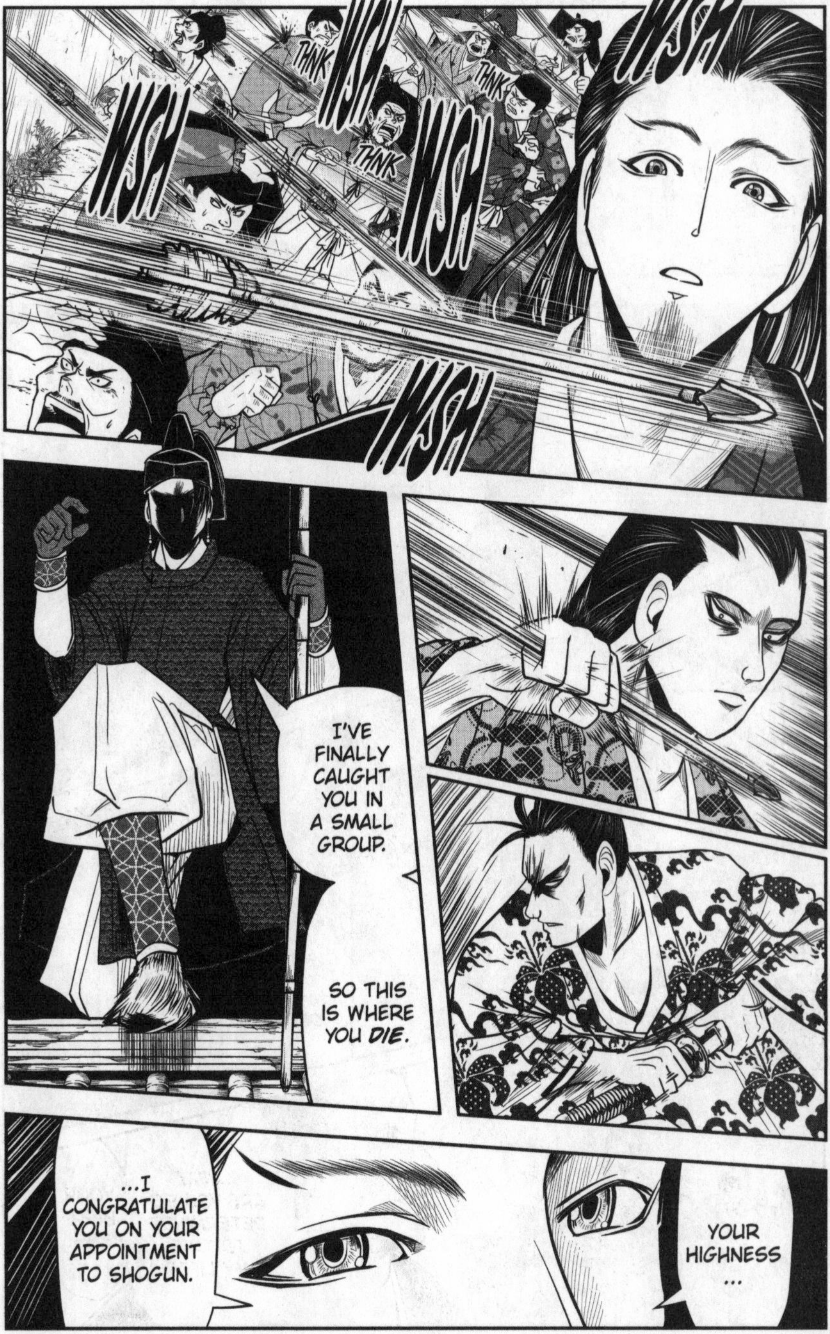
WSCH
WSCH
THNK
THNK
THNK
WSCH
WSCH
WSCH
I'VE FINALLY CAUGHT YOU IN A SMALL GROUP.
SO THIS IS WHERE YOU *DIE*.
YOUR HIGHNESS ...
...I CONGRATULATE YOU ON YOUR APPOINTMENT TO SHOGUN.

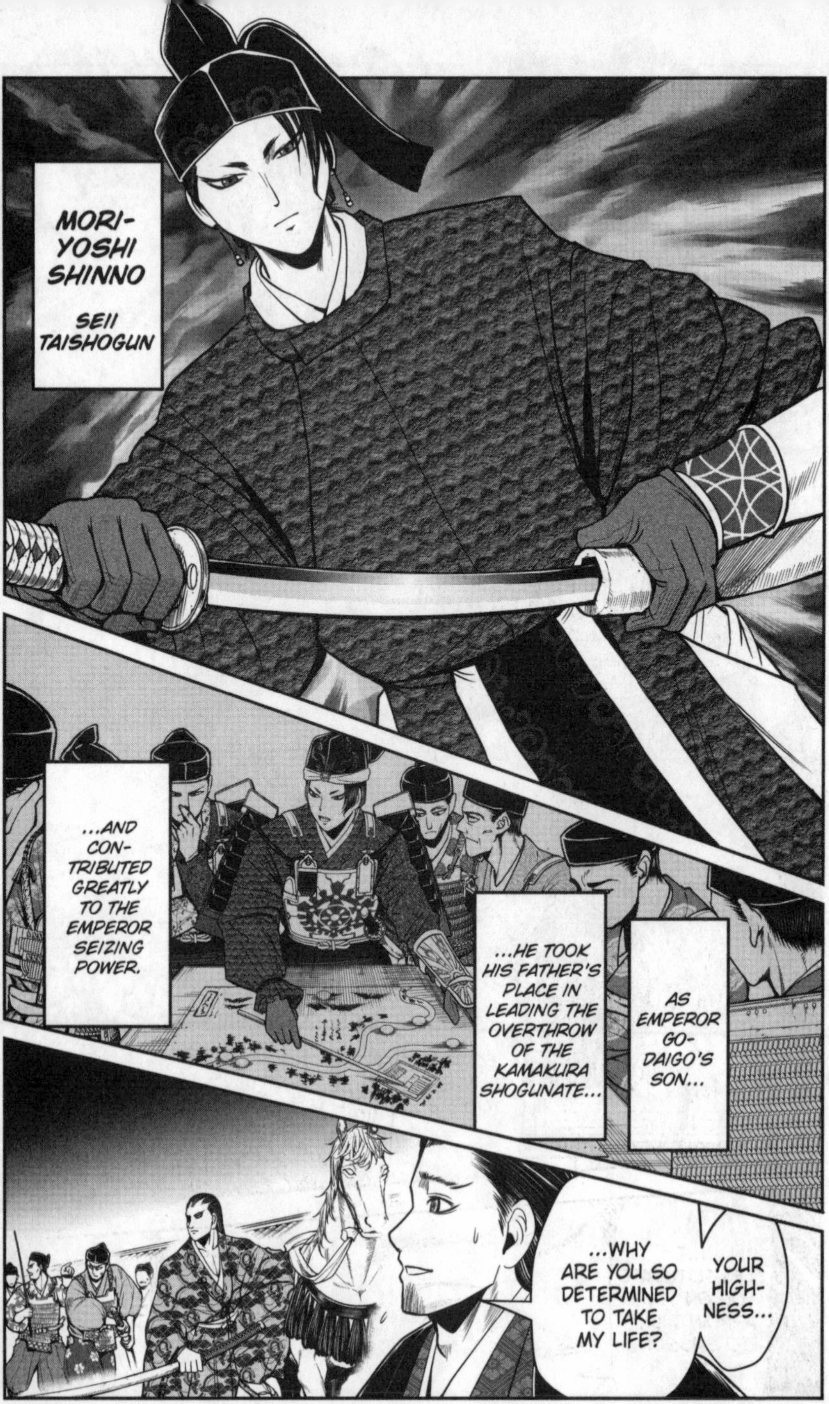
MORI-YOSHI SHINNO
SEII TAISHOGUN
AS EMPEROR GO-DAIGO'S SON...
...HE TOOK HIS FATHER'S PLACE IN LEADING THE OVERTHROW OF THE KAMAKURA SHOGUNATE...
...AND CON-TRIBUTED GREATLY TO THE EMPEROR SEIZING POWER.
YOUR HIGH-NESS...
...WHY ARE YOU SO DETERMINED TO TAKE MY LIFE?

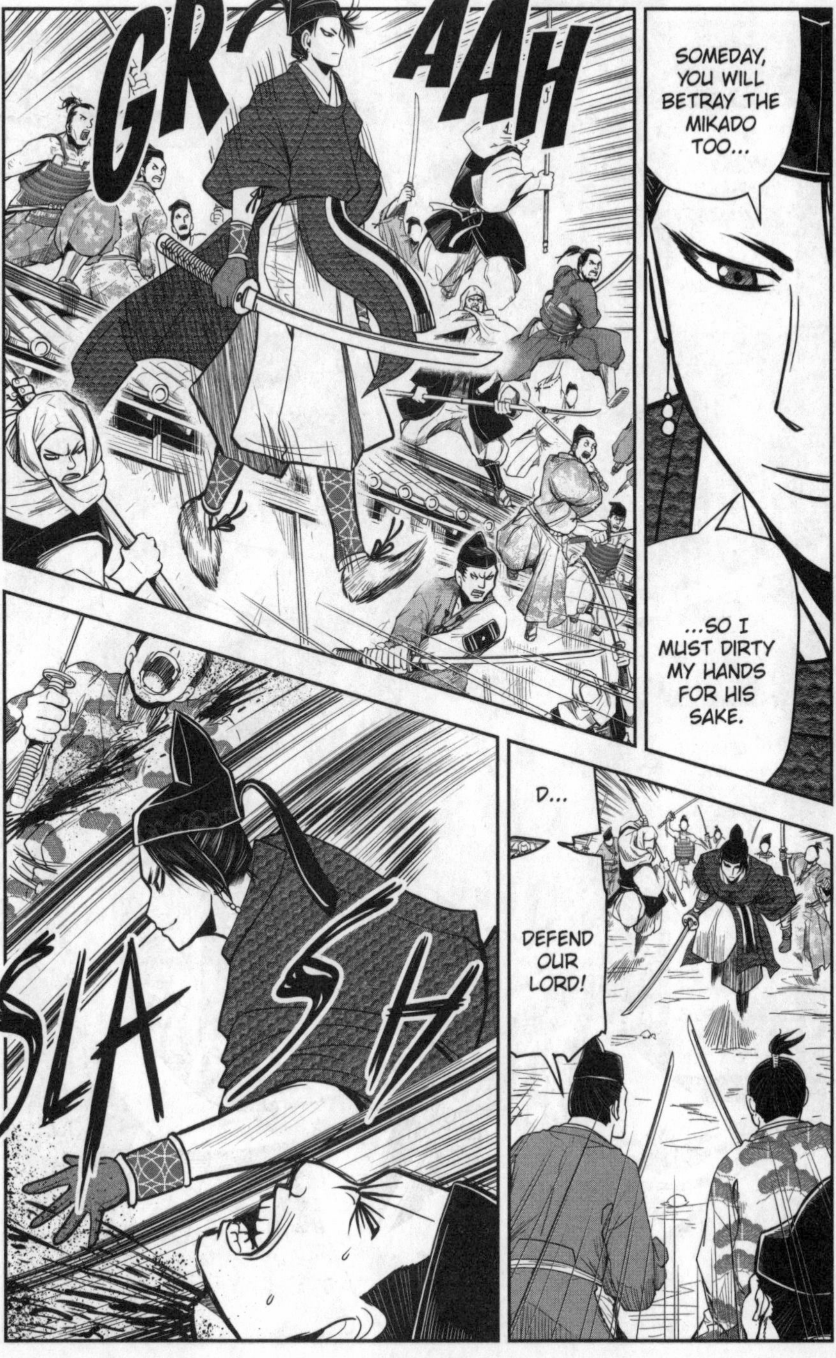
SOMEDAY, YOU WILL BETRAY THE MIKADO TOO...
...SO I MUST DIRTY MY HANDS FOR HIS SAKE.
GR AAH
D...
DEFEND OUR LORD!
SLASH

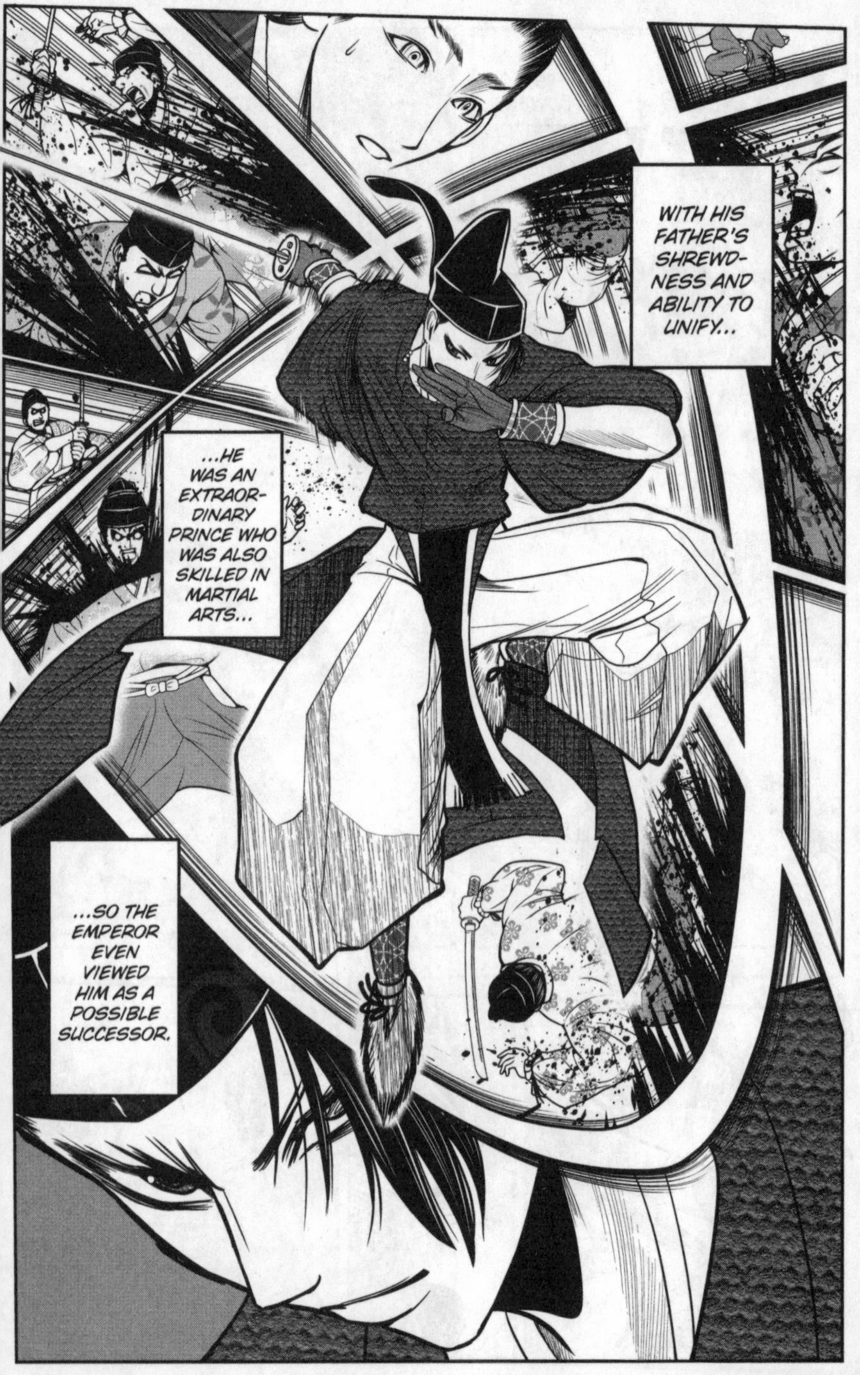
WITH HIS FATHER'S SHREWD-NESS AND ABILITY TO UNIFY...
...HE WAS AN EXTRAOR-DINARY PRINCE WHO WAS ALSO SKILLED IN MARTIAL ARTS...
...SO THE EMPEROR EVEN VIEWED HIM AS A POSSIBLE SUCCESSOR.

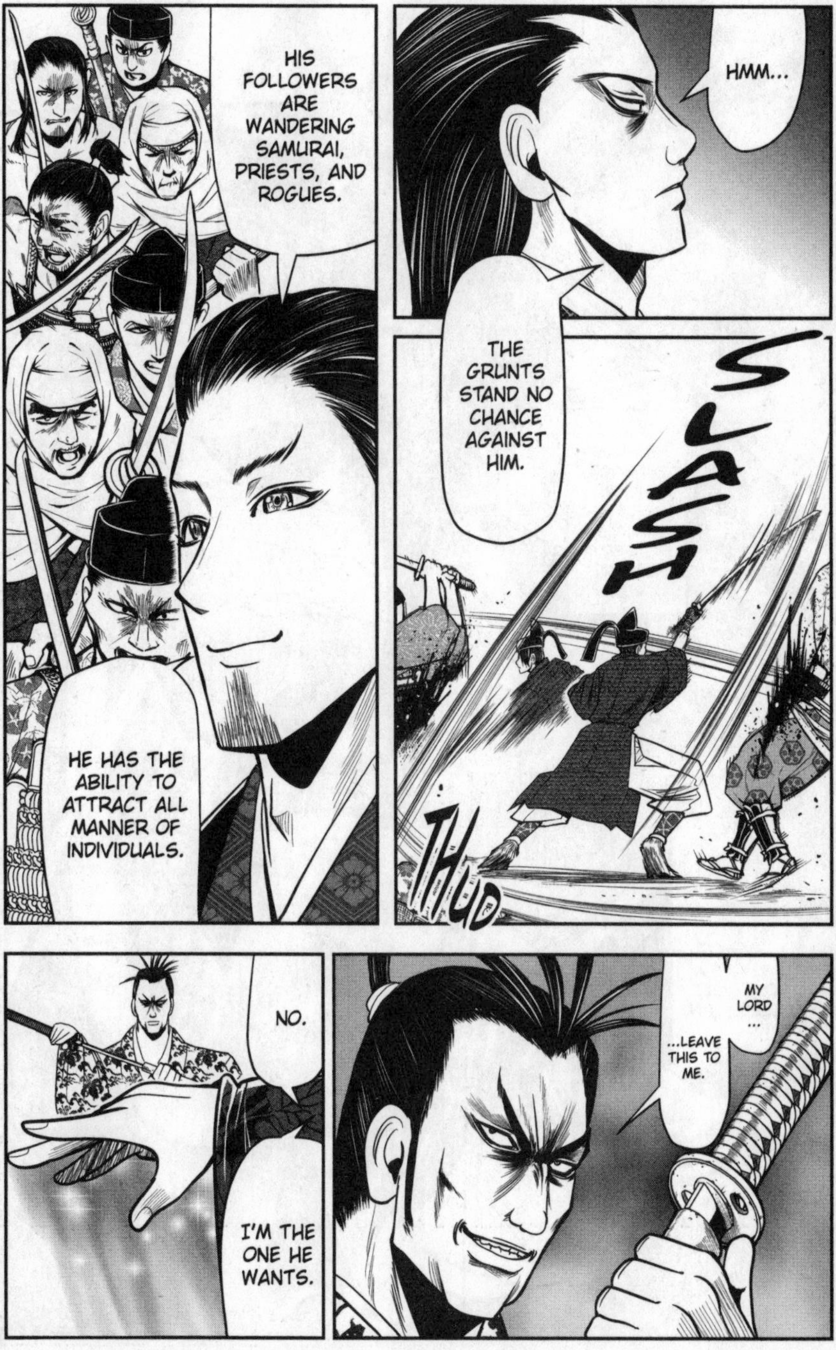
HMM...
THE GRUNTS STAND NO CHANCE AGAINST HIM.
SLASH
THUD
HIS FOLLOWERS ARE WANDERING SAMURAI, PRIESTS, AND ROGUES.
HE HAS THE ABILITY TO ATTRACT ALL MANNER OF INDIVIDUALS.
MY LORD ...
...LEAVE THIS TO ME.
NO.
I'M THE ONE HE WANTS.

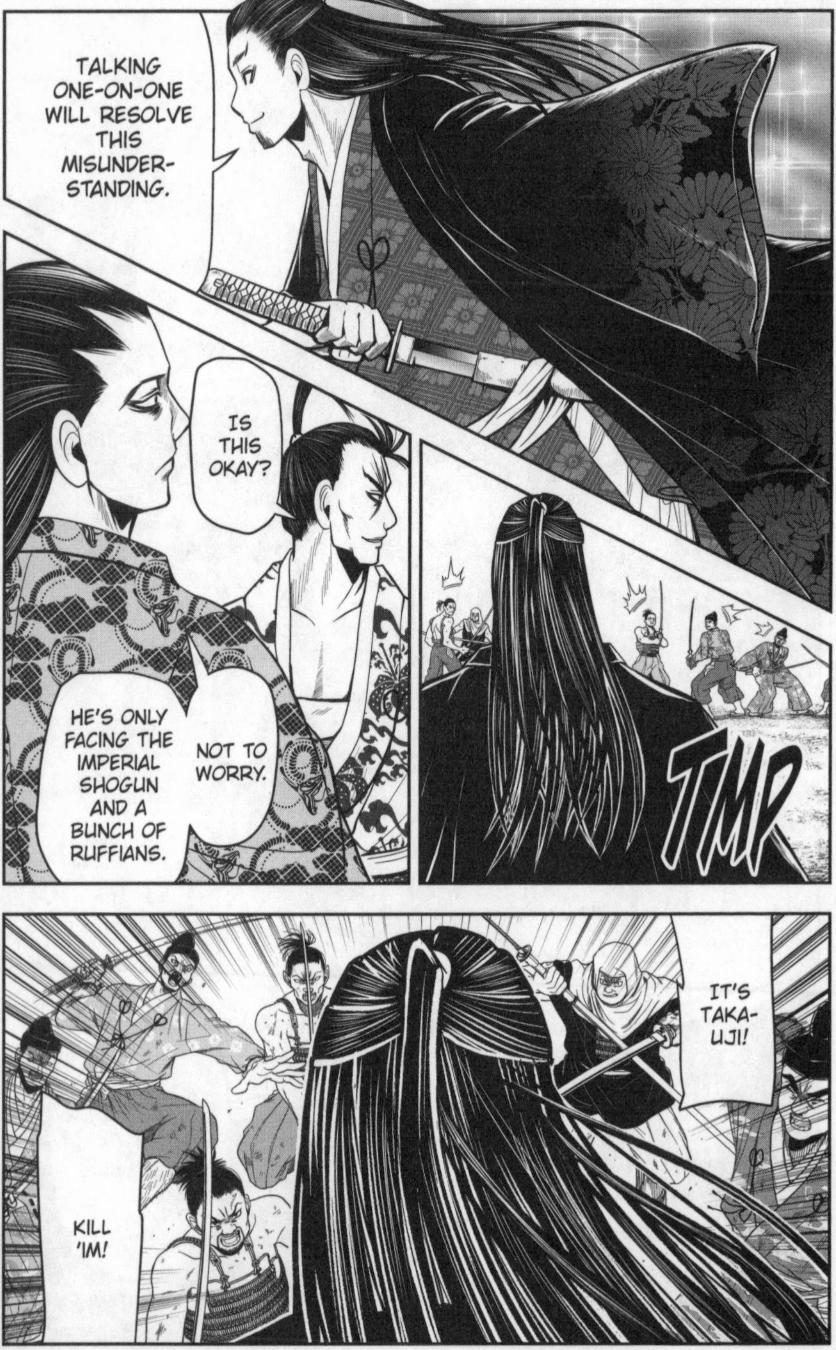

TALKING ONE-ON-ONE WILL RESOLVE THIS MISUNDER-STANDING.
TMP
IS THIS OKAY?
NOT TO WORRY.
HE'S ONLY FACING THE IMPERIAL SHOGUN AND A BUNCH OF RUFFIANS.
IT'S TAKA-UJI!
KILL 'IM!

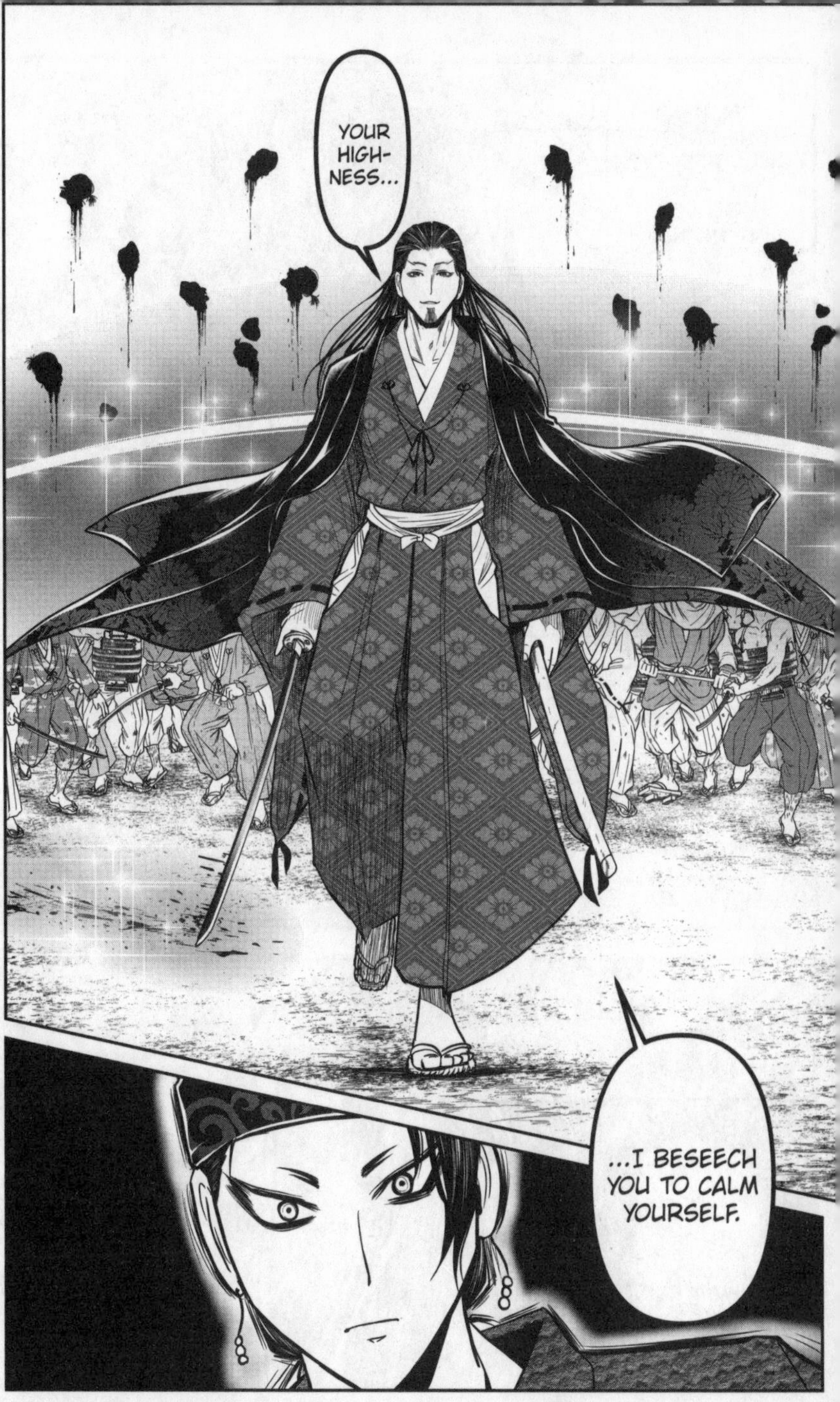
YOUR HIGH-NESS...
...I BESEECH YOU TO CALM YOURSELF.

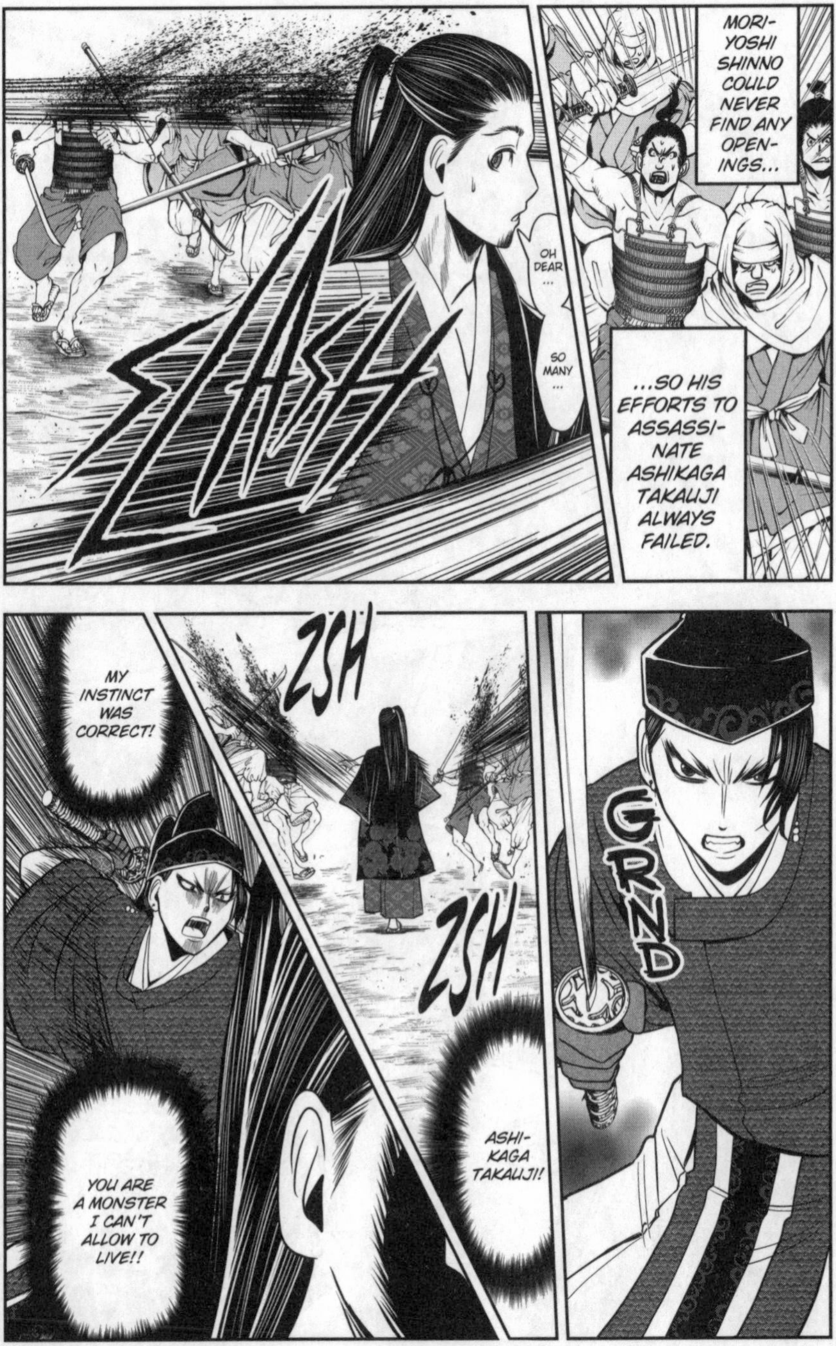
MORI-YOSHI SHINNO COULD NEVER FIND ANY OPEN-INGS...
...SO HIS EFFORTS TO ASSASSI-NATE ASHIKAGA TAKAUJI ALWAYS FAILED.
OH DEAR ...
SO MANY ...
SLASH
GRND
ZSH
ZSH
MY INSTINCT WAS CORRECT!
ASHI-KAGA TAKAUJI!
YOU ARE A MONSTER I CAN'T ALLOW TO LIVE!!

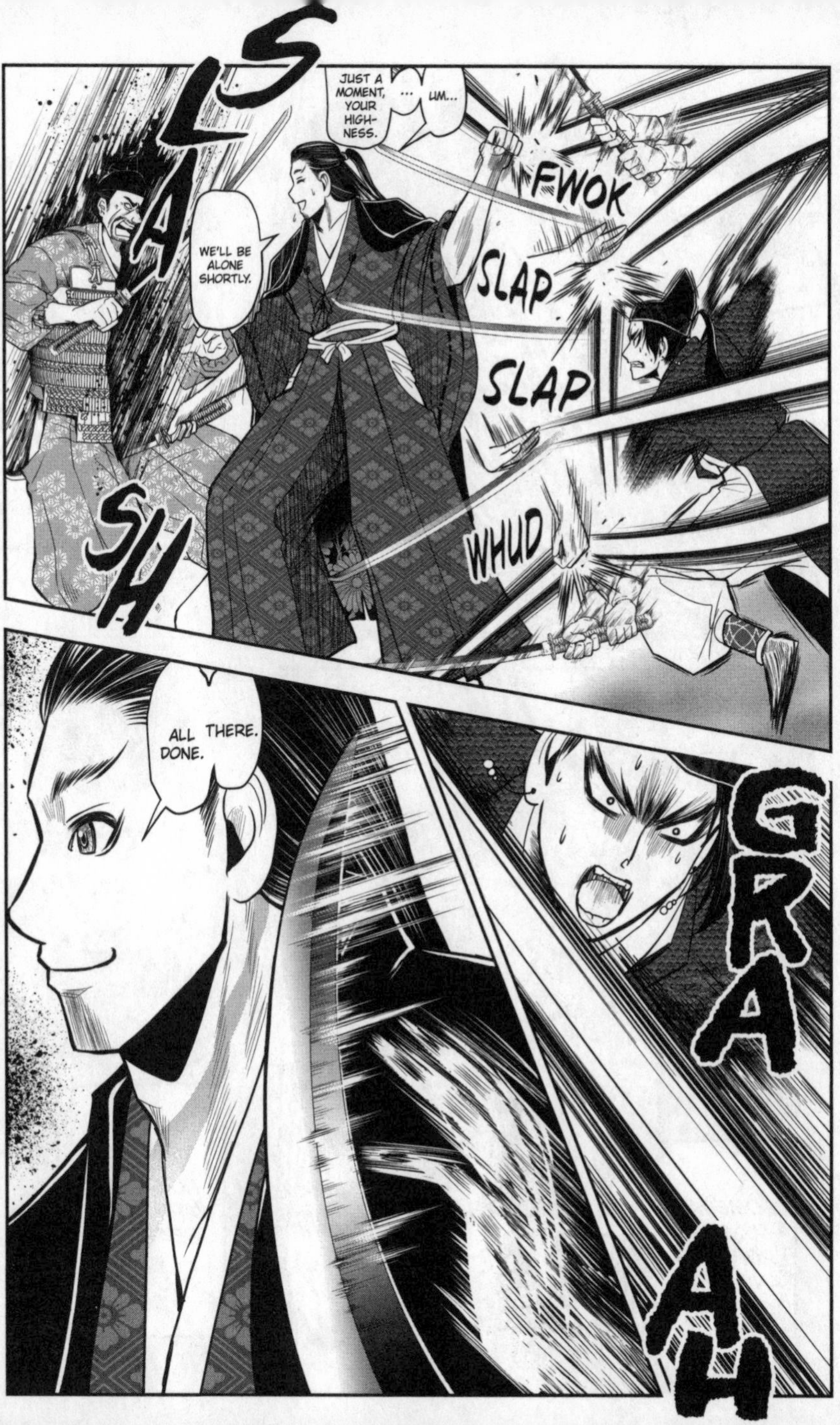
... UM...
JUST A MOMENT, YOUR HIGHNESS.
FWOK
SLAP
SLAP
WHUD
WE'LL BE ALONE SHORTLY.
SLASH
GRAAAH
THERE. ALL DONE.

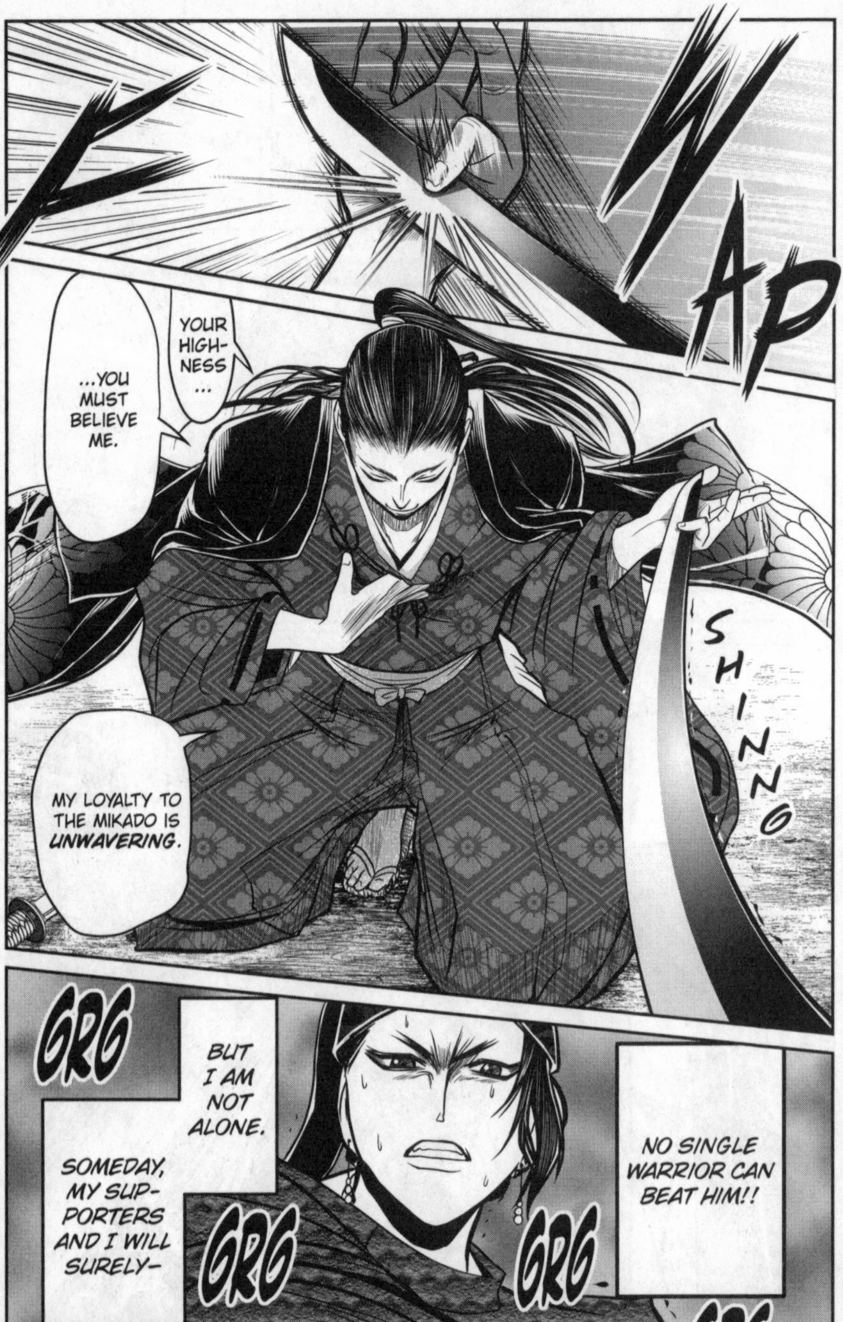
SNAP
YOUR HIGHNESS...
...YOU MUST BELIEVE ME.
SHINNG
MY LOYALTY TO THE MIKADO IS UNWAVERING.
GRG
NO SINGLE WARRIOR CAN BEAT HIM!!
BUT I AM NOT ALONE.
SOMEDAY, MY SUPPORTERS AND I WILL SURELY-
GRG
GRG
GRG

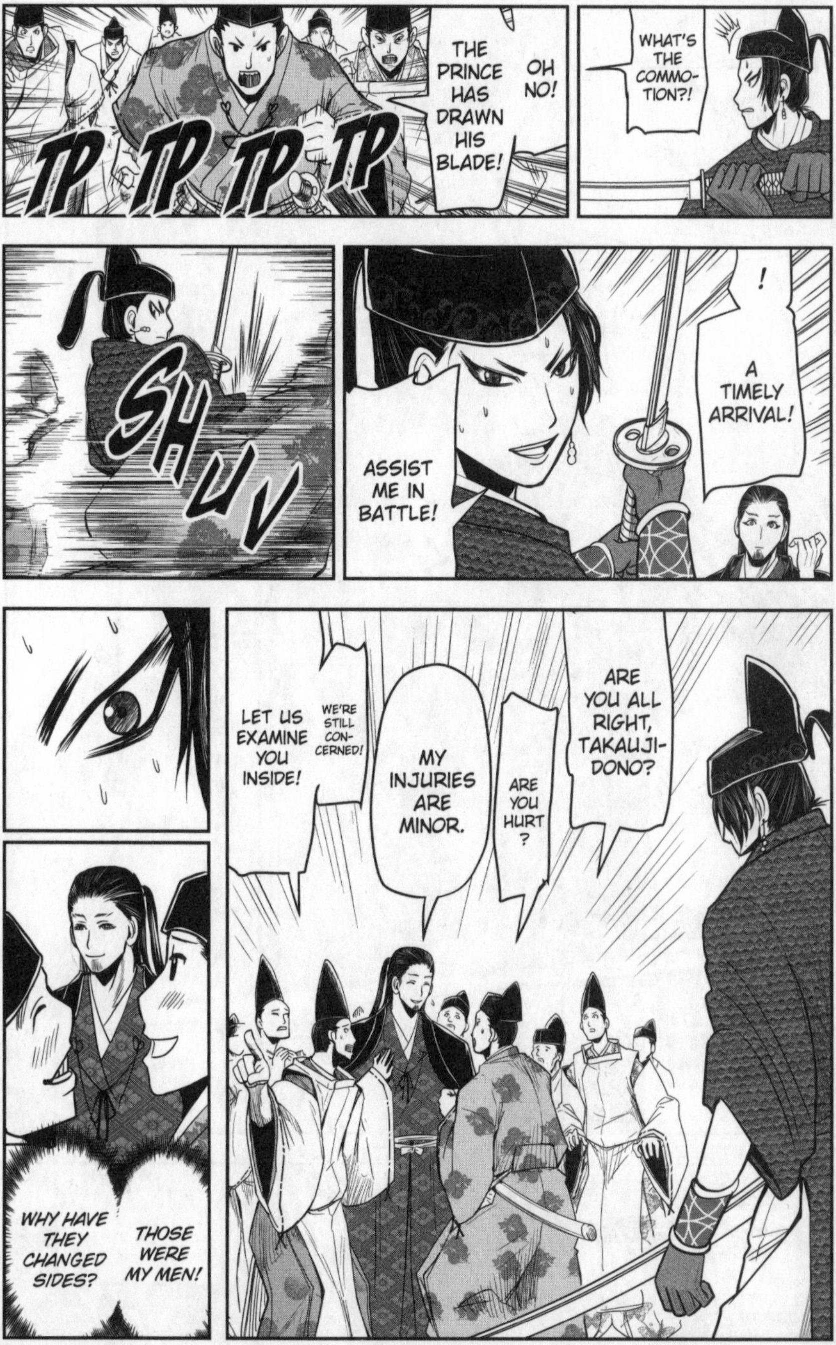
WHAT'S THE COMMOTION?!
OH NO!
THE PRINCE HAS DRAWN HIS BLADE!
TP TP TP TP
!
A TIMELY ARRIVAL!
ASSIST ME IN BATTLE!
SHUV
ARE YOU ALL RIGHT, TAKAUJI-DONO?
ARE YOU HURT?
MY INJURIES ARE MINOR.
WE'RE STILL CONCERNED!
LET US EXAMINE YOU INSIDE!
THOSE WERE MY MEN!
WHY HAVE THEY CHANGED SIDES?

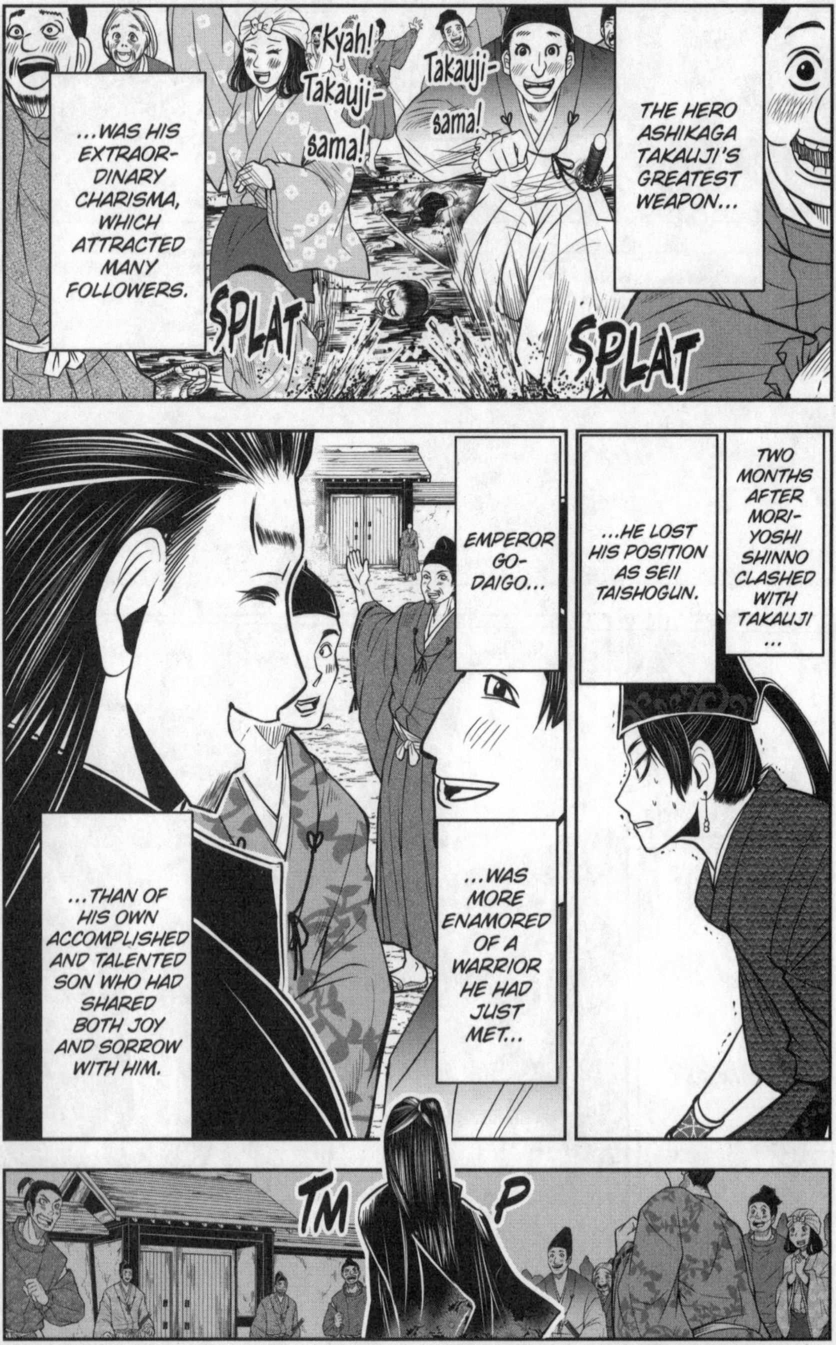
THE HERO ASHIKAGA TAKAUJI'S GREATEST WEAPON...
Takauji-sama!
Kyah! Takauji-sama!
...WAS HIS EXTRAOR-DINARY CHARISMA, WHICH ATTRACTED MANY FOLLOWERS.
SPLAT
SPLAT
TWO MONTHS AFTER MORI-YOSHI SHINNO CLASHED WITH TAKAUJI ...
...HE LOST HIS POSITION AS SEII TAISHOGUN.
EMPEROR GO-DAIGO...
...WAS MORE ENAMORED OF A WARRIOR HE HAD JUST MET...
...THAN OF HIS OWN ACCOMPLISHED AND TALENTED SON WHO HAD SHARED BOTH JOY AND SORROW WITH HIM.
TMP

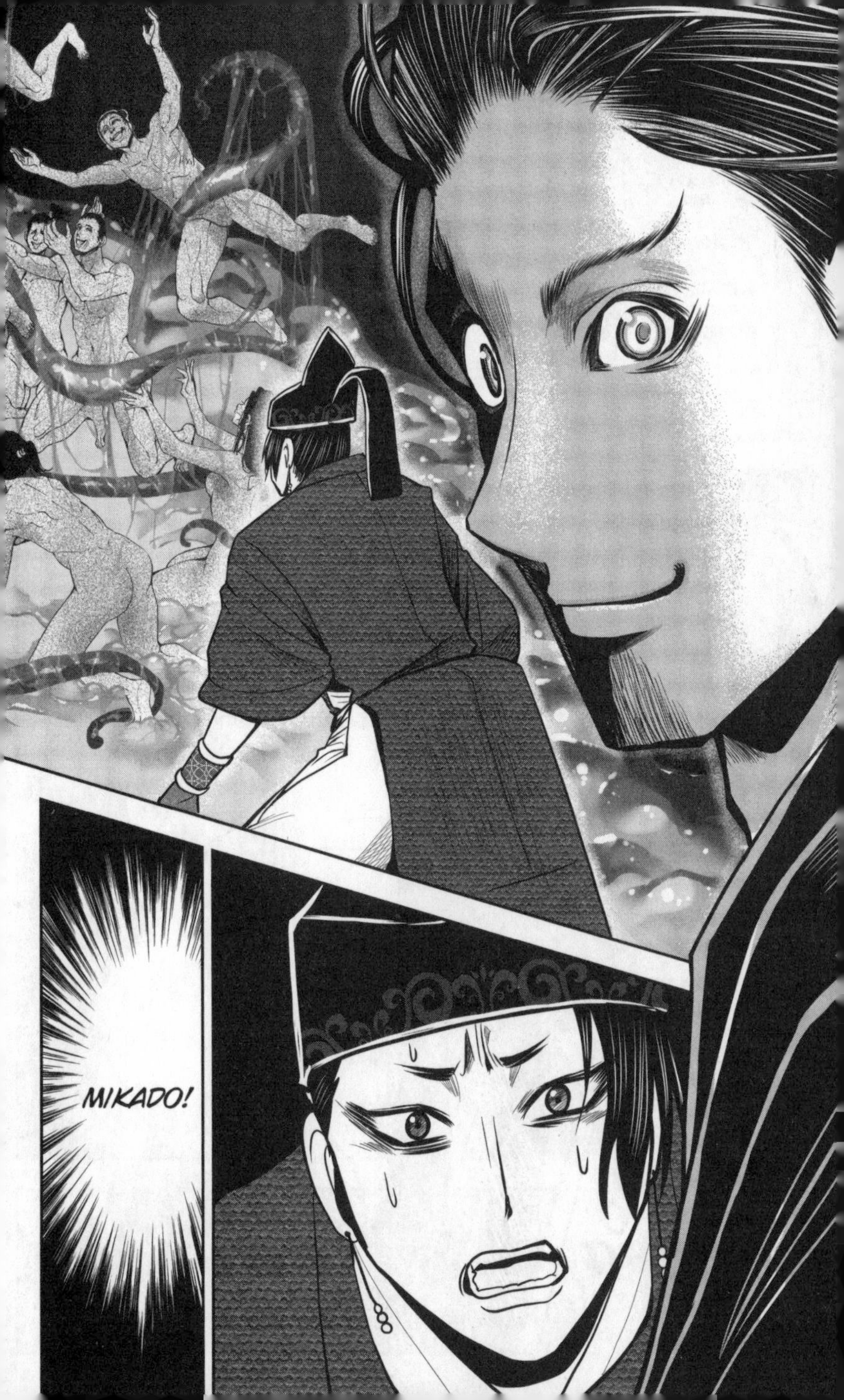
MIKADO!

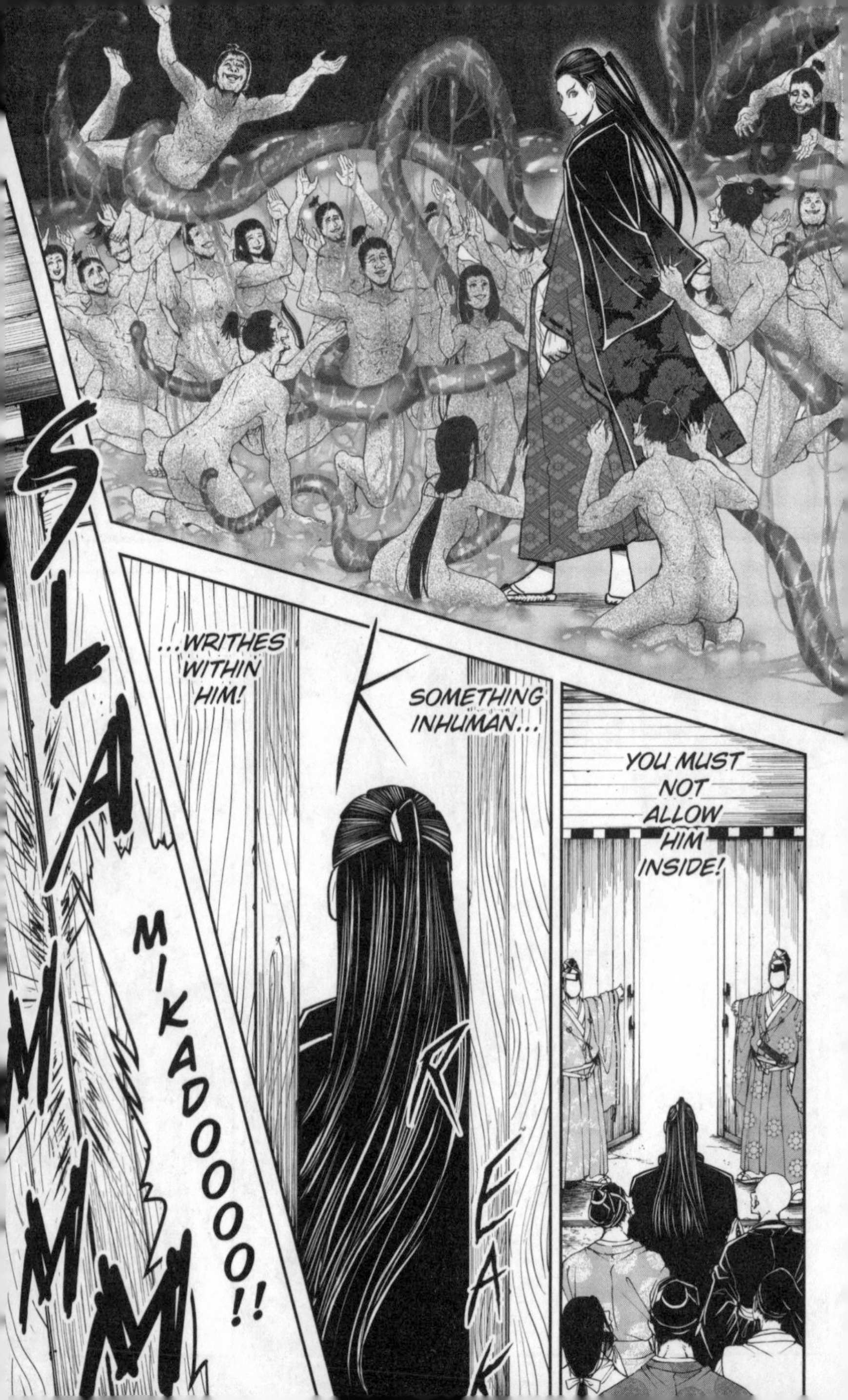
YOU MUST NOT ALLOW HIM INSIDE!
SOMETHING INHUMAN...
...WRITHES WITHIN HIM!
KREAK
SLAMMM
MIKADOOOOO!!

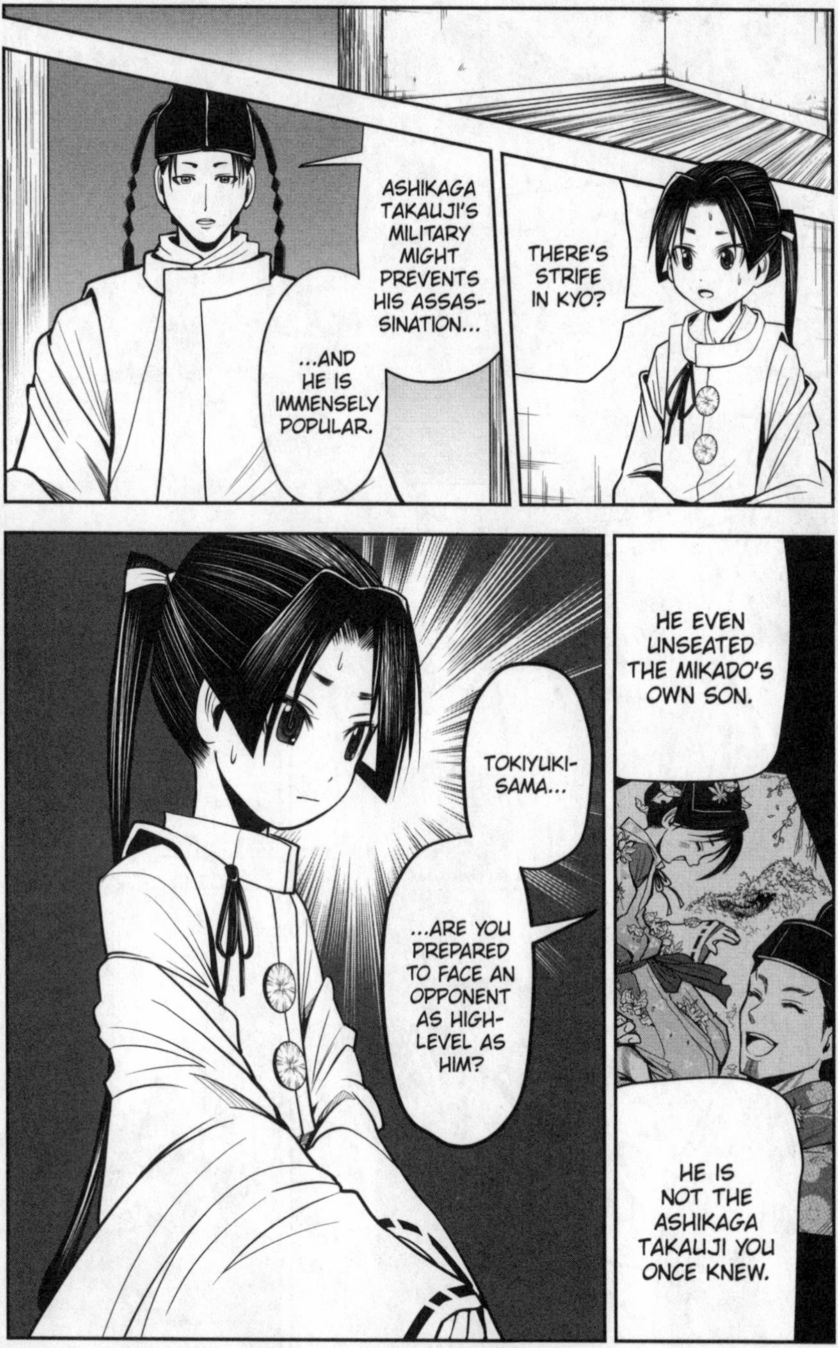
THERE'S STRIFE IN KYO?
ASHIKAGA TAKAUJI'S MILITARY MIGHT PREVENTS HIS ASSASSINATION...
...AND HE IS IMMENSELY POPULAR.
HE EVEN UNSEATED THE MIKADO'S OWN SON.
HE IS NOT THE ASHIKAGA TAKAUJI YOU ONCE KNEW.
TOKIYUKI-SAMA...
...ARE YOU PREPARED TO FACE AN OPPONENT AS HIGH-LEVEL AS HIM?

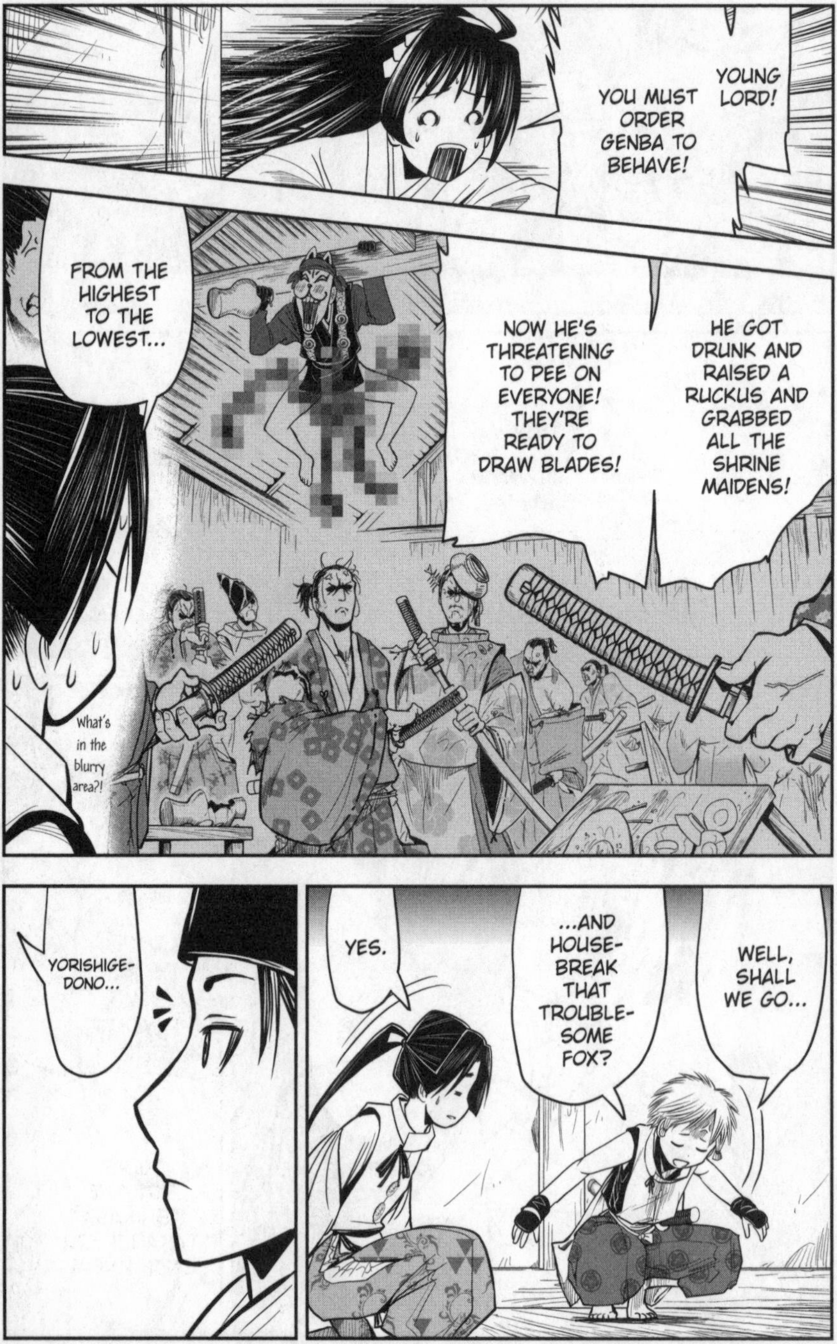
YOUNG LORD!
YOU MUST ORDER GENBA TO BEHAVE!
HE GOT DRUNK AND RAISED A RUCKUS AND GRABBED ALL THE SHRINE MAIDENS!
NOW HE'S THREATENING TO PEE ON EVERYONE! THEY'RE READY TO DRAW BLADES!
FROM THE HIGHEST TO THE LOWEST...
What's in the blurry area?!
WELL, SHALL WE GO...
...AND HOUSE-BREAK THAT TROUBLE-SOME FOX?
YES.
YORISHIGE-DONO...

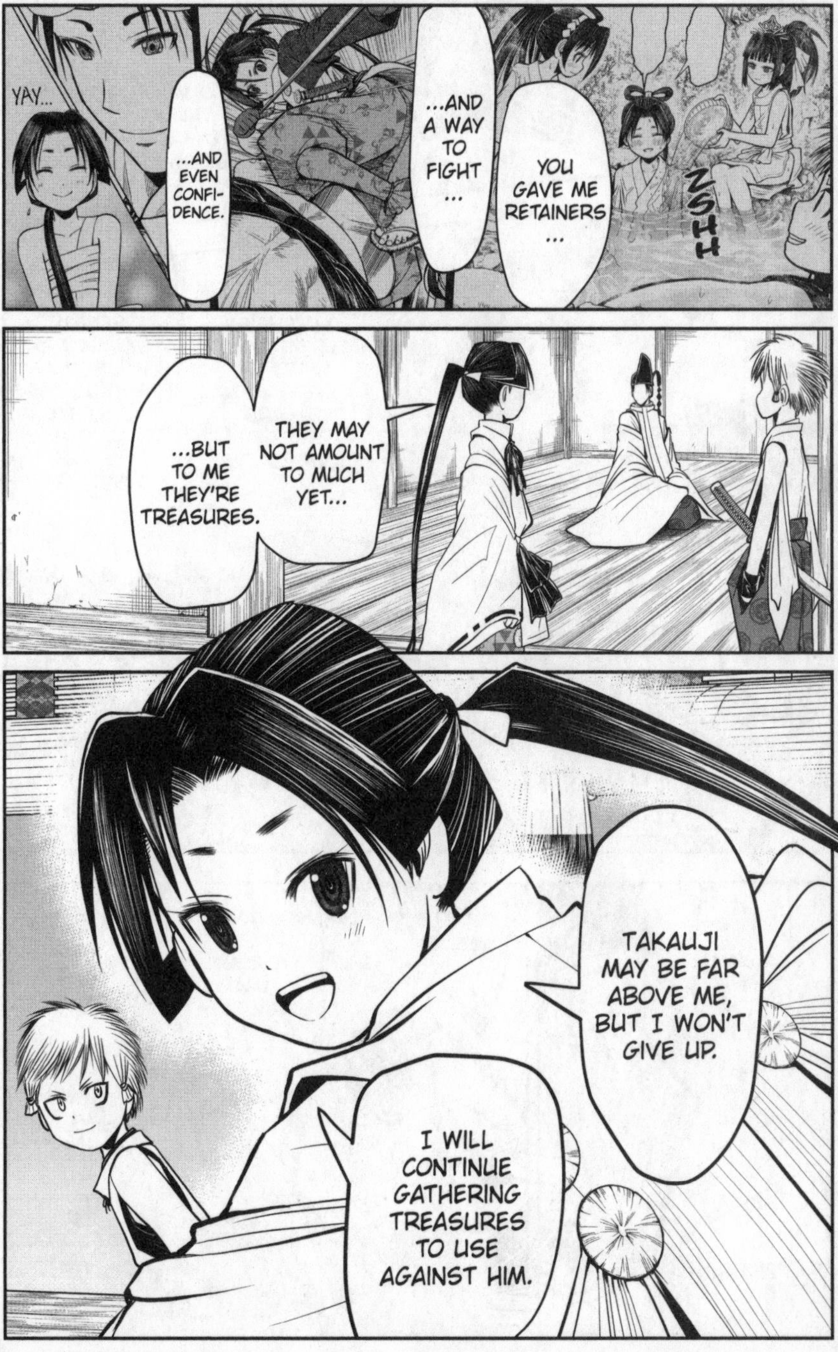
YOU GAVE ME RETAINERS...
ZSHH
...AND A WAY TO FIGHT...
...AND EVEN CONFIDENCE.
YAY...
THEY MAY NOT AMOUNT TO MUCH YET...
...BUT TO ME THEY'RE TREASURES.
TAKAUJI MAY BE FAR ABOVE ME, BUT I WON'T GIVE UP.
I WILL CONTINUE GATHERING TREASURES TO USE AGAINST HIM.

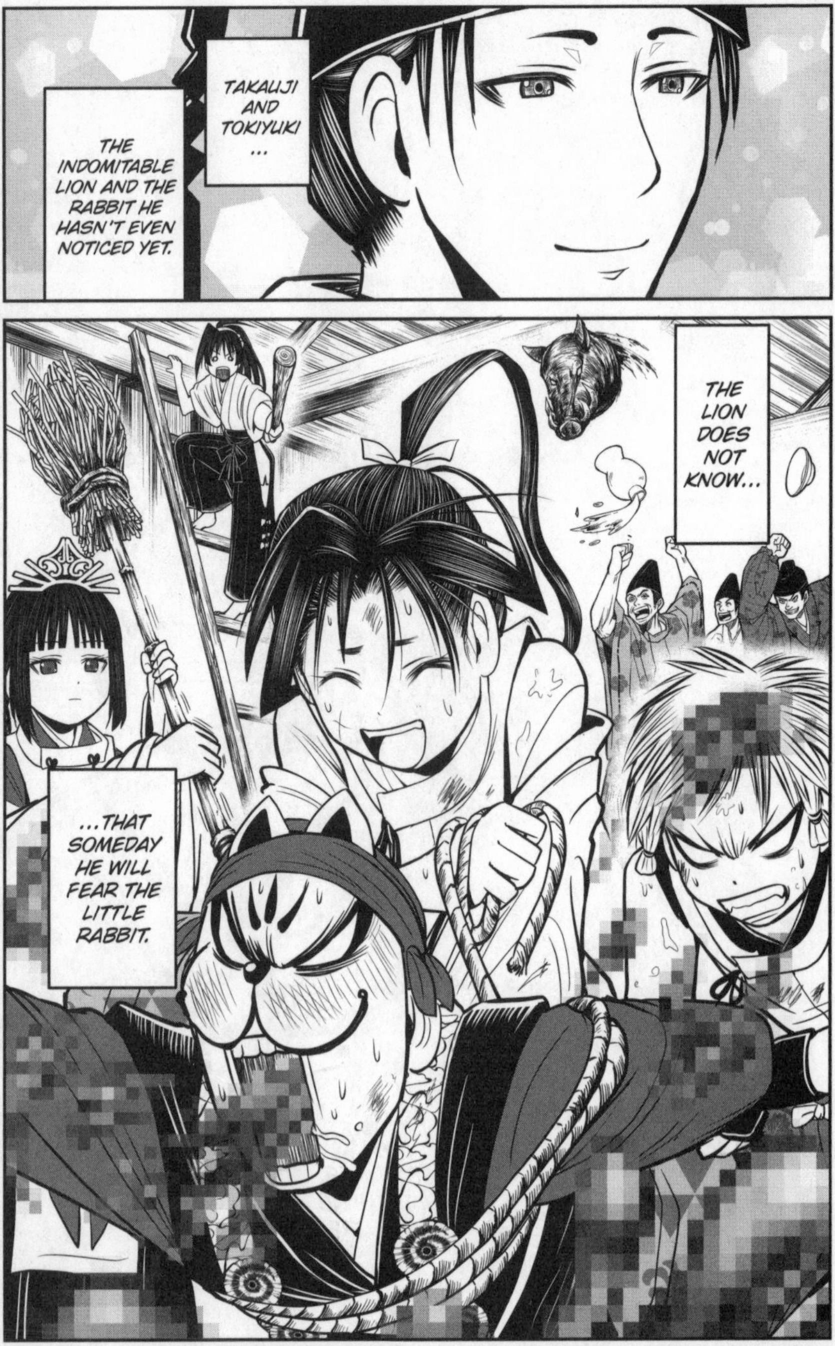
TAKAUJI AND TOKIYUKI...
THE INDOMITABLE LION AND THE RABBIT HE HASN'T EVEN NOTICED YET.
THE LION DOES NOT KNOW...
...THAT SOMEDAY HE WILL FEAR THE LITTLE RABBIT.

CHAPTER 16: WORRIED 1334

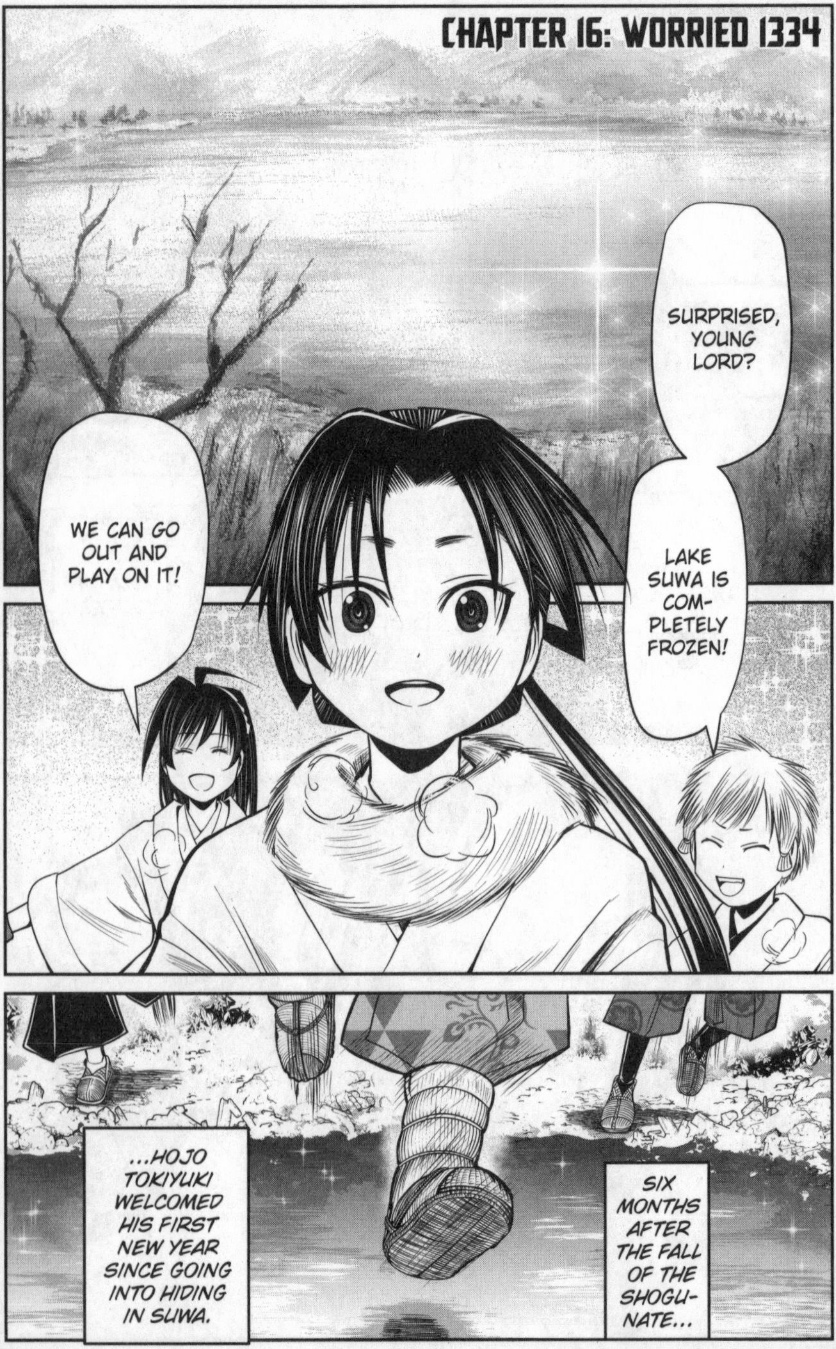
SURPRISED, YOUNG LORD?
LAKE SUWA IS COMPLETELY FROZEN!
WE CAN GO OUT AND PLAY ON IT!
SIX MONTHS AFTER THE FALL OF THE SHOGUNATE...
...HOJO TOKIYUKI WELCOMED HIS FIRST NEW YEAR SINCE GOING INTO HIDING IN SUWA.

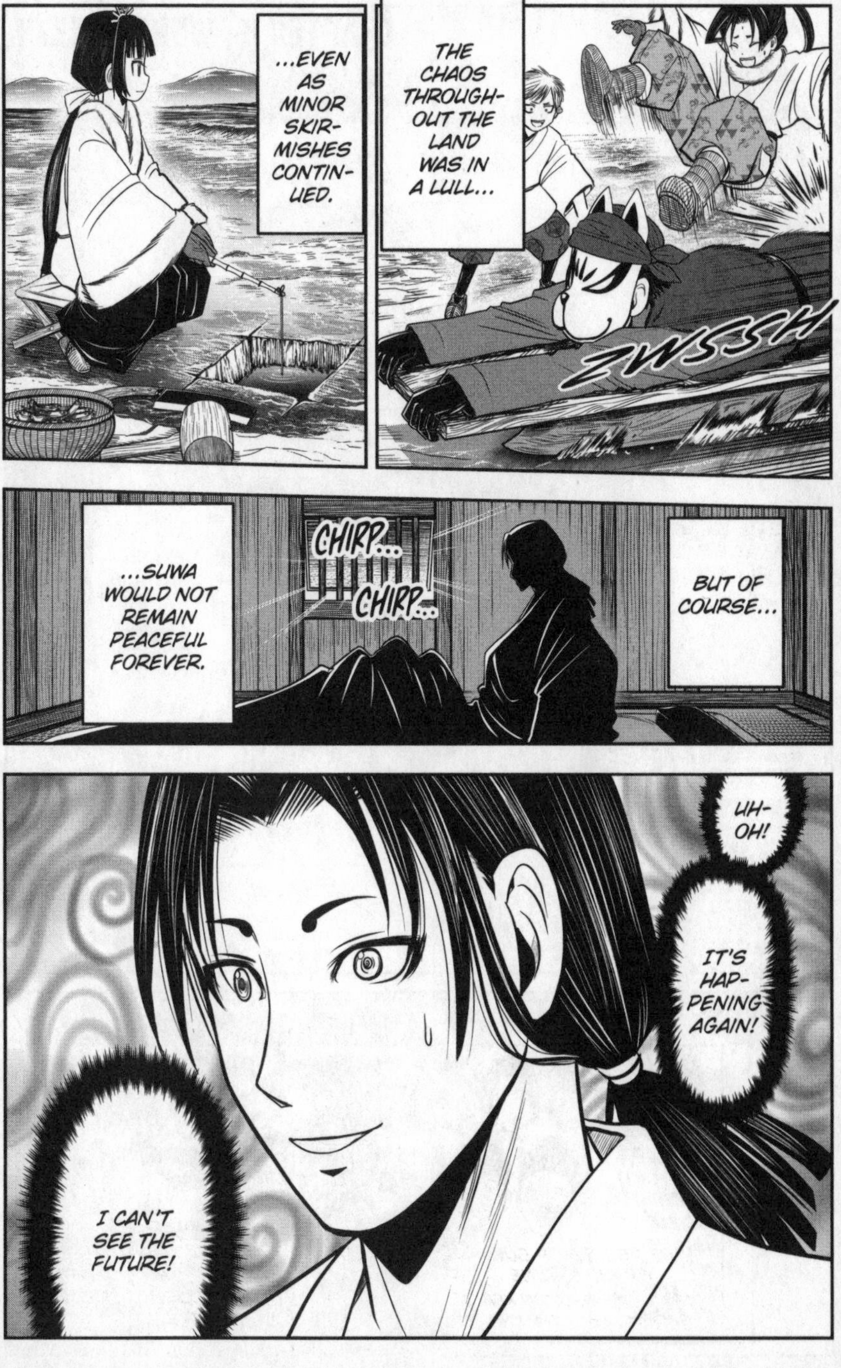
THE CHAOS THROUGHOUT THE LAND WAS IN A LULL...
ZWSSH
...EVEN AS MINOR SKIRMISHES CONTINUED.
BUT OF COURSE...
CHIRP... CHIRP...
...SUWA WOULD NOT REMAIN PEACEFUL FOREVER.
UH-OH!
IT'S HAPPENING AGAIN!
I CAN'T SEE THE FUTURE!

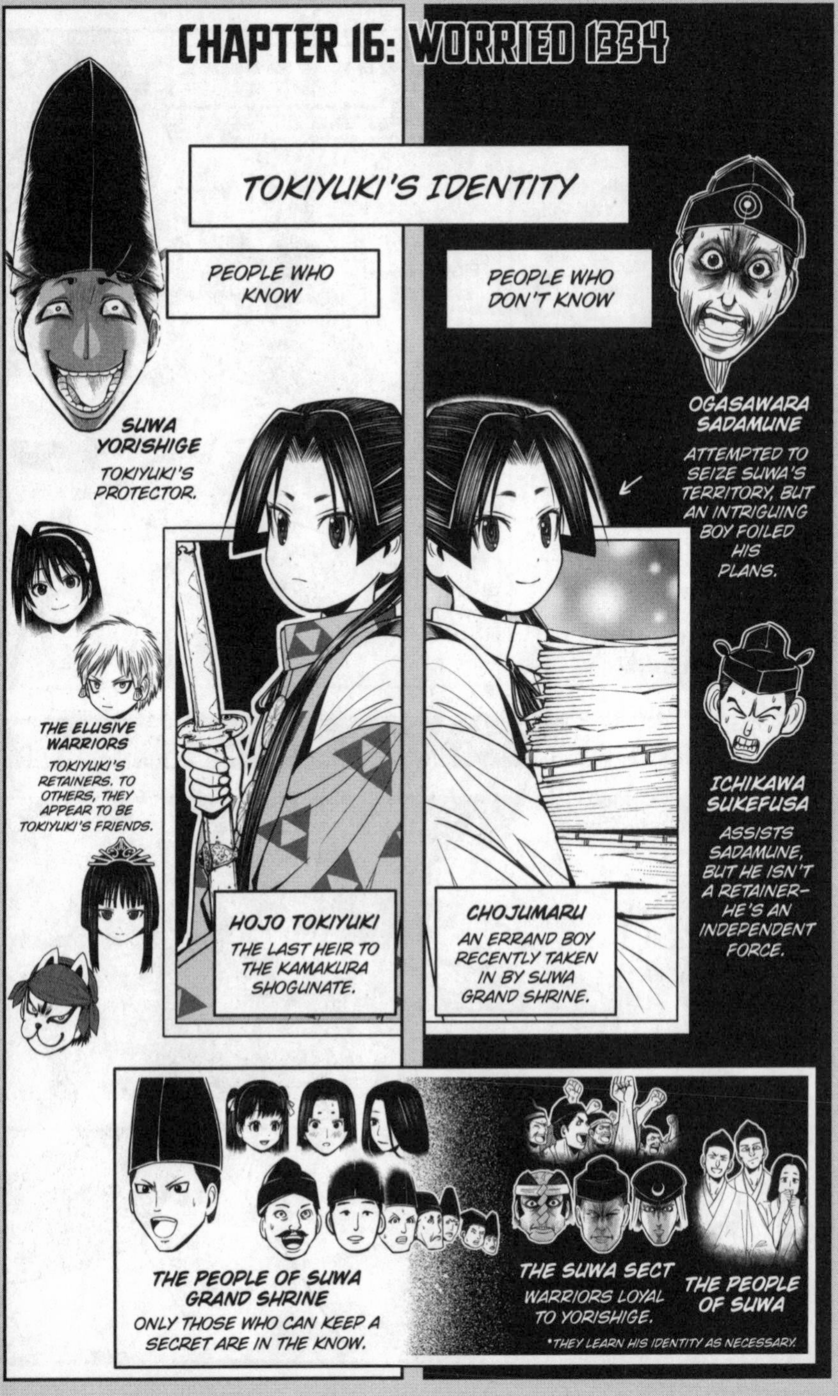
CHAPTER 16: WORRIED 1334
TOKIYUKI'S IDENTITY
PEOPLE WHO DON'T KNOW
OGASAWARA SADAMUNE
ATTEMPTED TO SEIZE SUWA'S TERRITORY, BUT AN INTRIGUING BOY FOILED HIS PLANS.
CHOJUMARU
AN ERRAND BOY RECENTLY TAKEN IN BY SUWA GRAND SHRINE.
ICHIKAWA SUKEFUSA
ASSISTS SADAMUNE, BUT HE ISN'T A RETAINER– HE'S AN INDEPENDENT FORCE.
PEOPLE WHO KNOW
SUWA YORISHIGE
TOKIYUKI'S PROTECTOR.
HOJO TOKIYUKI
THE LAST HEIR TO THE KAMAKURA SHOGUNATE.
THE ELUSIVE WARRIORS
TOKIYUKI'S RETAINERS. TO OTHERS, THEY APPEAR TO BE TOKIYUKI'S FRIENDS.
THE PEOPLE OF SUWA
THE SUWA SECT
WARRIORS LOYAL TO YORISHIGE.
THE PEOPLE OF SUWA GRAND SHRINE
ONLY THOSE WHO CAN KEEP A SECRET ARE IN THE KNOW.
*THEY LEARN HIS IDENTITY AS NECESSARY.

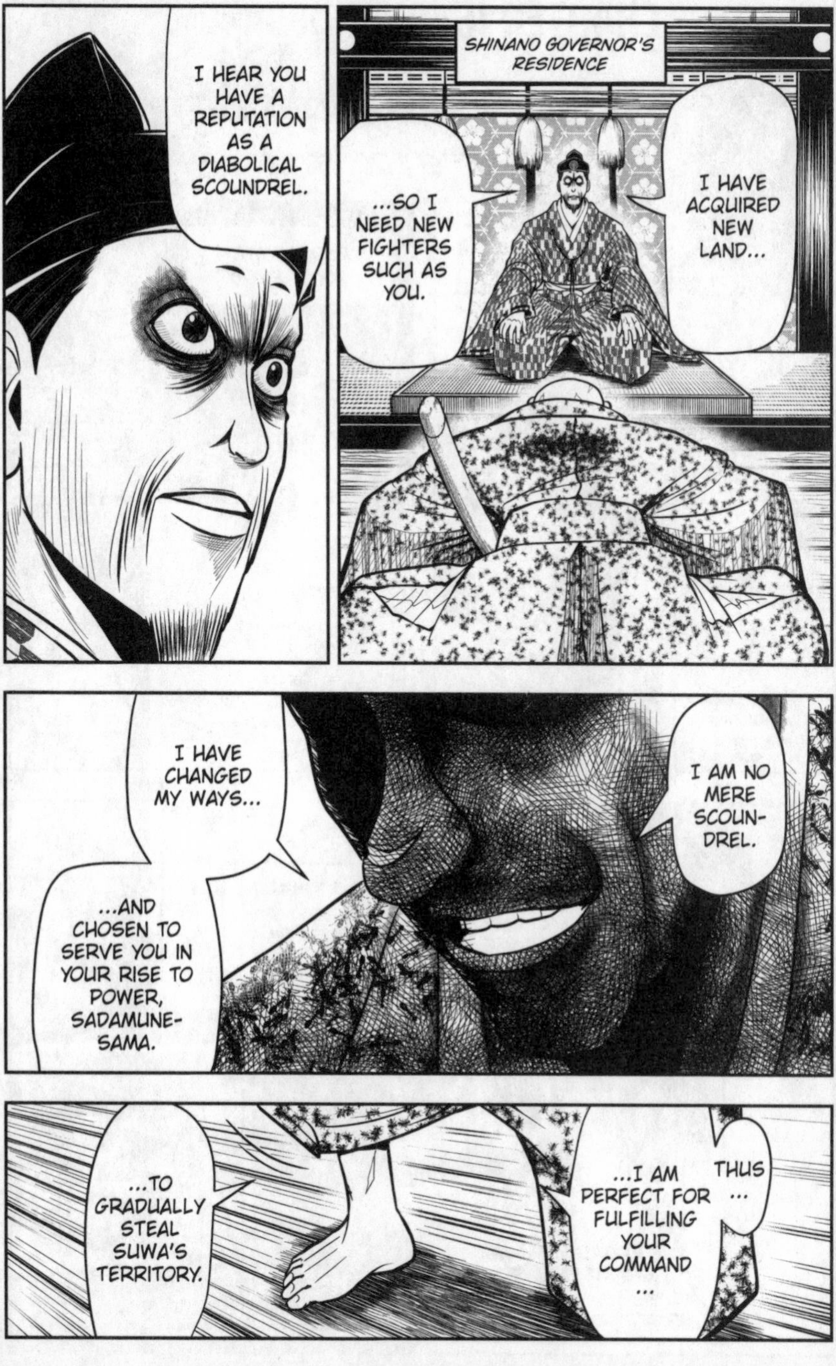
SHINANO GOVERNOR'S RESIDENCE
I HAVE ACQUIRED NEW LAND...
...SO I NEED NEW FIGHTERS SUCH AS YOU.
I HEAR YOU HAVE A REPUTATION AS A DIABOLICAL SCOUNDREL.
I AM NO MERE SCOUN-DREL.
I HAVE CHANGED MY WAYS...
...AND CHOSEN TO SERVE YOU IN YOUR RISE TO POWER, SADAMUNE-SAMA.
THUS ...
...I AM PERFECT FOR FULFILLING YOUR COMMAND ...
...TO GRADUALLY STEAL SUWA'S TERRITORY.

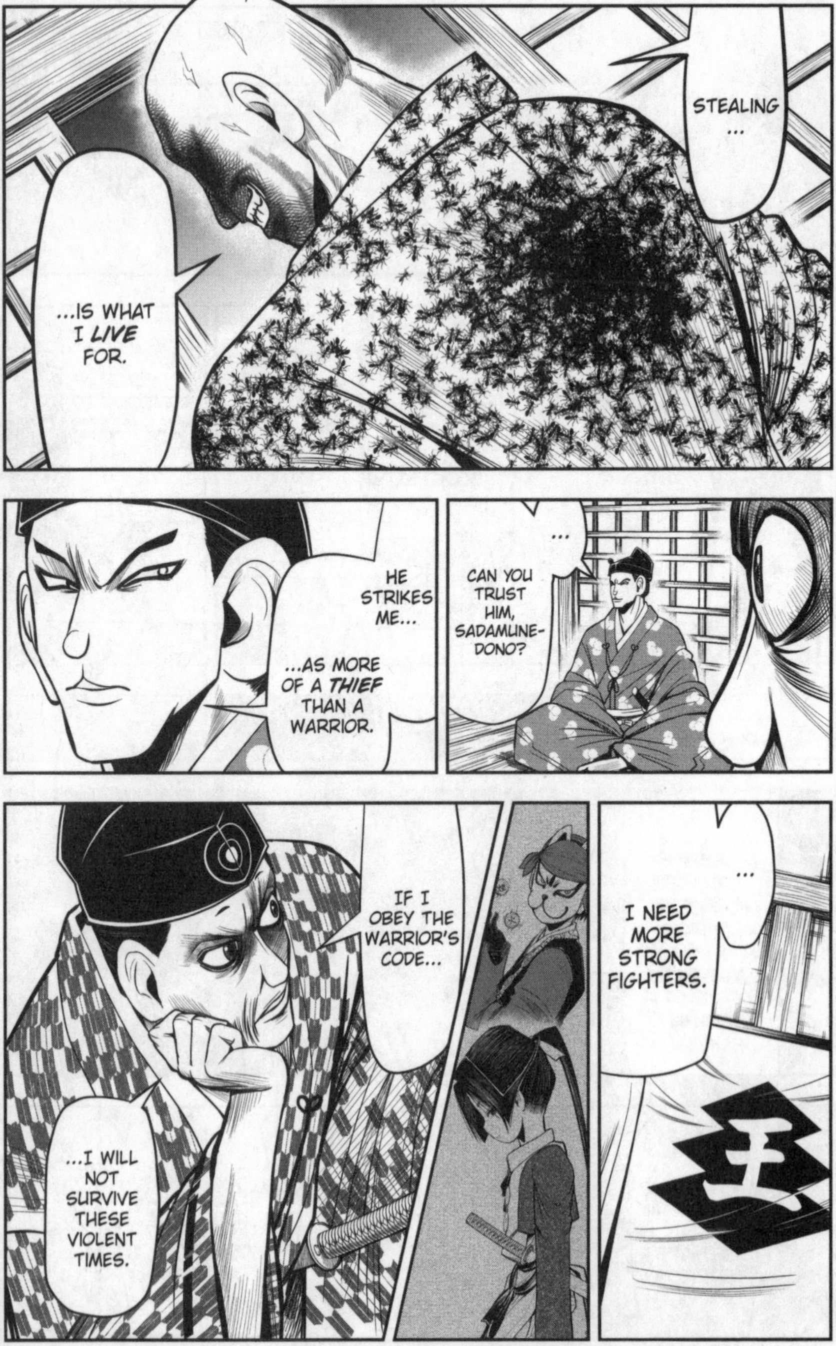
STEALING ...
...IS WHAT I *LIVE* FOR.
...
CAN YOU TRUST HIM, SADAMUNE-DONO?
HE STRIKES ME...
...AS MORE OF A *THIEF* THAN A WARRIOR.
...
I NEED MORE STRONG FIGHTERS.
IF I OBEY THE WARRIOR'S CODE...
...I WILL NOT SURVIVE THESE VIOLENT TIMES.

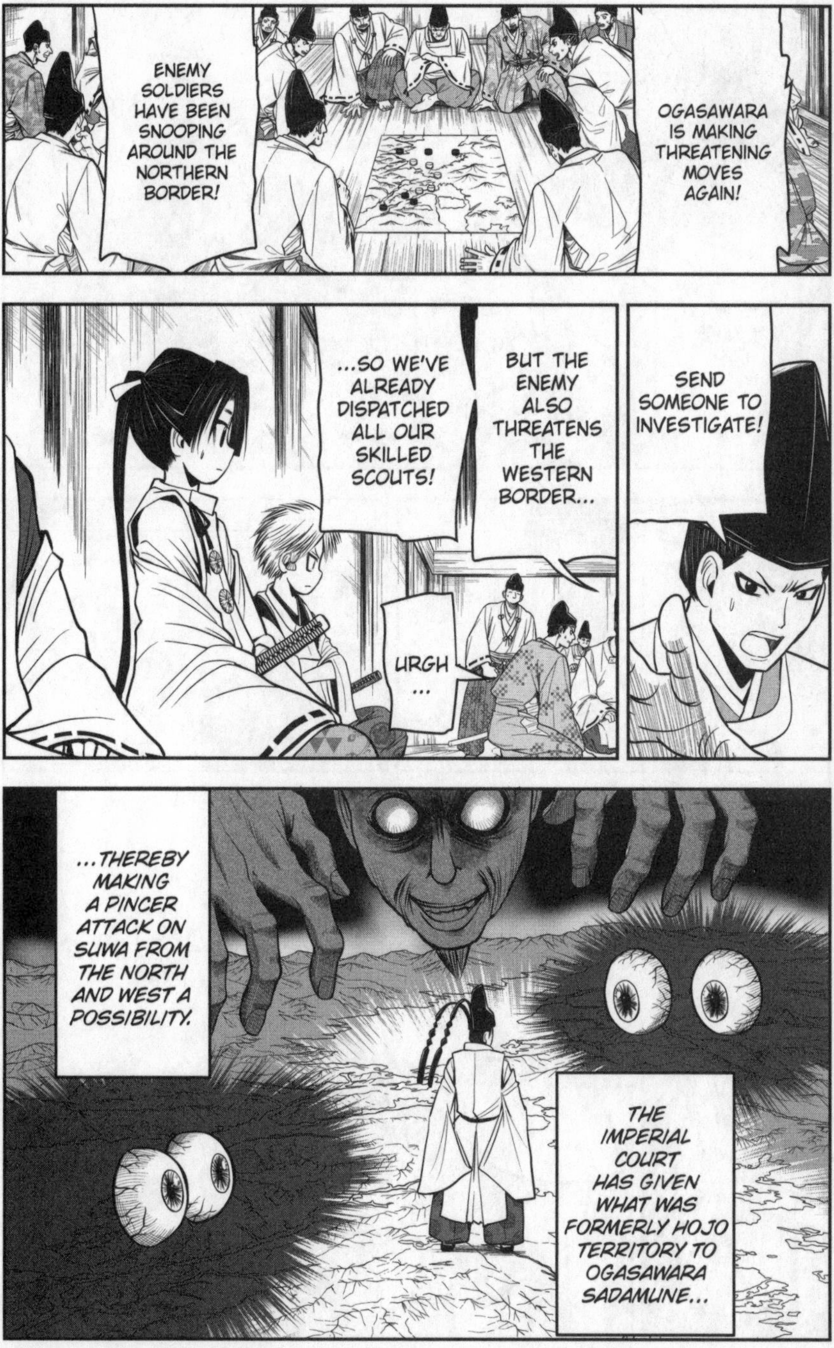

OGASAWARA IS MAKING THREATENING MOVES AGAIN!
ENEMY SOLDIERS HAVE BEEN SNOOPING AROUND THE NORTHERN BORDER!
SEND SOMEONE TO INVESTIGATE!
BUT THE ENEMY ALSO THREATENS THE WESTERN BORDER...
...SO WE'VE ALREADY DISPATCHED ALL OUR SKILLED SCOUTS!
URGH ...
THE IMPERIAL COURT HAS GIVEN WHAT WAS FORMERLY HOJO TERRITORY TO OGASAWARA SADAMUNE...
...THEREBY MAKING A PINCER ATTACK ON SUWA FROM THE NORTH AND WEST A POSSIBILITY.

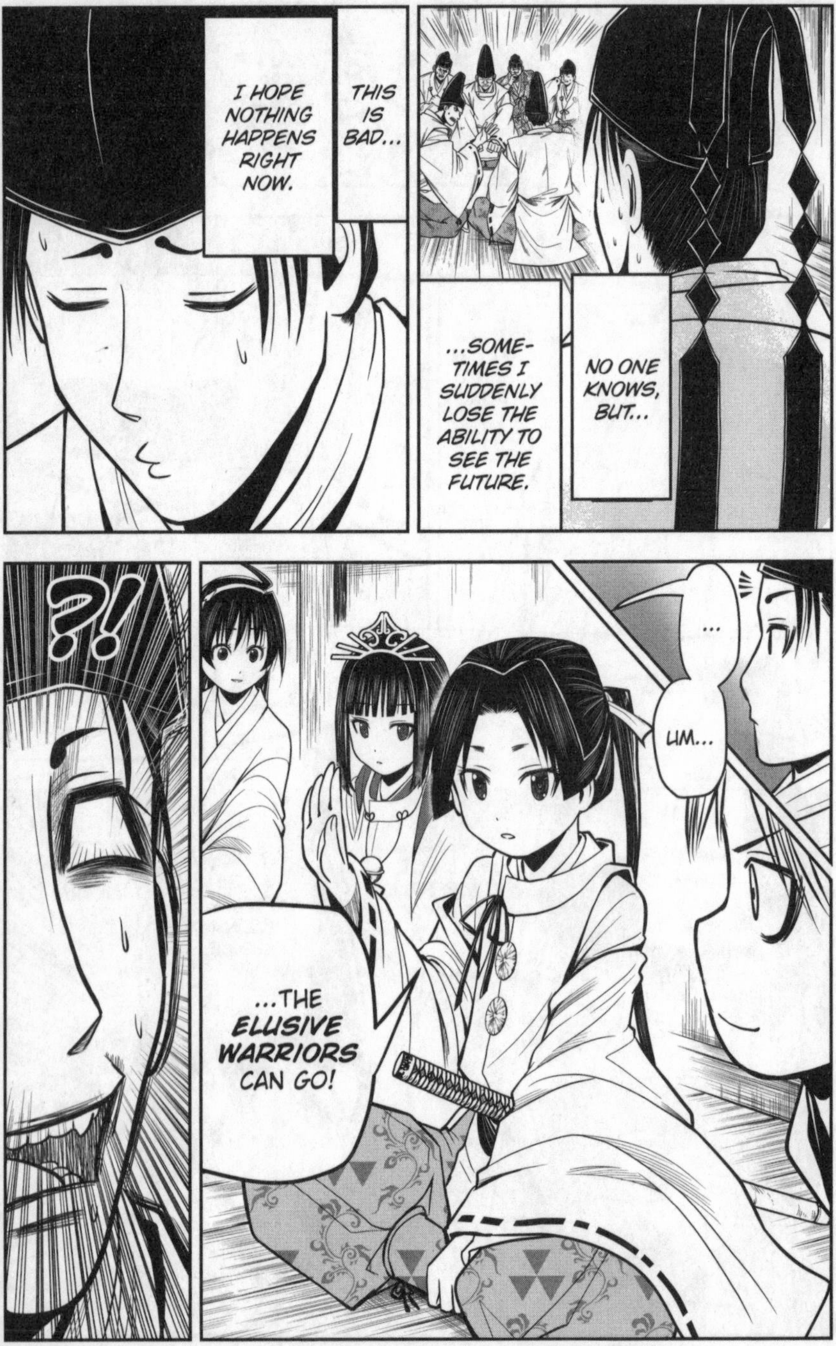
NO ONE KNOWS, BUT...
...SOME-TIMES I SUDDENLY LOSE THE ABILITY TO SEE THE FUTURE.
THIS IS BAD...
I HOPE NOTHING HAPPENS RIGHT NOW.
...
UM...
...THE ELUSIVE WARRIORS CAN GO!
?!

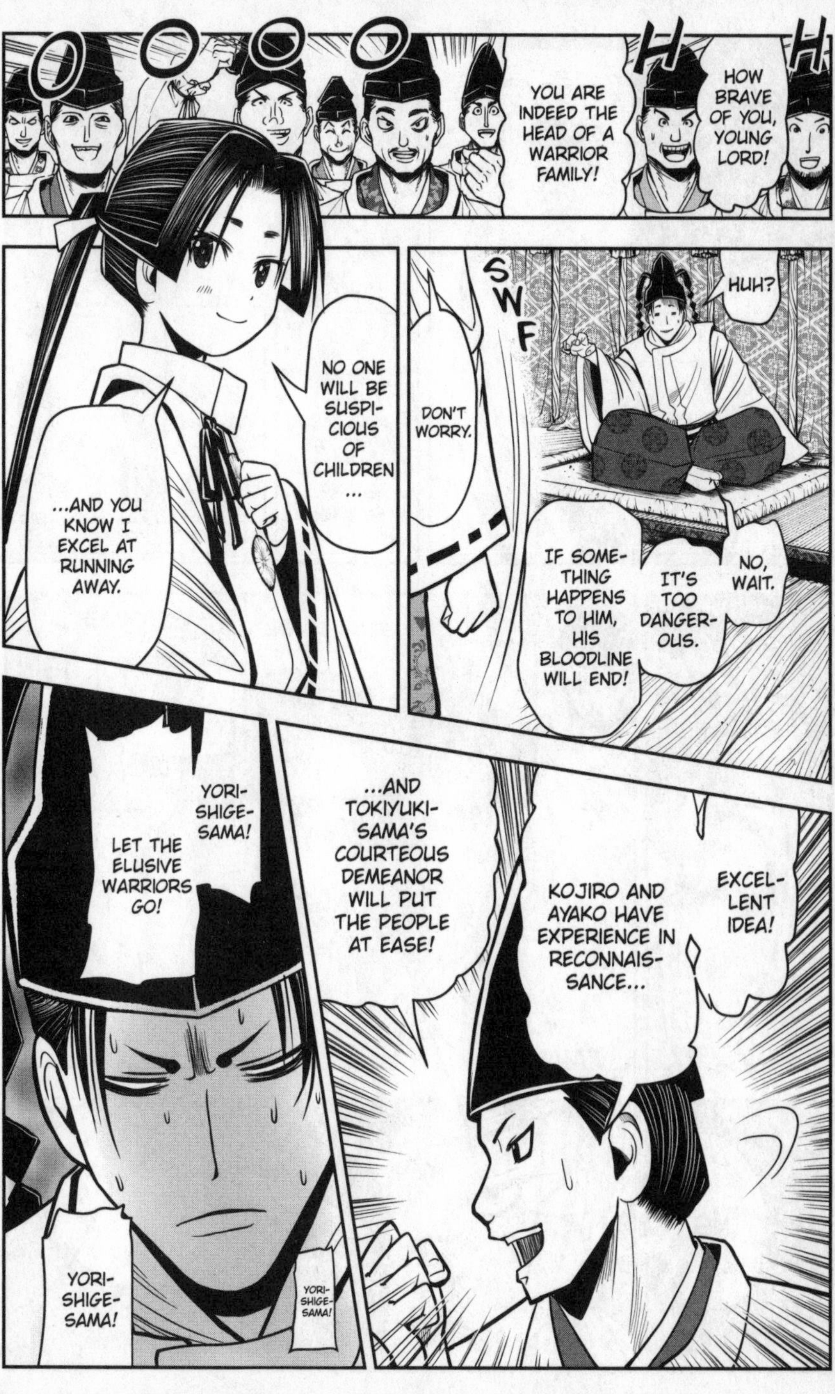
HH
OOOO
HOW BRAVE OF YOU, YOUNG LORD!
YOU ARE INDEED THE HEAD OF A WARRIOR FAMILY!
HUH?
NO, WAIT.
IT'S TOO DANGEROUS.
IF SOMETHING HAPPENS TO HIM, HIS BLOODLINE WILL END!
SWF
DON'T WORRY.
NO ONE WILL BE SUSPICIOUS OF CHILDREN...
...AND YOU KNOW I EXCEL AT RUNNING AWAY.
EXCELLENT IDEA!
KOJIRO AND AYAKO HAVE EXPERIENCE IN RECONNAISSANCE...
...AND TOKIYUKI-SAMA'S COURTEOUS DEMEANOR WILL PUT THE PEOPLE AT EASE!
YORISHIGE-SAMA!
LET THE ELUSIVE WARRIORS GO!
YORISHIGE-SAMA!
YORISHIGE-SAMA!

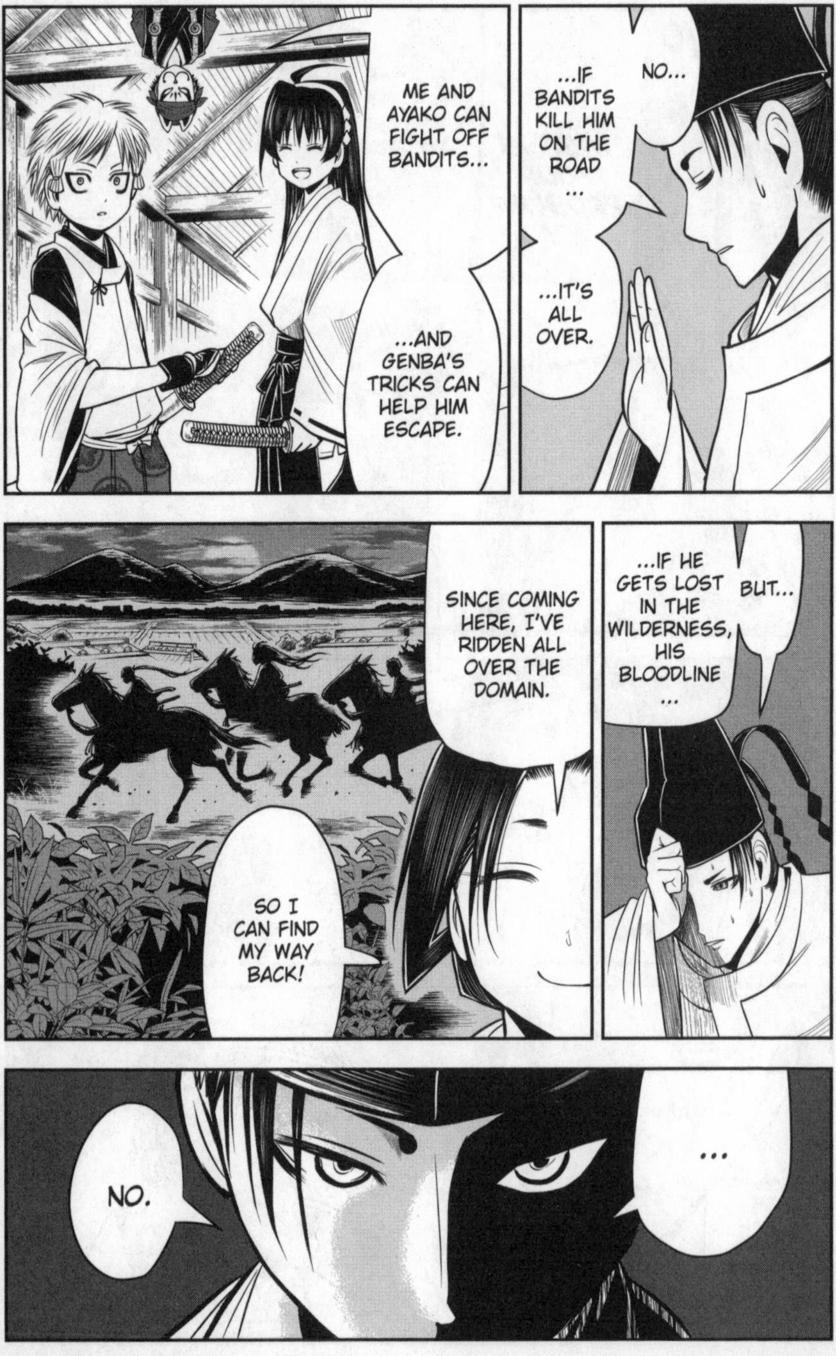
NO...
...IF BANDITS KILL HIM ON THE ROAD ...
...IT'S ALL OVER.
ME AND AYAKO CAN FIGHT OFF BANDITS...
...AND GENBA'S TRICKS CAN HELP HIM ESCAPE.
BUT...
...IF HE GETS LOST IN THE WILDERNESS, HIS BLOODLINE ...
SINCE COMING HERE, I'VE RIDDEN ALL OVER THE DOMAIN.
SO I CAN FIND MY WAY BACK!
...
NO.

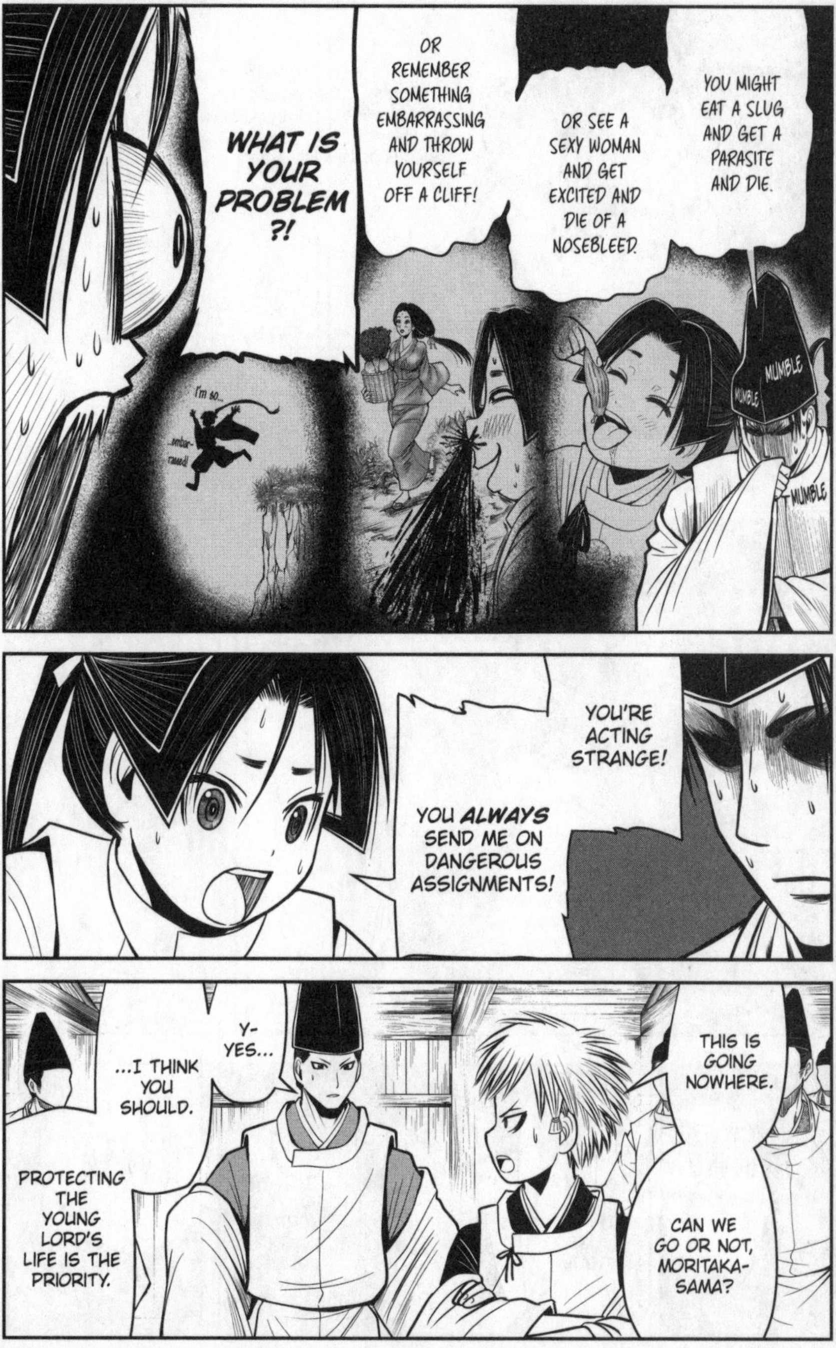
MUMBLE MUMBLE
MUMBLE
YOU MIGHT EAT A SLUG AND GET A PARASITE AND DIE.
OR SEE A SEXY WOMAN AND GET EXCITED AND DIE OF A NOSEBLEED.
OR REMEMBER SOMETHING EMBARRASSING AND THROW YOURSELF OFF A CLIFF!
I'm so... ...embar-rassed!
WHAT IS YOUR PROBLEM ?!
YOU'RE ACTING STRANGE!
YOU ALWAYS SEND ME ON DANGEROUS ASSIGNMENTS!
THIS IS GOING NOWHERE.
CAN WE GO OR NOT, MORITAKA-SAMA?
Y- YES...
...I THINK YOU SHOULD.
PROTECTING THE YOUNG LORD'S LIFE IS THE PRIORITY.

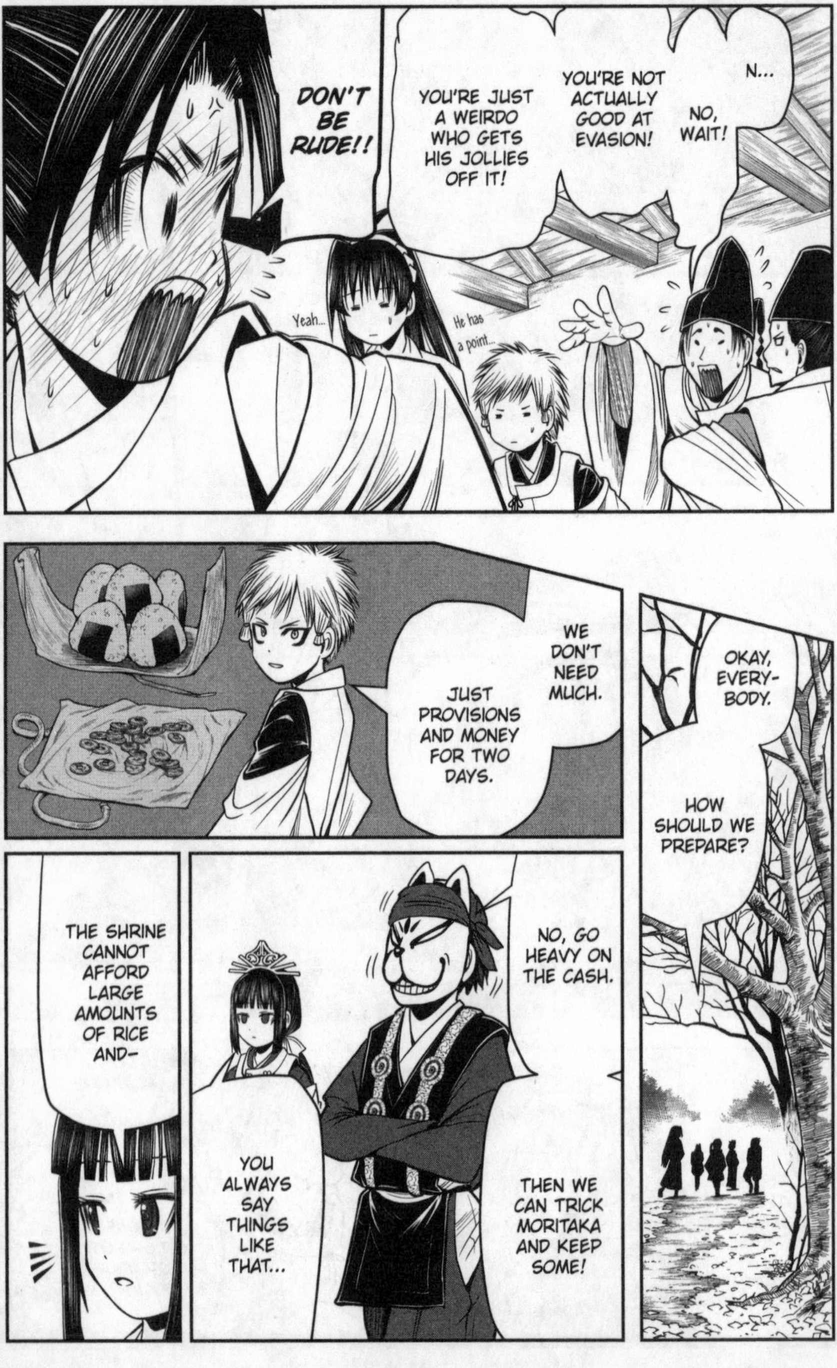
N...
NO, WAIT!
YOU'RE NOT ACTUALLY GOOD AT EVASION!
YOU'RE JUST A WEIRDO WHO GETS HIS JOLLIES OFF IT!
He has a point...
Yeah...
DON'T BE RUDE!!
OKAY, EVERYBODY.
HOW SHOULD WE PREPARE?
WE DON'T NEED MUCH.
JUST PROVISIONS AND MONEY FOR TWO DAYS.
NO, GO HEAVY ON THE CASH.
THEN WE CAN TRICK MORITAKA AND KEEP SOME!
YOU ALWAYS SAY THINGS LIKE THAT...
THE SHRINE CANNOT AFFORD LARGE AMOUNTS OF RICE AND–

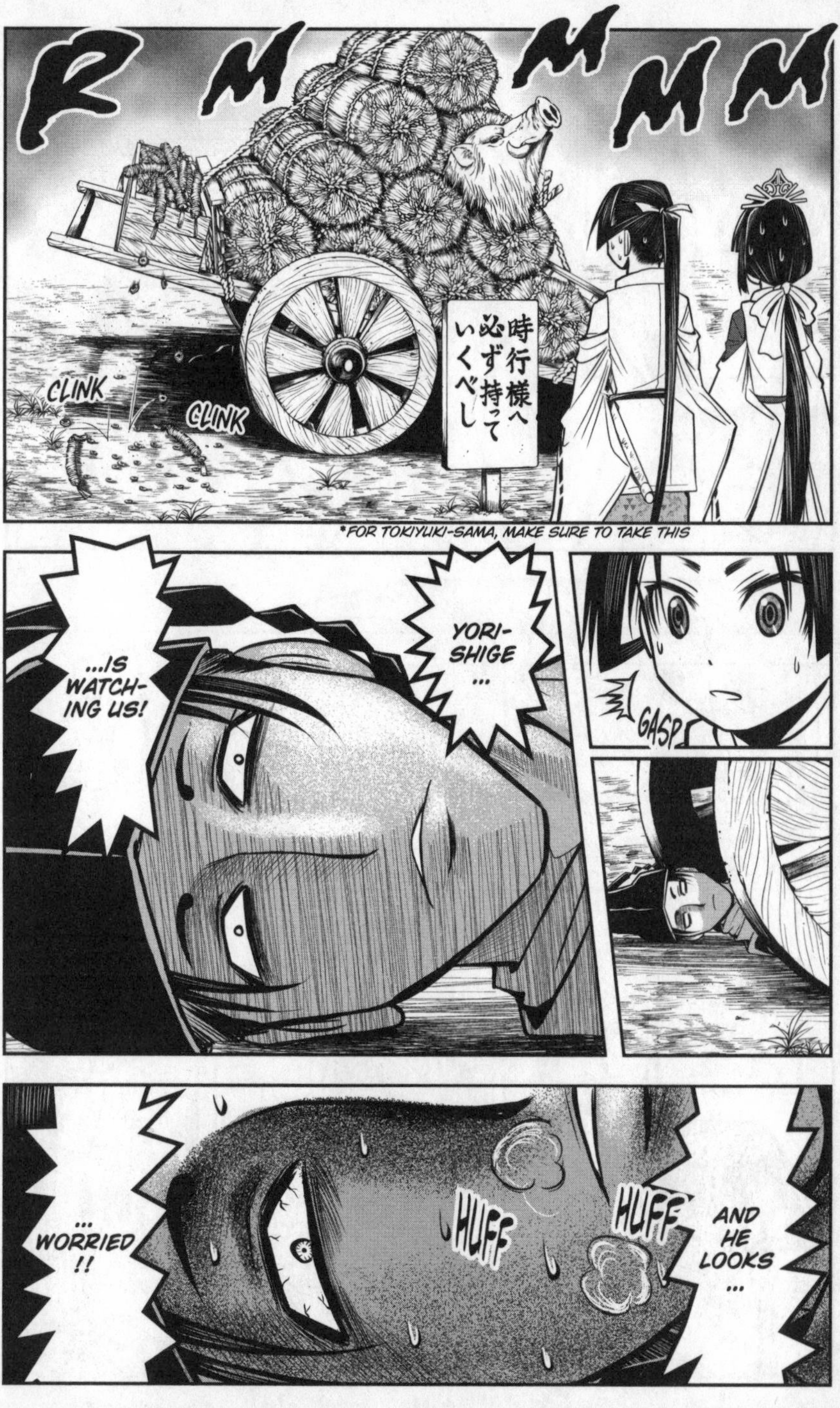
RMMMMM
時行様へ必ず持っていくべし
CLINK
CLINK
*FOR TOKIYUKI-SAMA, MAKE SURE TO TAKE THIS
GASP
YORI-SHIGE ...
...IS WATCHING US!
AND HE LOOKS ...
HUFF
HUFF
... WORRIED !!

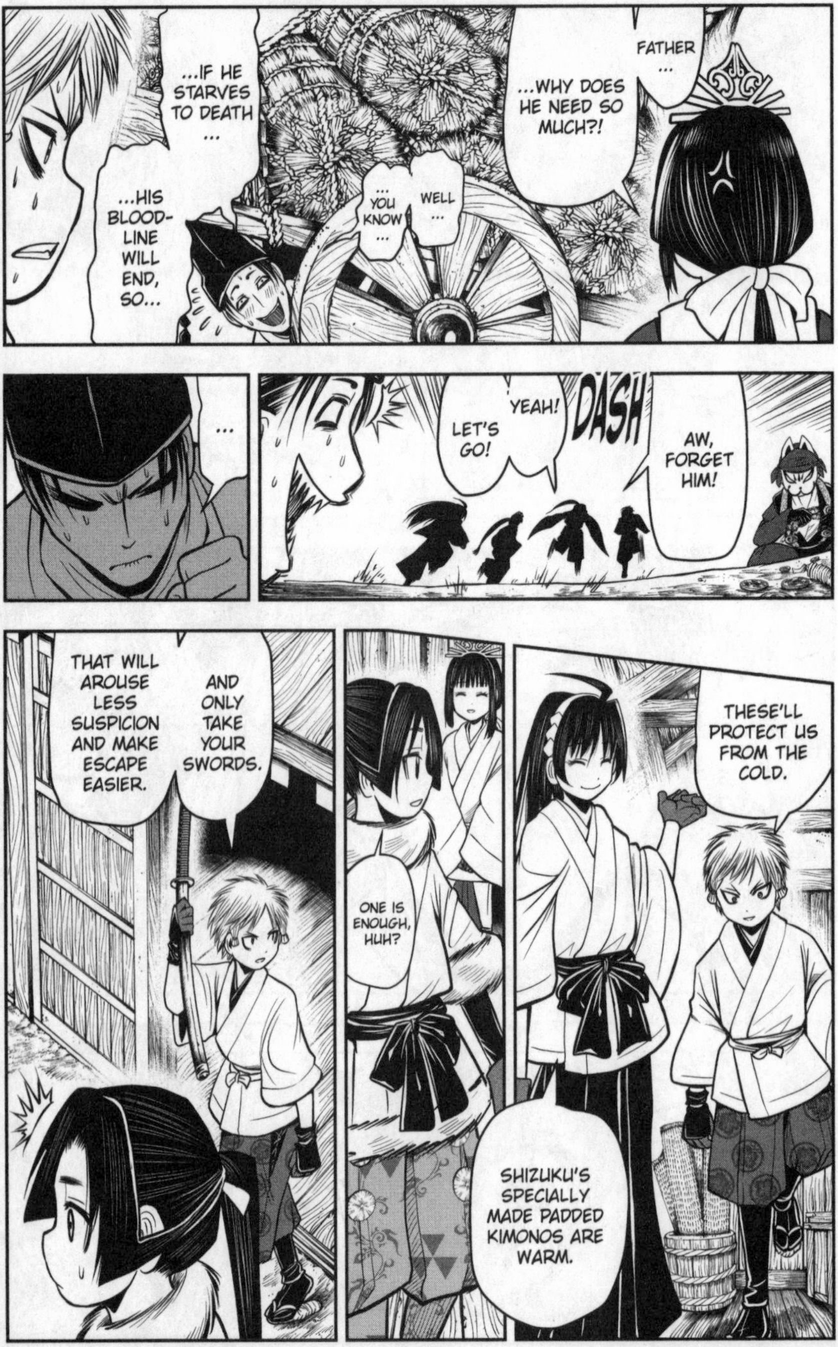
FATHER ...
...WHY DOES HE NEED SO MUCH?!
WELL ...
... YOU KNOW ...
...IF HE STARVES TO DEATH ...
...HIS BLOODLINE WILL END, SO...
AW, FORGET HIM!
DASH
YEAH!
LET'S GO!
...
THESE'LL PROTECT US FROM THE COLD.
SHIZUKU'S SPECIALLY MADE PADDED KIMONOS ARE WARM.
ONE IS ENOUGH, HUH?
AND ONLY TAKE YOUR SWORDS.
THAT WILL AROUSE LESS SUSPICION AND MAKE ESCAPE EASIER.

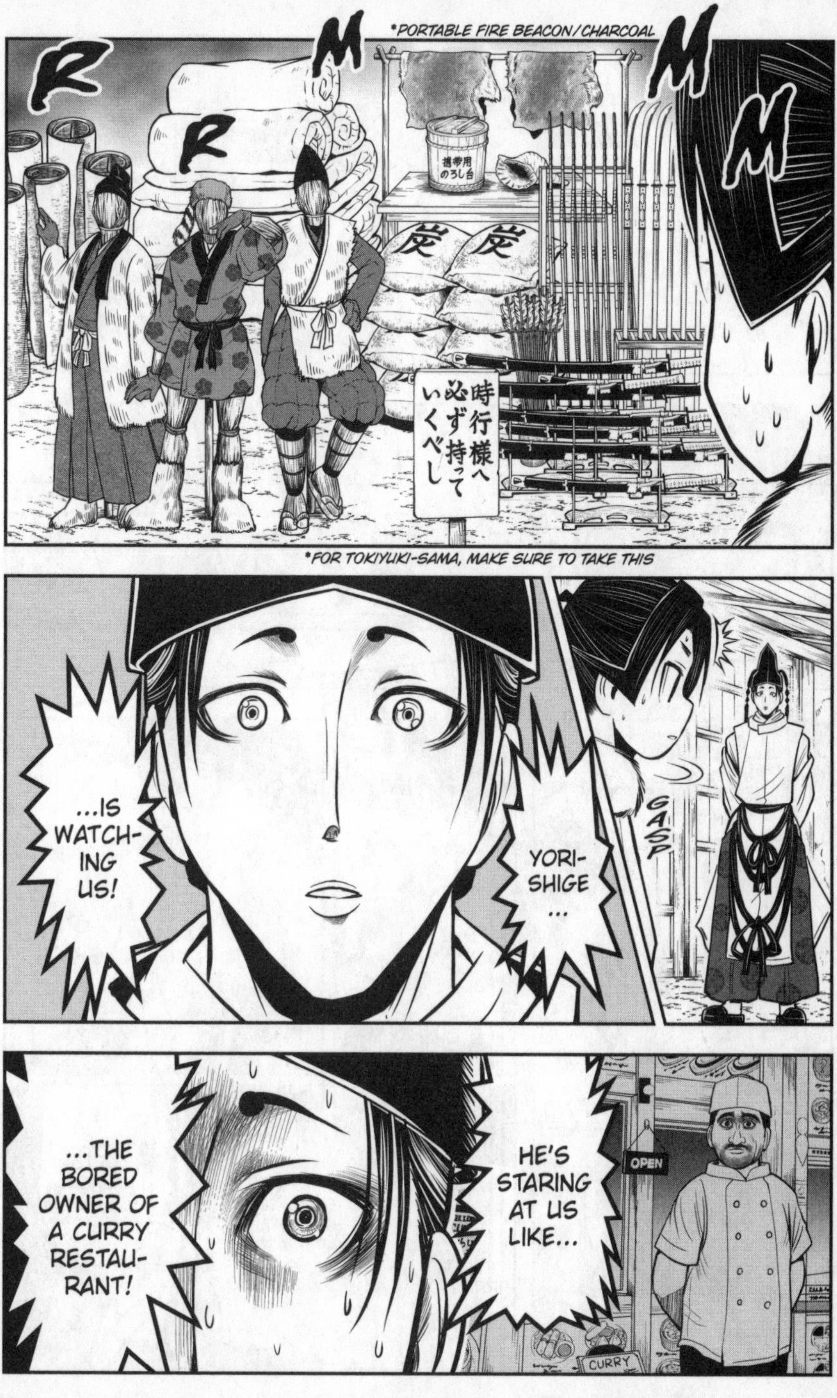
*PORTABLE FIRE BEACON/CHARCOAL
M M M
R R
携帯用のろし台
炭
炭
時行様へ必ず持っていくべし
*FOR TOKIYUKI-SAMA, MAKE SURE TO TAKE THIS
GASP
YORI-SHIGE...
...IS WATCHING US!
HE'S STARING AT US LIKE...
...THE BORED OWNER OF A CURRY RESTAURANT!
OPEN
CURRY

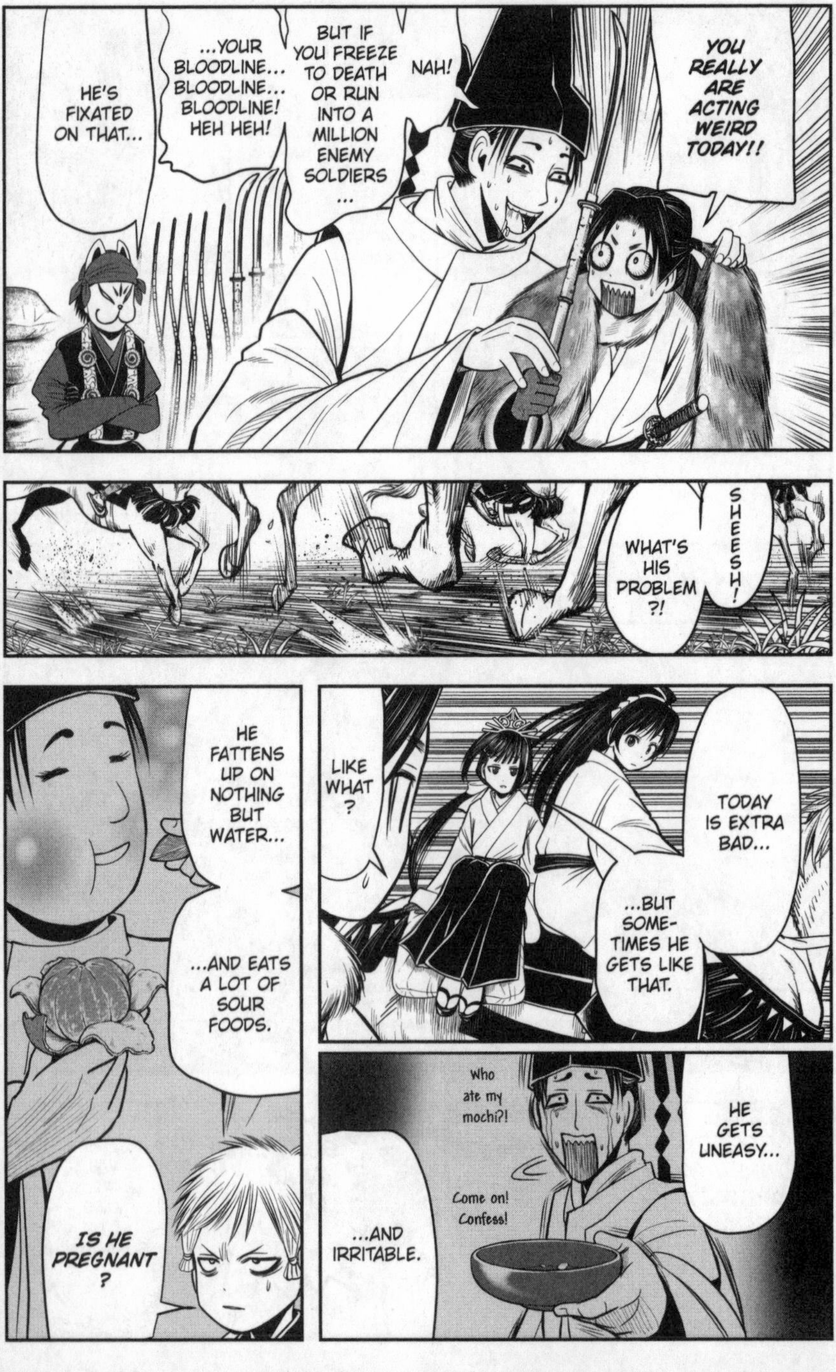
YOU REALLY ARE ACTING WEIRD TODAY!!
NAH!
BUT IF YOU FREEZE TO DEATH OR RUN INTO A MILLION ENEMY SOLDIERS...
...YOUR BLOODLINE... BLOODLINE... BLOODLINE! HEH HEH!
HE'S FIXATED ON THAT...
SHEESH!
WHAT'S HIS PROBLEM?!
TODAY IS EXTRA BAD...
...BUT SOMETIMES HE GETS LIKE THAT.
LIKE WHAT?
HE GETS UNEASY...
Who ate my mochi?!
Come on! Confess!
...AND IRRITABLE.
HE FATTENS UP ON NOTHING BUT WATER...
...AND EATS A LOT OF SOUR FOODS.
IS HE PREGNANT?

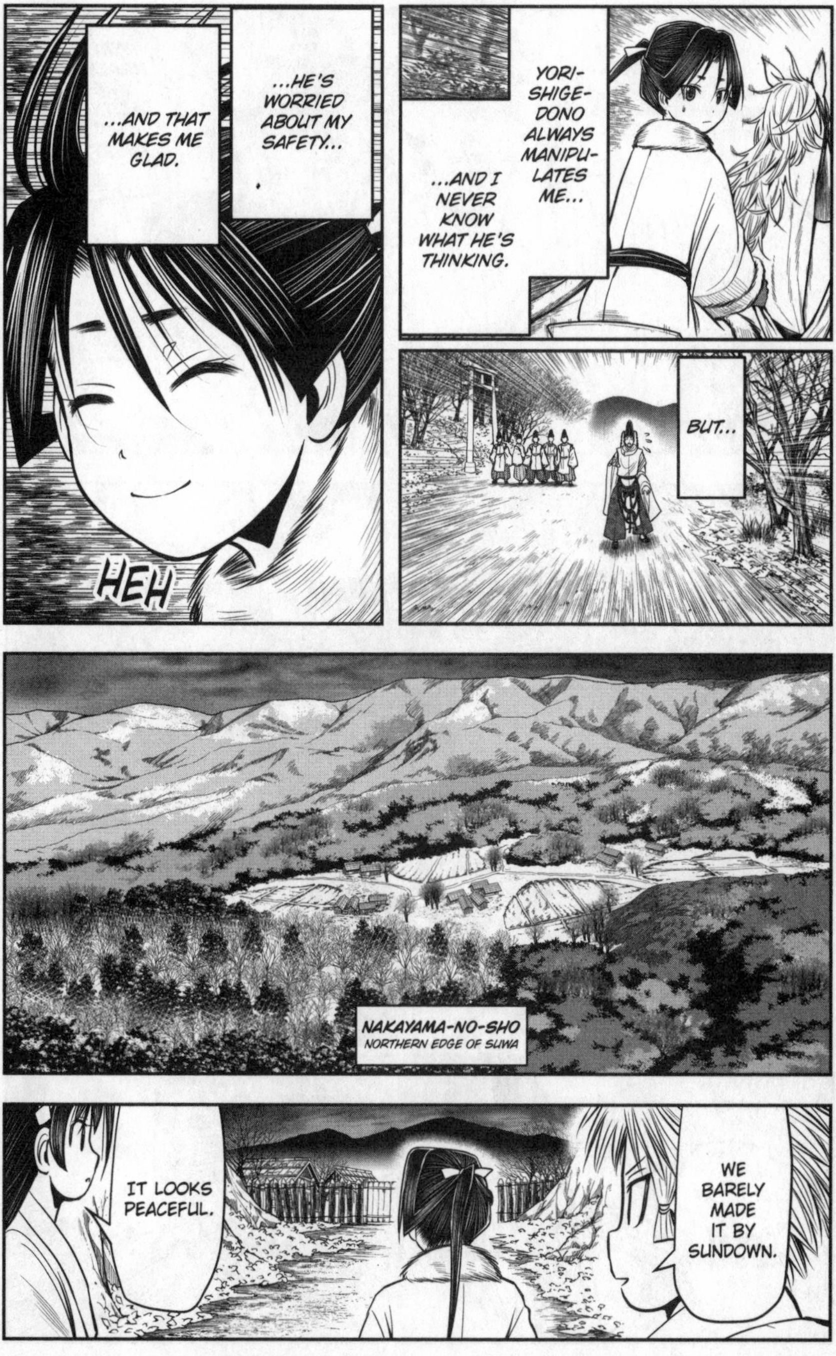
YORI-SHIGE-DONO ALWAYS MANIPU-LATES ME...
...AND I NEVER KNOW WHAT HE'S THINKING.
BUT...
...HE'S WORRIED ABOUT MY SAFETY...
...AND THAT MAKES ME GLAD.
HEH
NAKAYAMA-NO-SHO
NORTHERN EDGE OF SUWA
WE BARELY MADE IT BY SUNDOWN.
IT LOOKS PEACEFUL.

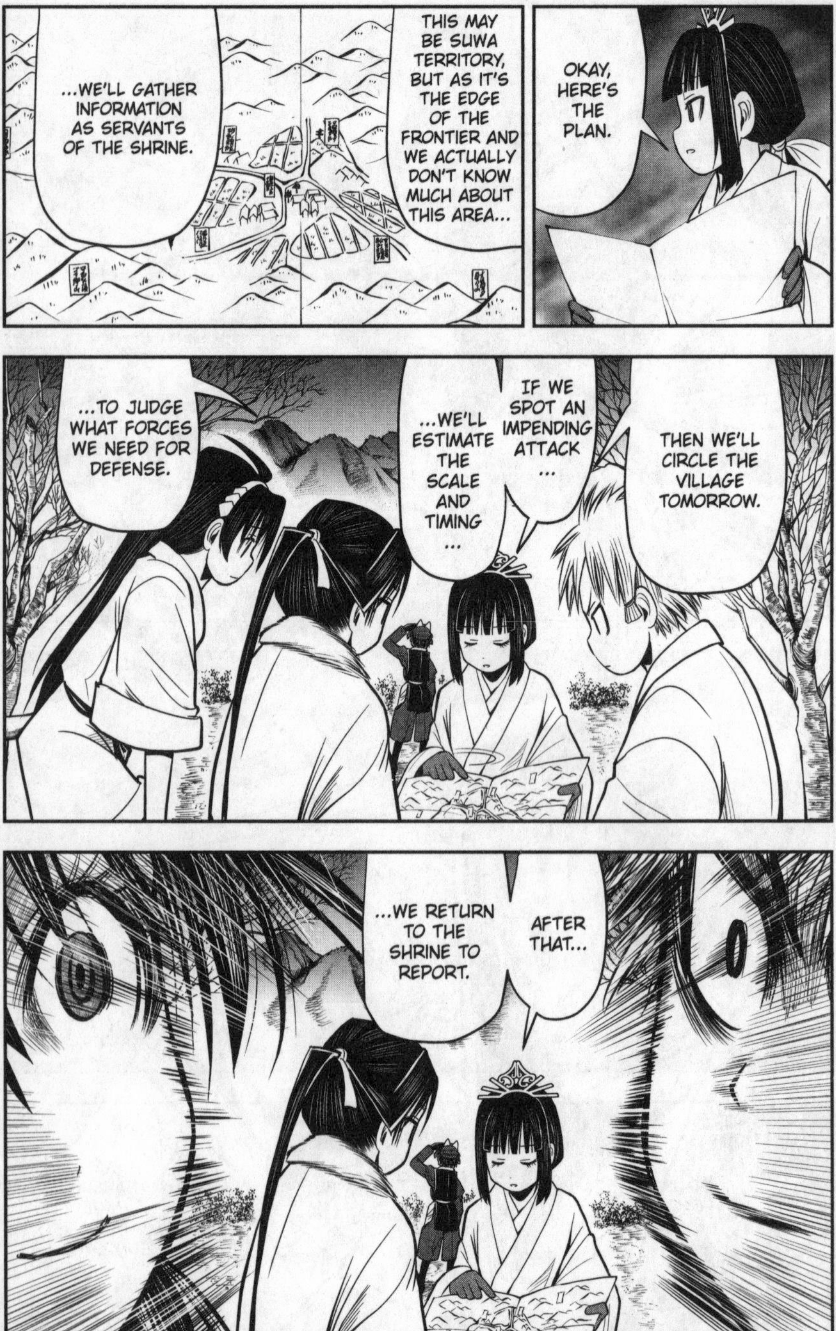
OKAY, HERE'S THE PLAN.
THIS MAY BE SUWA TERRITORY, BUT AS IT'S THE EDGE OF THE FRONTIER AND WE ACTUALLY DON'T KNOW MUCH ABOUT THIS AREA...
...WE'LL GATHER INFORMATION AS SERVANTS OF THE SHRINE.
THEN WE'LL CIRCLE THE VILLAGE TOMORROW.
IF WE SPOT AN IMPENDING ATTACK ...
...WE'LL ESTIMATE THE SCALE AND TIMING ...
...TO JUDGE WHAT FORCES WE NEED FOR DEFENSE.
AFTER THAT...
...WE RETURN TO THE SHRINE TO REPORT.

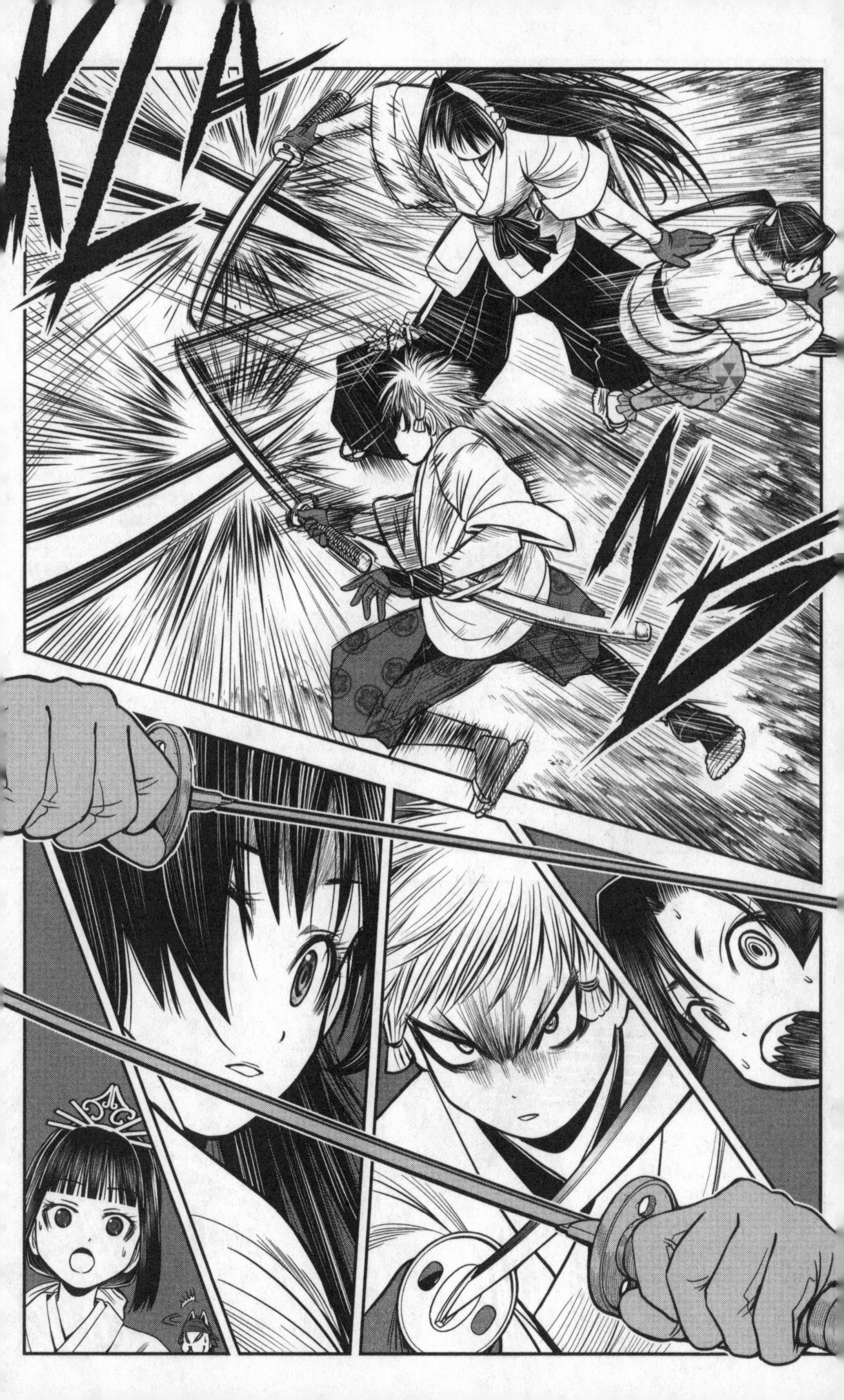
KLANK

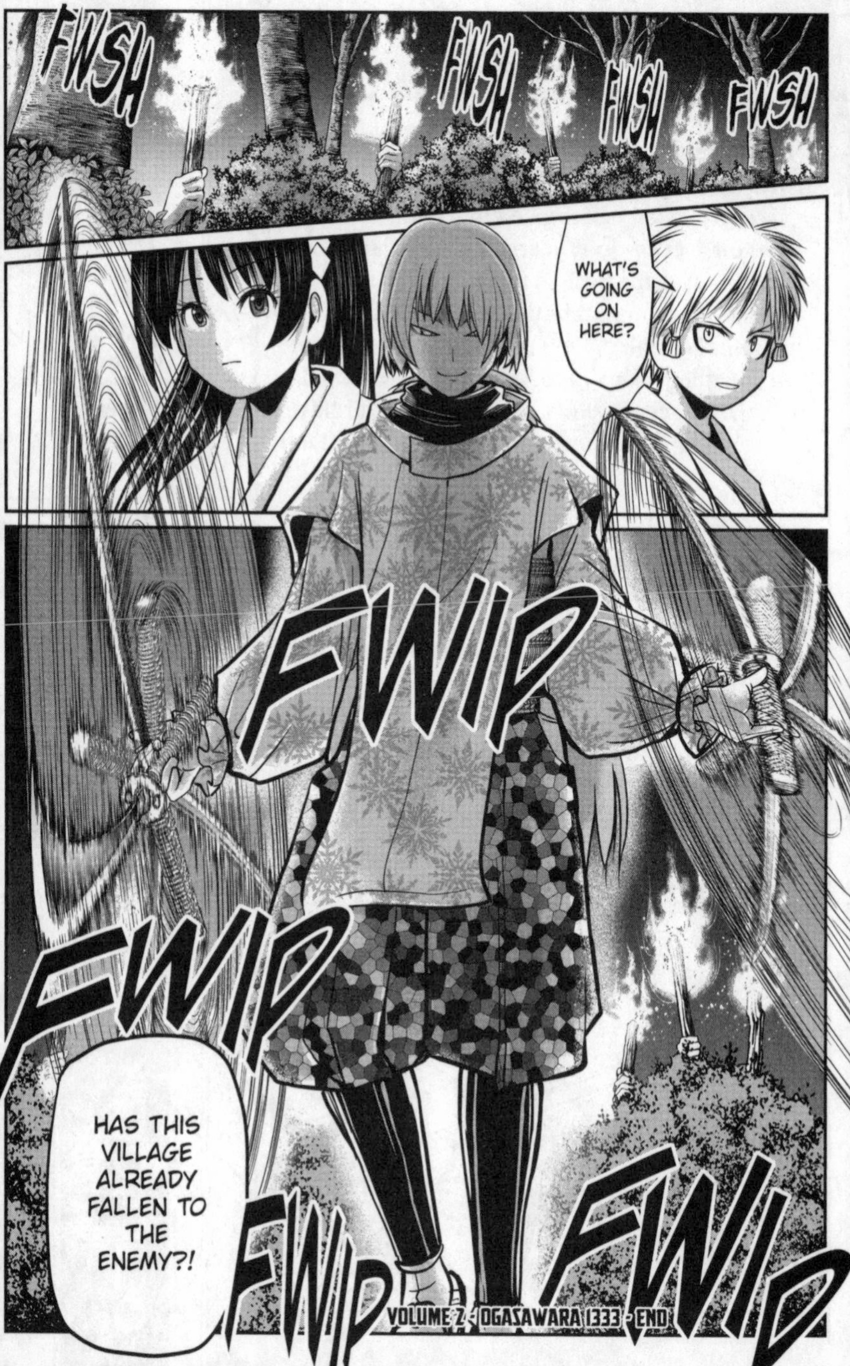
FWSH
FWSH
FWSH
FWSH
WHAT'S GOING ON HERE?
FWIP
FWIP
FWIP
HAS THIS VILLAGE ALREADY FALLEN TO THE ENEMY?!
FWIP
VOLUME 2 - OGASAWARA 1333 - END

In the Heian period, *bushi* were originally warriors whom the *kokushi* (like a prefectural governor today) summoned to a hunt, or *okari*, held once every four years as an official event. Hunting was the bushi's foremost skill. They hunted wild animals in thickly wooded mountains. Unless they could handle horses as well as the jockey Take Yutaka and possessed excellent archery skills, they would never have been able to take down animals fleeing for their lives.

For that reason, bushi trained in hunting from an early age, and dog shooting was part of that.

They would mark off a sizable area with a fence and release a number of wild dogs into it. Then they would ride in on horseback and shoot the dogs with arrows. Illustrations of this often appear in textbooks.

DOG SHOOT-ING...

...WAS A MAJOR SPORT BACK THEN.

THE ELUSIVE SAMURAI

INCREASE YOUR ENJOYMENT OF THIS MANGA BY LEARNING THE REAL HISTORY BEHIND IT!!

ANALYSIS
KAZUTO HONGO

You may wonder what happened to the dogs. If the arrows had sharp heads, the dogs would die, but scrolls don't show the dogs bleeding. Perhaps they removed the arrowheads? As a dog lover, I would find that to be a relief, but even without a point, an arrow would have considerable force, so the dogs would still probably die, the poor things... The dogs weren't pets, though. They were wild, slavering beasts. Maybe it was a kill-or-be-killed type of situation.

METE TO THE NECK! FIVE POINTS!

THWIP

WHAT GAMES AND SPORTS DID BUSHI PLAY?

Bushi weren't particularly smart, so when it came to board games, they probably only had something like *sugoroku*, which was like backgammon and thus useful for polishing strategic skills. The game go already existed in Japan, but that was for the nobility. It's unknown whether the bushi ever played it.

Bushi were good at physical activities, so they engaged in *kurabe-uma*, which was like horse racing, and *kari-yumi*, which was archery for points. The way they played *kemari* was like lifting in soccer, but only high-ranking bushi played that.

AH HA HA!

BOMP

WHAT WERE THE BOWS AND ARROWS LIKE?

The young Oda Nobunaga engaged in many battles to unify Owari Province. One such battle was the Battle of Ukino in the first year of the Eiroku era (1558). I won't include an explanation of the battle, but during the fighting there was a duel between Hashimoto Ippa, an expert musketeer who was Nobunaga's shooting instructor, and a famous archer. A bullet hit the archer, but an arrow struck the musketeer in the side and he died. The archer received a fatal wound but was still alive, so the archer won (according to the *Nobunaga Kōki*).

Various experiments, some of them on YouTube, have shown that a bow's force is considerable. In range and penetration, it is comparable to a matchlock gun. Firearms came to dominate because they're easier to handle and even inexperienced combatants such as farmers could operate them. By comparison, the bow is difficult to master and can't be used without a great deal of training.

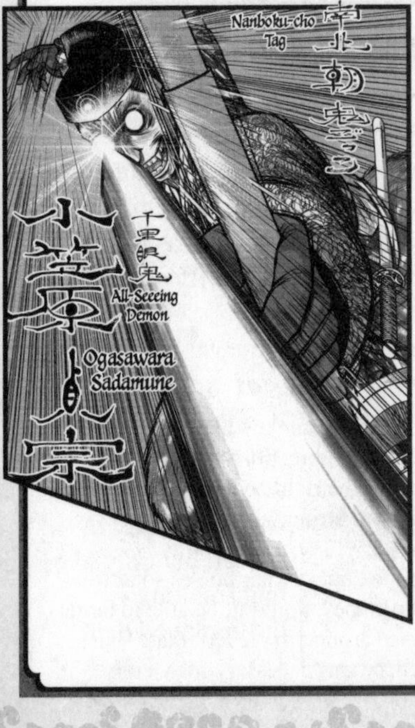
南北朝鬼ごっこ
Nanboku-cho Tag
千里眼鬼
All-Seeeing Demon
小笠原貞宗
Ogasawara Sadamune

As mentioned before, bushi originally rode horses and used bows, so they were mounted archers. In other words, their principal weapon wasn't the katana. It was the bow, which the bushi trained with daily from childhood. Thus, the warrior who was strong and could draw a bow with a high draw weight was admired in medieval Japan.

Another detail I'll add is that the Ogasawara clan of Shinano taught archery to other bushi at a famous school of the Seiwa Genji line. The Ogasawara clan unified the Ogasawara-ryū school of etiquette that spread in the Edo period, and archery was central to it.

WHEN DID WARRIORS START FIGHTING ON HORSEBACK?

In the eighth century, Emperor Kanmu, who built Heian-kyo, also undertook military reform by instituting the *kondei* system. He assigned from 30 to 200 professional soldiers specialized in military affairs to each province (like today's prefecture), and they preserved the peace in those areas.

The appointed warriors excelled in horsemanship and archery. We cannot confirm whether the kondei led to the appearance of the bushi as a class approximately 150 years later, but it's reasonable to think that at least the concept of warriors as masters of riding and archery, and thus as mounted archers, existed in the early Heian period.

Furthermore, Japan's bushi used the Japanese longbow (*wakyu*) while wearing heavy armor on horseback. Bow-armed heavy cavalry like this was rare in other parts of the world. Light cavalry with short bows and light armor that made use of speed to defeat their enemies was predominant. Japan is an island nation, so its arms and fighting methods may have developed in a unique way.

HOW DID MOUNTED WARRIORS FIGHT?

In the homes of the bushi in Japan, left-handed children learned to be right-handed. So bushi wore their katana on the left side and drew it with their right hand. There were no left-handed swordsmen.

It was the same with a bow. The archer held it with the left hand and fitted the bow to the string with the right hand. That was considered the proper way, and they did it while on horseback. For that reason, they called the left hand *yunde* (bow hand). The right hand gripped the reins, so it was the called *mete* (horse hand).

Today, when a shrine hosts *yabusame* mounted archery displays, it's easy to see that the arrows are loosed to the left of the direction in which the horses are running. The archers can't shoot to the right because they hold the arrow with their left hand and draw the bowstring with their right.

That's why mounted warriors in battle had to control their horses so as to put their opponents on the left. If they didn't, they wouldn't be able to target them. Of course, their opponents would race around to prevent that. Thus, proficiency in both horsemanship and archery was necessary for victory.

WHAT DID IT MEAN TO GIVE LAND?

Tokiyuki mentioned giving land to Genba. He meant a province, but what did that entail? It's a little difficult to explain.

Suppose Oda Nobunaga granted someone a province. For example, he says to Takigawa Kazumasa, his fourth-ranking retainer, "You worked hard to destroy the Takeda clan, so I'll give you Kozuke Province (Gunma Prefecture)." Then everything in Gunma Prefecture—the land, the people living there, the forests and rivers, and the wild boars and fish—would belong to Takigawa. That much is easy to understand.

In Tokiyuki's time, however, it meant appointing the recipient as *shugo* of Kozuke Province as well. A shugo wasn't a feudal lord like a daimyo. He was a government official. He organized the province's bushi but was a leader among his peers. A part of the province's taxes and other products would contribute to his income, but he couldn't take everything. Nonetheless, influential bushi wanted to become shugo, and the power to make that appointment belonged to the main line of the Hojo clan. You may view Tokiyuki's comment in this context.

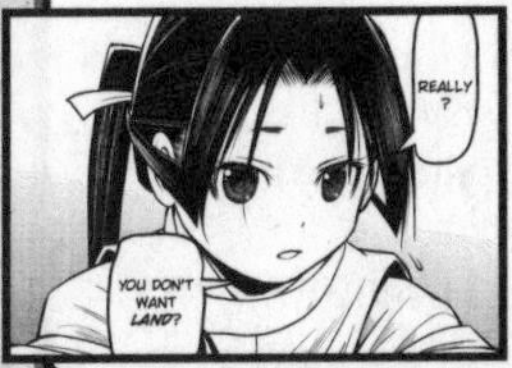
REALLY?
YOU DON'T WANT *LAND*?

WAS THE SHOGUNATE RICH?

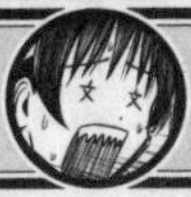

How much wealth did the Kamakura shogunate have? No account books remain, so we don't know. We do have documentation of the following transactions, however. Toward the end of the Kamakura period, the powerful vassal Ashikaga was trying to save money by lowering the cost of a familial memorial service that cost 20 *kan*. However, the Ashikaga forked over 200 kan for a Buddhist service held by the Hojo clan's main line (by Tokiyuki's father Takatoki).

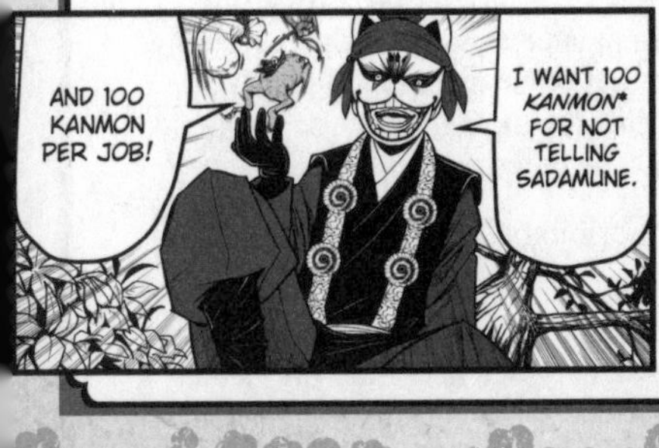
I WANT 100 *KANMON** FOR NOT TELLING SADAMUNE.
AND 100 KANMON PER JOB!

A single kan was about 50,000 yen in modern currency. That means the main line of the Hojo clan, which had dozens of vassals in a single prefecture, was able to collect money in the millions to tens of millions of yen. I'd say that's pretty rich. So Tokiyuki was indeed a spoiled brat.

HOW WAS LAW AND ORDER PRESERVED?

This question almost always shows up in high school textbooks. There's an illustrated scroll called *Obusuma Saburo Ekotoba* that relates a tale set in the late Heian period to the Kamakura period. It portrays the life of an important bushi named Obusuma Saburo, who was fighting to dominate Musashi Province.

Obusuma Saburo was a warrior in the Bando region who was passionate about the military arts. He was so dedicated to this pursuit that he married an ugly woman he had heard about because he knew that if he married a beautiful woman, he would become besotted and neglect his training.

Whenever ascetics or beggars, whether male or female, passed in front of Saburo's residence, his followers rushed outside and violently assaulted them until the victims met a horrible end. Saburo would say, *"Maniwa no sue ni namakubi tayasuna, kirikakeyo."* Which basically means, "Make it so that the corner of the garden never runs out of severed heads. Kill them all." In other words, they attacked and decapitated innocent people who had done nothing but walk by! Scary...

Everyone knows the bushi had callous dispositions, but this story is incredible, especially since Saburo is one of Musashi's foremost warriors. The Kamakura shogunate generally appointed talented bushi to be shugo with orders to capture murderers. Saburo could have served as shugo in Musashi and thus should have been cracking down on crime, but instead he committed crimes! The creation of this scroll shows that daily life in Kanto was fraught with danger.

I'll end this by saying that Hojo Shigetoki, one of the moderates supporting Hojo Tokiyori in the Kamakura shogunate, once told a child (Nagatoki, who served as regent), "Understand? No matter how angry you are, you must never kill another person." Seriously?!

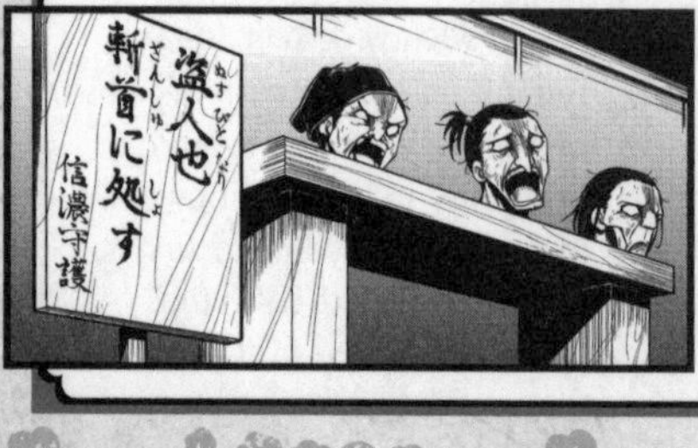
盗人也
斬首に処す
信濃守護

WAS BETRAYAL COMMON?

In bushi society, the most important personal ties were master-servant relationships. Retainers were willing to go into battle and sacrifice themselves for their liege lord, who in return granted them favor for their deeds. This is the well-known value system of "reward and service," of which land grants were typical.

There is a saying that goes, "Parents and children in one world, married couples in two, and masters and servants in three." This means that the relationship between parents and their children is restricted to this life. The relationship of marriage extends into this life from the previous one (or from this one into the next life). A master-servant relationship exists in the previous life, in this life, and in the afterlife. In other words, the bond between master and servant is strongest.

However, that pertains to bushi society in the Edo period. In the Kamakura, Muromachi, and Sengoku periods, master-servant relations were largely contractual. A bushi might think, "I worked hard, so my lord will compensate me accordingly," and treat it matter-of-factly.

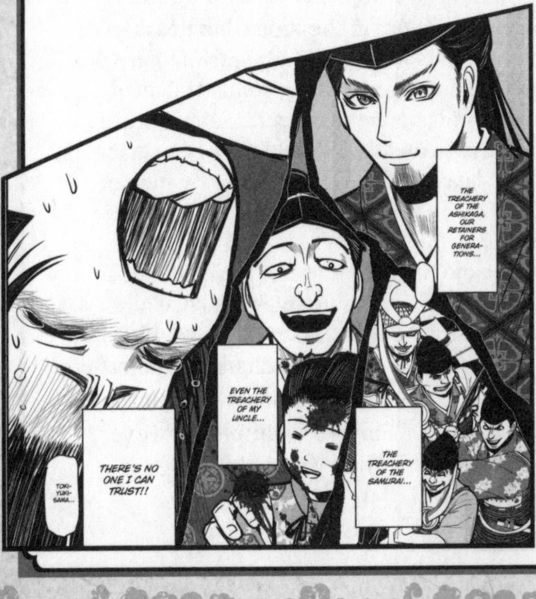
THE TREACHERY OF THE ASHIKAGA, OUR RETAINERS FOR GENERATIONS...
EVEN THE TREACHERY OF MY UNCLE...
THE TREACHERY OF THE SAMURAI...
THERE'S NO ONE I CAN TRUST!!
TOKI-YUKI-SAMA...

But some might think, "I worked hard, but my lord's stingy. I have no choice but to serve a different lord," and society would recognize that. In an extreme form, that might lead to treachery, so more than a few bushi betrayed their lord and his household.

There were no ninja who could singlehandedly take out 10,000 soldiers like Naruto, but ninja did exist and they did gather information. In a time without any advanced means of communication, television, smartphones, or anything like that, it was incredibly difficult to obtain information about faraway places. For that reason, enterprising bushi used ninja as their eyes and ears, ordering them to investigate other regions.

ENTER... THE NINJA!

Some ninja excelled in military arts. In the first year of the Chōkyō era (1487), the ninth shogun, Ashikaga Yoshihisa, led an army of 20,000 on a campaign of subjugation against the

Rokkaku clan in Omi Province. But a small number of elite fighters on the side of the Rokkaku pulled off multiple surprise attacks on Yoshihisa's larger force, severely affecting morale. It's said that Rokkaku's elites were ninja of the Koga school.

Ninja closely guarded their secrets, so we don't know much about their achievements. Given the above example, however, they probably played a significant role.

WHAT DID MORIYOSHI SHINNO DO?

Otonomiya Moriyoshi Shinno was also called Daitonomiya Morinaga Shinno. However, today's Japanese historians read his name as Otonomiya Moriyoshi Shinno, using the pronunciation "O" instead of "Dai," because documents came to light with kanji indicating that reading. His younger brother Emperor Go Murakami's name was Noriyoshi, so he also used the similar reading "Moriyoshi." To assume firm control of Mount Hiei, which was home to a group of warrior monks, Moriyoshi's father, Emperor Go-Daigo, sent Moriyoshi as his third son and seated him as the head abbot of the Tendai sect. At that time, he was known as Prince Son'un. In 1331, when Emperor Go-Daigo's plot to overthrow the shogunate was leaked, the shogunate seized the emperor and exiled him to the Oki Islands. Son'un then returned to secular life, taking the name Moriyoshi, and began leading his attendant bushi in guerilla raids. Without a thought for the danger to his own life, he aimed to overthrow the shogunate.

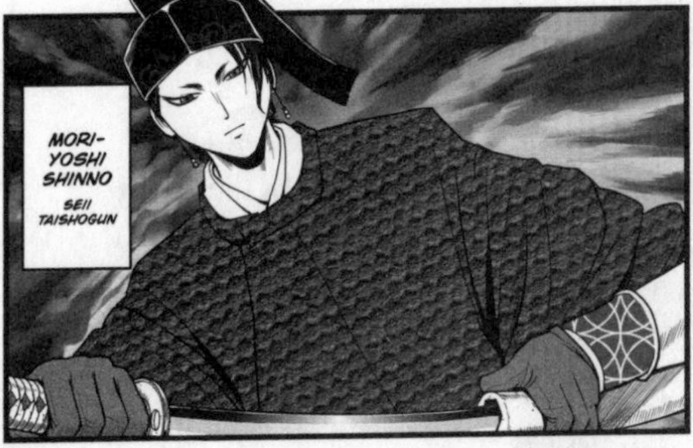
MORI-YOSHI SHINNO
SEII TAISHOGUN

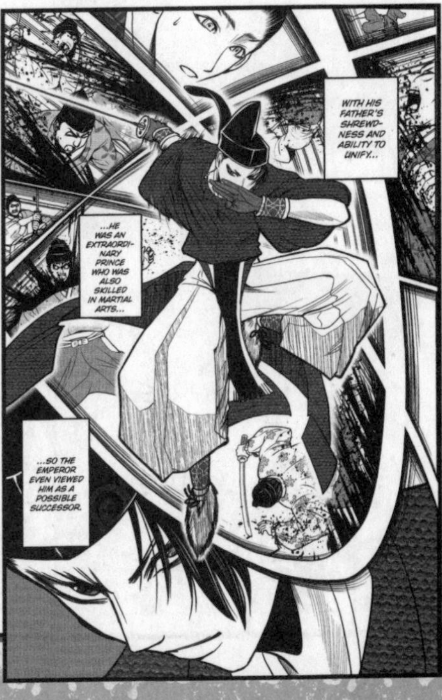
WITH HIS FATHER'S SHREWD-NESS AND ABILITY TO UNIFY...
...HE WAS AN EXTRAORDI-NARY PRINCE WHO WAS ALSO SKILLED IN MARTIAL ARTS...
...SO THE EMPEROR EVEN VIEWED HIM AS A POSSIBLE SUCCESSOR.

While Emperor Go-Daigo was in exile, it was Moriyoshi Shinno who commanded Kusunoki Masashige and Akamatsu Enshin and summoned powerful bushi in the Kinki region to topple the shogunate. When the shogunate finally fell, it was due to Shinno's continuous efforts. Thus, he contributed to the Kamakura shogunate's demise in equal measure to Ashikaga Takauji.

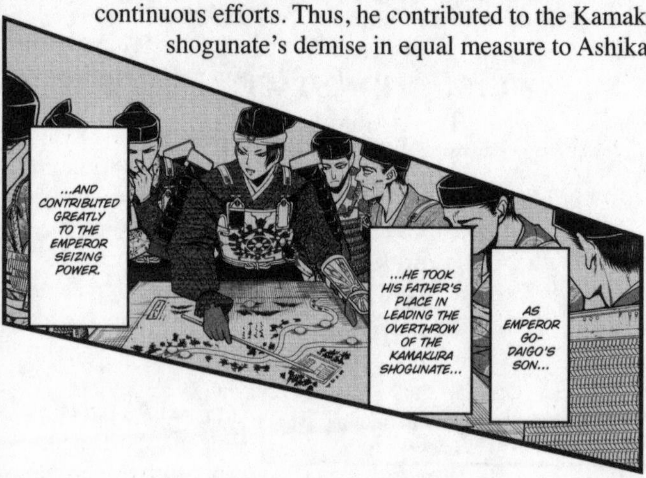
AS EMPEROR GO-DAIGO'S SON...
...HE TOOK HIS FATHER'S PLACE IN LEADING THE OVERTHROW OF THE KAMAKURA SHOGUNATE...
...AND CONTRIBUTED GREATLY TO THE EMPEROR SEIZING POWER.

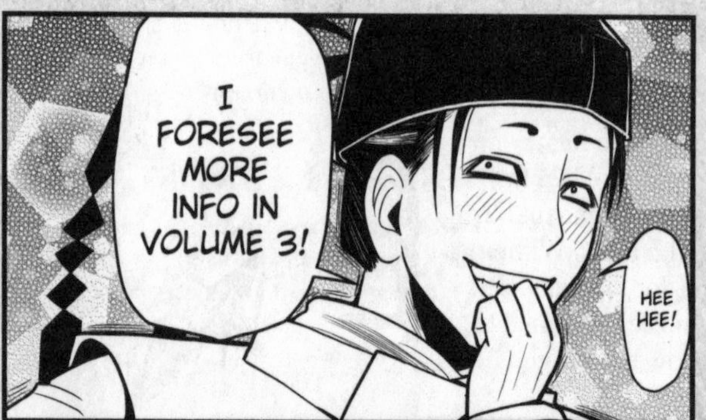
HEE HEE!
I FORESEE MORE INFO IN VOLUME 3!

SPECIAL THANKS

I borrow a lot of people's talents for *The Elusive Samurai*.

PRODUCTION STAFF
TEI ASHIGAKI
YUUKI IMADA
*His series *MINI4KING* begins in *CoroCoro Comic* in August 2021!
DAISUKE ENOSHIMA
SAKUJU KOIZUMI
WAHARE KOYOI
KEIJI INOUE

They help me create the art. They're my Kamakura warriors
who're almighty in drawing what I want.

EDITOR
RIKI AZUMA
He's an editor for *Weekly Shonen Jump*. He's from a high-class upbringing,
so he's got a taste for fine food despite being so young.

GRAPHIC NOVEL EDITOR
SATOSHI WATANABE
He handles stuff related to the graphic novel, and he's got really thin legs.

DESIGNER
YUKI MATSUMOTO (BANANA GROVE STUDIO)
She's in charge of the logo and design for the graphic novel.
She's a licensed art curator.

JAPANESE-STYLE ARTIST
TAKAFUMI ASAKURA
I asked him to take care of the background and patterns for the graphic novel cover.
He has so much skill and dignity that it's hard to believe we're the same age.

CALLIGRAPHY
KAMARI MAEDA
I ask him to letter the scenes introducing the demons.
A person of many talents, he's got a lot of energy and excellent presentation skills.

ADVISER AND ARTICLE WRITER
KAZUTO HONGO
I call upon him to supervise the historical details in the series and to write the pages
of historical analysis. Anything that departs from history is the author's own creation
or personal interpretation.

PERSONAL SYMBOL DESIGNER
MARIKA MATSUMOTO (& CAT)
She designs patterns for some of the characters' kimonos.
She's very service oriented, so she proposes numerous patterns.

WATER AND INK ARTIST
TOKURO KITAMURA
He does the water and ink art in the manga. I think it would
be great if he contributed his wonderful work to creators in various genres.

3D CG MODELING
MELTA KABUSHIKI GAISHA
They do 3D modeling for things like armor, helmets, and swords that aren't for sale
commercially. The biggest element for this time period, about which there aren't
many manga, is armor. And that's a real pain, so I'm thankful to them and their
digital-age skills for solving that problem.

SUWA RESEARCH COOPERATION
MICHIHO ISHINO
She helped me with research about Suwa. She's had all kinds of experiences and has
a lot of curiosity, so she knows everything, not just about Suwa.

ILLUSTRATOR
SHIE NANAHANA
She creates colorful backgrounds. As befits their startlingly high data volumes,
her illustrations are beautiful and vivid.

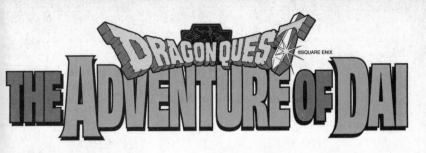

DRAGON QUEST THE ADVENTURE OF DAI

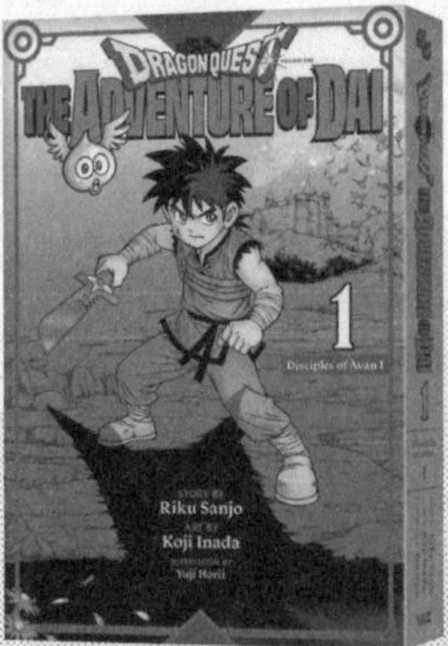

DRAGON QUEST
THE ADVENTURE OF DAI
1
Riku Sanjo
Koji Inada

Story by Riku Sanjo Art by Koji Inada
Supervision by Yuji Horii

Raised by monsters in a battle-scarred world, Dai has the heart of a hero! He sets off on a grand journey with brave friends, traveling the world to take down the Dark Lord's minions. Along the way, Dai must awaken the hero he was meant to be and master his dormant powers.

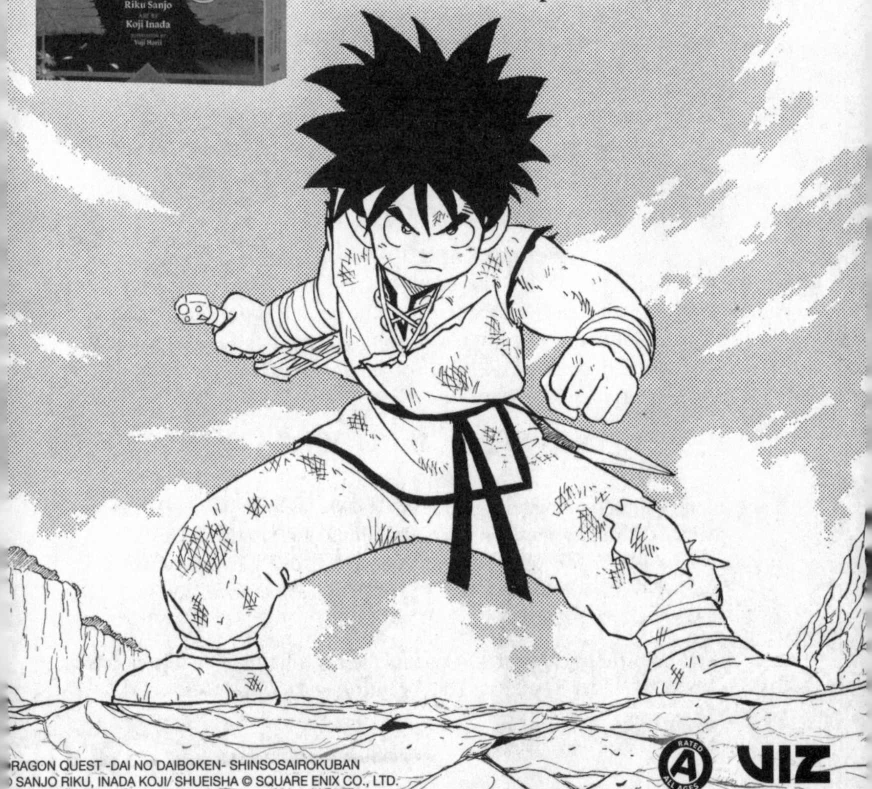

RATED A ALL AGES

VIZ

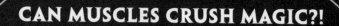

CAN MUSCLES CRUSH MAGIC?!

MASHLE

MAGIC AND MUSCLES

STORY AND ART BY
HAJIME KOMOTO

In the magic realm, magic is everything—everyone can use it, and one's skill determines their social status. Deep in the forest, oblivious to the ways of the world, lives Mash. Thanks to his daily training, he's become a fitness god. When Mash is discovered, he has no choice but to enroll in magic school where he must beat the competition without revealing his secret—he can't use magic!

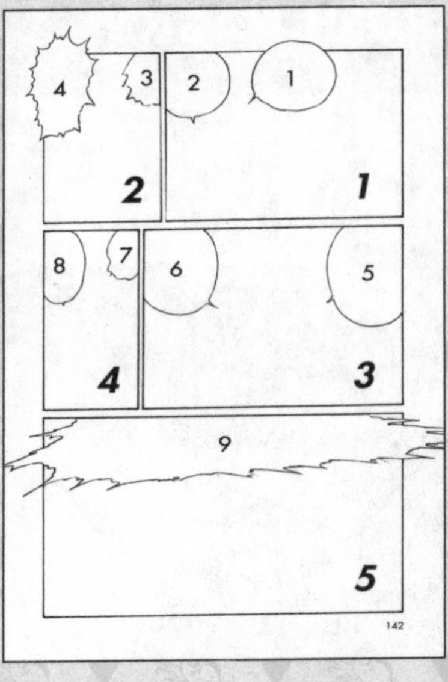
1
2
1
3
4
2
5
6
3
7
8
4
9
5
142

YOU'RE READING THE WRONG WAY!

THE ELUSIVE SAMURAI reads from right to left, starting in the upper-right corner. Japanese is read from right to left, meaning that action, sound effects, and word-balloon order are completely reversed from English order.

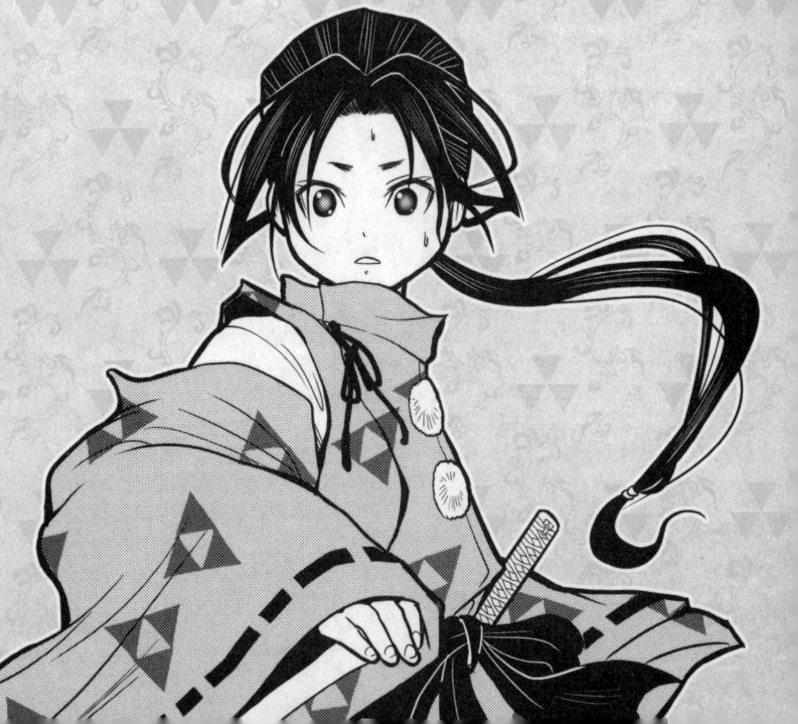

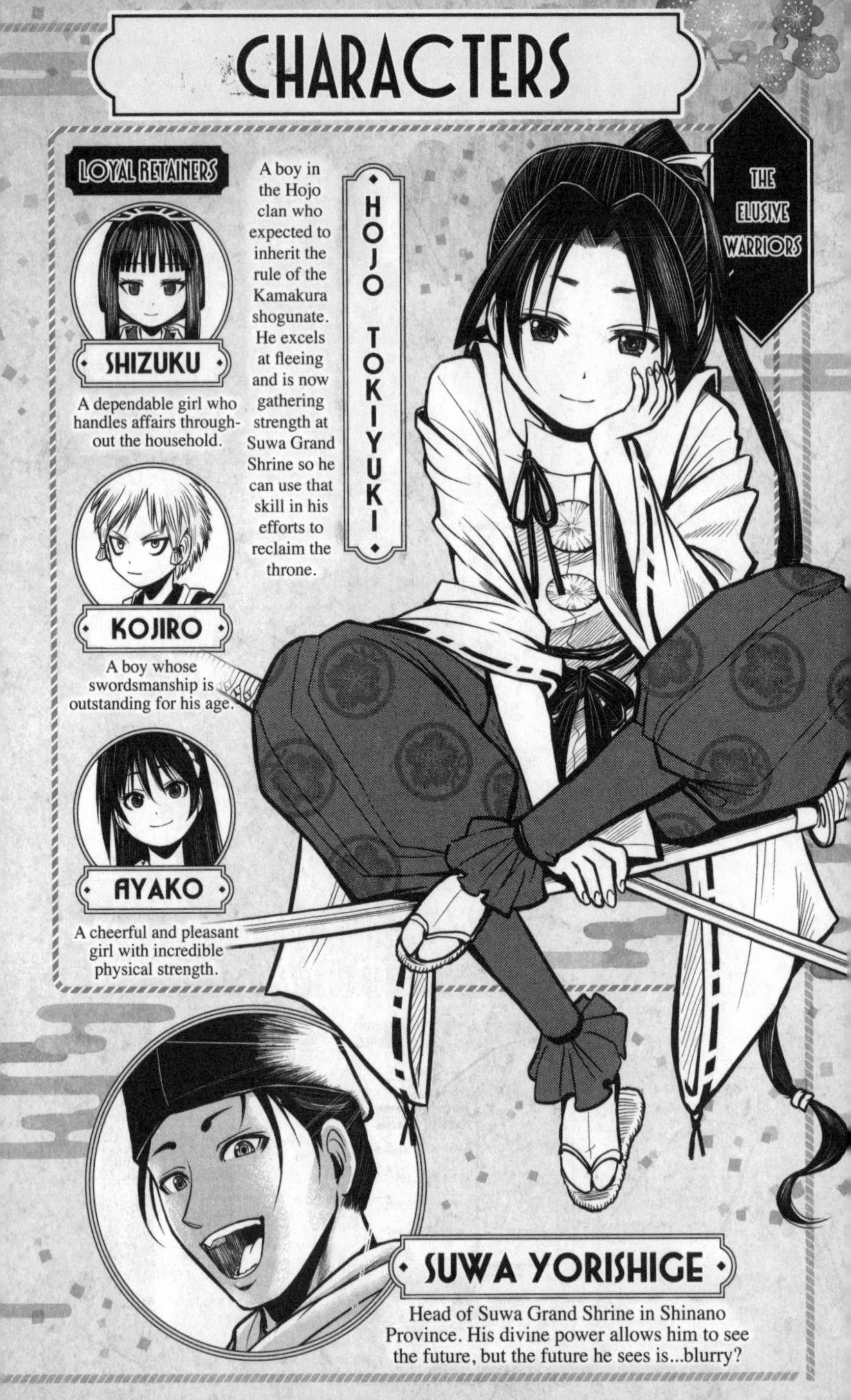
CHARACTERS
LOYAL RETAINERS
SHIZUKU
A dependable girl who handles affairs throughout the household.
KOJIRO
A boy whose swordsmanship is outstanding for his age.
AYAKO
A cheerful and pleasant girl with incredible physical strength.
HOJO TOKIYUKI
A boy in the Hojo clan who expected to inherit the rule of the Kamakura shogunate. He excels at fleeing and is now gathering strength at Suwa Grand Shrine so he can use that skill in his efforts to reclaim the throne.
THE ELUSIVE WARRIORS
SUWA YORISHIGE
Head of Suwa Grand Shrine in Shinano Province. His divine power allows him to see the future, but the future he sees is...blurry?

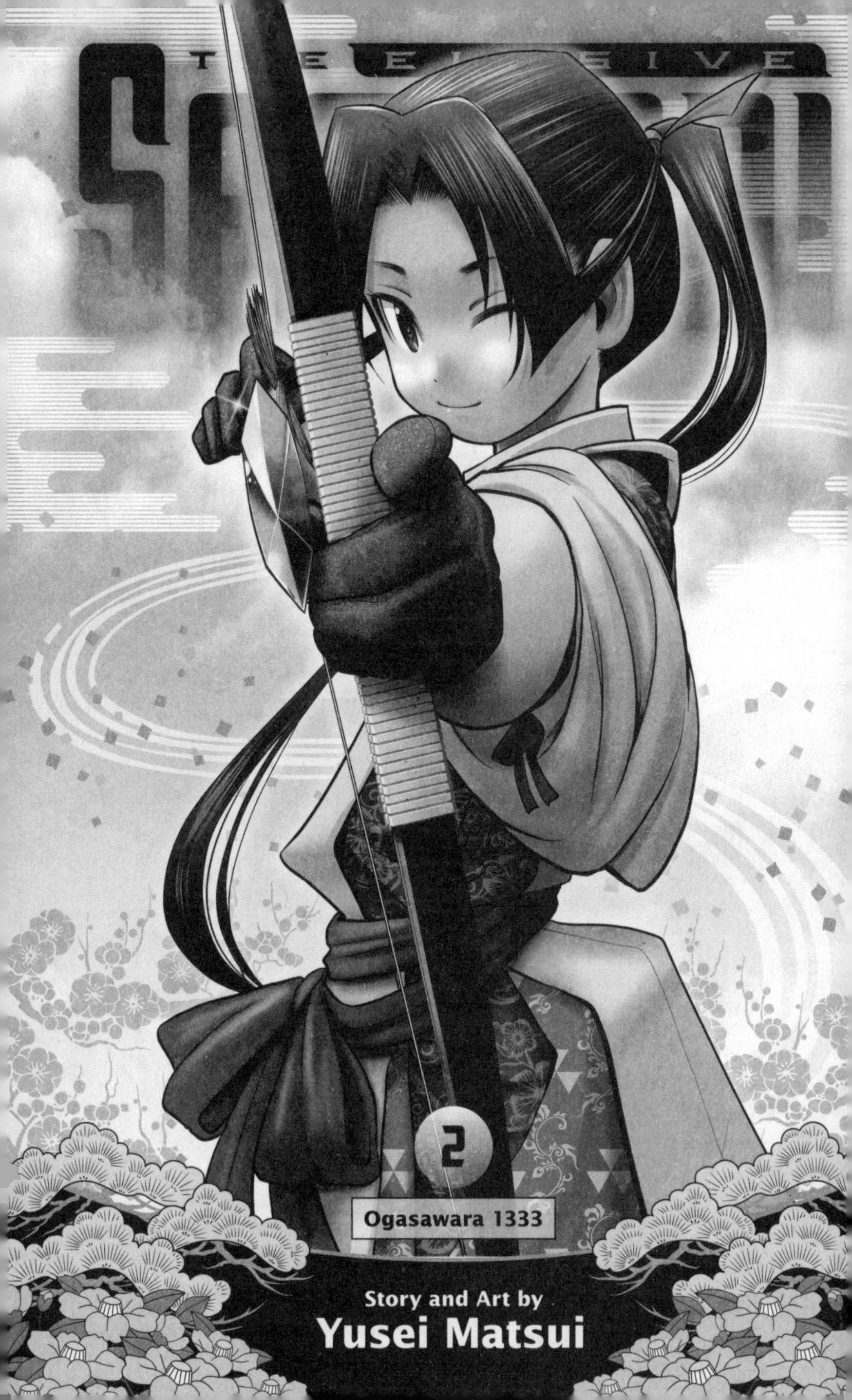
2
Ogasawara 1333
Story and Art by
Yusei Matsui